When they
were kids

To Elizabeth, best mother and best friend

C.O.M.

To my sister, Susan, and my brother, David,
with whom I shared a happy childhood

A.E.

When they were kids

Over 400 Sketches of Famous Childhoods

CAROL ORSAG MADIGAN

AND

ANN ELWOOD

RANDOM HOUSE

NEW YORK

When They Were Kids
© 1998 Carol Orsag Madigan and Ann Elwood

This book is available for special purchases in bulk by organizations
and institutions, not for resale, at special discounts. Please direct your
inquiries to the Random House Special Sales Department, toll-free
888-591-1200 or fax 212-572-4961.

Please address inquiries about electronic licensing of this division's
products, for use on a network or in software or on CD-ROM, to the
Subsidiary Rights Department, Random House Reference &
Information Publishing, fax 212-940-7370.

Library of Congress Cataloging-in-Publication Data

Madigan, Carol Orsag, 1948–
When they were kids : over 400 sketches of famous childhoods / by
Carol Orsag Madigan and Ann Elwood.—1st ed.
p.   cm.
Includes bibliographical references and index.
ISBN 0-375-70389-6 (alk. paper)
1. Celebrities—Biography.   2. Children—Biography.   I. Elwood,
Ann.   II. Title.
CT105.M24   1998
920.02—dc21   98-17690
                                        CIP

Typeset and printed in the United States of America.

Visit the Random House Web site at www.randomhouse.com

First Edition
0 9 8 7 6 5 4 3 2 1
September 1998
ISBN 0-375-70389-6

Design by Robert Bull Design.

CONTENTS IN BRIEF

CONTENTS

LIST OF ILLUSTRATIONS

INTRODUCTION

When They Were Kids is a book of stories about the childhoods of famous people. It covers a wide variety of personalities through-out history—political figures, artists and writers, entertainers, inventors, scientists, military leaders, industrialists, educators, explorers, re-ligious leaders, civil rights activists. Presented in list form, the book cuts a wide swath through the experience of childhood, which we have taken to mean the years until a person is seventeen or goes to college. We looked at everything from sibling rivalries to humiliating incidents to supernatural ex-periences and brushes with death.

In writing this book, we cast our net wide, starting out with a list of nearly 1,000 personalities. In the end we selected stories about three hundred seventy-four people. Why were some people included and others excluded? In making the decision, we asked ourselves these questions: Are childhood stories available about these people? Do these stories fit into the subject cat-egories set up in the book? And above all, are they good stories?

We focus primarily on home life, school life, and social life—bringing in people who were important to our subjects such as parents, teachers, best friends, and first loves. We look at events that had a profound impact on impressionable minds—especially situations that were in some way tragic or enlightening or frightening. We try to peer into the minds of our subjects by looking at their diaries, their dreams and nightmares, their earliest memories, their fears and phobias. And we look at the fun; the joy and excitement of childhood: a beloved pet, a first kiss, toys and hobbies, pranks and daredevil stunts.

Intertwined in the stories are all the ingredients that have molded our famous personalities: love and security or the deprivation of both, emotional and physical attributes, role models or the lack of them, bitter disappointments and early victories. The ways in which these ingredients came together ultimately formed the character, influenced the development, and led to the career of each person.

It was never our intention to psychoanalyze the childhoods of the famous, that is, to find the common threads that explain how someone moves from obscurity to fame, and sometimes fortune. We simply wanted to pull out the themes of childhood that we can all identify with—hopes and dreams, fears and anxieties, acceptance and rejection.

For us, only one thing is clear: There are many different roads to success. Some of our famous men and women were born in the lap of luxury, whereas others were constantly struggling to escape poverty. Some grew up in intellectually stimulating homes and went to good schools; others had an inferior education or no education at all. Some showed brilliance early and seemed destined for success, whereas others seemed—well, just plain ordinary. Some knew what careers they wanted to pursue; others just stumbled into work in which they excelled.

The stories we present run the emotional gamut, from funny through poignant and sad to shocking and bizarre. We hope you enjoy reading them.

A special note: We are indebted to Charles Levine, our publisher at Random House, whose talent and insight never cease to amaze us, and to his assistant editor, Megan Schade, who diligently and enthusiastically combed through the endless facts contained in this book. And we give a special salute to Heide Lange, our literary agent, who possesses endless amounts of spirit and fortitude.

Carol Orsag Madigan
Ann Elwood

CHAPTER ONE

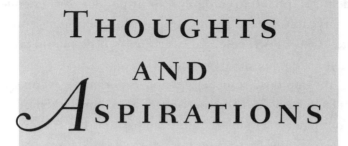

THOUGHTS
AND
*A*SPIRATIONS

What goes on in children's minds?

Most of us remember only tantalizing fragments of our early childhoods. But the memories we do have come up bright and distinct, floating up out of oblivion like the paper words in one of those black fortune-telling toy balls. The famous are no different. At age three, Miles Davis saw a blue gas stove flame that remained "as clear as music" in his mind when he grew up. Georgia O'Keeffe never forgot "the brightness of the light—light all around" she saw at the age of six months as she lay on a patchwork quilt spread out on the grass. All her life, Golda Meir remembered the sound of hammers as her father nailed boards across the door to barricade their home against a pogrom.

In the universe of childhood, perceptions are sharp-edged. Imaginary creatures rise from the mind to become intensely real. Angels comfort sad and frightened children. Monsters chase their victims down the corridors of nightmares. Imaginary worlds gave their now famous creators ways to cope. For instance, little H. G. Wells commanded his phantom orderlies to wipe out his enemies. Other imaginary worlds were testing grounds for a brilliant future, like the Brontës' Glass Town colony or Carl Jung's little mannikin in a pencil box or Jules Verne's desert island.

For the famous, some childhood experiences were real turning points because of how they perceived them. For Kareem Abdul-Jabbar, the experience was looking at a photograph. For Alexander Graham Bell, it was a visit to London to stay with his grandfather. For Napoleon, a sermon. For Burt Reynolds, a footrace. For journalist Ida Tarbell, an insult.

Children dream of the future. Sometimes their aspirations surprise us. Carol Burnett yearned to be a cartoonist, Burt Lancaster to be an opera singer, k. d. lang a roller derby queen. And who could guess that Ethel Barrymore and Madonna wanted to be nuns, and Vince Lombardi and Joseph Stalin to be priests?

EARLY MEMORIES

HENRY ADAMS (1838–1918), U.S. historian
In his autobiography, *The Education of Henry Adams*, he wrote of his young self in third person: "He first found himself sitting on a yellow kitchen floor in strong sunlight. He was three years old when he took this earliest step in education; a lesson of color." This style has fascinated readers ever since, turning his autobiography into a classic.

ISAAC ASIMOV (1920–1992), Russian-born U.S. science writer
He sat in a chair turning the pages of a book, but when he looked for the book again, it was gone. Years later, he told his mother about his early memory of the precious object that was lost. She said, "I remember the book. You were two years old at the time and you loved it." When he asked where it had gone, she replied that he had torn out every page as he turned it.

SIDNEY BECHET (c. 1897–1959), U.S. musician
His three older brothers—Homer (string bass), Leonard (trombone), and Albert Eugene (violin)—loved music and played instruments. Sidney wanted to play too. When he was very little, he found a douche belonging to his mother and tried to blow the nozzle to make a sound like a clarinet. The world continued to be filled with musical objects for him.

ALEXANDER GRAHAM BELL (1847–1922), Scottish-born U.S. inventor

His first memory was of a wheat field outside Edinburgh, Scotland. The wheat was high, higher than his head, and he sat in the middle of the field trying to hear it growing. After a while, he realized that he was alone and lost; he became frightened. He searched, but to no avail. Finally, he cried himself to sleep. Then he heard his father calling, "Aleck! Aleck!" He ran toward the voice, came out of the wheat, and leapt into his mother's arms.

Ruth Fulton (later Ruth Benedict) as an infant. Wick, Norwich, NY.

Courtesy of Special Collections, Vassar College Libraries, Poughkeepsie, NY.

RUTH BENEDICT (1887–1948), U.S. anthropologist
She began her autobiography with this sentence: "The story of my life begins when I was twenty-one months old, at the time my father died." Her grief-stricken, hysterical mother took her to view the body. To Ruth, her dead father seemed calm and young. From then on she lived in two worlds: "the world of my father, which was the world of death and was beautiful, and the world of confusion and explosive weeping, which I repudiated."

INGMAR BERGMAN (1918–   ), Swedish film director
His earliest memory anticipates his career as a filmmaker. Looking in a plate of food, he kept shifting his head to get different perspectives on it. His memories of his childhood are abnormally sharp. "Sometimes in the night, when I am on the limit between sleeping and being awake, I can just go through a door into my childhood and everything is as it was—with lights, smells, sounds and people."

JACKIE COOPER (1921–   ), U.S. actor
In Jackie Cooper's first memory, he was five years old hiding with his grandmother behind the living room couch. The doorbell was ringing and ringing, but his grandmother did not answer it. Instead, she put her hand over his mouth to keep him from saying anything. Then he heard footsteps walking away. His grandmother walked sneakily to the window, saying to Jackie, "You keep goddamn quiet, you hear?"

Not long after, the mailman came to the door, and she opened it. She pinched Jackie's rear end as she told him to say hello. The pinch was a kind of punctuation to show that she meant what she said. Jackie was angry but did nothing except try to talk to the mailman and keep an eye on her. She might pinch again—or even kick!

MILES DAVIS (1926–1991), U.S. musician
His earliest memory was of a gas flame on a stove. He wrote, "I remember being shocked by the whoosh of the blue flame leaping off the burner, the suddenness of it. . . . That stove flame is as clear as music is in my mind. I was three years old." He felt hotness, fear, and a "weird joy." The experience led him to a new place in his head, "the edge, maybe, of everything possible. . . . In my mind I have always believed and thought since then that my motion had to be forward, away from the heat of that flame."

CHARLES DICKENS (1812–1870), English writer
He rode downstairs in the arms of a woman, "holding tight to her, in the terror of seeing the steep perspective below." Downstairs people celebrated New Year's Day, "a very long row of ladies and gentlemen sitting against a wall, all drinking at once out of little glass cups with handles, like custard-cups. . . . [It was] very like my first idea of the good people in Heaven, as I derived it from a wretched picture in a Prayer-book—and they had all got their heads a little thrown back, and were all drinking at once."

K. D. LANG (1961–   ), Canadian singer
Kathryn Dawn Lang was a competitive child who excelled in music and sports. At an early age, she believed she was the equal of any girl—or boy—

and refused to be placed in a subservient position. As an adult, k.d., a self-proclaimed lesbian, recalled a childhood incident that occurred when she was five and was play-acting with a few friends. She said: "There was a point in the play where we were going home to our spouses. I was playing with two little boys, and they said they were going home to their wives. I said I was going home to my wife, too. They said, 'You can't have a wife!' I said, 'Yes, I can.' "

MALCOLM X (1925–1965), U.S. black nationalist leader
Malcolm X (born Malcolm Little) was four when he was grabbed out of bed and taken outside because his family's house was burning. In his autobiography, he claims that the fire was purposely set by two white men, and as he recalled: "We were outside in the night in our underwear, crying and yelling our heads off. The white policemen and firemen came and stood around watching as the house burned down to the ground."

GOLDA MEIR (1898–1978), Israeli political leader
When Goldie was four, she lived in the Russian city of Kiev. One morning she heard that a "pogrom" was going to happen in her neighborhood, and she became terrified even though she wasn't quite sure what a pogrom was. She knew, however, that it was bad and that it happened to Jews. Many years later, she recalled how her family prepared for it: "I can remember how I stood on the stairs together with a neighbor's daughter of about my own age, holding hands, watching our fathers trying to barricade the entrance by nailing boards across the door. I can hear the sound of that hammer now. . . . I remember how scared I was, and how angry." The pogrom never took place, but Meir never forgot the memory, and she told the story throughout her life.

MARGARET MITCHELL (1900–1949), U.S. novelist
Margaret's mother, May Belle, was very active in the Georgia women's rights movement, and one of Margaret's earliest memories was of a suffragette rally. She wrote: "Mother tied a Votes-for-Women banner around my fat stomach, put me under her arm, took me to the meeting, hissing bloodcurdling threats if I did not behave, set me on the platform between the silver pitcher and the water glasses while she made an impassioned speech. I was so enchanted at my eminence that I behaved perfectly, even blowing kisses to gentlemen in the front row."

MARILYN MONROE (1926–1962), U.S. actor
One of her earliest recollections was about an incident that supposedly happened when Marilyn was thirteen months old. In her words: "I remember waking up from my nap fighting for my life. Something was pressed against my face. It could have been a pillow. I fought with all my strength." If the incident ever really occurred, the person holding the pillow was probably her grandmother, who was committed to a mental institution shortly thereafter. Marilyn often fabricated stories about her childhood, however, and most of her biographers cast a wall of doubt on this early memory.

Margaret Mitchell, animal lover, with one of her furry friends.

Courtesy of the Hargrett Rare Book and Manuscript Library, University of Georgia Libraries.

GEORGIA O'KEEFFE (1887–1986), U.S. painter

When Georgia was about six months old, she was taken outdoors and placed on a patchwork quilt spread out on the grass. According to O'Keeffe, her very first memory was of that day and "the brightness of the light—light all around." She was always able to recall the exact design of the quilt—little red stars and white flowers on a black and white background.

Did you know that Sidney Bechet tried to play his mother's douche like a clarinet.

MARY PICKFORD (1893–1979), U.S. actor

Her real name was Gladys Smith, and her father died when she was four years old. Gladys's mother held down a number of jobs, but the Smith family was always on the verge of poverty. At one time Gladys was almost given up for adoption. Although she grew up to become "America's Sweetheart" and amassed a great fortune, Mary Pickford watched carefully over every penny she ever earned. When asked to recall stories from her childhood, she usually told one with a money theme, like the time her sister accidentally dropped a nickel between two piano keys and young Gladys grabbed a hammer to pry it out. The piano survived demolition when her grandmother intervened.

NORMAN ROCKWELL (1894–1978), U.S. illustrator

Norman's mother made him wear a hand-me-down winter coat to school. Although the coat was in good shape, it was far too big for Norman, and the other kids howled with laughter when he walked into the classroom. He later recalled, "The first warm day of spring I lugged it out to the back yard, poured turpentine on it, and burned it. I can see myself, squatting on my heels before my grandfather's paddock coat as the flames eat into it, poking it with a stick, stirring it to make sure *nothing* is left, my boy's face grim and serious."

H. NORMAN SCHWARZKOPF (1934–   ), U.S. general

In his autobiography, *It Doesn't Take a Hero,* the man who commanded the Allied forces in the Persian Gulf War mentions an early memory of the first thing he ever killed. He was fooling around with his bow and arrow, shooting at all kinds of things, but hitting nothing. Then he aimed at a robin and hit it straight on. The bird didn't die immediately but flapped around on the ground for several minutes. Norman felt horrible. Recalling the incident, the adult Schwarzkopf writes, "I went inside, got the fanciest box I could find, lined it with the very softest fabric I could find, and buried the bird, digging a deep hole and saying all the prayers I could remember."

FRANK SINATRA (1915–1998), U.S. singer

When Frank was three years old, his mother, Dolly, had a job as a chocolate dipper in a candy store. Frank said, "I remember my first visit to the candy store. She had a bucket of ice water and a vat of hot, fudgy chocolate. . . . She gave me three pieces of chocolate. It was wonderful."

9

JOHN STEINBECK (1902–1968), U.S. novelist

He was only four when the great earthquake hit San Francisco in 1906, destroying much of the city and killing hundreds of people. John's hometown of Salinas, one hundred miles south of San Francisco, was spared the devastation that the city suffered, but some local buildings were toppled. Steinbeck remembered the day his father took him by the hand and walked him down the main street of Salinas. They stopped frequently to survey the ruins. The Steinbeck home was spared, but the family phonograph fell to the floor and was damaged beyond repair.

LAWRENCE WELK (1903–1992), U.S. bandleader

In his autobiography, *Wunnerful, Wunnerful,* Welk wrote: "My earliest clear memory is of crawling across the floor of our sod farmhouse toward my father, who was smiling and holding out his accordion. And I can still recall the wonder and delight I felt when he let me press my fingers down on the keys, which were round and shiny like pearl buttons, and squeeze out a few wavering notes!"

HANK WILLIAMS (1923–1953), U.S. singer

Born in Alabama, Hank went to church every Sunday with his mother, Lillie, who played the organ in the Baptist church. Lillie sang out strong and clear during church services, and Hank liked to join in. He said, "My earliest memory is sittin' on that organ stool by her and hollerin'. I must have been five, six years old, and louder 'n anybody else."

IMAGINARY FRIENDS AND IMAGINARY WORLDS

W. H. (WYSTAN HUGH) AUDEN (1907–1973), English poet

When he was little, his parents took him to the gasworks down the road from their home in Solihull, England, because they thought the fumes were good for his bronchitis. He adored the pipes and meters. Nothing fascinated him more than the factories the family visited on vacation until, on a holiday in Derbyshire, he saw some old abandoned lead mines on the moors. The rusty machinery lying in the grass and the ruined chimneys enthralled him. In the world of his imagination he became a mining engineer. He described it like this: "I spent a great many of my waking hours in the construction and elaboration of a private sacred world, the basic elements of which were a landscape, northern and limestone, and an industry, lead mining." He was the "sole autocrat" of this world, which also contained narrow-gauge railways and waterwheels. All his world's machinery had to be real, something he saw in a catalog or book or actuality. Yet he did not want to know how the machinery worked.

He read textbooks about mining, such as *Machinery for Metalliferous Mines.* He looked at maps and at diagrams of mining equipment. He explored real mines when his parents let him. This preoccupation gave adults the notion that young Wystan should become a scientist. But he had no talent for science and did not care about it. The mines represented romance, pure and simple. More than anything he loved the vocabulary of mining. He later said, "A word like *pyrites* was for me not simply an indicative sign; it was the Proper Name of a Sacred Being . . ." These are clearly the words of a poet, not a mining engineer.

CHARLOTTE BRONTË (1816–1855), **EMILY BRONTË** (1818–1848),
and **ANNE BRONTË** (1820–1849), English writers;
PATRICK BRANWELL BRONTË (1817–1848), their brother

In 1826, their father brought home twelve painted wooden soldiers as a gift for Branwell, then nine. He and his sisters called them the "Young Men" and began to make up stories about them. The first adventure of the Young Men was to explore Africa and establish a colony there. That colony, with its fantastic buildings, became Glass Town, later part of the kingdom of Angria. By the time three years had gone by, the original twelve personages had become many, mostly aristocrats; they spoke a Glass Town language, Young Men's Tongue. The children put themselves in the story as Genii or Geniuses.

Almost every day, often with the help of Emily and Anne, Charlotte and Branwell wrote stories about their imaginary world in tiny handwriting. When Emily was about eleven, she and Anne created a separate imaginary world, Gondal, much more like the Yorkshire countryside where they lived. Rife with feuds and jailings, loves, and killings, it later became part of the Glass Town narrative.

By the time Charlotte was fourteen, the siblings had compiled twenty-two volumes of work, most of it about Glass Town. Branwell wrote about rebellion, Charlotte about love. Often her prose turned purple, as when, for instance, she described the duke of Zamorna: "Zamorna. The god-like Zamorna, the idol of all my sex." Or when she put these words in the mouth of Zamorna's wife: ". . . were Zamorna to leave me and marry another. I should die, not of consumption, but of a sudden paroxysm of life-quenching agony that would cut me down like a scythe."

The Brontës continued writing about Glass Town until they were grown. Their imaginary world—an "enchanted sphere," according to Charlotte—sustained them through a lonely childhood on the English moors.

AGATHA CHRISTIE (1890–1976), English mystery writer

Educated at home during her first ten years, she had few real-life friends, so she developed imaginary ones. At first, her private world included Mrs. Benson and the Kittens, and Dick and Dick's mistress. Later it was expanded to a school of girls and a line of kings and queens, all make-believe.

Agatha chose a school for her imaginary world because it was "the only background into which I could conveniently fit seven girls of varying ages and appearances . . . instead of making them a family, which I did not want to do." They looked like people in Royal Academy pictures that she found in books and like the flowers in human form drawn by Walter Crane in *The Feast of Flora*. Her imaginary friend Sue de Verte, according to Agatha, was "curiously colourless, not only in appearance . . . but also in character"; she probably stood for Agatha herself, an observer. Sue had a stepsister, Vera de Verte,

Anne Brontë, age fourteen, a watercolor by her sister Charlotte.

Courtesy of the Brontë Society.

thirteen, who became a "raving beauty," with "her straw-coloured hair and forget-me-not blue eyes." Her parentage was romantically unclear. She very likely represented what Agatha wanted to become.

THOMAS DE QUINCEY (1785–1859), English essayist and critic
Both Thomas and his brother William devised imaginary kingdoms, in which they fought their sibling wars. William, more than three years older, ruled

over Tigrosylvania, while Thomas ruled over Gombroon. At first, all was peaceful. When William declared war, Thomas, unwilling to engage in hostilities, announced that his kingdom lay in the tropics, too far away from the northern locale of Tigrosylvania to be a threat. William would hear none of this. He said that, yes, Tigrosylvania was partly located in the north, but it also extended south to the tropics, making it neighbors with Gombroon.

Undaunted, Thomas stated that Gombroon was very poor, not worth invading. Oh, no, said William, he knew of a diamond mine there, which his kingdom would exploit.

Thomas was ridden with anxiety. He did not want to fight.

Then the boys' tutor brought a book by a second-rate anthropologist to William's attention. The book gave an account of primitive men of Nicobar who had tails like cats. William seized on this detail. He insisted that the inferior people of Gombroon had similar tails. Thomas abandoned the game.

PETER FINCH (1916–1977), English actor
Peter's father spirited him off to France to live with his paternal grandmother, Laura Finch, when he was only two. He claimed to have rescued the child from his wife, whose military officer boyfriends were giving Peter champagne. From then until he was fourteen, Peter was shunted around from place to place—France, India, Australia.

His grandmother—who knew Isadora Duncan, Nijinsky, and other celebrities—became entranced with spiritualism, and young Peter, not yet ten, joined in. He created imaginary characters from the spirit world—a gray man standing under the trees, a French officer in Napoleonic uniform, a monk, a medieval lady.

Did you know that the poet W. H. Auden dreamed of being a mining engineer?

Some of his grandmother's friends thought that Peter was clairvoyant. When he was about ten, he talked to fairies, who were his playmates. His grandmother typed up some of his stories about the fairies. One described how they dressed him like themselves in a green jacket, red belt, and green knee-high boots with curled toes. It began: "These little men began dancing on my feet, dancing, dancing, dancing. And as they danced, I grew smaller, smaller, smaller, until, lo and behold! I found myself the same size as my little friends!"

CARL JUNG (1875–1961), Swiss psychologist
He carved an end of his wooden school ruler into a mannikin in top hat, frock coat, and boots. In his pencil box, he made a bed for it out of wool and then

put it to bed with a stone "painted with water-colors to look as though it were divided into an upper and lower half." In secret, he took the pencil box to the attic and hid it under a floorboard. Once he did that, he felt enormous relief. "The tormenting sense of being at odds with myself was gone."

His biographer, Vincent Brome, interprets the stone as the "two sides of his own developing nature"; the mannikin both as his father, who was arguing with his mother, and a feared Jesuit. Brome says that Jung put these elements together in the pencil box to achieve harmony.

In any case, the pencil box became the focus of a ritual. When Carl felt anxious, he went to the attic and communicated wordlessly with the mannikin. Each time, he left in the box a scroll with messages, written in his own secret language. It was a tiny world, under his control. "The episode with the carved mannikin formed the climax and the conclusion of my childhood," he said later. To him, the mannikin was an example of the collective unconscious.

JACK KEROUAC (1922–1969), U.S. novelist and poet

After visiting Rockingham Park racetrack with his father, Jack reproduced the world of the track with marbles, a huge ball bearing, and a Parcheesi board. In this imaginary world, Jack owned a great horse, the greatest in the world. He named it Repulsion. In reality, Repulsion was the ball bearing. Jack also owned the track, rode the horses as jockey, trained the horses—in short, ruled all. The marbles were other horses. Jack chipped them to roll at random, and he figured the odds for them. At the beginning of a race, he made trumpet noises and played "Dardanella" on the Victrola. The "horses" first paraded along the top of the board, held by a ruler; then, after Jack removed the ruler, they raced down the board. Jack made up a track newspaper in which he kept careful records of each race and the horses in it, including their jockeys, colors, stables, and other details.

MARGARET ROSE OF YORK (1930–   ), British princess

The daughter of King George VI and sister of the present Queen Elizabeth II, Margaret had a fairy-tale childhood. On the day she was born, there were traditional gunfire salutes and celebrations throughout London. At an early age, she learned to sing, dance, play the piano, and ride horses. She and her older sister, Elizabeth, played hide-and-seek, cowboys and Indians, and hopscotch. The little princesses were dressed in royal finery and hordes of journalists were always around, trying to get photographs of the girls. At Margaret's fifth birthday party, James Barrie, author of *Peter Pan*, was in attendance.

Although the sisters spent most of their time together, they were quite different from each other. Elizabeth was more serious and disciplined; Margaret was boisterous and somewhat unruly. When Elizabeth was studying, Margaret had her head buried in a comic book. Both princesses had their own gardens. Elizabeth planted flowers; Margaret planted potatoes. They loved going to the theater and playing charades, but Margaret was the better actress.

Princess Margaret had two imaginary companions. One was called "Cousin Halifax" and the other was called "Inderbombanks." Her family was well aware of her invisible friends, since she sometimes spoke of them. Cousin Halifax was a particularly useful pal. When Margaret did something wrong, such as arriving late, she often blamed Cousin Halifax. No one, not even the princess, knows whether the friends were male or female.

A. A. MILNE (1882–1956), English writer

Alan Alexander had an enviable childhood. He and his two older brothers idolized their father, John. About his father Milne once said, "He differed from our conception of God only because he was shy, which one imagined God not to be, and was funny, which one knew God was not." About his mother, Maria, he said that she knew "that a mother's job is not to prevent wounds, but to bind up the wounded." Both parents were teachers but made learning fun and exciting, not boring and painful. In addition, Alan's parents had a solid, loving relationship that lasted for thirty-five years. As a family, the Milnes took vacations together, read books together, and went to theaters and music halls together. John and Maria trusted the boys and gave them a lot of freedom. Their large home was full of books and toys and animals.

When Alan was five, he and his older brother Ken (aged six) created a fantasy adventure, which they cherished secretly for a number of years. The foundation of the fantasy was simple: Everyone in the world was dead, except for Alan and Ken. On the surface, the fantasy seemed horrific and cruel, especially for two happy, well-adjusted brothers. In his autobiography Milne, who created the beloved Winnie-the-Pooh, describes the fantasy in great detail, noting that it wasn't about wishing harm to come to anyone but was really about freedom and adventure. If he and Ken were truly alone, they could eat whatever they wanted from every sweet shop in London. They could have their pick of bicycles in the bicycle shop. They could be the drivers of a horse bus (apparently, animals were spared extinction). For hours the boys would sit in bed and plan their excursions throughout London. As Milne summed it up, "So many things to eat, so many things to try."

ISAAC NEWTON (1642–1727), English scientist

Isaac was a premature baby, born on Christmas Day in the small village of Woolsthorpe. According to his mother, Hannah, he was so tiny that "they could put him into a quart pot." Isaac's father had died before Isaac was born. Shortly after Isaac's birth, Hannah, then in her late twenties, married a wealthy, sixty-four-year-old minister, Reverend Barnabus Smith, who lived in the nearby town of Witham. When Hannah moved in with her new husband, she left Isaac behind in the Newton family home to be cared for by his maternal grandmother. The new living arrangements lasted for eight years.

Isaac would climb atop a tree from which he could see the steeple of Reverend Smith's church. He longed for his mother's love and hated the stepfather who had taken her from him. Since the towns of Woolsthorpe and Witham were only about a mile apart, Isaac frequently visited his mother but always felt abandoned. Adding to the boy's distress was the fact that his mother and stepfather had three children, all of whom lived happily in the Smith household. After Reverend Smith died, Hannah moved back to her Woolsthorpe home.

During the years of abandonment, young Isaac had a recurring fantasy: Reverend Smith's house would go up in flames and burn to the ground; and everything in the house, including his mother and stepfather, would be destroyed. When Isaac was nineteen years old, he became very religious and felt the need to confess all the sins he had committed in his lifetime. So he wrote them all down and came up with a grand total of fifty-eight sins. Most of them were minor childhood transgressions, but number 13 on the list was the sin of wishing to see his mother and stepfather perish in the home they denied him.

JULES VERNE (1828–1905), French science fiction and adventure novelist

He was a lanky kid with bright red hair who grew up in the seaport city of Nantes. Son of a maritime attorney, Jules was a high-spirited boy who loved to sail down the Loire River in his homemade raft. He earned average grades in school, but his teachers were impressed by his overactive imagination.

When Jules was six years old, he attended a school headed by one Madame Sambain. For many years the schoolteacher had told all her students the tragic story of her life: She was married at a young age to a handsome sea captain who disappeared on a ship headed toward the Indies. With passion and conviction in her voice, she told Jules and his classmates that even though thirty years had passed, she didn't consider herself a widow. She believed her husband was stranded somewhere, like Robinson Crusoe, on a desert island. Someday he would return to her.

The story fueled the fires of Jules's mind. At home he had a book about Robinson Crusoe and he studied the pictures carefully. The young boy concocted his own version of Madame Sambain's story—how the captain's boat was capsized, what the desert island looked like, how he survived and lived all by himself, what measures he took to get rescued, and so on. Jules's elaborate expansion of the tale never left his mind, and elements of the creation would, many years later, find their way into his novels.

A fantasy of being alone in the world: "So many things to eat, so many things to try."

—the young A. A. Milne

H. G. WELLS (1866–1946), English novelist

Herbert George (called "Bertie") was a small boy with big blue eyes and an insatiable curiosity about life. His parents showed little affection toward him or toward each other. As an adult, he once remarked that his parents had a totally effective method of birth control: They slept in separate rooms. At fourteen, Bertie was sent away from home and apprenticed to a draper, then a druggist, then another draper. The apprenticeships all failed because Bertie was a daydreamer who couldn't keep his mind on the tasks at hand.

Bertie wanted to go to school and receive an education, but his parents refused to go along with his plan. Totally miserable and depressed at the thought of his abysmal future, he even contemplated suicide, but never did anything about it. To escape the drudgery of his life, Bertie read books—everything from *Gulliver's Travels* to the works of Thomas Paine. His daydreams were filled with exciting places and people and often revolved around military battles featuring Bertie as the hero. He once wrote, "I used to walk around Bromley, a small rather undernourished boy, meanly clad and whistling detestably between his teeth, and no one suspected that a phantom staff pranced about me and phantom orderlies galloped at my commands to shift the guns and concentrate fire on those houses below. . . ."

Bertie's mother finally gave in and sent him off to school, and he subsequently earned a degree in zoology. His daydreams, however, paid off handsomely when he turned to writing and created such works as *The Time Machine* and *The War of the Worlds*.

DREAMS AND NIGHTMARES

JANE ADDAMS (1860–1935), U.S. social reformer

In a recurring dream, everyone was dead except her. The only way to save the world and make life begin again was to make a wheel. And she had to be the one to do it. She described it: "The village street remained as usual, the village blacksmith shop was 'all there,' even a glowing fire upon the forge and the anvil in its customary place near the door, but no human being was within sight. They had all gone around the edge of the hill to the village cemetery, and I alone remained alive in the deserted world. I always stood in the same spot in the blacksmith shop, darkly pondering as to how to begin, and never once did I know how, although I fully realized that the affairs of the world could not be resumed until at least one wheel should be made and something started."

In her waking hours, she haunted the blacksmith shop, taking in all the details of wheel making and asking questions. She told no one about the dream, "for there is something too mysterious in the burden of 'the winds that come from the fields of sleep' to be communicated, although at the same time it is too heavy a burden to be borne alone."

NICOLAS CAGE (1964–   ), U.S. actor

As a four-year-old, he dreamed that a huge blonde genie, a laughing woman in a gold bikini, reached into the window and picked him up off the toilet seat. When he woke up screaming, his father came to his room and said,

"Think of a white horse. The white horse will come and take your bad dreams away." It worked. Cage has passed the technique on to his son, Weston.

JEAN COCTEAU (1891–1963), French writer, artist, and film director
His father died in 1898. Young Jean had a recurring dream that began when he was ten and did not stop until he was twenty-one. In the dream he and his mother were at the Pré Catelan, which seemed to be a combination of farms and the cockatoo terrace of the Jardin d'Acclimation. They were ready to sit down at a table when he realized that his father was alive and had turned into a parrot, of the kind whose squawking was "associated in my mind with the taste of foamy milk." His mother also knew that his father was a parrot, but was not aware that Jean knew. The problem: to discover "which of the birds it was that my father had turned into, and why he had turned into that bird." He woke up crying "because of the expression on her face: she was trying to smile."

Did you know that Stephen King's best-selling novel Salem's Lot *was based on his own childhood nightmare of finding a body hanging from a gallows and, when the wind turned the body, seeing his own face staring back at him?*

THOMAS DE QUINCEY (1785–1859), English essayist and critic
In a recurring dream about a lion, he would meet the lion and become frightened, "spellbound from even trying to escape," and lie down, shamed, in submission in front of the lion. Later he wondered if all children had this dream, and whether it might have something to do with original sin.

His most famous work as a writer was *Confessions of an Opium Eater*. He claimed that he was not dependent on opium because he had a natural gift for dreaming and kept in touch with his childhood world.

MARIANNE FAITHFULL (1945–   ), English singer
She dreamed a recurring dream: In the dream, she is three. It is a sunny day, and her mother is dressed in armor with a wreath of snakes around her head. Marianne is in bed. The curtains are blue, and the lawn is green. A voice

calls, "Come, Marianne, come." She floats to the windowsill, opens the curtains, and flies to the asparagus bed at the end of the garden. Her mother looms over her. She is raking the coals on an outdoor fire. Then she lifts Marianne and puts her on the fire. Marianne allows her mother to roast her, but there is no pain or fear.

In real life, her mother, Eva, was the Baroness Erisso, a member of the aristocratic Austro-Hungarian von Sacher-Masochs family from whose name the term *masochist* comes.

GRAHAM GREENE (1904–1991), English writer

When he was being psychoanalyzed after a breakdown, he had dreams in which he was in a place of beautiful colors and towers, and a voice said, "Princess and Lord of Time, there are no bounds to thee." A "troop of black-skinned girls who carried poison flowers which it was death to touch" accompanied the Princess of Time, who represented kindness as well as destruction. In the dream he touched the flowers and felt pain in his hands and feet. In a later dream someone told him to kill the princess and gave him a leather-bound book of ritual and a dagger to help him do it, but he did not succeed. The princess always showed up "cruel and reassuring" in those of his dreams that began with fear of some kind: falling, doors opening, ghostly presences.

CARL JUNG (1875–1961), Swiss psychologist

When he was less than five, he heard his clergyman father preaching at funerals, and his father's words brought a question to his mind: Why should he pray to this being, Jesus, who took people, which meant they were put in a black box and buried? Jesus also became associated in his mind with pallbearers, "gloomy black men in frock coats, top hats, and shiny black boots."

Playing in the sand one day, he saw a black-clothed figure come out of the woods. It turned out to be a Jesuit. He ran into the house, terrified. After that he closely connected Jesus with the Jesuits.

Not long after, he dreamed the following dream: He was in a meadow when he found a hole lined with stones. In the hole was a stairway, and though frightened, he went down it until he came to a brocaded curtain. He drew the curtain aside and saw a rock chamber with an arched roof. A red carpet led to a raised platform, on which stood a throne of gold. Sitting on the throne was what seemed to be a thick and mighty tree. The tree was covered with human skin, and it was made of flesh and blood. The top seemed to be a rounded head with one eye looking up. The light in the hole focused more and more on the head. Carl was afraid that the "tree" would leave the throne and crawl toward him like a worm. Terrified, he heard his mother's voice, "Yes—just look at him. That is the man-eater." He woke up in a panic. Jung later interpreted the dream. He said that the "tree" was a giant phallus, identified with Jesus and the Jesuit.

STEPHEN KING (1947–   ), U.S. writer

The king of horror writing encountered singular horror in a dream he had as a child, aged eight. The body of a hanged man hung from a gallows on a hill under a "noxious green sky, boiling with clouds." Black birds—rooks—stood on the corpse's shoulders. A sign on the body read: ROBERT BURNS. Then the wind turned the body, and he saw its face—it was his own face, "rotted and picked by the birds, but obviously mine." Then the corpse's eyes opened, and it looked at Stephen. He woke up, screaming. King used the dream as an image in his novel *Salem's Lot*. He changed the corpse's name to Hubie Marsten.

H. P. (HOWARD PHILLIPS) LOVECRAFT (1890–1937), U.S. writer

He was a lonely, sickly, nervous kid who loved to read books—everything from classical mythology to the tales of Edgar Allan Poe. His love of the bizarre and the supernatural undoubtedly led to childhood nightmares that were weird, terrifying, and sometimes violent.

When Howard was six or seven, he began to have one recurring dream that he was able to describe in great detail. The villains of the dream were "Night-Gaunts," and he said they were "black, lean, rubbery things with horns, barbed tails, bat-wings, and no faces at all." The creatures, who flew in groups of twenty-five or fifty, would swoop down on him and pick him up by his stomach. Then they would fly "through infinite leagues of black air over the towers of dead and horrible cities." Sometimes they would throw him back and forth. At the dream's conclusion, the Night-Gaunts would arrive at a "gray void" and Howard could see numerous mountain peaks below. Then they would drop him. Luckily, he said, he always woke up before he hit the mountains.

Lovecraft's obsession with anything supernatural turned him into a horror-fantasy writer, and he is acknowledged as a pioneer in science fiction writing. As an adult, he once wrote that he had no interest in "ordinary people" and then added, "It is man's relations to the cosmos—to the unknown—which alone arouses in me the spark of creative imagination."

MARILYN MONROE (1926–1962), U.S. actor

She grew up in a succession of foster homes and lived in an orphanage for 21 months. Despite her constant uprooting, she seemed to be a well-adjusted child. Marilyn was an average student in school, and her teachers described her as "bright and sunshiny." Yet her unstable family life made her feel somewhat isolated and deprived. In junior high school the other students called her "the mouse" because she was so quiet. All that changed, however, when her body matured. Her shapely figure plus the right clothes and makeup gave her a new nickname: "the Mmmm Girl."

On a number of occasions, the adult Marilyn described a recurring childhood dream. In one account she said, "I dreamed that I was standing up in church without any clothes on, and all the people there were lying at my feet on the floor of the church, and I walked naked, with a sense of freedom, over their prostrate forms, being careful not to step on anyone."

ELVIS PRESLEY (1935–1977), U.S. singer

The future "king of rock 'n' roll" started having nightmares when he was about six years old. The dreams were usually violent and revolved around people attacking him. The dreams were particularly frightening and vivid when he was a teenager, and they continued throughout his adult life. Often, he dreamed that a mob was coming at him with knives, and he would defend himself by hurling things around the room—everything from glasses to pillows. Or he would wake up screaming and punch his fist into a wall. His lifelong inability to fall into a restful sleep was one of the reasons that he eventually relied so heavily on drugs.

Elvis was also a sleepwalker who sometimes wandered outside to escape the terrors of his nightmares. Since his sleepwalking mentality could be violent, he had to be awakened in a gentle, soothing manner. At one point his mother, Gladys, became so fearful that Elvis might injure himself that she removed the doorknobs so that he couldn't go outdoors.

Elvis's family believed that the nightmares were hereditary, since his father also suffered from them. Elvis said that one night he and his mother and father all had the same nightmare, in which their home was flooded out and they all got out of bed and dragged a mattress up on the roof to escape.

MARY SHELLEY (1797–1851), English novelist
A lively, imaginative child with auburn hair and hazel eyes, she loved to write stories, but her greatest pleasure was "indulging in waking dreams." As an adult, she wrote: "My dreams were at once more fantastic and agreeable than my writings. In the latter I was a close imitator . . . but my dreams were all my own. I accounted for them to nobody; they were my refuge when annoyed— my dearest pleasure when free."

Did you know that four-year-old Nicolas Cage was plagued by a nightmare that a huge blonde genie in a gold bikini reached through his bathroom window and picked him up off the toilet seat?

Her indulgence in dreams paid off when Mary was eighteen and on vacation with poets Lord Byron, Percy Bysshe Shelley (who would become her husband), and several other friends. The group was staying in a villa near Geneva, Switzerland. To entertain themselves on rainy nights, members of the group sat before a fireplace and created ghost stories. One night, after hearing Byron and Shelley discuss the possibility of reanimating a corpse, Mary went to her room but was unable to fall into a deep sleep. Her mind conjured up a "hideous phantasm of a man" who showed signs of life "with an uneasy, half-vital motion." The ensuing horrific scenes, played out in her waking dream, became the basis for her novel *Frankenstein*.

ROBERT LOUIS STEVENSON (1850–1894), Scottish novelist and poet

The Stevenson family nurse, nicknamed "Cummy," was a religious fanatic who filled Robert's head with stories of ghosts and demons and body snatchers. Those tales, coupled with the boy's vivid imagination, were probably instrumental in creating the endless nightmares that plagued Robert throughout his life. He dreamed of hell and Judgment Day, of deformed people, and of horsemen galloping aimlessly through the streets. Always afraid to go to sleep, Robert said his childhood nightmares left him with "a flying heart, a freezing scalp, cold sweats, and the speechless midnight fear."

As an adult, Stevenson found a profitable outlet for his dreams and nightmares, since they inspired some of his best story ideas. In an essay on his dreams, Stevenson described how little people, called "Brownies," visited him in his sleep and created an assortment of entertaining tales. According to Stevenson, the Brownies made up the dreams, while he acted as adviser and writer: "I pull back and I cut down; and I dress the whole in the best words and sentences that I can find and make."

The Brownies, said Stevenson, were the coauthors of *The Strange Case of Dr. Jekyll and Mr. Hyde*. He had been struggling for a story to show "the strong sense of man's double being," when the Brownies came to the rescue: "I dreamed the scene at the window, and a scene afterward split in two, in which Hyde, pursued for some crime, took the powder and underwent the change. . . . All the rest was made awake and consciously, although I think I can trace in much of it the manner of my Brownies."

MARK TWAIN (1835–1910), U.S. writer

His real name was Samuel Langhorne Clemens, and his childhood in Hannibal, Missouri, was almost as adventurous as that of Tom Sawyer, the character immortalized in his books. Born on a night when Halley's Comet glowed in the sky, Sam was a highly imaginative, hyperactive kid with blue-gray eyes and red hair. His youth was filled with dreams, nightmares, and sleepwalking—sometimes as a result of his fascination with the supernatural and sometimes as a result of actual incidents that had a traumatizing effect on him.

One recurring dream involved a gang of robbers, who would come into his bedroom and steal his bedclothes; Sam would sleepwalk around the room, collect the bedclothes, and hide them. When he was about nine and on a river cruise with his older brother, Sam dreamed of fire and explosions; he woke up and ran into the ladies' saloon, screaming that the boat was on fire and everyone should jump ship. Sam also witnessed a murder when he was nine (a local farmer shot a businessman) and endured many subsequent nightmares in which he "gasped and struggled for breath."

Sam's father died when he was eleven, and the ever-curious boy, with his eyes glued to the keyhole of the doctor's office, watched a partial autopsy of the body. On the day his father was buried, Sam appeared, late at night, sleepwalking at his mother's bedside; covered in a big white sheet, he circled her bed. When he was seventeen, Sam gave some matches to a tramp, who was later arrested and put in jail. In the middle of the night the tramp accidentally set his cell on fire, and Sam watched as Hannibal's citizens tried unsuccessfully to free him. Feeling horribly guilty because he had been the provider of the matches, Sam had "hideous" dreams featuring the tramp's face behind the iron bars of the cell as the fire raged.

FEARS, PHOBIAS, AND OBSESSIONS

JOAN BAEZ (1941–   ), U.S. singer and civil rights activist
An intense fear of throwing up has plagued her all her life, though only rarely has she actually vomited. In junior high and high school, nausea caused her to shake and shiver with heat and cold. Terrified, she would climb into her parents' bed. Her parents would stand by the toilet as she fought not to throw up—and finally succeeded in suppressing the impulse. Her mother would hold her hand and talk her through it. In her mind's eye, Joan would see a graph, whose line would drop below the page at the worst part of her nausea. She would breathe through her nose. The fear often left her when her mother said the magic words, "You won't be sick." As the nausea subsided, her mother would say, "You're getting better now. I can feel it in your hands."

Her father, a physicist, was less sympathetic. He tended to comment on what might have brought about her nausea—something she ate, or a bug. Once, when she asked him just to tell her she wouldn't vomit, he replied, "What's so bad about throwing up?" and sent her into a panic.

Did you know that Elvis Presley carried his own set of silverware to school?

INGMAR BERGMAN (1918–   ), Swedish film director
When the black blind in the nursery was drawn, everything became "alive and frightening; the toys changed and became unfriendly or just unrecognizable . . . there were figures there . . . *something for which no words existed.*"

Ruthlessly, the figures came out of the curtains, to disappear only when Ingmar fell asleep or the quality of the light changed.

A wardrobe in the hallway contained a little dwarf who chewed off the feet of bad children, a teenaged girl told him. He was so afraid of being shut up in the wardrobe that he would confess to any transgression. The wardrobe image shows up in Bergman's films as a "torture chamber." Actually, according to his sister, he was put in the wardrobe only once. Perhaps that was enough.

SALVADOR DALI (1904–1989), Spanish painter

Though as a boy he first loved grasshoppers, Dalí developed an inexplicable fear of them when he saw that their faces resembled that of a "drooler," a little fish. This fear was intensified when a girl cousin threw a half-dead and mushy grasshopper against his neck, causing him to scream and nearly faint. His classmates found out about the incident and proceeded to plague him with dead insects. He later said that grasshoppers terrified him partly because even on the brink of death, they could still seize him with their legs, "as if all of a sudden the spring of their capacity for suffering had reached the breaking point, and they had to fling themselves, no matter where—on me!"

One day, Salvador made a paper rooster and told all his tormentors that he was a thousand times more afraid of it than of a grasshopper, though he was not afraid of the rooster at all. Thereupon, they tormented him with paper birds, so when he found one in his cap, he began to scream and would not handle it, but instead spilled ink on it. He said, "Dyed blue, it doesn't scare me any more," then threw it at the blackboard. The Father Superior expelled him from school for impudence.

CLARENCE DARROW (1857–1938), U.S. lawyer

His carpenter father, Amirus, made coffins and became an undertaker to add to the family income. Coffins were piled in a corner of the shop. Clarence "stayed as far away from them as possible, which I have done ever since." At night when he was trying to go to sleep, it seemed to him that his room was peopled with ghosts and bogeymen who had escaped from his father's workshop. All his life, he feared death. Seeing it firsthand did not make it any less horrible. To him life was just a journey toward "the waiting grave."

CHARLES DICKENS (1812–1870), English writer

He was afraid of many things: of "the terrible old woman hobbling out of the box" (from *Tales of the Genii*), of seeing a chain gang, and most especially of a chalk figure that he once saw on a church door, of which he said, ". . . it horrified me so intensely—in connection with the churchyard, I suppose, for it smokes a pipe, and has a big hat with each of its ears sticking out in a horizontal line under the brim, and is not in itself more oppressive than a mouth from ear to ear, a pair of goggle eyes, and hands like two bunches of carrots, five in each, can make it. . . ." He ran home, afraid it was following him. The hands reminded him of those of a retarded man, the Chatham "Idiot"; they were a "dreadful pair of hands that wanted to ramble over everything—our own face included."

Did you know that Mozart would become physically ill at the sound of a trumpet?

GRAHAM GREENE (1904–1991), English writer
Playing on a haystack brought on an attack of hay fever. All night he coughed and fought for breath. He later figured out that this experience gave him his obsessive fear of drowning. "I was able to imagine the lungs filling with water," he said. He dreamed of being drawn to the edge of the water; as time went on, even awake, he felt his feet attracted to the water's edge. Reports in the local paper of inquests of those who had drowned in the Grand Junction Canal probably intensified his fears. He said, "I cannot to this day peer down . . . the sheer wet walls, without a sense of trepidation."

WOLFGANG AMADEUS MOZART (1756–1791), Austrian composer
A child prodigy, as a very young boy Wolfgang was enamored of all things musical but terrified of the sound of a trumpet when the instrument was blown alone. The sound made him physically sick. As one observer noted, "To hold a trumpet in front of him was like aiming a loaded pistol at his heart." No one, including the boy, understood why the trumpet sound was so frightening. Fortunately, however, the phobia inexplicably disappeared before Wolfgang's ninth birthday.

ELVIS PRESLEY (1935–1977), U.S. singer
He was a mama's boy, an only child (his twin brother died at birth) who was overprotected and idolized by his mother, Gladys. She sent him off to school with his own silverware to protect him from germs. At home his dishes and silverware were washed and stored separately, and no one else was allowed to use them. Elvis got angry if anyone tried to mess with his eating utensils. As he grew older, he would sometimes lift food from other people's plates, but for a while he still carried around his own silverware. When Elvis went into the army, he abandoned the practice.

STEVEN SPIELBERG (1946–   ), U.S. film director
His parents often had to turn off the television set because little Steven was scared of just about anything he watched and could end up crying. At the movies he was terrified by the wicked witch in *Snow White and the Seven Dwarfs* and shook through the entire screening of *Fantasia*. In the real world, Steven had a phobia about all snakes and insects. He imagined little people emerging from a crack in the wall beside his bed. When the branches of the trees outside his bedroom window blew in the wind, he saw frightening shapes such as detached arms and long, grasping tentacles.

As an adult, Spielberg capitalized on his childhood fears in many of his movies, such as *Poltergeist*. In a personal essay in *Time* magazine he wrote, "I liked being scared. It was very stimulating. In my films I celebrate the imagination as a tool of great creation and a device for the ultimate scream, and even as a kid I liked pushing myself to the brink of terror and then pulling back."

DIARISTS

LOUISA MAY ALCOTT (1832–1888), U.S. writer

Louisa's father was a transcendentalist philosopher who believed in educating his children at home. As part of their education, he required that they keep journals. Louisa obeyed, but her journals, which she kept from the age of ten, clearly meant more to her than the dutiful fulfillment of an assignment. They reveal the agonies of conscience and rebellion of an intelligent little girl. Though a true child of the nineteenth century, she rejoiced in her own irrepressible individuality.

September 1, 1843: ". . . Father asked us what was God's noblest work. Anna said *men*, but I said *babies*. Men are often bad, babies never are. We had a long talk, and I felt better after it, and *cleared up*. . . .

"As I went to bed the moon came up very brightly and looked at me. I felt sad because I have been cross today, and did not mind Mother. I cried, and then I felt better, and said that piece from Mrs. Sigourney, 'I must not tease my mother.' I get to sleep saying poetry—I know a great deal."

September 14, 1843: ". . . I had a music lesson with Miss P. I hate her, she is so fussy. I ran in the wind and played be a horse, and had a lovely time in the woods with Anna and Lizzie. We were fairies, and made gowns and paper wings. I 'flied' the highest of all. . . ."

March, 1846: ". . . I have made a plan for my life, as I am in my teens, and no more a child. I am old for my age, and don't care much for girl's things. People think I'm wild and queer, but Mother understands and helps me. I have not told any one about my plan, but I'm going to *be* good. . . ."

SALVADOR DALI (1904–1989), Spanish painter

When he was fifteen, Dalí kept a diary that was packed with references to girls—pretty art students, the sister of a friend ("lady of the nights"), a girl in a railroad station. The girls were unattainable—he was too shy to approach them—yet he embraced the idea of love: ". . . I went to sit on one of the boulevard benches. . . . There I saw enamoured couples . . . walking before my eyes, showing their happiness . . . up and down, up and down, whispering their rapturous feelings. They gazed at one another and in their faces there was a smile of happiness . . . I thought about how happy they must be, and I smiled."

The diary describes his adolescent life: He plays soccer and billiards, goes to the movies, does his math homework at 1 A.M. In withering detail, he tells of his confession to a Catholic priest: ". . . a well-fed and overweight clergyman covered me with the old, fading purple shade. 'Ave Maria purissima' . . . he sighed, raising his eyes to the sky. I answered like a robot, 'Bless me, father, for I have sinned.' " His favorite painters, he writes, are the French impressionists, and at a picnic, he watches light striking glass objects on the tablecloth and the curving line of the sea.

Did you know that Beatrix Potter wrote her diary (totaling 200,000 words) in a secret code that took nine years to decipher?

Surprisingly for such a self-absorbed young boy, Dalí also writes of politics—terrorism in Barcelona, for example: "Today a magnificent armed attack took place against one of the vilest men; he was really a full-fledged terrorist." And he talks scathingly of the "loathsome militarism of the German people," as he predicts the war to come.

AGNES DE MILLE (1905–1993), U.S. choreographer

When Agnes de Mille was about eight, the family moved from the East Coast to Los Angeles, where her father, William, a playwright, was writing screenplays for Hollywood. Agnes kept a diary, which gives a picture of early Hollywood and her own growing sensibilities with astounding fidelity.

She was there when her uncle, Cecil B. DeMille, shot scenes for *Joan the Woman*. William, who was assisting, wore a cavalry officer's uniform as he put a group of actors through their paces. "I was a little afraid that Father would get hurt, but he didn't. The French came charging across the field with Joan at their head carrying her standard. . . . They jumped the stockade and fought the English and they won. It was the most beautiful scene I've ever seen."

Before she was eleven, she wrote about the making of *Ivan the Terrible*: "I hate it, and so does he. They were taking a scene where they were beating a man. There were great big lashes on his back and the blood was pouring down. It nearly made me sick. While I was looking, suddenly a strange feeling came over me, and everything got blurred. I could hardly see. My eyes aked [*sic*]. The people became dim figures moving all around. I sat down in a dark corner of the room where they keep the armor for 'Joan of Arc.' I declared the truth and slowly things began to be clear til I was all right."

MARLENE DIETRICH (1901–1992), German-born U.S. actor

When she was ten and a half, her Aunt Valli gave her a red diary bound in morocco leather and embossed with gold. She called it Red. It was the first of many diaries in which she recorded her life and loves, sometimes in Berlin slang. She describes falling in love with boys:

"Dessau. 9 November 1916. . . . I saw him [Fritz] later at violin lessons. . . . He swooned over me in Hartsbad. He was sort of interesting. What was especially interesting was his hot kissing in the dark hallway, for which I got real angry at him. He is 14 years old but behaves like 17. . . . The day we were leaving, he rode by on his bicycle. I had some roses from Tante Elsa, so I pretended I had gotten them from an admirer and told him they should have been from him. . . . I think I'll write to him and reawaken his ardor. . . ."

And not long after, she describes falling in love with a wounded soldier:

"13 January 1917. . . . I love him. With all my love. And what is so beautiful about the whole thing is that he likes me! . . . Before I knew nothing of love. Tomorrow I will see you on the promenade, Fritzi. I will see you, you, you, you angel—you, you wonderful you! . . . I hope Mutti doesn't spoil it all for me.

"16 January 1917. Now it's all over. The whole thing didn't mean a thing to him. And I let myself go and showed him how much I liked him. . . ."

And she tells of her attraction to women:

"17 July 1917. Countess Gersdorf, your feet are pink my heart is set on fire for you!

"I am dying of love for her, she is beautiful like an angel, she is my angel. . . .

"I kissed her hand, she had sweet gray leather gloves on and said, 'Little Leni, you are not going to kiss that dirty glove, are you?'

"14 August 1917. . . . If she weren't married, I would do anything to win her heart and get her before Count Gersdorf. Even now, I'd like to be him. I long for her. She does not know it. She comes here [Berlin] in September and maybe she'll ask me to accompany her to the races to pass the time and have me as her 'boy.' . . . Sometimes my love is like a baby's, although it is serious, like a grown-up. It is the kind of love I could feel for a man. . . ."

ANNE FRANK (1929–1945), German-Dutch Holocaust victim

Anne Frank was perhaps the most famous diarist of modern times. Though she died in her teens, the whole world knows who she was. For three years, the Franks—Anne and Margot and their parents—hid from the Nazis in what they called the secret annex, behind Mr. Frank's business offices. They were joined there by Mr. and Mrs. Van Damm and their son, Peter, and Dussel, a dentist.

Anne began her diary, which she called "Kitty," when she was thirteen. In it, she recorded teenage outrages, loves, and insecurities; her problems with her mother and sister; the peculiarities of the Van Damms and Dussel; and her infatuation with Peter.

In her last entry, August 1, 1944, she wrote: ". . . if I'm quiet and serious, everyone thinks it's a new comedy and then I have to get out of it by turning it into a joke, not to mention my own family, who are sure to think I'm ill. . . . if I am watched to that extent, I start by getting snappy, then unhappy, and finally I twist my heart round again, so that the bad is on the outside and the good is on the inside and keep on trying to find a way of becoming what I would so like to be. . . ."

Three days later, the Gestapo arrested the inhabitants of the secret annex. Anne died eight months later in the concentration camp at Bergen-Belsen. Elli Vossen and Miep Van Santen, who had helped the Franks, found the diary's pages scattered on the floor. They gave them to Anne's father, Otto, who survived the war. Otto published it in 1947.

J. EDGAR HOOVER (1895–1972), U.S. FBI director

By 1908, when he was about thirteen, he was detailing the minutiae of his life in a diary, with the following notation in the front: "Mr. Edgar Hoover, private." In a way the diary was his dossier on himself, as his biographer Anthony Summers has noted. He kept track of everything: the temperature; rain and clouds; the money he made from jobs; lists of his hat, sock, and collar sizes. Some diary entries tell of his railway and streetcar trips throughout the District of Columbia and beyond—all alone. His niece Dorothy said, "All the family had that horrible thing about organization. Everything had to be organized and catalogued, and the pictures had to be straight on the wall—always. It sounds crazy, but we were all like that." He describes how he "gave out Valentines" when he was fourteen, how he fooled people on April 1, and what he did on Groundhog Day. He even records his birth, with a shaky notion of person: "On Sunday, January 1, at 7:30 A.M. J. Edgar Hoover was born to my father and mother. The day was cold and snowy but clear. The Doctor was Mallen. I was born at 413 Seward Square, S.E. Wash. DC. . . ."

SINCLAIR LEWIS (1885–1951), U.S. novelist

Sinclair, called "Harry," began keeping a diary when he was fifteen years old. In it are the musings of a small-town boy who would come to immortalize his community of Sauk Centre, Minnesota, in his bestselling book *Main Street*. The diary, written partly in a secret code, revealed everything from his daily activities to his unrequited love for a girl named Myra: "O, what a charming girl she is and how I love her. But, alas, she does not like me." Harry wrote about the pranks he pulled off in chemistry class, about the rousing "school yells" he composed for his high school, about how angry his father would get when Harry came home very late in the evenings.

Harry's diary suggested that he was an average teenager, actively involved in school and family life. In truth, Harry was a loner who had a very difficult time making friends.

ANAIS NIN (1903–1977), French-born U.S. novelist

Her father, a Spanish concert pianist, deserted the family when Anaïs was eleven years old, and her mother, Rosa, decided to take Anaïs and her two brothers to the United States. On board the boat from Spain to New York City, the young girl began to keep a journal of her new life, "a diary written to persuade my absent father to return." What began as a childish effort to re-

*A meticulously groomed
J. Edgar Hoover, age four.*

Courtesy of the National Archives.

gain her father turned into a lifelong obsession. Nin kept a diary for over fifty years (more than 35,000 pages). She called her journal her "shadow," her "only friend," her "mate for life." Hailed as the "high priestess of diary writing," Nin wrote short stories and novels; portions of her extensive diaries first began to appear in print when she was sixty-three years old.

At age twelve the highly introspective child, who never got over being abandoned by her father, wrote: "I would like that nobody should ever know me. I would like to live isolated and alone. I envy the lives of those souls who can feel such peace, such sweetness in solitude. In one of my stories I uncover the sweetness of this solitude which everybody fears, why? Because they are sick, and blind."

ROBERT PEARY (1856–1920), U.S. Arctic explorer

Generally acknowledged as the first person to reach the North Pole, Peary started keeping a detailed diary when he was a teenager. He wrote about what he did every day, about his observations of nature, and about the things he could do to improve himself. The only child of a widowed mother, he was something of a loner who liked to read, to hike, to sail and explore.

During his junior year in high school in Portland, Maine, Robert became enamored of a classmate known only as "Em" in his diary. One winter day, after Robert and Em walked home over slippery streets, he wrote, "She clung to me closer than usual which, of course, was pleasant for me." Two weeks later he wrote, "I am going to see how she would take it if I should kiss her one of these evenings." After another two-week period, he wrote, "I asked for a kiss. Of course, she refused but it was not a very decided one, and I am going to take one some evening." A subsequent entry, in the form of a poem, exudes great excitement over a kiss from a girl named Lillie—probably the much-fancied "Em."

BEATRIX POTTER (1866–1943), English writer of children's books

Nine years after Potter died, her diary was discovered hidden in the attic of her home. Consisting of a bunch of school exercise books and loose sheets of paper, the diary was written in a secret code that took almost nine years to decipher. It covered the period of her life from age fifteen to thirty and totaled about 200,000 words.

For the most part the diary was a fact-filled, impersonal account of Potter's life. There were no secret revelations, no fantasies about boys, no bitter feelings about her parents or younger brother. Mostly she filled the pages with accounts of her summer vacations in Scotland, her love of nature and animals. She wrote about visits to museums and zoos and commented on stories she had read in the newspapers. An obedient, mild-mannered girl, Beatrix occasionally allowed herself to make a few critical comments, like how she felt about one of her art tutors: "It is tiresome when you do get some lessons, to be taught in a way you dislike and to have to swallow your feelings out of considerations at home." The most revealing entries in the journal are those that show her to be a lonely child who was subject to bouts of depression: "How much I have to be thankful for, but these odious fits of low spirits would spoil any life." Perhaps that is why she committed the rest of her life to creating books that brought joy into the childhoods of others.

RUTH WESTHEIMER (1928–   ), German-born U.S. sex therapist

When she was ten years old, Karola Ruth Siegel was among a group of German-Jewish children put on a train to Switzerland to escape persecution from the Nazis. Left behind were her parents and grandparents—all subsequently killed in concentration camps. For six years Ruth lived in Heiden in a children's home while she waited for news from her parents, who had planned to leave Germany and send for her. Life at the home was safe and secure but lonely and filled with hard work and "a daily schedule that would make Cinderella's life look leisurely."

Did you know that Anaïs Nin's childhood diary grew to become her lifelong obsession, eventually totaling over 35,000 pages?

Ruth's biggest source of comfort was her diary, which she began keeping two years after she arrived in Heiden. She called it her "tool for knowledge" and her "best confidant" and hoped that one day she would give the diary to her parents to read. The diary was really a collection of small blue composition notebooks, and she wished that someday she would have a real diary—one that could be locked with a key. A sample entry from her diary: "Will I be able to stick it out? I don't know. . . . One word keeps coming back: alone, one is so alone in this world. One has to keep on struggling—but: alone, always alone. I do miss my parents terribly. No friend can take their place. Oh, how I long for them, how homesick I am!"

TURNING POINTS

KAREEM ABDUL-JABBAR (1947–   ), U.S. basketball player

He was born Lew Alcindor into a middle-class family in Harlem. In 1950, the family moved to another part of Manhattan. Lew was an obedient and bright child, the best academically and the tallest in his class in parochial school. In third grade, a classmate brought a Polaroid camera to school, and the teacher took a class picture in front of the blackboard. Lew was in the center of the back row. When the picture was ready, the teacher passed it around to the students, who had gone back to their seats. When Lew saw himself in the picture, he said to himself, "Damn, I'm dark and everybody else is light!" He had never paid much attention to his color before.

He told no one of his revelation, but when he came upon Hans Christian Andersen's story, "The Ugly Duckling," he identified with its main character.

In his own version of the story, the duckling grew up to be a beautiful black swan, not a white one.

HANNAH ARENDT (1906–1975), German-born U.S. philosopher

Her parents, Paul and Martha, were highly educated socialists, who wanted to bring up their daughter as part of the educated elite. Martha kept an *Unser Kind* (Our Child) book that was a detailed record of Hannah's development— her diet, her routines, her illnesses, her achievements, personality traits. In the beginning Hannah was "a real sunshine child"—cheerful, obedient, eager, loving. Her first three years were spent in a gregarious household, visited by many friends and relatives for piano playing, singing, and storytelling. Soon, however, signs of Paul Arendt's illness, syphilis, which he had contracted before his marriage but thought was cured, became very apparent. By the fall of 1910, Hannah could no longer invite her friends over because her father needed quiet. She became a "little mother" to her father, patiently playing card games with him. In 1911, he was institutionalized.

When her grandfather, Max Arendt, died in the spring of 1913, she seemed untouched. And when her father died in October of that year, she said to her mother, "Remember, Mama, that it happens to a lot of women."

However, the "sunshine child" began to develop illnesses and become "difficult." Throughout 1916, she was a "fever child," suffering nosebleeds, headaches, throat infections. In 1917 she developed diphtheria, and her personality turned "mysterious." The illnesses often occurred right before a journey. Her biographer, Elisabeth Young-Bruehl, notes that she had watched people go away and never return. The illnesses seemed to be a physical manifestation of her fears of abandonment. She remained psychologically sensitive for the rest of her life.

ALEXANDER GRAHAM BELL (1847–1922), Scottish-born U.S. inventor

The inventor of the telephone came from a line of inventive men interested in the problems of speech. His grandfather, also Alexander, worked first as an actor and then as a speech teacher. He had presence: a booming voice, energy, a rugged face. A scandal involving the seduction of his wife by one William Murray brought him a small settlement of three hundred pounds, as a result of which he went to London, bringing his fourteen-year-old son, also Alexander, with him. In London he gained modest fame as a speech teacher and eventually remarried. After a stay in Newfoundland, his son returned to Scotland and later married a deaf Englishwoman, Eliza Grace Symonds, the love of his life. They lived in Edinburgh with their three boys. Their second child was the third Alexander Bell, who grew up to invent the telephone. He was, however, a late bloomer. His older brother, Melville (Melly), and younger brother, Ted, put him in the shade. His schoolwork was mediocre.

When he was fifteen, Alexander went to London to live with his grandfather, then over seventy years old. The elder Alexander Bell had been busy teaching speech, lecturing, and writing. But his second wife had died, and he was lonely.

Grandfather Bell took care of first things first. He sent provincial Aleck to a London tailor to be outfitted, down to cane and gloves and tall silk hat. Grandfather and grandson became "companions and friends." Grandfather Bell worked on Aleck's declamation and elocution and pushed him into serious reading and study. In the spring of 1863, when Grandfather Bell became ill, Aleck took care of him devotedly. The year had turned him "from a boy somewhat prematurely into a man," he said later. "From this time forth, my intimates were men rather than boys, and I came to be looked upon as older than I really was." In a letter, his father said, "You will have cause for thankfulness all your life that you had the benefit of such a training as my father has lovingly afforded you." Aleck agreed. He later called his sojourn in London "the turning point of my whole career."

CARL BERNSTEIN (1944–   ), U.S. journalist

Coauthor with Bob Woodward of the newspaper investigation that exposed the Watergate scandal, Carl Bernstein came from a politically aware family. His parents, members of the Communist Party USA, helped to organize the campaign to save Julius and Ethel Rosenberg from execution. On June 19, 1953, when Carl was nine, the event they had tried to stop occurred: Ethel and Julius Rosenberg died in the electric chair. Freckle-faced Carl was in tears. He was in tears because whatever forces killed the Rosenbergs could kill his mother, too. He hated his parents for making themselves so vulnerable. The activist child who, with his parents, had walked with blacks up to white lunch counters lost his enthusiasm for activism.

Alarming events continued to happen. The Bernsteins were brought up before committees set on flushing out Communists. His mother ended up on the front pages of three Washington, D.C., newspapers. This affected Carl; for one thing, other kids were not allowed to play with him any more.

When Carl became old enough, he requested a bar mitzvah ceremony. His parents, who were not religious, resisted the idea. Carl wrote them a note accusing them of being "atheistic Jewish Communists." They gave in. The FBI came to the bar mitzvah. As an adolescent, Carl shunned politics, especially left-wing politics. He agreed with his parents on only one thing: that Richard Nixon was bad.

NAPOLEON BONAPARTE (1769–1821), French general and emperor

He was born in Ajaccio on the island of Corsica on a holy day dedicated to the Virgin Mary; Napoleon's mother, Letizia, had her first labor pains in church. As a young boy, Napoleon dutifully attended church, but he really disliked going to high mass on Sunday since the service was so long. However, whenever he tried to skip high mass, he was soundly slapped by his mother. Napoleon attended religious schools in Ajaccio from the age of five, and when he turned nine, the Bonapartes decided to send him to France to attend a military academy.

The Brienne Military Academy was run by the Order of St. Francis. Every day Napoleon went to mass and was expected to take communion every two months and go to confession every month. While he studied subjects like Latin and mathematics, Napoleon really immersed himself in the study of military history—great battles, soldiers, and statesmen. When he was eleven, he listened to a sermon in which the friar emphatically stated that both Cato and Caesar were in hell. From that moment on, the boy would question his beliefs in Christianity. He was outraged to hear that "the most virtuous men of antiquity would burn in eternal flames for not having practiced a religion they knew nothing about."

MICK JAGGER (1943–   ), English singer

His father, Basil ("Joe"), taught physical education in Dartford, England. He later distinguished himself as a national expert on basketball. When Mick was three, Joe started him on callisthenics. Mick was going to be an athlete. At eleven, he passed the "eleven plus" exam that qualified him for grammar school, the elite track that led to university. At twelve he was teaching physical education at a U.S. Army base to children of GIs. After José, an African-American cook at the base, introduced him to black music, Mick and three other boys started a blues band, Little Boy Blue and the Blue Boys. Jagger, the singer, tried to sound like an African American from the Deep South.

In spite of his love affair with music, Mick continued to play basketball at school, eventually becoming captain of the Dartford Grammar School team. Surprisingly, basketball affected his singing. In one game Mick knocked into another player, bit off the tip of his own tongue, and swallowed it. He couldn't talk or sing for days. But when he did, his voice was transformed. He no longer sounded British at all; his voice had a grainy, gutsy, hard-edged sound. "We were shocked," said Dick Taylor, his then drummer. "He sounded so weird—the way he sounds now, actually. That accident just changed his voice completely. Biting off the tip of his tongue may have been the best thing that ever happened to Mick Jagger."

Did you know that Burt Reynolds's life might have been vastly different "if not for the outcome of a single footrace"?

DAVID LETTERMAN (1947–   ), U.S. talk show host and comedian

At Broad Ripple High School in Indianapolis, Indiana, Dave participated in basketball and track but wasn't a star athlete. He was a funny guy who was well liked but wasn't part of the "in crowd." His academic performance was less than stellar. Although he didn't agonize over what his life would be like after graduation, he did try to figure out what he was good at, what he liked, and how the answers to those questions would translate into a career.

Dave's musings on his future all came together one day in speech class when he had to give an impromptu speech. The task turned out to be easy, he was very good at it, and he was overwhelmed with praise. Years later, Letterman recalled the incident: "Wait a minute! I can actually get a grade here, just standing up and telling stories? How do you apply this? And then I found out you could study broadcasting in college, and I thought, 'Holy cow! There you go! It's a miracle.' "

NORMAN VINCENT PEALE (1898–1993), U.S. clergyman

The man who would write *The Power of Positive Thinking*, one of history's all-time bestselling books, was born in Ohio, the son of a Methodist minister. Norman was a shy, awkward kid who worshipped his father, Charles. Of his father Norman once said, "My father loved people, all sorts and conditions of people, good or bad. To him there was no distinction."

According to Peale, an incident took place when he was nine or ten that would have a profound impact on his life and on his decision to become a pastor. One evening the madame of a whorehouse in Cincinnati called the Peale home and asked if Norman's father would come to visit a nineteen-year-old prostitute who was dying. Charles agreed to go and took young Norman along despite his wife's objections. The boy watched as his father gently talked and prayed with the young woman and assured her that the Lord would forgive her sins.

In his autobiography, Peale gives an emotional account of the evening at the prostitute's bedside and recalls, "Even though I was still so young, the experience awed me by its beauty. This unholy place of evil became holy because, for a fact, the Lord was there. In that moment I saw the wonder and glory of the ministry, the majesty and power of the work of the pastor."

RICHARD PRYOR (1940–   ), U.S. comedian and actor

He grew up a poor black kid in Peoria, Illinois. Most of the students in Richard's elementary class were white. He knew he was different, but he had no idea how or why being black really made him different from the rest of the kids. The distinction, however, became somewhat clearer when he was seven and developed a crush on a white girl. Richard gave her a present—an erase-a-slate writing board—and was elated that she happily accepted the gift. The next day, the girl's angry father came to school and yelled at Richard, warning him never again to give any presents to the girl. For the first time, Richard began to understand the meaning of racism.

The boy was confused. He didn't want to be white, but he wasn't sure he wanted to be black. So he gave himself a new identity. In his autobiography, Pryor says, "I called myself Sun the Secret Prince. As Sun the Secret Prince, I was colorless. I was just light and energy, caroming off the planets. No boundaries. Simply alive."

BURT REYNOLDS (1936–   ), U.S. actor

Burt wanted to be called "Buddy," but his classmates called him "Greaseball" or "Mullet" because of his Italian-Indian heritage. After school at Central Junior High in West Palm Beach, Florida, Burt would wander into Beth's Soda

Shop, the local hangout, where social standing was based on which corner you sat in—nerds, cheerleaders, greasers, or jocks. Burt joined the greasers but longingly watched the jock corner filled with guys in letterman sweaters.

One day, after winning a race in gym class, fourteen-year-old Burt was approached by a few athletes who challenged him to run a footrace against Vernon Rollison, the best sprinter at Central High. Buddy agreed, and on the morning of the race a large crowd gathered on the football field to watch Greaseball the underdog run against Rollison the star athlete. At first Rollison took the lead, but Burt—running barefoot—kept his eyes on the goalpost; at the five-yard line, he raced past his opponent to win.

After his victory, Burt went out for the football team and became an all-star player. He also participated in baseball, basketball, and track. The big red Cs sewn on his white letterman sweater symbolized his transition from outcast to local hero. And everybody called him "Buddy." In his autobiography, Reynolds writes, "As much as I'd like to think everything I've done is based on a lot of luck and some talent—all the movies, TV shows, plays, adventures, and predicaments—it all might've been different, and perhaps never taken place, if not for the outcome of a single footrace."

ALBERT SCHWEITZER (1875–1965), Alsatian-German medical missionary
He was a philosopher, biblical scholar, musician, and humanitarian. But Dr. Albert Schweitzer is best remembered for his missionary work in the hospital he founded in Lambaréné in French Equatorial Africa (now Gabon), where he worked for more than fifty years. He believed that all living beings were somehow interrelated and called his ethical philosophy "a reverence for life." In 1952 he was awarded the Nobel Peace Prize.

Son of a Protestant minister, Albert grew up in the village of Günsbach in Alsace, the borderland between Germany and France. As a very young boy, he was bothered by the fact that the evening prayers he was taught included only human beings. So he made up his own ending: "Bless and protect all things that have breath, guard them from evil, and let them sleep in peace."

Did you know biting off the tip of his tongue changed Mick Jagger's voice and future forever?

One day Albert's friend Henry Brasch asked him to go bird shooting. The boys grabbed their slingshots, headed up a hill, and patiently waited for birds to gather on tree branches. Before getting off a shot, Albert heard church bells ringing in the distance—a sign to him of divine intervention. As the commandment "Thou shalt not kill" flashed into his mind, the boy dropped his weapon, excitedly shooed away the birds, and ran home. He later wrote, "This early influence upon me of the commandment not to kill or to torture other creatures is the great experience of my childhood and youth. By the side of that all others are insignificant."

RED SKELTON (1913–1997), U.S. comedian and actor

Red's father, a circus clown, died two months before Red was born. Ida Mae, Red's mother, was a charwoman in a vaudeville theater in Vincennes, Indiana. The boy and his three brothers grew up in a two-room shack; many of his early memories were of being hungry. At age seven, Red took his first job: selling newspapers on street corners. It was the first of many part-time jobs he took to put food on the table.

When Red was about ten, a stranger paid for his ticket to a local vaudeville show starring comedian Ed Wynn. Mesmerized by Wynn's performance, Red went backstage to get an autograph and in an excited voice told Wynn that he planned to become a comedian. The vaudeville star chatted with the boy, signed the back of Red's sweatshirt, and offered some career advice. The incident cemented Red's determination to make it big in show business. Forty years later, after Skelton had become famous (creating such zany characters as Freddy the Freeloader and Clem Kadiddlehopper) and Wynn's career was in trouble, Skelton stepped in to help his boyhood idol.

SYLVESTER STALLONE (1946–   ), U.S. actor and screenwriter

He was born in a charity hospital in New York City, and the forceps used in the delivery damaged a nerve on one side of his face, leaving it partly paralyzed. A scrawny, insecure kid with a speech impediment, Sylvester caused a lot of trouble in school, thinking it would win him attention and respect. Instead, the kids made fun of his silly first name and decided to call him "Binky," then "Stinky." He was in and out of a number of schools (sometimes expelled), and when he was eleven, his parents divorced.

Stallone says that a turning point in his life happened when he was fifteen and moved to Philadelphia to live with his mother and stepfather. In an interview with *Parade* magazine, he described how he went to a church dance and a big man approached him and said, "At the count of three, I'm going to break your face." Then the guy slugged him. Stallone recalled, "I walked home, each step feeling more self-contempt. I'd been struck by a stranger for no reason, treated like a nothing. I turned around and came back and fought my heart out." Even though the fight ended without a decisive winner, the fifteen-year-old walked away with newfound confidence and self-respect.

IDA TARBELL (1857–1944), U.S. journalist

One of America's first investigative journalists, Ida Tarbell grew up in the 1860s in the booming oil towns of western Pennsylvania. She was a rebellious, independent girl who rode horses, climbed trees, and skipped school to take long walks in the hills. Yet she was also an excellent student, an avid reader, and an imaginative girl whose mind created wonderful adventure stories. Crusaders of some sort always seemed to be visiting the Tarbell home, since Ida's father, an independent oil man, was always railing against oil barons like John D. Rockefeller and her mother was active in women's rights groups. By the time she was fifteen, Ida was filled with ambition.

One summer Ida went to a camp and participated in a science program led by two women lecturers. Fascinated by the microscope demonstrations, Ida waited for the proper moment to approach the women and told them that she wanted to become a scientist and would they please give her some advice. When she finished her little speech, Ida was humiliated and angry at the response she received. She later recalled, "The two ladies smiled down from their height, so plainly showing they thought me a country child with a queer behavior complex. 'Quite impossible,' they said and turned back to their conference.' " At that moment, Ida clenched her fists and resolved that one day she would "show them"; she would do something important.

She didn't turn out to be a scientist but did become a writer. Her book *History of the Standard Oil Company* exposed the ruthless business practices of big business. She wrote on a variety of American issues in *McClure's* magazine, a muckraking publication, and interviewed prominent figures of her time, including Benito Mussolini and Louis Pasteur.

WHAT THEY WANTED TO BE AS GROWNUPS

FRED ALLEN (1894–1956), U.S. comedian
His earliest ambition was to be a streetcar motorman.

Did you know that Shirley Temple Black originally dreamed of being an FBI agent?

MARIAN ANDERSON (1897–1993), U.S. singer
A child who doctored her dolls and bandaged her friends, she harbored the ambition to be a surgeon.

ELIZABETH ARDEN (1891–1966), U.S. businesswoman
She said as a child, "I want to be the richest little woman in the world." With a chemist, she created a cream to cure skin blemishes. Its success launched her career—and she went on to make a fortune in cosmetics.

ETHEL BARRYMORE (1879–1959), U.S. actor

She wanted to be a nun, then a concert pianist. She won a silver medal at school for playing a Beethoven sonata.

SAMUEL BECKETT (1906–1989), Irish dramatist

His music teacher asked him what he wanted to do when he grew up. His answer was, "Play." "Music?" she asked. "No, I want to play cricket for Ireland," he replied.

Did you know that k. d. lang wanted to be a roller derby queen when she grew up?

JACK BENNY (1894–1974), U.S. comedian

Though his violin playing was a running joke in his comedy act, as a boy Benny wanted to be a professional violinist. His parents gave him a half-size violin for his sixth birthday, and he began lessons. While still in school, he played for pay at parties and in a theater orchestra.

SHIRLEY TEMPLE BLACK (1928–   ), U.S. actor and politician

She wanted to be a G-woman (FBI agent). When her mother told her she was not the type, she said she would fool the robbers because they wouldn't suspect her.

CAROL BURNETT (1933–   ), U.S. comedian

Her ambition was to be a cartoonist. She created a strip called "The Josephson Family," whose characters included Joseph (the father), Josephine (the mother), Jody (a teenaged girl), Joey (a boy), and Jo-Jo (the dog). When she and her grandmother worked as night cleaning ladies at a Warner Bros. office building, she left one of her sketches on an artist's desk, hoping to be discovered. The next night, she found a note on the desk, telling her just to clean the office, period.

TRUMAN CAPOTE (1924–1984), U.S. writer

He wrote: "One day, when I was nine or ten, I was walking along the road, kicking stones, and I realized that I wanted to be a writer, an artist. How did that happen? That's what I ask myself. My relatives were nothin', dirt-poor farmers. I don't believe in possession, but something took over inside me, some little demon that made me a writer. How else can it be explained?" At five or six, he took a little dictionary, paper, and pencil with him everywhere. Later he set up a writer's corner in his room, with a typewriter, where he wrote stories.

SALVADOR DALÍ (1904–1989), Spanish painter

At age six he wanted to be a cook, but a year later he wanted to be an emperor, like Napoleon Bonaparte. It began when he saw a picture of Napoleon on a keg of *maté* (a kind of tea). "At the time, if I were lagging as we came back from a long walk, all I needed was to be told, 'Lead the way, Napoleon,' and immediately all my fatigue was forgotten as I hopped on my trusty warhorse."

CLARENCE DARROW (1857–1938), U.S. lawyer

He always wanted to write a book. "I remember when I was very small, and used to climb on a chair and look at the rows of books on my father's shelves, I thought it must be a wonderful being who could write all the pages of a big book, and I would have given all the playthings that I ever hoped to have for the assurance that some day I might possibly write down so many words and have them printed and bound in a book."

ANGELA DAVIS (1944–   ), U.S. political activist

She saw doctors and nurses almost every day because she went to the nursery school next door to the Children's Home Hospital, where, at age two, she had her tonsils removed. White-uniformed hospital personnel fascinated her, and she decided that she wanted to be a pediatrician. This ambition lasted until high school, when her intense interest in political activism began.

MILES DAVIS (1926–1991), U.S. musician

His girlfriend's little brother, William, died when an uncaring doctor refused to treat him, saying that he would be dead by morning. Furious and heartsick, Miles Davis decided he wanted to be a doctor to try to save the lives of people like William. But then, as he said, "Music just moved medicine out of my head."

DANIEL DAY-LEWIS (1957–   ), English actor

A skilled woodworker, he considered making cabinetmaking his life's work. As a teenager, he made a Welsh dresser and a dining room table of pine and walnut with accompanying caned chairs. After finishing school, the multitalented Daniel applied for a job as an apprentice with a foremost cabinetmaker and also to the Old Vic Theatre School. In the end, he chose acting.

MALCOLM FORBES (1919–1990), U.S. publisher

Even as a grade-school student, he had the ambition to be president of the United States. He said once, "It's the Holy Grail, the gold at the end of the rainbow."

DUSTIN HOFFMAN (1937–   ), U.S. actor

He took up classical piano in 1952. When speakers failed to show up for school assemblies at Los Angeles High School, he was sometimes called upon to play the one song he knew, "Bumble Boogie." He also played at parties, hoping that a girl would sit down next to him on the piano bench and notice his sensitive hands.

WILLIAM JAMES (1842–1910), U.S. psychologist
Though he had talent as a scientist, he wanted to be an artist. By the time he was ten, he was spending a great deal of time drawing. At fourteen, he so impressed the French painter Léon Coignet with his drawings that Coignet allowed him into his atelier. His father thought art was a shallow profession, yet he later agreed to let William study painting under William Morris Hunt. Within the year, William changed his mind and decided to study science.

C. EVERETT KOOP (1916–   ), U.S. surgeon general
From the time he was small he wanted to be a surgeon. He practiced cutting pictures from magazines with both hands and tying knots in small places with one hand. When he was a teenager, he operated on animals with his mother as his anesthetist.

BURT LANCASTER (1913–1994), U.S. actor
He wanted to be an opera singer and sang in the church choir until he was fifteen. Burt listened to opera on the radio, and since he lived in New York City, he frequently attended programs at the Metropolitan Opera. According to Lancaster, when his voice broke, he was forced to abandon his ambition.

K. D. LANG (1961–   ), Canadian singer
As a teenager, she wanted to be a roller derby queen. A gifted athlete, Kathryn Dawn Lang watched roller derby shows on television and then perfected her style and technique in the basement of the Lang home.

ANDREW LLOYD WEBBER (1948–   ), English composer
He loved ancient ruins and wanted to become a historian. Andrew, at age seven, even knew the exact position he wanted: chief inspector of ancient British monuments. Before he reached his teens, Andrew wrote a number of meticulously researched and illustrated essays on ancient monuments.

VINCE LOMBARDI (1913–1970), U.S. football coach
The legendary coach ("winning isn't everything; it's the only thing") of the Green Bay Packers, Lombardi originally wanted to be a priest. He even attended a preseminary school but dropped out. An incident that occurred in his senior year at a Jesuit high school shows that Vince's decision *not* to become a priest was probably a good one: A teacher, who had to leave the classroom, asked Vince to be in charge of the recitation of the "Hail Mary." When the teacher came back, he found Vince hitting another boy's head against the blackboard. The action was warranted, said Vince, because "He wouldn't say the 'Hail Mary.' "

MADONNA (1958–   ), U.S. singer and actor
Until she was fifteen, Madonna Louise Ciccone attended Catholic schools. For a short while, she thought about becoming a nun. However, she said, "When I realized that nuns didn't have a sex life, I was incredibly disenchanted."

to us. The radiance of Harry's visit has not faded yet & I come upon gleams of it 3 or 4 times a day in my farings to and fro, but it has never a bit diminished the lustre of far off shining Newport all silver and blue & this heavenly group below (all being more or less failures, especially the two outside ones) The more so as the above mentioned Harry could in no wise satisfy my cravings to know of the family and friends as he

A sketch young William James made to illustrate a letter he wrote in 1861; his brother, Henry, holds their father's arm.

Shelf mark bMS Am 1092.9 (2501).
By permission of the Houghton Library, Harvard University.

HENRY LOUIS MENCKEN (1880–1956), U.S. editor and critic

In his early teenage years Henry planned on a career as a chemist. Holed up in his room, he conducted all sorts of experiments in his makeshift laboratory. But then he endured two years of lessons from a chemistry teacher. As Mencken described it, the teacher's "inept tutelage confused and disheartened me. He had a great influence on my life. He taught me the useful lesson that fools are often potent in this world."

POPE JOHN PAUL II (1920–   ), Polish-born head of the Catholic Church

Born in Wadowice, Poland, Karol Wojtyla was a good soccer player and a good dancer. He liked poetry and literature, and most of all he liked the theater. In high school he often had the starring role in theatrical productions. In addition, he sometimes directed the plays or acted as set designer. Karol seemed destined for a theatrical career. In his book, *Gift and Mystery,* Pope John Paul II says, "I must admit that the whole experience of the theater left a deep impression on me, even though at a certain point I came to realize that *this was not my real vocation.*"

JOSEPH STALIN (1879–1953), Soviet dictator

One of the harshest dictators in world history, Joseph Stalin was originally destined to be a priest. He spent six years (ages nine to fourteen) at the Gori Theological School and then entered the Tiflis Theological Seminary. He remained at Tiflis for five years but was expelled for his political activities. According to one of his classmates, Stalin "saw everywhere and in everything only the negative, the bad side, and had no faith at all in the idealistic motives or attributes of mankind."

Did you know that as a child Salvador Dalí first wanted to be a chef, and then an emperor like Napoleon Bonaparte?

JAMES STEWART (1908–1997), U.S. actor

His father wanted him to be an engineer, but for a while all Jimmy wanted to be was an aviator. He had a big scrapbook in which he pasted articles about flying. When talking about his early ambition, the Oscar-winning actor once said, "Airplanes were the last thing I thought about every night and the first thing I thought about in the morning."

JOSIP BROZ TITO (1892–1980), Yugoslavian political leader

Tito once wrote: "My ambition when I was a small boy was to be a tailor, a natural result of the wish of every little peasant in Zagorje to have nice clothes." At fifteen he left home and moved to Sisak to take a job as a waiter in an army canteen because a friend told him that the waiters got nice clothes to wear. Throughout his life, Tito had a taste for expensive clothes and fine accessories.

QUOTATIONS ABOUT CHILDHOOD

SHERWOOD ANDERSON (1876–1941), U.S. writer
"A man, if he is any good, never gets over being a boy." (From *Tar*.)

INGMAR BERGMAN (1918–   ), Swedish film director
When he finally gained his independence from his parents, he said it was "like emerging from an iron lung and finally being able to breathe for oneself." He also said, "My parents did their best to destroy the lives of their children."

ESTHER DYSON (1951–   ), Swiss-born U.S. writer and entrepreneur
When she was five, her mother ran off with a mathematician. Her response was, "Oh, who needs a mother after the milk is gone."

GRAHAM GREENE (1904–1991), English writer
He said of childhood that we are all "emigrants from a country we remember too little of . . . we can't remember how happiness felt or the quality of the misery, we watch our children's eyes for hints: knowledge has altered the taste of every emotion."

STEPHEN KING (1947–   ), U.S. writer
"People of my generation, twenty-five to forty, we were obsessive about our own childhoods for a long time. We went on playing for a long time, almost feverishly. I write for that buried child in us, but I'm writing for the grown-up too. I want grown-ups to look at the child long enough to be able to give him up. The child should be buried."

BURT LANCASTER (1913–1994), U.S. actor
"My background was potluck, and everybody had to share. I wore my brothers' hand-me-down clothes, but when you're that young that just doesn't matter."

WLADZIU VALENTINO LIBERACE (1919–1987), U.S. pianist
"Except for music, there wasn't much beauty in my childhood. We lived in one of those featureless bungalows in a featureless neighborhood."

ABRAHAM LINCOLN (1809–1865), U.S. president
"All that I am or ever hope to be I owe to my angel mother."

GEORGE LUCAS (1944–   ), U.S. film director and producer
"I had a good life when I was a kid, a normal, tough, repressed childhood filled with fear and trepidation all over the place. But generally, I enjoyed it; it was good."

BETTE MIDLER (1945–   ), U.S. singer and actor

"I didn't belong as a kid, and that always bothered me. If only I'd known that one day my differentness would be an asset, then my early life would have been much easier."

GEORGE ORWELL (1903–1950), English novelist and essayist

"I had the lonely child's habit of making up stories and holding conversations with imaginary persons, and I think from the very start my literary ambitions were mixed up with the feelings of being isolated and undervalued."

JOHN STEINBECK (1902–1968), U.S. novelist

"I remember the sorrow at not being part of things in my childhood."

GLORIA SWANSON (1899–1983), U.S. actor

"I hated being a child and I hated school. . . . I couldn't wait to wear long skirts and put my hair up on top of my head and wear a wedding ring and be Mrs. Somebody with twelve children—six on each side of the dining-room table."

PETER USTINOV (1921–   ), English actor, writer, director, and producer

"The most painful function of a parent is to be the bone on which the young may sharpen its teeth. I am forever grateful to my father for supplying such a resolute bone."

OSCAR WILDE (1854–1900), Irish poet and dramatist

"Children begin by loving their parents; as they grow older they judge them. Rarely, if ever, do they forgive them."

CHAPTER TWO

$\mathcal{H}$OME LIFE

> *"Happy families are all alike; every unhappy family is unhappy in its own way."*
> LEO TOLSTOY, *ANNA KARENINA*

Home: a downy nest second only to the womb, perhaps a cradle of genius. Home: a hell where children's hearts break, sometimes forever. Home: inhabited by parents, who dote and doubt, nurture and hurt.

In the biographies of the famous we find great evidence of parental love, some of it excessive. Mary Baker Eddy's mother wrote, "sometimes I fear I worship mary instead of the great jehovah." Freud was his mother's "golden Sigi." How did the children react to this love? Take mother love, for instance, with its mixed press. William Randolph Hearst said that he was "a mother's boy" but was "mighty glad of it." However, the poet W. H. Auden, in an unpublished poem, wrote: "Tommy did as mother told him / Till his soul had split; / One half thought of angels / And the other half of shit."

Parents could do their children real damage. Sometimes it was not

47

their fault because they were mentally ill. Temperance leader Carry Nation had a mother with intemperate notions—she thought she was Queen Victoria and wore a long purple velvet gown and crystal and cut-glass crown to prove it. Beat poet Allen Ginsberg's mother wore cooking pots on her ears to keep out the voices she heard, yet Ginsberg loved her always and called her "the beautiful Garbo of my Karma."

Brothers and sisters played a role, too. Fierce sibling rivalry shows up in the biographies of the famous. Both Dwight Eisenhower and John F. Kennedy contested with powerful older brothers. Salvador Dalí fought the ghost of the brother who died before he was born.

Some famous people had unhappy childhoods. In fact, unhappiness drove a few to run away. And poverty stalked more of the famous than you might think. Dick Gregory was so poor as a child that he ate library paste because he was hungry. Other eminent people remember their childhoods as supremely happy. For instance, Duke Ellington described his parents as "very strict about seeing that I got everything I wanted."

Was Tolstoy right about happy and unhappy families? Read the following pages and judge for yourself.

FAVORITE CHILDREN

HUGO BLACK (1886–1971), U.S. Supreme Court justice

His mother, Della, was within five days of giving birth to him when her adored little daughter, two-year-old Mary Ardella, died. Hugo, born in a time of great grief, became her comfort. She babied him, and as he grew, he tried to take care of her.

Hugo's father, Faet, owned the largest store in the county, read the best books, and involved himself in politics. He was also a binge drinker, and had less and less control over his drinking as time went on. When Faet stayed out late, Hugo, who slept in his parents' room until he was twelve, consoled Della.

Daisy, one of Hugo's six older siblings, said, "Hugo wanted to please everybody no end." And Black himself said, "I was the family pet." He believed he was Della's favorite child.

MARY BAKER EDDY (1821–1910), U.S. founder of Christian Science

Even before Mary, the last of six Baker children, was born, her mother told a neighbor that "she could not keep her thought away from the strange conviction that this child was holy and consecrated and set apart for wonderful achievements. . . . "In an 1844 letter to Mary herself she went even further: "sometimes I fear I worship mary instead of the great jehovah."

Because of her illnesses and her special place as baby of the family, Mary usually got her own way, which reinforced her sometimes autocratic behavior. She threw monumental tantrums, and no one was able to stop her. Because he feared for her health, even her stern father failed to make her work or obey. Though she could be difficult, the whole family favored her over the other children. Her sister Abigail said, "I loved Mary best of all my brothers and sisters."

SIGMUND FREUD (1856–1939), Austrian neurologist

As the firstborn son, he had a leg up on being the favorite child. And more— he was born in a caul (the amniotic sac), a sign of good luck. In spite of the fact that he was born covered with black hair, his young mother, Amalia, called him her "golden Sigi." (In German, *Sieg* means "victory.") In addition, a venerable peasant woman predicted his greatness shortly after his birth.

His position as favorite son endured even after the births of his six siblings, five sisters and a brother. After he graduated from the Sperl Gymnasium *summa cum laude,* his position in the family grew even more exalted. For example, he lit his room with an oil lamp; the other children had candles. When he complained about the noise from his sister Anna's piano lessons, the piano was taken away.

He later said "that if a man has been his mother's undisputed darling he retains throughout life the triumphant feeling, the confidence in success, which not seldom brings actual success along with it."

OSCAR HAMMERSTEIN II (1895–1960), U.S. composer

Because young Oscar was a "delicate boy," his mother, Allie, coddled him, letting him stay home to read when he looked ill, "heavy under the eyes." He also adored her: "I did not fear her, but somehow I couldn't have borne the thought of displeasing her. I adored her with all my heart." He was clearly her favorite, destined for greatness. His brother, Reggie, on the other hand, disappointed, not least because he was supposed to be a girl. Allie said, "Oscar's the genius—Reggie's the clown." It was a self-fulfilling prophecy. The boys' maternal grandmother, Grandma Nimmo, taught Oscar letters and numbers before he went to school. He went on to do well in school, while Reggie was left behind. Oscar later observed, having faced the demands of life outside the maternal cocoon: "I might have run from the task in the light of a very bad upbringing, and yet the bad upbringing seems to have been good for me in many ways." Perhaps significantly, he always felt secure in himself, aware of his own value.

ELIA KAZAN (1909–   ), Turkish-born U.S. film director

As he himself put it, he and his mother, Athena, engaged in a "secret conspiracy" against his father. In the evenings, when his father and his cronies played cards and his younger brothers went early to bed, Elia and his mother sat together and read. He always felt that it was during those evenings that she made him her special child.

Did you know that Frank Lloyd Wright's mother was so certain that young Frank would be an architect that she hung framed pictures of cathedrals in his bedroom?

When he was twelve, his eighth-grade teacher, Anna B. Shank, took a shine to him. She admired his beautiful brown eyes and saw "great possibilities" in him. She decided that he should go to Williams College in Massachusetts. She and Athena worked together to get Elia into Williams without telling his father, who wanted Elia to go into his rug business. Elia called it the "beautiful brown eyes conspiracy."

Elia was accepted at Williams. When his father found out, he hit Athena in the face, and she fell to the floor. Six months later, Elia came home from college. His brother George told him that their parents were sleeping in separate rooms. He said, "I think it was something about you."

CALVIN KLEIN (1942–   ), U.S. clothing designer
"My son is going to be famous," Calvin's mother, Flo, bragged to her friends. One of their neighbors said, "Flo wasn't a mother to any of her children, except Calvin." Calvin did not make his bed or pick up after himself—Flo, ruler of the household, did that. Mother and son shared a love of clothes; Flo sent Calvin to kindergarten as a willing fashion plate in pastel-colored shirts.

Barry, Calvin's older brother, called him "the King." Barry was far from the favorite child. Like Flo's father, Barry was a compulsive gambler; gambling was a habit Flo detested. Flo also did not give much affection to her daughter, Alexis, born in 1950, perhaps because she was a girl. Alexis was once so resentful that she threw Flo's perfume down the toilet.

ALAN JAY LERNER (1918–1986), U.S. lyricist and dramatist
Joseph Lerner had three sons; but Alan, the middle son, was the one who got special attention. Joseph, a wealthy New York businessman, squired his son around the city, taking Alan to boxing matches at Madison Square Garden and to all the hit musicals on Broadway. Father and son went out to dinner together, discussed everything from politics to women, and shared a love of language and writing.

Although their relationship was close, Alan's father was not a sentimental man and was not overtly affectionate. Even when Alan grew up to create some of the most successful musicals in Broadway history (*Brigadoon, Paint Your Wagon*) and won an Academy Award for the screenplay of *An American in Paris,* Joseph Lerner was rarely heard to praise his son. Yet Alan always felt that his father was enormously proud of him.

Diagnosed with cancer of the jaw at age fifty, Joseph underwent fifty-seven operations, and whenever possible Alan was by his side in the hospital. In his autobiography, *The Street Where I Live,* Lerner expresses great sadness that his father died before his biggest hit, *My Fair Lady,* was completed. In addition, he wrote, "Directly or indirectly, by intention or accident, by admiration, rebellion or resistance, it was my father who created the child who became the father of the man."

FLORENCE NIGHTINGALE (1820–1910), English nurse

William and Fanny Nightingale, Florence's parents, both came from wealthy families; and their combined fortunes allowed Florence and her older sister, Parthe, to grow up in the lap of luxury. The girls were raised on two large estates in the English countryside, were educated by private tutors, and wore clothes bought in Paris. On vacation the family traveled through Europe in a custom-made carriage. William and Fanny planned the same future for both their daughters: Each would marry well and take her proper place in English society.

Florence was prettier and cleverer than Parthe. While Florence could be shy and introspective, she was also impulsive, stubborn, and outspoken. Compared with Florence, Parthe seemed plain and reticent. William Nightingale loved both of his daughters, but Florence was his favorite, and he often told friends that she had "quite a man's mind." He was, however, shocked when Florence abandoned her social standing and wealth and decided to spend her life taking care of the sick and needy.

Florence Nightingale, called "the Lady with the Lamp," is considered to be the founder of modern nursing. In 1907 she became the first woman to receive Britain's Order of Merit. Her autobiographical notes and journals are surprisingly critical of her family and upbringing. She called her early years a "petty, stagnant, stifling life." In addition, she portrayed her father as a weak, ineffectual person, "a man who has never known what struggle is . . . and having never by circumstances been forced to look into anything, to carry it out."

NELSON ROCKEFELLER (1908–1979), U.S. politician

Nelson's father, John, son of oil baron John D. Rockefeller, was a workaholic who set strict standards of behavior for his six children. The young Rockefellers had to recite Bible verses every day, keep a journal of how they spent their allowance money, abstain from all alcohol and tobacco, and always refrain from acting vain or boastful about the family wealth. On the other hand, Nelson's mother, Abby, was a spontaneous, energetic woman who was passionate about art and music and loved elegant clothes and good times. In addition, she was unabashedly devoted and loving toward her husband and children.

Of all the Rockefeller siblings, Nelson was the most like his mother. He had a zest for life that filled everything he did, whether he was earning extra spending money with a rabbit-breeding business, playing soccer, or building a wood cabin on one of the family's estates. One of the Rockefeller servants summed up the essence of the thirteen-year-old boy: "Nelson is so full of life, he doesn't know what to do with himself." The high-spirited Nelson was always considered to be his mother's favorite child.

Abby usually overlooked Nelson's mischievous behavior. When he hid a bunny in her muff before the family went off to church, she pretended not to notice the animal and sat in church with the muff, and the bunny, in her lap. When Nelson, an undiagnosed dyslexic, got poor grades in school, Abby was always around to offer positive advice. Although she coddled the boy, Abby never forgot that her son would one day be at the helm of the family business and philanthropic endeavors. When Nelson was a teenager, she wrote to him: "I am eager that you shall be much above the ordinary in character and achievement. The world needs fine men, there is great work waiting to be done. I want you to train yourself to meet any opportunity the future may hold in store for you."

FRANK LLOYD WRIGHT (1867–1959), U.S. architect

When Anna Wright was going through her first pregnancy, she was certain of two things: that her child would be a boy and that he would grow up to be an architect. Before the baby's arrival, Anna took ten pictures of old English cathedrals (torn from a magazine), had them framed, and put them on the walls of the baby's bedroom. Both of Anna's predictions came true, by nurture or nature, and as Wright once said, "I had grown up from childhood with the idea that there was nothing quite so sacrosanct, so high, so sacred as an architect, a builder."

Frank had two sisters, but he was always the obvious center of his mother's universe. Desperately unhappy in her marriage to Frank's father, a Baptist preacher, Anna transferred all her dreams and ambitions to Frank. She praised and pampered him, made sure he always ate healthy meals, and encouraged his creativity. Anna divorced her husband when Frank was seventeen, and until she died at the age of eighty-four, she remained entwined in her son's life. She paid his bills when he was short of funds, interfered in his romantic relationships, and was always offering advice of some sort.

In his autobiography Wright wrote about the relationship between him and his parents: "Anna's extraordinary devotion to the child disconcerted the father. He never made much of the child, it seems. No doubt his wife loved him no less but now loved something more, something created out of her own fervor of love and desire. A means to realize her vision."

CHILDREN OF MENTALLY ILL PARENTS

INGMAR BERGMAN (1918–   ), Swedish film director

Both of the morose filmmaker's parents suffered nervous breakdowns when he was a boy: His mother, Karin, came from a family with a history of "nervous instability," and his father, Erik, had a morbid streak. For instance, when Erik was a boy, after his father and younger sister died, his favorite game was playing at being a minister at a funeral. He became a minister when he grew up.

During the early years of their marriage, Erik and Karin did not have enough money, and Sweden was undergoing a food shortage. Between June 1918 and February 1919 an influenza epidemic hit in three waves, and Erik was kept busy burying people and consoling the survivors. During these difficult times, Karin struggled to be a good minister's wife, but the role did not come naturally to her; tired, bored, and desperate, she kept a diary about her anguish.

Her romance with another minister, Torsten Bohlin, came out in the open about 1925, the same year her brother died in an airplane crash. At first she and Bohlin planned to run away together, and the Bergmans talked about a divorce. Then both she and her lover had second thoughts. The Bergmans stayed together. However, the marriage was troubled, even after the romance between her and Bohlin ended. Erik became "pathologically jealous" and suffered a nervous breakdown that left him in poor health for five years; Karin suffered from mental problems too. One of Bergman's sisters, Margareta, remembers that both her parents were "frequently absent for longish periods at a time, my father in nursing homes; likewise my mother. The psychoneurotic storms of that time must have been terrible indeed."

Did you know that, in Allen Ginsberg's poem "Kaddish," "the beautiful Garbo of my Karma" refers to his mother?

NICOLAS CAGE (1964–   ), U.S. actor

Throughout his childhood, Nicolas Cage's mother, modern dancer Joy Vogelsang, was shuttled in and out of mental institutions. His father, artist-inventor Nicolas Coppola, brother of Francis Ford Coppola, tried to keep the volatile marriage going in spite of these disruptions. In one of their many fights, Joy told him that Nicolas was not his child, even though father and son are look-alikes. They divorced when Nicolas was twelve.

Nicolas remembers well his apprehension when walking down the long hallway to go to see her in institutions. Yet he also lovingly views films of her playing with him when he was little and calls her a "tender mother." She spoke what he identifies as poetry, "beautiful but scary." She is, he says, "the driving force" in his creativity.

In a *Playboy* interview, Cage said, ". . . even when things got really bizarre, I was able to detach and look at it with a scientific curiosity." He believes that "it made my life rich and gave me a depth of emotion; it's a blessing in disguise. . . . It gave me an insight and a sensitivity that I don't think I would have had." His mother is now well.

PATRICIA CORNWELL (1960–   ), U.S. mystery writer
Patricia Cornwell says of her childhood, "I didn't always know what was going to happen." At Christmas, when she was five, her father left home. "It killed me," she says. "I . . . wrapped around one of his legs like a little tree frog and I was screaming, 'Don't go! Don't go!'" In that same year, she was molested by a security guard. Two years later her mother, Marilyn, moved the family from Miami to Montreat, North Carolina. At Christmas, when Patricia was nine, her mother suffered a nervous breakdown and wanted to check into a hospital to be treated for clinical depression. The family was destitute—without food, fuel, or clothes. The family car was mired in snow. Desperate, Marilyn walked the three children up the hill to the home of evangelists Ruth and Billy Graham, whom she did not know, and attempted to give the children to them. Ruth Graham graciously made the family spaghetti for lunch. Though she didn't take the children herself, she found a home for them with some missionaries and opened an account for them at a department store while their mother was hospitalized. In 1983, Cornwell published a loving biography of Ruth Graham, who became a close friend. Graham describes Cornwell as "plucky and smart as a whip."

Cornwell's mystery novels about a detective, Dr. Kay Scarpetta, who is a medical examiner, have made her rich. In 1996, she received a $24 million advance for three crime novels. In spite of her success, she still feels insecure. She keeps a Smith & Wesson .38 by her bedside.

JANE FONDA (1937–   ), and **PETER FONDA** (1939–   ), U.S. actors
Jane and Peter Fonda's mother, Frances, an American heiress descended from British nobility, suffered from mood swings and a shattered ego throughout most of her marriage to actor Henry Fonda. Obsessed with her looks, she taped "frownies" to her forehead to prevent wrinkles and constantly changed the color of her hair, an uncommon practice then. If she became fat, she once said, she would use a knife to cut the fat off. She often spent days "sick" in bed. The marriage was rocky.

Frances thought the marriage might improve when in 1948 the family moved to Greenwich, Connecticut, so that Henry could pursue a Broadway career. It didn't. If anything, things grew worse. Frances said to a friend, "Henry doesn't satisfy me sexually anymore." Henry was satisfying other women, though—he often spent the night in his New York apartment, enjoying affairs with a series of girlfriends. He told Frances in December 1949 that he planned to divorce her and marry Susan Blanchard, Oscar Hammerstein's daughter, who was only twenty-one. Frances was devastated. In February 1950, she signed herself into Craig House, a mental institution in Beacon, New York. In mid-March, when she came home for a visit, accompanied by two nurses, Jane and Peter did not want to see her.

A month later, on April 14, Frances went into the bathroom at the nursing home where she was then staying and, using a razor blade she had secreted in the backing of a framed photograph, slit her own throat. A note attached to the door read, "This is the only way."

Jane and Peter did not know at first that their mother had committed suicide. They were told that Frances had died of a heart attack. Jane did not cry, but instead dealt with her emotions by going on food binges. Peter did cry—he had been dreaming that his mother might die. Not long after, Jane saw the truth in a magazine article about Henry, and that summer at camp, she woke up screaming from nightmares about her mother. "I knew from the beginning that she wouldn't last. I knew she was too fragile to make it," Jane said, much later.

Did you know that after writer Patricia Cornwell's mother suffered a nervous breakdown, in a fit of desperation, she tried to give young Patricia to evangelists Ruth and Billy Graham?

ALLEN GINSBERG (1926–1997), U.S. poet

Allen Ginsberg remembered watching his mother, Naomi, flowers wreathed in her hair, play the mandolin in a New Jersey meadow when he was very little. Very few of his memories of her were that happy—her mental instability shadowed his childhood.

She was in and out of mental institutions from the time he was three. Diagnosed as a paranoid schizophrenic, she accused her mother-in-law, and later others, including Mussolini, of wanting to kill her. She heard voices so alarming that she would put cooking pots on her ears to try to keep them out. She believed that messages were being sent to her through wires in her head and sticks in her back implanted by doctors at Greystone, a public mental institution.

When she was at home, far from cured, either Allen or his older brother, Gene, would often stay home from school to care for her. Her paranoid fantasies escalated, she imagined that her enemies were calling her a prostitute and that an agent was out to kill her for it. One afternoon in 1941, she became very agitated. Allen, home alone with her, tried to reason with her, but she would hear none of it. At one point she leaned out the window and shouted, "Go 'way, you rotten thing!" to someone she thought was the agent. Finally, she convinced Allen to take her to a rest home in Lakewood. They endured a nightmare bus journey to get there. While Naomi was being admitted, she said electricity had ruined her blood and she needed a transfusion. The authorities at the rest home turned them away, saying, "This is not an insane asylum." Finally, Allen found her a room in another rest home. Wishing his mother dead, he told her to be quiet and took a bus back to Paterson.

A week later she was back at Greystone, and she spent the rest of her life in and out of mental hospitals. She was no longer "the beautiful Garbo of my Karma," said Allen later in his poem "Kaddish," but he loved and cared for her all his life.

H. P. (HOWARD PHILLIPS) LOVECRAFT (1890–1937), U.S. writer

His childhood was almost as bizarre as the horror-fantasy tales he would later write. When Howard was two years old, his father, Winfield, a traveling salesman, began to suffer from hallucinations, probably a symptom of untreated syphilis. Five years later he died in a mental institution at the age of forty-four.

After the death of his father, Howard and his mother, Susie, moved to Providence, Rhode Island, to live with her father. Susie Lovecraft appeared to be a doting mother who looked after her son's cultural education by frequently taking him to concerts and plays. In reality she was a neurotic woman who never displayed physical affection—Howard called her a "touch me not"—and pulled her "sick" boy out of school several times for illnesses that were probably psychosomatic.

Although Howard was an average-looking child, his mother told everyone that he "was so hideous that he hid from everyone and did not like to walk upon the streets where people could gaze at him . . . because he could not bear to have people look upon his awful face." Under the watchful, and always critical, eye of his mother, Howard was shy and timid. He later described his mother's behavior toward him as "devastating." Susie, like her husband, was eventually institutionalized and died when Howard was thirty-one. Sixteen years later, Lovecraft himself died of intestinal cancer.

MARILYN MONROE (1926–1962), U.S. actor

Marilyn's mother, Gladys, was unable, financially and psychologically, to care for a child and had Marilyn (born Norma Jean) placed in foster homes. Gladys lived in fear of mental illness (her own mother, Della, had been institutionalized when Norma Jean was a baby) and was prone to fits of depression and hysteria. However, when Norma Jean was seven years old, Gladys bought a home in Hollywood, moved Norma Jean in with her, and enrolled the girl in school. The reunion, however, was short-lived.

One morning about six months after Gladys had moved into her own home, she became crazed and uncontrollable, and the English couple who rented part of the house called an ambulance. By most accounts, the scene that ensued was both frightening and sad. When Gladys saw the ambulance attendants, she became violent, and the attendants strapped her to a stretcher. She was taken to a hospital and later transferred to a state asylum. The diagnosis: paranoid schizophrenia.

> *Did you know that although H.P. Lovecraft was a perfectly normal looking child, his deranged mother told people that he "was so hideous that he hid from everyone and did not like to walk upon the streets where people could gaze at him . . . because he could not bear to have people look upon his awful face"?*

Norma Jean was in school when her mother was taken away. When she came home, the English couple told her that her mother was ill and had had to go to a hospital. From then until she turned sixteen and got married, Norma Jean lived in a succession of foster homes. During one period, between the ages of nine and eleven, she lived in an orphanage for twenty-one months.

CARRY NATION (1846–1911), U.S. temperance leader and social reformer

The hatchet-wielding crusader grew up on a number of farms in Kentucky and Missouri. Her father, George, was a teetotaling, hardworking man who read the Bible daily to his six children. Carry always said, "If I ever had an angel on earth, it was my father." That testimonial stemmed in large part from how George kept the family together in spite of an ever-present problem: Carry's mother, Mary.

Mary believed she was Britain's Queen Victoria. She appeared at the breakfast table in a long purple velvet gown and with a crown of crystal and cut glass atop her head. She asked everyone to address her as "Your Majesty" and at times wouldn't talk to anyone, including her husband and children, unless they scheduled an appointment. Mary was forever talking about the problems of being a monarch and even made detailed plans for her abdication, in case she should ever be forced to give up the throne.

Carry's father, committed to keeping his family together, prayed that Mary's hallucinations would disappear and patiently endured his wife's ridiculous appearance and behavior. Rather than argue with his hyperactive wife, George usually indulged her royal fantasies; he even built her a royal carriage. It had rubber tires, a red upholstered interior, and silver-mounted harnesses. Dressed in her regal finery, Mary would travel the countryside to visit the farmers in her kingdom. One of the family's slaves would accompany her and would blow a horn to announce her arrival. Sometimes Mary would berate the farmers; on other occasions she would bestow a knighthood upon them.

Mary's mental instability was a great embarrassment to the family. In addition, there was a dark side to her comical behavior. She flew into rages, slapped the children, and then went off to her room to cry for hours. Carry grew up afraid of her mother and without any maternal nurturing. Mary was eventually placed in the Missouri State Hospital for the Insane, where she died.

GLORIA STEINEM (1934–   ), U.S. writer/publisher and feminist

Ruth Steinem, Gloria's mother, had her first nervous breakdown in 1930, before Gloria was born. She was an attractive, auburn-haired woman who had studied math and history in college, loved to read books, and had a natural flair for writing. She was energetic and hardworking and did her best to support her husband's numerous entrepreneurial activities and take care of Gloria's older sister. The first breakdown, according to Gloria, "followed years of trying to take care of a baby, be the wife of a kind but financially irresponsible man with show-business dreams, and still keep her much-loved job as reporter and newspaper editor."

Gloria's parents were divorced when she was ten, and for the next seven years mother and daughter lived together, mostly in Toledo, Ohio, where the young Gloria was primarily responsible for her mother's care. Ruth was often depressed, always anxious about money, subject to hallucinations, and rarely left her home. When Gloria wasn't in school or working at an after-school job, she was tending to her mother, "an invalid who lay in bed with eyes closed and lips moving in occasional response to voices only she could hear." At the time, the only treatment given to Ruth was something called "Doc Howard's medicine," a potent liquid that put Ruth in a stupor and hampered her physical coordination.

Ruth was eventually institutionalized and diagnosed with "an anxiety neurosis." When she was released from the hospital, she was able to resume a somewhat normal life, enjoying vacations with Gloria, holding down various part-time jobs, making new friends. For a while she was even able to live alone, yet she was always vulnerable to depression. After Ruth died at the age of eighty-one, Gloria wrote "Ruth's Song," an essay about her mother. In it, she said, "I realize that I've always been more touched by old people than by children. It's the talent and hopes locked up in a failing body that gets to me; a poignant contrast that reminds me of my mother, even when she was strong."

MAMAS' BOYS

W. H. (WYSTAN HUGH) AUDEN (1907–1973), English poet

From the time Wystan was born, the youngest of three children, his mother, Constance, wanted to have (in his words) "a conscious spiritual, in a sense, adult relationship" with him. When he was only eight, she taught him the highly erotic love-potion scene from Wagner's *Tristan and Isolde*. They sang it together as a duet—he was Isolde.

His doctor father joined the army in World War I. "To some degree I lost him psychologically," Auden later said. His relationship with his mother assumed great importance. In an unpublished poem, he wrote later: "Tommy did as mother told him / Till his soul had split; / One half thought of angels / And the other half of shit." He owed much to his mother, he believed—his sense of security, for one, and his intelligence, for another: "No one thinks unless a complex makes him." He also believed that his homosexuality stemmed in part from his identification with her. Even as an adult, her judgments ruled him. "Mother wouldn't like it" was his response to bad behavior.

In 1941 she died. On the day of her death he and his lover, Chester Kallman, were supposed to have dinner with Admiral King of Newport, Rhode Island. Kallman tried to break the news gently: "We're not going to King's." "Goody, goody," said Auden. "The reason is your mother has died." Auden was quiet; then he said, "How like her that her last act on earth should be to get me out of a social engagement that I didn't want." After that he began to cry. When a letter from her arrived after her death, he was unable to open and read it.

Did you know that when General Douglas MacArthur was U.S. Army chief of staff, he left the office every day to have lunch with his mother?

ANDREW CARNEGIE (1835–1919), Scottish-born U.S. businessman and philanthropist

He said that his mother, Margaret Morrison Carnegie, was "the power that never failed in any emergency." When his father, William, a weaver, began to lose his ability to make a living because of competition from steam-loom textile factories, his mother opened a shop to help keep the family solvent. But it was to no avail, and in 1848, when Andrew was thirteen, the family sailed for the United States in the hope of improving their fortunes. William found a job as a hand-weaver, and Margaret went to work too, as a shoe binder.

Carnegie claimed that his mother was the sole reason for his success. He dedicated his first book, *An American Four in Hand in Great Britain* (1888), to her: "To my favorite Heroine My Mother."

Even as a young boy, he vowed never to marry as long as his mother was alive. True to his promise, Carnegie didn't wed until six months after Margaret's death, when he was fifty-one years old.

ROY COHN (1927–1986), U.S. lawyer

Al Cohn might very well have married Dora Marcus because he needed money. Dora was short and dumpy, but her father was powerful and rich. The couple came to hate each other. Still, they produced a child, Roy, a name that means "king." And indeed, according to a cousin, "Dora brought Roy up as the crown prince." She left Al out of the process—Roy was her baby, hers alone. Their relationship was "not normal," as his Aunt Libby put it. Dora spoiled Roy rotten. For instance, one day when Roy was eleven, mother and son went to a restaurant with a relative. Roy asked for the menu and ordered a sandwich. When it came, he arrogantly sent it back, and Dora let him get away with it.

When he went to summer camp, she stayed in a nearby hotel and went to the camp every day to tell them what Roy could or could not do. Once, a man whose son went to Roy's school called to say he was taking the boys to a sports event. Dora said, "That's nice. You can learn a lot from my son."

Dora and Roy lived together until she died in 1967. He was then forty-two. Before she died, he dated women, among them Barbara Walters; after her death, he dated boys.

Did you know that upon hearing that the reason for his evening's plans being canceled was that his mother had died, W.H. Auden replied, "How like her that her last act on earth should be to get me out of a social engagement that I didn't want"?

WILLIAM RANDOLPH HEARST (1863–1951), U.S. publisher

When the future publishing tycoon was very young, his mother Phoebe hired a phrenologist (an expert on analyzing people through the shapes of their skulls) to tell her about her child's character. Part of the final report read: "[He] is very strongly attached to his mother, provided she treats him lovingly. . . . He will always be under petticoat government." Both mother and son were stubborn, spirited, and deeply devoted to each other. A passionate woman, Phoebe lavished praise and attention on her only child, whom she called "Sonny" and "Billy Buster." She chronicled his childhood in letters to relatives and friends: "Bless his little heart. . . . His being with me so constantly has made him perfectly devoted to me. He is a real little calf about me." Willie slept with her until he was three and a half.

Willie's father, who made a fortune in mining and land speculation, had little interest in his wife's deep enthusiasm for culture. When he became involved with another woman, the marriage survived, but Phoebe turned to young Willie even more than before. Afraid of being called a sissy, young Willie became a smart aleck who loved to shock his mother with outrageous pranks, knowing that nothing he did would ever diminish Phoebe's love and loyalty.

In 1873, Phoebe took Willie on an eighteen-month-long tour of Europe. In Paris, he and a friend tied a string around the tail of a cat, who shredded some draperies in its distress; started a fire in one hotel room; and blew a hole in the ceiling of another. On the other hand, the trip gave him an appreciation of art, architecture, and antiquities. When he saw Windsor Castle, he said, "I would like to live there"; and he also asked Phoebe to buy him the Louvre. As an adult, Hearst admitted that he was "a mother's boy" but declared he was "mighty glad of it."

J. EDGAR HOOVER (1895–1972), U.S. FBI director

Married to a man who suffered from chronic depression, Annie Hoover continually pushed her son Edgar to be perfect, to excel at everything he tried. He was the fourth and last child, conceived while his parents were in mourning over the death of their three-year-old daughter from diphtheria. As a little boy, Edgar was high-strung, sickly, and never strayed far from his mother. According to Dorothy Davy, "Edgar, of all her children, was the one she spoiled."

He tried all his life to live up to her expectations. In high school the boy who would become "the head of our thought police," according to poet Theodore Roethke, was a high achiever, a star pupil, and a champion debater. A member of the Cadet Corps, Hoover was distraught when his drill team failed to win a regional competition; a friend later wrote him, "I wondered if you were crying because you were mad or were mad because you were crying."

As an adult, Hoover said, "I have always held girls and women on a pedestal. They are something men should look up to, to honor and worship." He sometimes dated women but never married and constantly denied that he and his best friend, Clyde Tolson, were homosexual lovers.

When his father died in 1921, he became the man of the house, and he and Annie were inseparable. On Mother's Day 1924, she gave him a diamond-studded star sapphire ring; he wore it for the rest of his life. He also bought expensive jewelry for her.

Annie and Edgar lived together until Annie died at the age of eighty. When she passed away, Edgar was at her side in the bedroom where he was born.

HARRY HOUDINI (1874–1926), Hungarian-born U.S. magician

Born in Hungary to Samuel and Cecilia Weiss, his real name was Ehrich. When he was a baby, if he was unhappy, his mother would hold him to her breast and her heartbeat would calm him. He seemed to sleep very little, and whenever she went to look in on him, he would gaze up at her with his blue-gray eyes.

The family sailed to New York shortly after he was born and eventually settled in Milwaukee. He showed his talent for legerdemain early on. As a young boy, he was able to pick the lock on his mother's pastry cupboard and steal her jam tarts.

Did you know that when Roy Cohn went to summer camp his mother would stay at a nearby hotel and would go to the camp each day to tell the camp authorities what Roy could and could not do, and that Roy lived with his mother until he was forty-two years old?

When Houdini was twelve, his father asked him to promise that he would always care for his mother. The boy agreed, and the next morning he left home to make his fortune. Soon after that, the family moved to New York, and the young Houdini came home. When he got his first paying job as an entertainer, Houdini asked to be paid in gold coins, which he poured into his mother's lap. He became a professional magician at seventeen.

His mother was always the center of his concerns. As his biographer, Kenneth Silverman, put it, "The royal box in his mental theater was occupied by

Cecilia." When he was thirty-three, after leaping off a bridge in chains, he wrote in his diary, "Ma saw me jump!"

His strong attachment to her didn't end when she died at seventy-two. He fell to the floor in a faint when he got the news. "I seem to have lost all ambition," he wrote. Houdini tried to contact her spirit but only ended up exposing a host of fraudulent mediums. On a number of occasions, he lay face down on his mother's grave, talking to her and hoping that she would get a message to him.

LYNDON BAINES JOHNSON (1908–1973), U.S. president

Rebekah, his mother, called him her "beautiful" child and "the most wonderful baby in the world." Her first, he was a very bright child. He knew the alphabet when he was two, recited Longfellow and Tennyson at three, and could read at four: "I'll never forget how much my mother loved me when I recited those poems. The minute I finished she'd take me in her arms and hug me so hard I sometimes thought I'd be strangled to death."

When the family moved to Johnson City, Texas, a town of only 323 people in the middle of "an ocean of land," Rebekah felt isolated and unhappy. At age three or four, Lyndon saw her crying at the water pump. His father was away, and she said she was afraid to be alone. Lyndon vowed he would take care of her. Because of her need of him, he felt "big and important. It made me believe I could do anything in the whole world." In first grade he chose a poem to read to the class and parents. It was "I'd Rather Be a Mama's Boy."

Rebekah made Lyndon take lessons in dancing and violin. When he quit the lessons at eight, she pretended he was dead. Her love was conditional— she wanted him to fulfill her ambitions and become an important man. He did. "I think except for her I might not have made it through high school and certainly not through college," Lyndon later said. To him, she was "faith, pure gold, the greatest female I have ever known, without any exceptions."

WLADZIU VALENTINO LIBERACE (1919–1987), U.S. pianist

Probably the highest-paid pianist of all time, Liberace was always very effusive about his devotion to his mother, Frances. He often told two stories about his childhood: the time his mother saved his life by nursing him through a bout of double pneumonia, and the time Frances ignored a doctor's recommendation to amputate his badly infected finger and instead saved the finger—and his career—by applying an old-time poultice remedy. Despite his worldwide popularity, Liberace was often hammered by music critics for his flamboyant style and extravagant costumes, as well as for being "the biggest sentimental vomit of all time" who "slobbered over his mother." One critic invented a term, "Momism," for Liberace's relationship to his mother. Liberace's reply: "I am never bothered about things that are written about me. But I must admit that I do become bitter when my love for my mother is described as any kind of ism, whether it's Communism, Fascism, or Momism."

DOUGLAS MACARTHUR (1880–1964), U.S. general

Descended from a long line of military men, MacArthur spent his preschool years on army posts in the Southwest. His mother, Mary "Pinky" MacArthur, was a southern belle who taught her son not to cry, always to do what was right for his country, and to "never lie, never tattle." Nonetheless, she increased Doug's dependence on her by dressing him in skirts and keeping his hair in long curls until he was eight years old. Pinky was strong-willed and had great ambitions for Doug. She engineered his entrance into West Point, and during her son's stay at the academy she moved into a nearby hotel where she could see if the lights were on or off in his dorm room (to see if he was studying). Throughout MacArthur's military career, Pinky wrote letters to his superiors, suggesting that her son be promoted. When MacArthur took a mistress at the age of 54, his biggest fear was that his mother would find out about the liaison. When he was army chief of staff, based in Washington, D.C., MacArthur, a four-star general and highly decorated World War II hero, left the office every day to have lunch with his mother. Pinky died at the age of eighty-four.

ELVIS PRESLEY (1935–1977), U.S. singer

The king of rock 'n' roll slept in the same bed with his mother, Gladys, until he reached puberty. Until Elvis entered high school, Gladys walked him back and forth to school every day and made him take along his own silverware so that he wouldn't catch germs from the other kids. She forbade him to go swimming or do anything that might put him in danger. Mother and son communicated in a special "baby" language, comprised of words that no one else could understand. As Elvis grew up, Gladys was the only person he trusted, the only one he could pour out his heart to. When he became famous, Elvis moved her into Graceland, a twenty-three-room mansion in Memphis. While Gladys constantly worried that Elvis would die young, a victim of his hectic life style, she herself was dead at the age of forty-six. At her funeral, Elvis's grief was uncontrollable. He cried and howled, spoke baby talk, and threw himself on top of his mother's casket.

MARCEL PROUST (1871–1922), French novelist

From a very early age the French author of *Remembrance of Things Past* was excessively sick, suffering from hay fever, asthma, stomach problems, and anxiety attacks: He learned that he could control his mother through his illnesses. Although his father was a doctor, it was Marcel's mother, Jeanne, who always gave the boy her undivided attention and read to him while he lay in bed. When she left for an evening at the theater, Marcel would stay awake, fearful that she would die and never return to him. Proust became incurably dependent on his mother, and when she died at age fifty-six, the thirty-four-year-old novelist wrote: "From now on my life has lost its one aim, its one sweetness, its one love, its one consolation."

FRANKLIN DELANO ROOSEVELT (1882–1945), U.S. president

When he was very young, Franklin wore dresses and Lord Fauntleroy suits, and his mother, Sara, didn't cut his long blond curls until he was five years old. The future president of the United States wasn't allowed to take a bath unsupervised until he was almost nine years old. Taught by private tutors until he was fourteen, Franklin was supposed to fulfill his mother's dream and become a country squire. When he finally left home to attend school at

Groton, he was a tall, awkward child who was perceived as a spoiled "mama's boy"; the girls he knew said that F. D. stood for "feather duster." Sara continued to protect and dominate her son throughout much of his life, even though she was unable to stop him from marrying his distant cousin, Eleanor Roosevelt. As an adult, FDR is known to have cried only once—after his mother's death, when he accidentally came upon a collection of childhood mementos that she had put together for him.

Franklin D. Roosevelt, age five, with his mother, Sara Roosevelt.

Courtesy of the Franklin D. Roosevelt Library.

> *". . . I do become bitter when my love for my mother is described as any kind of ism, whether it's Communism, Fascism, or Momism."*
>
> —*Wladziu Valentino Liberace*

PËTR ILICH TCHAIKOVSKY (1840–1893), Russian composer

He was a lonely and emotionally frail young boy whose mother, Alexandra, praised his musical talents and was his only source of happiness. She died of cholera when he was fifteen, and he never got over the pain of losing her. Every year, on the anniversary of Alexandra's death, Tchaikovsky wrote about his separation from his mother in his diary. Throughout his life the great Russian composer would break down in tears whenever he picked up a packet of his mother's letters.

HAPPY CHILDHOODS

ELIZABETH BARRETT BROWNING (1806–1861), English poet

Most people know her as the invalid poet who eloped with the romantic Robert Browning because her despotic father, Edward, would not allow her to leave the house. Yet what we know of her early life would lead us to predict a far different future. At least until adolescence, her childhood was a free and happy one. She grew up in a fantastic, Turkish-inspired house Edward had dreamed up. It had minarets, like something out of *The Arabian Nights*. The grounds were a child's paradise: woods with twisted paths, a stream, and a deer park; grottoes; ponds; cottages—and an underground passage from house to garden.

Elizabeth, the first child, adored her many siblings (eight boys and two girls). It was she who concocted activities and bossed and inspired the other children into carrying them out. The children put on plays, went fishing, made a camp in the grotto from which they sent letters to their mother asking for "a few saussages [sic]."

All the Barrett children loved their parents. When their father came home, they were delighted to see him. Elizabeth said life was no fun without her father, and her little brother Septimus said, "You are a funny old fellow and I hope you will be as funny when you are a nice old man. . . ."

With adolescence Elizabeth developed health problems so severe that by age fifteen, she was taking opium for pain. She was unhappy because she could not go away to school like her brothers. Her enchanted childhood was over.

"I had a good life when I was a kid, a normal, tough, repressed childhood filled with fear and trepidation all over the place. But generally, I enjoyed it; it was good."

—George Lucas

LEWIS CARROLL (CHARLES LUTWIDGE DODGSON) (1832–1898), English mathematician and writer

Under the floor in the Croft Rectory, someone found a piece of wood on which he supposedly wrote as a carefree child, "And we'll wander through the wide world, and chase the buffalo." He was the oldest son of eleven children and probably his mother's favorite. His father was the perpetual curate of Daresbury, Cheshire, the home of his famous Cheshire cat. Their home was a loving one.

Charles and his siblings never lacked for fun. They created a railway line in the garden. Charles was the ticket agent, believing that he deserved that exalted position because it was he who made the train out of a wheelbarrow, truck, and barrel. The railroad had rules like this: "Station master must mind his station and supply refreshments: he can put anyone who behaves badly to prison, while a train goes round the garden: he must ring for the passengers to take their seats, then count 20 slowly, then ring again for the train to start. . . ." The children also climbed in the marl pits, where they found granite balls, sea shells, and sometimes a fossil. With the help of a carpenter, Charles built a marionette theater, for which he made marionettes and wrote plays.

The stories he wrote for children, such as *Alice in Wonderland*, sometimes hint at a childhood so happy that he regretted leaving it. All his life, he enjoyed spending time with children, almost as one of them.

ELIZABETH II (1926–   ), British monarch

When she was a baby, her parents doted on her. They wanted to bring her up like any other child of her class. Her father, then just a royal duke, and his wife, Elizabeth ("the Little Duchess"), loved each other. Elizabeth II's mother had had a happy childhood herself. She once said to a friend, "I have nothing but wonderfully happy memories of childhood days at home. We had fun, kindness, and a marvellous sense of security." This was not so true for her husband, who became King George VI in 1936. "The House of Hanover, like ducks, produces bad parents. They trample on their young," said the royal librarian, Owen Morshead. George's father, George V, terrified him. In fact, George V supposedly once said to Lord Derby, "My father was frightened of his mother, I was frightened of my father, and I'm damned well going to see that my children are frightened of me!" Elizabeth's father wanted his children to have a happier childhood than he had had.

When Elizabeth was only a few months old, her parents went off on a six-month tour of the empire. Her mother hated leaving the baby behind. In fact, she was so distraught that she asked the driver taking her to the railway station to drive around Grosvenor Gardens twice so that she could compose herself.

Elizabeth and her younger sister, Margaret, were normally mischievous, but the family avoided spoiling them. The princesses even did their Christmas shopping at Woolworth's. When their father worked in the garden, one of his favorite pastimes, the children helped. A charming film of the royal family shows him pretending to cut the girls' hair with pruning shears. They were a happy, fun-loving family, as their father had vowed they would be.

EDWARD KENNEDY (DUKE) ELLINGTON (1899–1974), U.S. musician and composer

His parents "were very strict," he once said, "about seeing that I got everything I wanted." He admired his father, J. E. (James Edward), who had a great sense of style. His mother, Daisy, called Duke her "little jewel." She said to him once, "Edward, you are blessed. You don't have anything to worry about. Edward, you are blessed." She and Duke were devoted to each other. He always liked blue because his mother dressed him in blue on Sundays. At a White House reception in 1969, more than thirty years after her death, he said, "There is no place I would rather be tonight, except in my mother's arms."

Though they were not rich, the Ellingtons were better off than most black families. Both parents worked, J. E. as a blueprint maker and caterer and Daisy as a domestic. Duke said his father "lived like a man who had money, and he raised his family as though he were a millionaire."

His parents told Duke that he and his sister, Ruth, could "do anything anyone else can do." According to Ruth, she and Duke grew up in a house "full of love, where people did not talk about hostile incidents." Their parents' positive attitudes gave Duke a lifelong confidence in himself.

Duke himself thought he had lived a very happy childhood. He nostalgically remembered chasing rabbits in the park, reading detective stories, dreaming about being an athlete, and singing with the family and friends.

ABBIE HOFFMAN (1936–1989), U.S. political activist

"Out of left-wing literature, sperm, licorice and a little chicken fat" he invented himself, or so he said. He was the quintessential rebel, who went underground in the sixties and then resurfaced as a Yippie turned stockbroker.

In his autobiographical writings, he established a romantic past as a rebel. Not true. Born in Worcester, Massachusetts, he grew up in a "happy-go-lucky

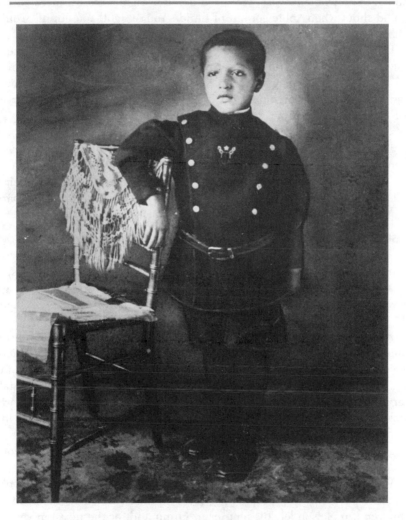

Duke Ellington as a boy,
his mother's "little jewel."

Courtesy of the Duke Ellington Collection, Archives Center, NMAH, Smithsonian Institution.

household," according to his brother, Jack. Abbie was the oldest of three children—Jack was born in 1939 and Phyllis in 1941. People came over to his family's house to play cards, for holiday gatherings, or just to sit around and talk.

His mother protected him, even to the point of giving him an alibi when he was picked up by the police at the age of thirteen for changing license plates on cars. His father was the disciplinarian, though he had a soft spot for Abbie. "The whole world's wrong, and you're right!" his exasperated father would shout when Abbie got out of hand. "You're right! You got it!" would be Abbie's fresh reply.

In the summer the family would go to a farm, where they would feed the cows, collect eggs, and do other farm chores. During World War II, Abbie and his friends liked to play war games in which they "got Hitler." Abbie was patriotic—he hero-worshipped his Uncle Schmully because he had served in the army during the war.

Though Abbie and his Republican father had their differences, they remained fond of each other. In the 1950s they watched boxing on television, went to Boston Celtics games, and rooted for the Red Sox together. Even during the time when Abbie, as a Yippie, advocated that children kill their parents (his way of shocking people), he would call home and tell his parents "not to worry," and he still came home for holidays.

NELSON MANDELA (1918–   ), South African political leader

Of his childhood, Mandela once wrote: "I have the most pleasant recollections about the Transkei of my childhood, where I hunted, played sticks, stole mealies on the cob and where I learned to court; it is a world which is gone. A well-known English poet had such a world in mind when he exclaimed, 'The things which I have seen I now can see no more.' "

His father was a tribal chief (with four wives and thirteen children) who called his youngest son "Rolihlahla" (meaning "troublemaker"). Upon entering school, however, the troublemaker was given a new name, Nelson, by his teacher. As a young boy, Nelson roamed the fields around his village, taking care of sheep and cattle. He picked fruits and roots for food, fished with a makeshift rod of twine and wire, and used a slingshot to shoot birds in the sky. He made toy animals from clay and was a proficient stick fighter who was known for his agility and fancy footwork. In the evenings, Nelson listened to his parents tell tales of African legends and heroes.

When Nelson was nine, his father died. Chief Jongintaba, regent of the Thembu people in Mqhekezweni, offered to raise Nelson as one of his own children. So Nelson left his mother in Qunu and for the next ten years was reared and guided by Jongintaba. He attended school, worked as a ploughboy and shepherd, played and danced with the other children in the tribe. Most important, he was allowed to attend tribal meetings, where he was groomed to eventually become a counselor to the chief. He listened intently as the chief's chosen advisers, as well as the local citizenry, discussed important issues such as an impending drought or the implementation of new laws. Nelson said the Thembu meetings were "democracy in its purest form." Always concerned that the boy get a good education, Jongintaba subsequently sent Nelson to a good boarding school and then on to college.

Nelson Mandela became a worldwide symbol of the struggle against apartheid in South Africa. His relentless fight to overcome racial oppression caused him to be imprisoned for twenty-seven years. When he was released, he continued to lead the fight, and in 1994, when South Africa held its first multiracial, democratic elections, Mandela won the race for president. He was later awarded the Nobel Peace Prize.

COLIN POWELL (1937–   ), U.S. general

The center of Powell's universe has always been his family. The young Colin, who would become a four-star general and chairman of the Joint Chiefs of Staff, was raised on Kelly Street in the South Bronx while his parents, Luther and Maud (Jamaican immigrants), worked in New York City's garment district. Living in the Powells' neighborhood were a group of aunts and uncles and their offspring, as well as a number of close family friends. In his autobiography, *My American Journey,* Powell wrote, "I was a contented kid, growing up in the warmth and security of the concentric circles my family formed. . . . Family members looked out for, prodded, and propped up each other."

Gatherings at the Powell home were frequent and festive. Jamaican delicacies, like plantain and roasted goat, were usually served, and calypso music permeated the air. Sometimes as many as fifty guests showed up on Christmas Day. On many occasions Colin would listen to his relatives talk of the "old days" in Jamaica where many of them had grown up.

Although his neighborhood was rife with petty crime and street-gang violence, Powell remembers it as a fairly safe place where "racial tolerance prevailed." He and his friends roamed through the numerous candy stores, ethnic grocery stores, and bakeries. They played more than thirty street games, from kite fighting and stickball to punchball and sluggo. Colin did belong to a neighborhood gang, but the boys' worst offense was playing poker in the back of a shoe repair store. On Saturdays he usually went to the movies, and on Sundays the family went to their Episcopalian church, where Colin was an acolyte. In high school he got average grades and earned a letter in track and field.

Colin adored his parents. Maud was a big-hearted woman with "a melting smile." Luther was a hardworking, optimistic man who loved to dress in suits and hats and was known for his gracious manners and generosity. According to Powell, his father never backed off from making an important decision and in the neighborhood "became the Godfather, the one people came to for advice, for domestic arbitration, for help in getting a job. . . . Luther Powell never let his race or situation affect his sense of self."

JANET RENO (1938–   ), U.S. attorney general

When Janet Reno was asked to come to Washington, D.C., to be interviewed for a possible position in President Bill Clinton's administration, she was caring for her dying mother at the Reno family home in South Florida. Reno replied that she was not available for consideration while her mother, Jane, was still alive and needed her. Jane Reno, a former newspaper reporter, was an outspoken, independent woman gifted with indomitable will and perseverance. When Janet was ten years old, Jane decided to build a three-bedroom home in south Miami on a piece of rural property that lay on the outskirts of Everglades National Park. Determined to construct the house by herself, Jane sought out the advice of various craftspeople; then she dug the home's foundation, bought building supplies, and started from scratch. With the help of her husband, Henry, Jane completed the home in two years—even doing all the plumbing and electrical work.

Janet's father, Henry, was a Pulitzer Prize–winning reporter for the *Miami Herald*. When he was not pursuing a crime story or driving his four children to school, Henry was working in his garden, growing roses and gardenias. The Reno clan was a tight family unit. They read books together, discussed politics and world events at the dinner table, went camping and fishing together. A tomboy, Janet had her own horse, preferred play clothes to dresses, and usually ran around barefoot. Sometimes she accompanied her father when he interviewed sources for a newspaper story, and on weekends she listened to lively conversations among her parents' friends and colleagues, who frequently stopped by to visit.

When asked to name her heroes, Reno frequently mentions American presidents such as Thomas Jefferson and Franklin D. Roosevelt, but at the top of her list are Jane and Henry Reno. The first woman ever to be appointed attorney general of the United States, Reno speaks often of her loving parents, her secure upbringing, and the house her mother built: "That house is a symbol to me that you can do anything you really want if it's the right thing to do and you put your mind to it."

CASEY STENGEL (1891–1975), U.S. baseball player and manager

Charles Dillon Stengel (called Charley) was a rambunctious, mischievous kid with powerful arms, long blond curls, and big ears. He grew up in Kansas City, Missouri, the son of an insurance agent. Charley's mother, Jennie, was a high-spirited, affectionate woman who lavished attention on Charley, the youngest of her three children. About his formative years, Stengel once commented, "The best thing I had was that the family allowed everybody to come to our home. My mother always liked everyone in the neighborhood, and they could all come and use our yard."

Charley's best friend was his brother, Grant, who was two years older than Charley. Inseparable siblings, the boys played cops and robbers, rode bikes, constructed huge snow forts, taught their dog how to climb a ladder. In addition, the brothers got into a lot of trouble together—sneaking onto trolley cars without paying, kidnapping the neighbors' pigeons, and consistently ignoring the Kansas City curfew law for kids.

Charley's boyhood was saturated with baseball. By the time Charley was nine, he was a pretty good athlete, usually playing second or third base, but Grant was always the better player, the son destined to win a place on a professional team. An unfortunate accident, however, left Grant with a permanent foot injury, ending his chances of a career in baseball. As Charley grew older, he got better and better and became the star pitcher on his high school baseball team. He dropped out of school just before graduation to sign on with a minor league team, the Kansas City Blues.

The angelic two-year-old Casey Stengel grew up to become one tough baseball player.

Courtesy of the National Baseball Hall of Fame.

Did you know that Abbie Hoffman said that he invented himself "out of left-wing literature, sperm, licorice and a little chicken fat"?

After his playing days, Stengel went on to manage a number of baseball teams. At the helm of the New York Yankees, he led the team to seven World Series wins. As long as his life centered on baseball, Stengel was a happy man. His wife once said, "He doesn't talk about anything else. He doesn't think about anything else. He has only one life, and that's baseball."

JAMES STEWART (1908–1997), U.S. actor

President Harry Truman once said, "If Bess and I had a son, we'd want him to be just like Jimmy Stewart." Whether he was playing George Bailey in the film classic *It's a Wonderful Life* or fighting for his country in World War II, Stewart was generally regarded as an all-American hero. The tall, lanky, folksy actor made more than seventy-five movies during his career, and both his on-screen image and his personal life led to his reputation as an honest, decent, charming gentleman.

Jimmy's boyhood reads like a Hollywood movie script. Raised in the small town of Indiana, Pennsylvania, Jimmy was a curious, talkative kid who played the accordion, joined the Boy Scouts, and went to church every Sunday. He and his friends put on magic shows and invented "rides," which they hoped to sell to carnivals that regularly came to town. Everyone in the Stewart family loved music, and Jimmy, his parents, and his two sisters spent many evenings at home singing together. Jimmy once said that his father "sang softly, so as not to cover up mother's clear, sweet voice."

Jimmy adored his mother and sisters, but the central figure in his life was his father, Alex. Owner of a hardware store, Alex spent a lot of time with his only son. He encouraged the boy to develop his mechanical abilities (he bought him a crystal radio set), took him to movies and baseball games, watched Jimmy's primitive theatrical productions, and gave him a summer job in the hardware store. To anyone who would listen, Alex bragged about Jimmy.

Stewart said that he and his father "were bound together by a comradeship of disobedience." Often, when Jimmy's mother said no to something, his father would become his ally. When Jimmy was ten, he was determined to take his first airplane ride with a barnstorming pilot, but his mother said the flight was too dangerous. Alex, however, caved in to the boy's pleas and drove him out to take the fifteen-minute flight. As Stewart told the story: "On the way out to the pasture, he [Alex] insisted on stopping to pick up the family doctor! And even that wasn't enough for him. The whole time I was up in the air he stayed in the car with the engine running, just in case a wing or something fell off and he had to rush to the crash site!"

HARRY S TRUMAN (1884–1972), U.S. president

Truman once said, "I had just the happiest childhood that could ever be imagined." He was born in the then frontier town of Independence, Missouri, at a time when there were no cars, movies, television sets, or radios. It was a town steeped in moral values, where neighbors talked to each other every day, families talked about world events at mealtimes, and a deal made on a handshake was as good as a deal closed with a signed contract. Harry was devoted to his parents and spent many hours playing games on the family farm with his brother, Vivian, and sister, Mary Jane.

Harry wasn't a popular kid, but he wasn't an outsider. At age six he started wearing eyeglasses (the other kids called him "Four Eyes"), and when his classmates were out roughnecking, Harry was usually reading a book or taking piano lessons. When the neighborhood boys were engaged in a shootout between the Dalton Gang and the Jesse James Gang, Harry would be off on the sidelines telling everyone the history of the gangs—who got killed, how, and when. He had plenty of pets, including a goat (his father was a livestock dealer), went to church regularly, got good grades in school, and had an after-school job in a drugstore.

In Harry's high school all the students competed for the attention of Tillie Brown, the English teacher. When graduation day rolled around, Harry's friend Charlie Ross was named valedictorian and the winner of Tillie Brown's English prize. At the commencement ceremonies, Brown stepped on stage and planted a big kiss on Charlie, her number one pupil. A number of the boys, including Harry, protested that they too deserved a kiss. Brown said that they would get one—if and when they went out into the world and accomplished something worthwhile. When Truman became the thirty-third president of the United States, he hired Charlie Ross to be his press secretary. One night in the White House, the president and his boyhood friend phoned Tillie Brown. Truman asked her if becoming president was a feat worthy of a kiss. The teacher calmly replied, "Yes, come and get it."

President Truman, who earned a reputation for being a no-nonsense, unpretentious chief executive, often spoke of the values and lessons he learned in his childhood. On his desk were two signs: "The buck stops here," and "Always do right. This will gratify some people and astonish the rest." About his background, he once said, "I wouldn't think much of a man that tried to deny the people and the town where he grew up. . . . You must always keep in mind who you are and where you come from."

POOR KIDS

SHERWOOD ANDERSON (1876–1941), U.S. writer

After Irwin Anderson, Sherwood's father, lost his job working for a harness maker, he became an itinerant and unsuccessful paperhanger and painter. Irwin wanted to play the alto horn and tell Civil War stories more than he wanted to support his family. When he did get a job painting, he would often walk off the job. To compound matters, he drank, and in his cups he would come home and roar, "I have tried being a man, but I cannot make it. . . ." Sherwood's mother, Emma, took in washing to help make ends meet.

The family never stayed long in one house during their long stay in the town of Clyde, Ohio. More than once they were evicted for nonpayment of rent. Often, they could not afford to rent a wagon to move, so they carried their belongings from the old place to the new on their backs. They finally ended up living on the edge of town. The house was rickety; they had to nail cloth and wood to the holes in the house to keep warm.

Luckily, Emma was ingenious about getting food. On Hallowe'en, it was a favorite trick for children to throw cabbages at people's houses. When they did, Emma would rage at them until they threw more. After the children had gone, the family would bury the cabbages in a trench, to be saved as food for spring.

MARY MCLEOD BETHUNE (1875–1955), U.S. educator

She was the fourteenth of seventeen children. Her family owned thirty-five acres of land, a pine cabin, a cow, a mule, and a plow. Her father, an ex-slave, grew cotton on the land, and the whole family worked at keeping the weeds out all summer. The year that the mule died, the children took turns pulling the plow. They lived on fatback and grits. Their mother took in washing from the family to which she had belonged as a slave.

Mary wanted to go to school from the day when two white children told her to put down a book she had picked up, saying "*You* can't read." When the Mission Board of the Presbyterian Church came to their town of Mayesville, South Carolina, to start a school for African-American children, Mary got to go. She walked five miles there and five miles back all through elementary school. Then she won a scholarship and went to Scotia Academy for seven years. The scholarship did not even cover her basic needs, so when school was not in session she worked for white families as a cook, laundress, or chambermaid. For a while she owned only one blouse, which she washed out every night to wear the next day.

ALBERT CAMUS (1913–1960), Algerian-born French writer

His family on his father's side was originally French, but migrated to Algeria. Camus's father was placed in a Protestant orphanage when he was a year old. He ran away, according to family legend, and ended up as an apprentice laborer in a vineyard. His mother, whose family was originally Spanish, was one of nine children. Illiterate and partially deaf, she mispronounced words, at least partly because the shock of her husband's death in World War I, before Albert was a year old, affected her speech.

In a four-room apartment lived Albert, his mother, his brother, his grandmother, and his two uncles. Albert slept in a room with his mother and brother. The family shared a toilet with two other families. They brought their water from a street fountain in wooden buckets. The children's toys were made of fruit pits or other valueless materials—they even made kites of codfish tails. All the family lived partly on Uncle Etienne's wages as a cooper. Albert's mother worked as a domestic. As a young student, Albert had no desk to work at. He used the dining room table, and after he was done, he had to return his books to his book bag.

When Camus was grown up and famous, a critic noted that he had not learned about freedom from Karl Marx. Camus replied, "It is true: I learned it in poverty." But the Algerian sun, he said, compensated for his poverty.

CHARLES CHAPLIN (1889–1977), English-born U.S. actor

His mother, Hannah, had been a singer, but her voice failed when he was five. His father, an alcoholic music hall star, came and went. To support Charlie, his brother, and herself, Hannah worked in London as a seamstress and nurse and pawned their belongings for cash. She made clothes for the boys out of her old dresses—and she taught Charlie to act. He wrote: "I learned from her everything I know. She was the most astounding mimic I ever saw. . . . It was in watching and observing her that I learned not only to translate motions with my hands and features, but also to study mankind." In 1896, in spite of Hannah's efforts, she and the boys entered the Lambeth Borough workhouse and were soon separated. The boys were moved to the Hanwell School for Orphans and Destitute Children.

When Charlie was nine, his mother was put into a lunatic asylum at Cane Hill. The courts placed the boys in their father's house, but their father was rarely there or, if home, was either drunk or hung over. His mistress, Louise, resented the boys and sometimes she locked them out. The Royal Society for the Prevention of Cruelty to Children stepped in, and sent Charlie to live with Hannah, who had just been released from the lunatic asylum. In 1901, Charlie's father died of alcoholism. One day that same year, Charlie found his mother in the attic, completely deranged. He took her hand and led her to the infirmary for the insane. Luckily, it was not long afterward that he became a successful actor and was on his way to fame and fortune.

DICK GREGORY (1932–   ), U.S. comedian and civil rights activist

"We ain't poor, we're just broke," his proud mother, Lucille, said. His father was long gone. The family was on relief in St. Louis, and his mother worked on the sly cleaning houses to make a little extra. They kept a telephone hidden in a closet because people on welfare were not allowed a telephone. Dick slept in a bed with four other people. The places they lived in were cold and infested with rats. If his mother spent money for medicine, there was no money to pay the rent.

In order to have clean clothes when the pipes were frozen, Dick would get chopped ice from a soda machine at the grocery store, melt it, and wash his clothes by hand in the resulting cold water. If the clothes were not dry in the morning, he wore them to school anyhow.

In school he was often put in the idiot's seat—a seat in the back of the room surrounded with a chalk circle to designate it as the place for those who misbehaved or were not too bright. Dick was bright enough; it was just that he was so hungry he couldn't focus and learn. He ate library paste and sometimes stole from other kids' lunches.

Once, when the teacher was collecting money from the children for the Community Chest, he raised his hand to pledge a nonexistent fifteen dollars from his nonexistent father. The teacher said, "We're collecting this money for you and your kind, Richard Gregory. If your Daddy can give fifteen dollars then you have no business being on relief." When he continued to talk, she said, "And furthermore, we know you don't have a Daddy." After that, shame, understandably, kept him from school for a while.

MALCOLM X (1925–1965), U.S. black nationalist leader
Earl Little, Malcolm's father, was a Baptist preacher whose meager earnings were never enough to support his wife and seven children. The family lived in East Lansing, Michigan, and were able to survive only by growing their own food in a large garden. Reverend Little died (possibly murdered) when Malcolm was six, and the family began a steady decline into poverty. Malcolm's mother, Louise, made some money by doing housework and the older children took on odd jobs, but the family had to rely on food and clothing supplied by the state welfare department.

In his autobiography, Malcolm X notes that he and his brothers and sisters were "so hungry we were dizzy." He and his brother trapped small animals for food and caught bullfrogs to sell for a nickel apiece. On a good day the family ate oatmeal or cornmeal. On a bad day, his mother would boil dandelion greens. Malcolm sometimes stole food but was punished if his mother found out.

In 1939 Louise Little suffered a nervous breakdown and was placed in a mental institution, where she remained for twenty-six years. The two oldest children were allowed to remain in the family home, but the other children, including Malcolm, were placed in foster care.

ROBERT MAXWELL (1923–1991), Czech-born British publisher
His publishing empire—books, magazines, and newspapers—enabled him to enjoy an opulent life style. He had his own yacht and helicopter, and at one time estimates of his worth exceeded one billion dollars. Maxwell was obsessive about cultivating his image as a powerful, savvy business tycoon. When he died in mysterious circumstances in a boating accident, that image was shattered as investigations into his financial dealings led to charges of deception and fraud.

Maxwell was born Abraham Lajbi Hoch in a peasant village in Czechoslovakia. His father earned a meager living by buying and selling cattle and sometimes worked as a laborer. Abraham and his six brothers and sisters grew up in a two-room wood shanty with dirt floors and no running water. Meals consisted mostly of potatoes and other vegetables grown in the garden; sometimes, on holidays, a small piece of meat would miraculously appear. The Hochs, like many families in the village, were grateful for, and dependent upon, food and clothing supplied by charities in the United States.

While Maxwell did receive a rudimentary education in village schools, he usually claimed that he was "self-taught." When going to school, the Hoch children had to share the few pairs of shoes that the family owned. When recalling his childhood, Maxwell said that he remembered always being hungry, always being cold. He once commented, "The poverty, indignity, and hunger have engraved themselves on my heart."

AUDIE MURPHY (1924–1971), U.S. soldier and actor

About his childhood, the World War II hero wrote: "I am one Texan boy who never had a pair of cowboy boots. I am one native-born and native-bred American male who actually doesn't know the rules of our national pastime— baseball. I never had time to play or the paraphernalia you play it with. I never had a bike. It was a full-time job just existing."

Audie was working in the cotton fields when he was five. One of nine children, he lived in a succession of rundown shacks. When the family hit rock bottom, they sought shelter in a boxcar. Audie's father, a sharecropper, was a drunk who deserted the family when Audie was twelve. Audie's mother, a proud, religious woman, was forced to accept charitable contributions from her church. While there were plenty of poor families in Hunt County, Texas, most folks considered the Murphys among the very poorest. Some families wouldn't allow their kids to play with the Murphy children because the Murphys were considered to be at the bottom of the economic heap.

Did you know that publishing tycoon Robert Maxwell grew up with six brothers and sisters in a two-room shack with dirt floors and no running water?

Audie had one pair of ill-fitting pants when he went to school. Some of the kids felt sorry for him because he never had any toys and didn't get any Christmas presents. In addition, he often appeared hungry and undernourished. However, Audie was a bright student who got good grades and loved to read books.

Audie dropped out of school when he was fourteen and went to work—as a farmhand, cotton picker, grocery store clerk, gas station attendant. When he was eighteen, he joined the army and went off to fight in World War II.

DOLLY PARTON (1946–   ), U.S. singer and songwriter

She was born in a one-room shack in the mountains of Tennessee, and the attending doctor was paid off with a sack of cornmeal. One of twelve children, Dolly grew up in houses with leaking roofs, no running water, and newspapers used for insulation on the walls. Her clothes were homemade hand-me-downs, and about the only store-bought items the Parton children ever received were ugly, durable leather shoes purchased at the start of the school year.

Dolly's mother made a doll, "Tiny Tasseltop," for her out of a corncob, and her father whittled small, wooden toy cars. The kids tied June bugs to a string to make "lectric kites." For the most part, Dolly was not acutely aware of how poor her family was; she once said, "I have found that poverty is something you don't realize while you're in it." Occasionally, however, the economic differences between Dolly and some of her classmates were painfully evident. In school the kids would be asked what they ate for breakfast, and Dolly would answer like the rest of the kids, "Sausage and eggs and waffles" (she really had biscuits and gravy). At Christmas she apprehensively pulled a name for the gift exchange out of the grab-bag box but worried that she wouldn't be able to afford a gift for the person whose name she had drawn.

In her autobiography Dolly Parton spins tales of a warm, loving family life filled with childhood traumas and triumphs. About her humble beginnings, she writes: "When I think about survival and the things Mama and Daddy did to keep us all alive and reasonably healthy, I am aware that it was not just their wills and wits that kept us going. It was a legacy passed down from every mountain dweller who had ever learned anything about surviving hundreds of years before, starting with the Native Americans."

UPTON SINCLAIR (1878–1968), U.S. novelist and social reformer

He was born in Baltimore, Maryland, and many of his earliest memories dwelt on the theme of smashing bedbugs in the one-room rental units in which his family usually lived. Upton's father, an alcoholic, was rarely employed, and his mother, who came from a respectable southern family, did her best to ignore the pathetic circumstances of her marriage. The family was always moving from one cheap room to another, and Upton spent much of his boyhood sleeping across the foot of his parents' bed.

The Sinclairs moved to New York City when Upton was ten, but the move did nothing to improve their economic condition. They again lived in dingy boardinghouses and hotels in poor neighborhoods. There was never enough money for food and clothing. When things got desperate, Upton's parents sent him back to Baltimore for a few months to live with wealthy relatives (on his mother's side of the family). Thus the boy literally moved from rags to riches. At age fifteen, Upton started selling jokes and short stories to magazines and earned enough money to support himself and his parents.

Sinclair became instantly famous in 1906 after publishing *The Jungle*, an indictment of the meat-packing industry in Chicago. He wrote more than ninety books and frequently acknowledged that his favorite theme was showing the contrasting worlds of the rich and the poor. He explained, "As far back as I can remember, my life was a series of Cinderella transformations; one night I would be sleeping on a vermin-ridden sofa in a lodginghouse, and the next night under silken coverlets in a fashionable home. . . . No Cophetua or Aladdin in fairy lore ever stepped back and forth between the hovel and the palace as frequently as I."

SIBLING RIVALRIES

SALVADOR DALI (1904–1989), Spanish painter
One Salvador Dalí was born on October 12, 1901, and died on August 1, 1903 in Figueres, Catalonia. On May 11, 1904, ten months later, another Salvador Dalí was born—the dead child's brother and imagined reincarnation, the Dalí destined to become a famous, eccentric artist.

Dalí's cousin reported that the boy's parents "made comparisons between the two every day. They used the same clothes and gave him the same toys." Dalí saw his dead brother as a rival: "I deeply experienced the persistence of his presence as both a trauma—a kind of alienation of affections—and a sense of being outdone."

The death of the first son made Salvador's parents obsessively afraid that Salvador might die, too, even though he was healthy and strong. And death haunted the boy himself. When Salvador looked at a large photograph of his dead brother, he was so terrified that his teeth started to chatter. Trying to take his shirt off over his head made him feel as if he would suffocate. In his autobiography, he tells how praying at his brother's tomb made him wonder whether he was alive or dead.

His parents babied him, which made him into a manipulative little tyrant, attuned to every emotional nuance and ready to take advantage of it. When he started school, he did not know how to tie his shoes. He was prone to raging temper tantrums when he did not get his way.

Salvador felt he was loved, but not for himself. The sibling rivalry forever haunted him. He once wrote, "Before all and at whatever cost: myself—myself alone! Myself alone! Myself alone!"

DWIGHT DAVID EISENHOWER (1890–1969), U.S. president
In the Eisenhower family, Dwight David, future president of the United States, was always "Little Ike"; his brother Edgar, less than two years older than he, was always "Big Ike." The two were always competing, and Edgar always won, except in shooting. Of course, they fought each other, too. Their parents, strong Christians, did not stop them—they felt that fighting was natural for boys, even character building. Though Little Ike refused to buckle under easily, he later told his brother, "I was just the tail to your kite."

The family was poor, and Dwight and Edgar dressed in hand-me-downs. The boys either went barefoot or, facing ridicule, wore their mother's old

*Dwight D. Eisenhower,
age three, 1893, with his
competitive brothers.
Arthur holds Roy, and Edgar
stands behind Dwight.*

Courtesy Dwight D. Eisenhower Library.

button-top shoes. Their poverty made them put aside their rivalry to sell vegetables from their three-acre farm to richer people in Abilene, Texas. Sometimes, too, they played hooky, fishing and hunting together. Little Ike once
said that it was possible, just barely, to "make you and me look like Tom
Sawyer and Huckleberry Finn." And once when their father beat Edgar, Little Ike said, "I don't think anyone ought to be whipped like that, not even a
dog."

After Big Ike became a lawyer and Little Ike a soldier, Little Ike wanted to
redress his grievances as the always defeated little brother. Big Ike cautiously
offered to meet him "with boxing gloves at forty paces." Yet it was also true
that, when grown, all six Eisenhower brothers presented, as Edgar said, "an
unbreakable ring" of affection for each other, even though Edgar became
such a right-wing Republican that he was often at loggerheads with his eminent brother.

JOSEPH HAYDN (1732–1809), Austrian composer

When Joseph Haydn was six, he performed for a visiting uncle, Johann Math-
ias Franck. The boy sang, showing off his "weak but pleasant voice" (as he
later described it) and sawed away at an imaginary violin, showing off his perfect time. Franck offered to take the talented Joseph home to Hainburg with
him so that he could go to a school where he was headmaster. Joseph's poor
parents—his father was a wheelwright—agreed. At this point, Joseph was the
Haydn child destined for greatness. His brother, Michael, then a baby, stayed
home.

When Joseph was eight, he went to Vienna to join the Vienna Boys' Choir
and soon afterwards began to compose music. Of course, as he grew older,
his voice changed, and he could no longer sing high notes. Joseph was a mischievous child. For instance, on one occasion he climbed the scaffolding at
Empress Maria Theresa's new palace in defiance of the empress, who asked
the choirmaster to beat him, which he was more than happy to do.

As Joseph's fortunes fell, Michael's rose. At age eight, Michael, a fast
learner with a beautiful soprano voice, more beautiful than Joseph's had ever
been, came to join the choir. The empress was so taken with Michael that
she gave him twenty-four golden ducats. Of Joseph, perhaps remembering
his exploits on her scaffolding, she said, "The elder Haydn boy sings like a
crow."

In 1749, the choirmaster threw Joseph out of the choir and into the
streets, with no money and in ragged clothes. Luckily for Joseph, a music
teacher whom he barely knew took him in, and later a friend of his father lent
him 150 florins, so he was able to survive. Living in an unheated attic, he
made money as an accompanist, violin player, singer, and teacher. More important, he spent long hours studying composition and composing music. He
was still a teenager when he wrote Mass in F.

Meanwhile, Michael became conductor to the Bishop of Grosswardein.
When Joseph heard this, it only made him more determined to compose, and
by 1758 was appointed music director to Count Ferdinand Maximilian von

Morzin of Bohemia. In the end, he took back his rightful place as the more talented brother.

WILLIAM JAMES (1842–1910), U.S. psychologist, and **HENRY JAMES** (1843–1916), U.S. novelist

Only sixteen months apart in age, the ebullient prankster William and the stoic and cerebral Henry James spent their contentious childhood overprotected by their father, whose own childhood had been visited by tragedy and pain. (He wore a cork leg, having lost his real one as the result of an accident involving fireworks.)

When William was eight, he started to take little trips around their hometown, New York City. Henry asked to go with him. William said no. "*I play with boys who curse and swear!*" Six-year-old Henry did not meet these criteria. However, sometimes William did let his little brother accompany him—to visit a little farm with peacocks on Eighteenth Street or to watch the building of the Hudson River Railroad, where dynamite often exploded.

At ten or eleven, Henry started writing. In one of his stories, there was a description of a storm: "the thunder sounded and the lightning followed." Future scientist William set him straight and would not let it go, teasing Henry so ruthlessly that his mother stepped in. After that, Henry wrote closeted in his room and kept his work under lock and key, retreating into reading and daydreaming.

As they grew older, the boys seemed to become closer. In Paris in 1856–57, they roamed galleries, as William lectured to Henry about art. Yet close as they were, Henry had a dream that perhaps revealed some of his hidden feelings about their relationship. He dreamed of chasing a figure that first tried to break into his room and then fled. He pursued it down the Galerie d'Apollon in the Louvre, which he recognized in a flash of lightning. The figure could have been William, some analysts say.

He later wrote that William's age put him so far ahead of him "as if he had gained such an advance of me in his sixteen months' experience of the world before mine began that I never for all the time of childhood and youth in the least caught up with him or overtook him. He was always around the corner and out of sight."

JOHN FITZGERALD KENNEDY (1917–1963), U.S. president

When they were kids, Joe and John ("Jack") Kennedy had a bicycle race in opposite directions around the block. As they approached each other at top speed, neither would yield. It took twenty-eight stitches to patch Jack up, though Joe was unhurt.

This story exemplifies their relationship: invincible and Olympian big brother Joe, injured and unyielding little brother Jack. Joe, less than two years older than Jack, acted as father to all the Kennedy children, all of whom accepted his tutelage with something like hero worship—except Jack. Once, during dinner at the Kennedy beach cottage, Jack wolfed down his chocolate cream pie and then stole Joe's piece and ate it before Joe could retrieve it. Joe chased Jack down to the breakwater, where Jack, trapped, got into position to dive into the ocean, fully clothed. Joe pulled him back and started laughing at his brother's face, full of terror and whipped cream.

Jack wanted to go to schools where his brother Joe was not enrolled, so that he would not have to face the competition. But they both ended up at Choate, an elite prep school, where Joe won the Harvard Football Trophy awarded for athletic and academic ability. As for Jack, he won a pie-eating contest and was a cheerleader.

In college, Joe was again the star—in athletics, social life, academics— while Jack failed to become president of the freshman class and did not win a post on the student council as a sophomore; his grades were mostly Cs. Their competition ended only with Joe's death in World War II.

JACK KEROUAC (1922–1969), U.S. novelist and poet

All his life, Jack Kerouac lived in the shadow of his older brother, Gerard, who died at the age of nine, a saintly victim of rheumatic fever. Jack adored Gerard; his parents, especially his mother, Mémère, adored him even more.

Gerard loved animals to the point that he rescued a mouse from a trap and put breadcrumbs on his windowsill for the birds. In his last years, confined to the bedroom of their house in Lowell, Massachusetts, he selflessly entertained Jack, five years his junior, by drawing animals and helping him make Erector set machines.

As death approached, Gerard cried, "Why do I hurt? I confessed." Jack, who slept in the same room, could hear him. To try to help, he spread pictures of holy figures on Gerard's bedspread, but to no avail. Gerard died in agony. Leo Kerouac, the boys' father, lost his faith. Their mother lost her teeth. As for Jack, he tried to be his brother, saving kittens from torture and performing other acts of mercy. Yet when Jack was in high school, Mémère said to him, "You should have died, not Gerard." His fame as king of the Beats and author of *On the Road* made no difference. He wrote, after thirty years had gone by, "there's no doubt in my mind that my mother loves Gerard more than she loves me."

When Mémère wanted to move to Florida, Jack took her there. He bought her a house with money he had received for selling his correspondence with Allen Ginsberg to Columbia University. It was there that he died, age forty-seven, from internal bleeding, perhaps brought on by alcoholism.

D. H. (DAVID HERBERT) LAWRENCE (1885–1930), English novelist

There were three girls and three boys in the Lawrence family. The star child of the family was Ernest, who was seven years older than David (called "Bert"). The older brother was tall, good-looking, intelligent, and athletic. He had a great sense of humor, wore stylish clothes, and loved to dance. Ernest's engaging personality and zest for life were infectious and made him very popular, especially among the young women who sought him out. Ernest's mother, Lydia, adored him and proudly displayed a glass inkstand, a prize he had won at the age of twelve in a school footrace.

Bert was the opposite of Ernest. He was skinny and frail and timid and missed a lot of school because he always seemed to be sick. The headmaster of his school was always comparing Bert to Ernest and told Bert that he wasn't fit to tie his brother's bootlaces. Bert's classmates called him a sissy because he refused to play games with the boys and preferred to hang around with the girls. The boys taunted him by chanting, "Dicky, Dicky Denches plays with the Wenches."

When Ernest went off to London to work, Bert was able to get more attention from his mother. While Bert was probably envious of Ernest's confidence and abilities, he nonetheless loved his brother. Whenever Ernest came home from London for a visit (he had become quite successful), the family flew into a frenzy of activity; Ernest was treated as the conquering hero. The

Future army officer and war hero George C. Marshall (right) with his sister, Marie, and his near-perfect brother, Stuart.

Courtesy of the George C. Marshall Research Library.

family was devastated, however, when Ernest suddenly became ill and died at the age of twenty-three. Lydia Lawrence was inconsolable and said that "she looked forward more to meeting her son Ernest in heaven than Jesus Christ himself."

GEORGE C. MARSHALL (1880–1959), U.S. general and statesman

George's only brother, Stuart, was older, brighter, more ambitious, and a near-perfect son in the eyes of his father, George Marshall, Sr. George, on the other hand, was a terrible student, somewhat lazy, and always seemed to be causing some kind of trouble. If Stuart broke a family rule, he was rarely punished. If George broke the same rule, he was promptly dispatched to the basement for a whipping from his father. Stuart could do no wrong; everything George did was wrong.

The boys' father, a Civil War veteran, was thrilled when Stuart enrolled in the Virginia Military Institute in Lexington, Virginia. However, instead of fulfilling his father's wish for him to become a career military officer, Stuart chose instead to become a chemist. Seeing a chance to best his older brother, George decided to attend the same school. One day, however, George overheard Stuart trying to talk their parents out of sending George to the school because he was a dunce and would only embarrass the family. The younger brother, however, won out, and attending the Virginia Military Institute turned out to provide structure and direction to his life. Many years later, George Marshall referred to the family squabble over his schooling, "I did finally get ahead of what my brother had done. That was the first time I had ever done that. . . . The urgency to succeed came from hearing that conversation."

The "urgency to succeed" propelled Marshall to become one of the most noted and respected military generals in U.S. history. He was U.S. Army chief of staff during World War II, and after the war served as secretary of state and secretary of defense. In 1953 he won the Nobel Peace Prize for the Marshall Plan, which provided crucial economic aid to postwar Europe. When President Truman awarded Marshall the Distinguished Service Medal, he said, "In a war unparalleled in magnitude and in horror, millions of Americans gave their country outstanding service. General of the Army George C. Marshall gave it victory."

RAN AWAY FROM HOME

JEAN COCTEAU (1891–1963), French writer, artist, and film director

In 1904, after being expelled from school, young Jean studied in a pension with a tutor, M. Dietz, who "sprawled, drooped, coiled and uncoiled" with his "odalisque poses," peering at his pupils "over his pince-nez and shaking with sarcastic laughter." Jean couldn't stand it. He ran away to Marseilles, where "an old Annamese woman found me absolutely lost and wandering up and down the waterfront." He told her that his family mistreated him (a lie) and that he never wanted to return home. In the Old Quarter, where she had taken him, he worked showing tourists the sights in the daytime and taking them dancing at night. Along the way, he took on the name and identity of a boy who had drowned. His uncle finally sent two policemen after him, and they brought him back home.

SAMUEL TAYLOR COLERIDGE (1772–1834), English poet

Samuel asked his mother to cut his cheese in a whole piece so that he could toast it; then he went into the garden. To "disappoint the favorite," his brother Frank cut the whole piece of crumbly cheese into bits. When Samuel came back and discovered the bits of cheese, he hit Frank. Frank fell down and pretended to be badly hurt. Frightened and guilty, Samuel acted solicitous of his brother, who then stood up, laughed, and hit Samuel in the face. Enraged, Samuel grabbed a knife. His mother took his arm. Fearing that she would spank him, Sam jerked away and fled to the bank of the Otter River not far away from the Coleridge home in Devon. He stayed there, reading prayers and thinking of his mother's anxiety over his absence. It grew dark, cold, and stormy. Even so, he fell asleep.

Meanwhile, his mother had waited for Samuel to come back. When he did not, she sent several men, including his father, and some boys to search for him. In three towns, the town crier announced that he was missing and that there was a reward for finding him. The river and ponds were dragged.

Samuel woke up on the riverbank at about 5 A.M., but he couldn't move. Sir Stafford Northcote found him and had his servant carry him to his father. Coleridge later wrote that he would never forget "Father's face as he looked upon me while I lay in the servant's arms—so calm, and the tears stealing down his face; for I was the child of his old age."

DAVID CROCKETT (1786–1836), U.S. frontiersman

At thirteen the future "king of the wild frontier" got into a big argument with the school bully and then ambushed the classmate after school. According to Davy: "I pitched out from the bushes and set on him like a wildcat. I scratched his face all to flitter jig, and soon made him cry out for quarters in earnest." He knew that the bully would tell on him. Afraid of a beating by either the teacher or his often intoxicated father, Davy would set off for school with his brothers and then hide in the woods. Later, the schoolmaster went to see his father to ask where Davy had been. Coming home, Davy saw his father with a big stick, so he ran away. His father chased him for a mile but then gave up.

Davy joined one of his brothers on a cattle drive and subsequently worked for a wagoner. After about three years, he decided to go home to Tennessee. On the last night of his journey, he crossed a raging river in a canoe. At his father's tavern, he didn't announce himself, and it was hours before his family realized who he was.

W. C. FIELDS (1880–1946), U.S. comedian and actor

Fields, who became one of America's foremost comedians, was born in Philadelphia. He and his father, James, who sold fruits and vegetables from a cart in the streets, were often at odds. W. C., then known as "Whitey" for his blond hair, would practice juggling with his father's oranges and lemons, often dropping and ruining them. His justifiably irate father would hit him with the back of his hand, which was missing the little finger. One day, when W. C. was eleven, he accidentally left a shovel in the yard. When James stepped on the shovel, it hit him in the shin, causing an injury. After hopping around for a while, the angry father picked up the shovel and whacked his son's head with it. To get even, a few days later young Fields dropped a wooden crate on his father's head. Fearing severe punishment, the boy ran off.

W. C. stayed on his own for several years, helped at first by his friends, who brought him food to a hole in the ground a mile from his home, where he slept for a while. He moved successively into a club room over a black-smith's shop, a livery stable, a barrel, and the woodbox near the furnace in a cellar. He stole food and took advantage of the free lunch in saloons. It was during these times that Fields developed his famous grandiose air (from hiding his insecurities), his bulbous nose (from being punched), and his cracked voice (from having too many colds.) He made money working as a pool shark and selling ice and papers. But it was his skill with juggling that eventually led him into vaudeville and launched his comedy career.

ERROL FLYNN (1909–1959), Australian-born U.S. actor

The childhood of the swashbuckling actor in Hobart, Tasmania, was marked by two themes: He kept getting bounced out of school, and he was a chronic runaway. Young Flynn liked his father, a marine biologist at a university who was frequently away from home, but had few kind words for his mother, who wielded authority over the rebellious youngster. After Flynn became famous, his mother loved to tell reporters that her son was "a nasty little boy." A nasty boy he was—he was a kleptomaniac, and he was cruel to animals. Once he pushed his baby sister down a hill on a sled into a lake—luckily his mother was just able to save the infant.

The first time he disappeared from home, he was six. He was staying with his family at a boardinghouse when he and a little girl of three, whose family was also staying there, took off. The Flynns called the police. It took a day and a night to find the children—on a roof in a slum. Three years later Errol left again. This time he was found sleeping in a cowshed on nearby Mount Wellington.

When Errol was a little older, he liked to go down to the wharves and look at ocean liners. He would say to his friends Angus Brammall and William Lacey, "Christ, I'd like to get away from this dump on one of those ships." Once he and another friend, Donald Love, stole a yacht from the Hobart Yacht Basin and sailed off for New Guinea. They ran ashore and were arrested, but the police did not charge them because their fathers were prominent men—Love's father owned a department store, and Flynn's father was a professor.

LILLIAN HELLMAN (1905–1984), U.S. writer

At age fourteen, when the Hellmans were living in New Orleans, she and her adored father got into a fight about a lock of hair. A boy had given it to her, and she had put in the back of her new watch. Her father asked the boy's name, but she refused to tell. The interrogation put her in a rage.

She ran away, beginning a forty-eight-hour odyssey into the city that began when she hid in a doll's house on the grounds of a mansion, sleeping on "a tiny Madame Récamier couch." She tried to buy a train ticket and went into Bourbon Street's red-light district, where a whore yelled at her. The second night, she slept behind a bush. The stares of two rats woke her. She had her first menstrual period, accompanied by cramps. She tried to rent a room in a black neighborhood, telling the landlord that she was a mulatto. Finally, her father found her and took her home.

SAM HOUSTON (1793–1863), Texan political leader

Sam's mother sent him to work as a clerk in a general store in Maryville, Tennessee, when he was fifteen. Hating the humdrum atmosphere, one day he just disappeared into the woods. Weeks later, two white poachers told the family that they had seen a boy like him living with a Cherokee band on tribal lands. According to one romantic source, months later, Sam was reading the *Iliad* in the shade of a tree when his brothers, John and James, found him with the Indians on an island. In any case, he flatly refused to go home. He said, "I prefer measuring deer tracks to measuring tape." The boy who would later become a leader in Texas's fight for independence stayed with the Cherokees for three years, learning their language and adopting their ways. The leader of the band, Ooleteka, adopted him and named him Kalanu ("The Raven").

LYNDON BAINES JOHNSON (1908–1973), U.S. president

When he was four and jealous of his younger siblings, he started running away from home. He would hide in the fields, listening to his parents calling for him. He remembered that his mother "became very frightened when she . . . couldn't find me. She had two smaller children in the house and couldn't locate me."

He finished high school when he was not yet sixteen. His parents sent him to take a preparatory set of courses at Southwest Texas State Teachers College in San Marcos, but he was kicked out. At about this time, he had a dream: He was sitting in a tiny cage with a pile of heavy tomes and a stone bench. An old woman walked in front of him, and he caught a glimpse of himself in the mirror she carried—no longer a boy but a brown-spotted, long-haired old man. The old lady would not let him out of the cage, and he woke up saying, "I must get away. I must get away." And so he did. Along with four friends, he hopped into a 1918 Model T Ford and headed to California in search of adventure. The thirty-sixth president of the United States would later recall that he had planned to tell his parents of his plans, "but when I reached the front door of my house, I began to shiver uncontrollably. . . . I lost my nerve." When Johnson and his friends got to California, they had only eight dollars among them. During his two years away from home, Johnson worked as an elevator operator, grape picker, dishwasher, law clerk, and auto mechanic.

CLARE BOOTHE LUCE (1903–1987), U.S. writer and diplomat

Author, member of Congress, and U.S. ambassador to Italy, Clare Boothe Luce was born in New York City. She was the daughter of a chorus girl and a professional violinist. At sixteen Clare left home with ten dollars in her pocket and took a job at a paper novelty company, where she made flowers, nut cups, and bonbon holders; she was paid eighteen dollars a week. Her independent streak lasted for only two months, however, until an appendicitis attack forced her to return home.

JULES VERNE (1828–1905), French science fiction and adventure novelist
He grew up in the seaport city of Nantes and was surrounded by sailing ships and boisterous sailors and tales of high adventure. Even though he was a well-adjusted boy, the lure of the maritime life was hard to overcome. When Jules was eleven, he posed as a cabin boy and took off on a boat called the *Coralie*. However, a few family friends had observed his movements, and when his parents started to look for their missing son, they quickly learned where Jules had gone. When the ship anchored at a nearby port, Jules's father (who had boarded a steam ferry) was waiting for him. After being punished, Jules supposedly said, "From now on, I'll travel only in my imagination."

PARENTS' ADVICE

"Life will give you many unpleasant tasks to do; your duty will be hard and disagreeable and painful to you at times, but you must do it. You may have pity on others, but you must not pity yourself. Do what you find to do, and what you know you must do, to the best of your ability."

HENRY FORD'S MOTHER

"All children must look after their own upbringing."

ANNE FRANK'S FATHER

"When in doubt, never do anything secret, which may bring discredit to one's cause or dishonor our people. Be brave and the rest will follow."

INDIRA GANDHI'S FATHER

"The other person may have the right to feel the way he or she does. Hear them out. You may learn something. They'll respect you for taking the time and are more likely to listen to your side."

BARRY GOLDWATER'S MOTHER

"I would not be too hard on the fools if I were you, Willie. If everybody were very clever, you and I might have a pretty hard time getting along."

WILLIAM RANDOLPH HEARST'S FATHER

"Don't take life or its happenings too seriously. Lift up the corners of that mouth that I gave you one moonlit night."

KATHARINE HEPBURN'S FATHER

"Give 'em more than they paid for."

DUSTIN HOFFMAN'S FATHER

"Never have partners."

HOWARD HUGHES'S FATHER

"Never get sick, Hubert; there isn't time."

HUBERT HUMPHREY'S FATHER

"Why walk when you can run?"

LEE IACOCCA'S FATHER

"Let me tell you something about women, son. You will have your troubles with them. We all do. There will be arguments; a marriage may not work; there may be times when you get into bed and not be able to function. But always remember this. No matter what happens, it's her fault."

ALAN JAY LERNER'S FATHER

"Before you can do what you want to do, before you can exist as an individual, the first thing you have to accept is duty, the second thing is respect for authority, and the third . . . is to develop a strong mental discipline."

VINCE LOMBARDI'S FATHER

"Never lie, never tattle."

DOUGLAS MACARTHUR'S MOTHER

"If there were more virgins, the world would be a better place."

MADONNA'S FATHER

"Remember this place, Rocky, and when you grow up be somebody. Don't ever work in a shoe factory."

ROCKY MARCIANO'S FATHER

"Never become involved with someone who can make you lose stature, if the relationship becomes known. Sleep up."

ARISTOTLE ONASSIS'S FATHER

"Sometimes you have to waltz around your enemy to fox-trot on his back."

GORDON PARKS'S FATHER

"Rathers never quit."

DAN RATHER'S FATHER

"Always think things through for yourself, lass. Don't take anything for granted, even things that have been repeated for centuries. You'll only grow up when you begin to think for yourself."

MARGARET SANGER'S FATHER

"Son, don't take life too seriously. You'll never get out of it alive."

RED SKELTON'S MOTHER

"Don't go around looking for trouble. But if you ever get into a fight, make sure you win it."

JOHN WAYNE'S FATHER

Howard Hughes, without partner, at seventeen with his motorized bike.

Courtesy of the Houston Metropolitan Research Center, Houston Public Library.

CHAPTER THREE

RECREATION

"First there's the children's house of make-believe,
Some shattered dishes beneath a pine,
The playthings in the playhouse of the children.
Weep for what little things could make them glad."
ROBERT FROST, "DIRECTIVE"

How we envy kids. At least in summer, they play all day, giving vent to their energy and imagination until they drop. The way they play sometimes foretells their later professions. Not always, though.

Like other kids, many of our subjects flirted with danger as children. Their ability to survive allows us to believe in their own childish perception of their immortality. Dancer Nijinsky balanced on the edges of roofs. William Wyler walked the edge of a zoo's bear pit. Hoping to fly, Samuel Beckett threw himself in a freefall off the top of a pine tree.

To the despair of their parents and teachers, quite a few of our subjects were pranksters. Marlon Brando wrote a dirty word in lighter fluid on the blackboard and set it on fire. Steven Spielberg brought a gruesome dish to the dining room table—a doll's head mounted on a plate of lettuce leaves.

The famous played with some fabulous—and some ordinary—toys. For instance, child star Shirley Temple, owner of a kids' dream of a dollhouse, had more fun with her slingshot, even pinging First Lady Eleanor Roosevelt. Among their pets were some unusual animals: Alvin Ailey's pet snake, Stephen Crane's trick circus pony, Margaret Mitchell's cantaloupe-eating cat who could salute like a soldier.

The hobbies of the famous astound us. Johnny Carson and Orson Welles were amateur magicians. The Dalai Lama liked to fix up cars. C. Everett Koop kept an amputated foot in a jar of formaldehyde.

Some of these notable people liked to read unlikely books as kids. Poet W. H. Auden was fascinated by *Mrs. Beeton's Book of Household Management* and *Dangers to Health,* a book about plumbing. Hitler liked to read westerns by Karl May. Who would have guessed?

DAREDEVILS

SAMUEL BECKETT (1906–1989), Irish dramatist

His nickname was "Family Jonah," for his ability to survive dangerous situations, after the biblical story of the bold Jonah, who ended up in the belly of a large fish. Luckily he and his brother Frank, four years older than he, were fearless and athletic, mostly because their competitive and jovial father had brutal ways of teaching them essential skills of life. For example, he taught them how to swim by throwing them into the water. They swam. Sam and Frank were very close. Both were tough. As local tennis champions, they had to play only with each other, because friends were afraid of the shots the Beckett boys aimed at their opponents' heads.

Sam liked to climb to the top of a pine tree and throw himself down in a spread-eagled free fall, hoping to fly, but counting on lower branches to break his fall. This terrified Frank, who was almost as fearless as Sam but not quite; so he told May, their mother, what Sam was doing. She proceeded to beat Sam to prevent him from doing other such foolhardy things. It didn't help much. Once, wanting to see what would happen, he dropped a lighted match into a can of gasoline. Luckily, the can was almost empty and all that happened was that he burned his eyebrows. For that escapade, May beat him with her hand so hard that her hand swelled up, so she had to resort to a stick to finish the job.

DAVID CROCKETT (1786–1836), U.S. frontiersman

David Crockett, who was then under twelve years old, was tracking a deer in the woods when he saw a shape in the bushes and shot at it. The shape turned out to be a neighbor, a farmer who had been gathering berries. The musket ball tore a great hole in the man's shoulder, and for days he lay near death, his fever rising and falling. David felt guilty, even though it had been an accident. In his mind's eye, he imagined himself standing at the man's coffin as people shouted "Murderer!" at him. Each daybreak he would keep watch at the neighbor's house for a sign of whether the man was alive or dead.

He longed to do something to help, and finally an idea came to him. He had one great talent—he was a champion tree climber, able to swing from limb to limb with great agility. One morning he went to the neighbor's house, climbed a venerable oak tree, and put on a dazzling, hourlong performance. He leapt from limb to limb and swung like a monkey, so far above the ground that he surely would have died if he had fallen. The neighbor, watching from a window, smiled and said, "That was a great show, young fellow. Didn't know you could do something besides shoot a gun."

AMELIA EARHART (1898–1937), U.S. aviator

In 1904, watched by her four-year-old sister, Muriel, she belly-slammed her sled down an icy hill. A horse and wagon coming from a side street were about to cross their path. A collision seemed inevitable. Amelia put her head down—and with perfect timing shot the sled under the horse's belly between its feet. She was unhurt.

Her experience on the sled was a typical exploit. When Amelia was seven, her family had attended the World's Fair in St. Louis, where she was fascinated with the roller coaster. When the family came home, she built a roller coaster, with the help of Muriel, friend Ralphie Morton, and her Uncle Carl. They nailed tracks of wood from the roof of a shed to the ground below and made a cart with wheels to fit the track. They greased the track with lard, hauled the cart to the roof, and then launched themselves down. When the test run resulted in a crash, they rebuilt the roller coaster so that the tracks had a gentler descent. Amelia said it was "just like flying." Unfortunately, her mother thought the roller coaster was dangerous and had it destroyed after a few runs.

KATHARINE HEPBURN (1907–   ), U.S. actor

A very young Katharine (Kathy) climbed trees, and when alarmed neighbors called about it, her mother replied, "Don't scare her. She doesn't know that it is dangerous." Her father, Dr. Thomas Hepburn, encouraged Katharine's daredevil tendencies. To teach her to ride a bike when she was three, he just put her on the bike and let it go down a long hill. She survived. When she and her brother Tom were older, he attached a swinging ladder to a tree limb sixty feet above the ground and put a trapeze on a pulley, which rode a rope from the limb to the ground. Kathy and Tom climbed the ladder and then rode the trapeze from the tree limb down.

Dr. Hepburn liked to drag the children on sleds attached to the car, trying to throw them off as he drove fast around corners. They loved it. It was a good thing that Kathy had natural agility and nerve. Skinny and tough, she became an accomplished athlete, afraid of nothing.

After the suicide of her brother, Tom, Kathy started breaking into houses with her friend Ali, reprising the moment she had opened the door to find him dead. They stole nothing. Kathy would first find a way to get into a house and then open the door for Ali. Once she dropped through a skylight, landing in a third-floor hallway, just missing a three-story fall to a marble floor.

ELIZABETH KENNY (1880–1952), Australian nurse

She was fearless. Soon after she learned to walk—at nine months—she started roaming, so that she had to be tied to a stump. At four or five, she tried to fly, using the stump as a launching pad. When she was out in the bush one day, a poisonous death adder stood in her path. She hit the snake with a stick, took it home, and dropped it, whereupon it came out of its stupor and wiggled away.

By the time she was six, she was "living on horseback," and two years later she was riding anything that moved—cows, calves, horses—bareback, sidesaddle, or man's saddle. She even rode an untamed stallion named Satan that no one else could ride—bareback.

At thirteen, when the Kennys were living in Headington Hill, Elizabeth leapt on a horse without looking to see if it was properly saddled. The saddle slipped and she fell, breaking her wrist. With her other hand, she tied the horse to a tree and walked home. Her father, Michael, drove her forty miles over a rough road to the house of the doctor, McDonnell, in Toowoomba. He set the wrist and kept her at his house until it healed. McDonnell liked Elizabeth. When she was trying to figure out how muscles worked, he gave her a little lecture about it and lent her some books. What she learned later played a part in her development of the Kenny method, which helped children paralyzed by polio to regain the use of their muscles. Elizabeth had to fight the medical establishment's opposition to the method with the courage that she had learned in the Australian bush.

JOHN MUIR (1839–1914), Scottish-born U.S. naturalist

Growing up in Scotland, the high-spirited, irrepressible Johnnie Muir loved "scootchers," the Scottish term for adventures done on a dare—one boy would so something scary or dangerous and then dare his friends to follow suit. He would sneak into a forbidden room in the Muir house (reputedly haunted by the ghost of the former owner), touch the belongings of the "ghost" and then challenge his younger brother Davie to do the same. Johnnie crawled out of his third-story bedroom window and dangled his small body over the end of a slippery, steep slate roof (his brother almost fell when duplicating the deed). Some of the best scootchers happened when crawling around the crumbled ruins of thousand-year-old Dunbar Castle.

At school he engaged in an almost daily series of fistfights and excelled at "Wee Willie Wastle," in which he stood at the top of a sandhill and defended his turf until he got knocked off. Another popular game was "Switches," in which two boys stood toe to toe and lashed out at each other's bare legs with switches of knotwood until the boy in the most pain gave in and was declared the loser. After school Johnnie and his friends made guns out of old gas pipe and improvised bullets from lead scraps; they shot at geese and seagulls flying overhead on the seashore. Another favorite pastime: putting explosive powder into a hole in the sand and then lighting a fuse to "make an earthquake." Unfortunately, the boys sometimes used too much explosive and ended up with singed hair and powder burns on their faces.

Many years later the noted conservationist and mountaineer reflected on his early scootcher-climbing days: "That I did not fall and finish my rock-scrambling in those adventurous boyhood days seems now a reasonable wonder."

AUDIE MURPHY (1924–1971), U.S. soldier and actor

The most decorated American soldier of World War II, Murphy was the son of a sharecropper and grew up in Hunt County, Texas. One of twelve children (only nine survived to adulthood), the boy lived in a succession of ramshackle homes and at times had to take shelter in a boxcar. Put into the cotton fields when he was five, Murphy had to drop out of school in the fifth grade to help support the family. His father, a poor provider and a drunk, deserted the family when Audie was twelve.

Short and undernourished, the boy never backed away from a fistfight and lured himself into dangerous situations. Even though he was a poor swimmer, he was always diving into water tanks or crossing treacherous creeks. Most of all, he took chances with guns. An expert marksman, he shot game for food, but he also played lots of games with guns. Sometimes he and his friends shot objects—like cigarettes or books—out of each other's hands; or they steadied bottles on their heads and shot them off. According to one observer, Audie and his brother Buck once tried to shoot marbles out of each other's lips.

VASLAV NIJINSKY (1890–1950), Russian ballet dancer

One of the greatest dancers and choreographers of his time, Nijinsky left audiences awestruck as he leaped across the stage, often giving the impression that he was suspended in midair. Even at the age of four, he was an artistic sensation, able to outperform all the students in his ballet class. He was also a hyperactive child, and his inability to remain still, together with his athletic talent, played a big part in his daredevil stunts.

He climbed tall trees and swung from branches. He raced across the tops of buildings and carefully balanced his body on the edges of the roofs. He ran through the woods and found his way into nearby gypsy camps, where he joined their singing and dancing.

When he was twelve years old, Vaslav pulled a stunt that almost ended his budding career. The incident took place at the Imperial School of Ballet in St. Petersburg. His fellow students dared him to jump over a high barrier they had put together—mostly a big wooden music stand. As Vaslav, deep in concentration, started running toward the music stand, one of the boys rubbed soap on the floor in front of the barrier and another boy added height to the barrier. Thus deprived of any chance of flying over the barrier, Vaslav hit it hard. He was taken to a hospital and remained in a coma for four days, having sustained excessive abdominal bleeding. In order to recover, he had to drop out of school for a semester.

Little daredevil Audie Murphy.

Courtesy of the Audie Murphy Research Foundation.

EDWARD RICKENBACKER (1890–1973), U.S. aviator

His whole life was one big adventure. Born and raised in Columbus, Ohio, Eddie Rickenbacker was one of the earliest racing car drivers on the national circuit. In World War I he flew many dangerous missions, shooting down twenty-six enemy aircraft and earning numerous decorations, including the congressional Medal of Honor. He was a pioneer in the automobile industry.

And in 1942, while on a wartime mission for the air force, his plane crashed in the Pacific Ocean. Rickenbacker and the other survivors spent twenty-three days in a life raft before being rescued.

When Eddie was eight, he and fellow members of the "Horsehead Gang" wandered over to a gravel pit in Columbus (closed on Saturdays). Intrigued by thoughts of a roller coaster ride down the 100-foot embankment, they pulled the steel cart, moored on a cable at the bottom of the pit, up the incline. They anchored it with blocks until several of the boys climbed in, pushed away the blocks, and then careened down the incline at an uncontrollable speed, as a result of which everyone was tossed out of the cart. All but Eddie were thrown clear, but the cart hit him hard several times before he ended up at the bottom of the pit. The young daredevil was bruised and bloody from head to toe, and one of his legs was cut to the bone.

The year after the roller coaster incident, Eddie decided he wanted to fly, so he bought a huge umbrella and secured it to a bicycle. The plan: to ride down the steep, slanting roof of a barn and take off into the air, soaring like a bird. For this feat, however, Eddie gave himself a measure of safety by building a little sandhill at the end of the barn. As soon as the flying contraption left the roof, the umbrella turned completely inside out—and down went Eddie into the sand. The bicycle and umbrella were destroyed, but Eddie survived.

WILLIAM WYLER (1902–1981), German-born U.S. film director
He won three Academy Awards and directed thirty-two movies including *Wuthering Heights, Jezebel, The Best Years of Our Lives, Ben-Hur,* and *Funny Girl.* About Wyler's directorial style, actress Bette Davis once said, "He could make your life a hell, but I would have jumped into the Hudson River if the man had told me to."

Born in the city of Mulhouse in Alsace, then a part of Germany, Wyler was a willing participant when friends dared him to do something. He grabbed a goldfish out of a bowl and ate it; he swam fully clothed across a river; he boldly tested ice on a frozen pond. His mother, Melanie, was particularly terrified of Willy's penchant for heights. Once he climbed two stories up the outside wall of the family's apartment building and surprised her as she looked through the kitchen window. Especially fond of the bear pit at the local zoo, Willy would scale the protective railings that circled the pit and gingerly walk around the top of the enclosure. He never fell in, but once he lost his hat, which the bears quickly ripped apart.

FAVORITE TOYS

SHIRLEY TEMPLE BLACK (1928–   ), U.S. actor and politician
With her prize slingshot, she could hit a Coca-Cola bottle at twenty feet. Edwin Burke, screenwriter for *The Littlest Rebel,* wrote a special sequence

for her in that movie so that she could show off her prowess with her favorite weapon.

In 1938 she gave First Lady Eleanor Roosevelt two of her special police badges, one for each of the First Lady's grandchildren. Shirley, who had created the police force, attached conditions to the gift: Mrs. Roosevelt had to inform her grandchildren of the rules of the force, including the fines for infractions, one of which was failing to wear the badge at all times.

Later that year, Shirley and her mother visited the First Lady at Val Kill, the Roosevelt family estate in Hyde Park, New York. In her lace purse Shirley had stashed her police chief's badge and her slingshot. She noticed that neither Mrs. Roosevelt nor the grandchildren, who were visiting, were wearing badges. Moreover, the two grandchildren laughed when she demanded a fine for their failure to follow the rules. Shirley was very irritated. As Mrs. Roosevelt leaned over the barbecue to turn the chops, the sundress she was wearing hiked up a bit, an irresistible opportunity for a shot. Shirley found a pebble, sneaked out her slingshot, and let fly, hitting the target right on. Mrs. Roosevelt flinched and straightened up quickly, but ignored the incident. Mrs. Temple did not. Back at their hotel, she smacked Shirley on the bottom and said, "See how *you* like it!"

TRUMAN CAPOTE (1924–1984), U.S. writer

When he was five or six, Truman had a little green tricycle made shaped like an airplane with a red propeller. He told his friends that he was going to ride it down the street, take off, and fly to China. No matter how hard he pedaled, he never left the ground.

AGATHA CHRISTIE (1890–1976), English mystery writer

Her dollhouse was so crowded with furniture that she could not fit it all in. So at her mother's suggestion, she turned a four-shelf wall cupboard into another dollhouse and put the original house on top. At their first meal the dollhouse family had roast chicken and "a rather peculiar pink pudding."

Agatha also loved her hoop, a big circular toy meant for rolling with a stick. To Agatha, it became "a horse, a sea monster, a railway train." She rolled the hoop-train on three railways that she had devised in the yard, calling out, "Lily of the valley Bed. Change for the Tubular Railway here. . . ."

On wet days she played in the greenhouse with a dilapidated American rocking horse named Mathilde. As she described it, "Mathilde had a splendid action—much better than that of any English rocking horse I have ever known. She sprang forwards and back, upwards and down, and ridden at full pressure was liable to unseat you. Her springs, which needed oiling, made a terrific groaning. . . ."

NOEL COWARD (1899–1973), English dramatist and actor

The future playwright and actor showed his passion for the stage as a young boy. One of his favorite toys was a little auditorium. In it he staged "Cinderella" and "Black-Eyed Susan" using cardboard cut-out figures as actors. When he was given a bigger auditorium, with scenery painted by his father,

Noel fashioned marionettes by attaching dolls to a wire circle so that he could manipulate them. He dressed the dolls in "long chiffon draperies of different colors" and made them dance.

DALAI LAMA (LHAMO THONDUP) (1935–　), Tibetan religious leader
Living at the monastery in Lhasa as the next incarnation of the Dalai Lama, he had many toys, some imported ones sent by an official on the Indian border, others gifts from foreigners. Among the toys were a complete Meccano set and a clockwork train. The boy also had a set of lead soldiers, with which he played war games. He would fashion tanks and airplanes from dough, next set them and the soldiers out in beautiful formations, and then have his armies engage in battles. When he grew older, he melted the soldiers down and recast them as monks.

ELIZABETH II (1926–　), British monarch
She preferred soldiers to dolls; she lined up the soldiers and walked up and down in front of them to review the troops, but threw the dolls around the room. She adored a clockwork monkey that was a present from her grandmother, Queen Mary. And she and her younger sister, Margaret Rose, owned a thatched cottage playhouse that was a gift from the Welsh people. But perhaps Elizabeth's favorite toys were thirty wheeled horses, each twelve inches high, that she saddled and bridled every day. At night, she would take off the saddles, feed and water the horses, and then stable them on the landing outside her bedroom.

WILLIAM FAULKNER (1897–1962), U.S. writer
His artistic maternal grandmother, Lelia Butler, whom he called Damuddy, carved him a nine-inch doll and made a blue policeman's outfit with brass buttons for it. Little Willie called the doll Patrick O'Leary, and he liked to make up stories about it as he played with it in the attic.

ANDREW LLOYD WEBBER (1948–　), English composer
The man behind *Cats* and *The Phantom of the Opera* was writing his own songs when he was only seven years old. When he was eleven, Andrew built his own toy theater out of wood and bricks. Grandiose and technically sophisticated, the theater had an orchestra pit and a revolving stage. Andrew used the theater to put on musical productions. As his younger brother, Julian, moved the "actors" (toy soldiers) around the stage, Andrew stood off on the sidelines, directing the show and banging out songs on the piano.

HENRY LUCE (1898–1967), U.S. publisher
The son of Presbyterian missionaries, Henry (who would grow up to launch *Time* magazine) spent part of his childhood in China. He had a large collection of tin soldiers and often annoyed his siblings by spreading them all over the floor in the children's playroom. He put up little forts, and his soldiers engaged in great battles. Henry became very disturbed if anyone dared move anything around on his battlefield.

Did you know that when the Dalai Lama was a boy, he played war games with soldiers? He then melted them down and made them into monks when he was older.

THOMAS MANN (1875–1955), German novelist

Born into a prosperous family, Thomas had a lot of extraordinary toys that he shared with his brothers and sisters, among them an elaborate puppet theater, a hobbyhorse with glass eyes and pony fur, lead soldiers, and toy lambs. The Mann children also had a grocery store complete with a counter, scales, and a crane for lifting sacks. One of Thomas's favorite playthings was "a complete knight's armor of iron-gray cardboard, with visored helmet, tournament lance, and shield."

GEORGIA O'KEEFFE (1887–1986), U.S. painter

She had four brothers and sisters, but Georgia liked to play by herself and built her own dollhouse. It was a simple, four-room contraption in which she placed tiny dolls. The dollhouse was completely transportable, and in the summer she would move it outside and create miniature outdoor surroundings for it. Sometimes Georgia would make a little park and carefully trim the grass, and sometimes she would make little paths out of stones and sand. A dishpan full of water served as a lake, and on the lake floated a sailboat.

EUGENE O'NEILL (1888–1953), U.S. dramatist

Eugene had his very own railroad. It was a big, coal-burning model, and the train's tracks ran all the way around his family's home in New London, Connecticut. The train was sturdy enough to carry the boy, and Eugene loved to stoke up the engine and then proudly ride the train as it chugged around the tracks. One of Eugene's cousins said that the boy sometimes used as much as half a ton of coal a day.

B. F. SKINNER (1904–1990), U.S. psychologist

A small-town boy who grew up in Susquehanna, Pennsylvania, Burrhus Frederic was a very smart, inquisitive child who loved to build things. The Skinner house and yard were always cluttered, and Fred never had to look far to find materials for his gadgets and inventions. Among the toys he made for himself were merry-go-rounds and wagons, roller skate scooters, sleds, and rafts. A music lover, Fred also crafted his own kazoos and whistles and made violins out of cigar boxes. In addition, he created a game called Teno-Ball, a version of table tennis. As an adult, Skinner once wrote, "Making do . . . that has always been a favorite theme of mine. To make the most of what you have."

HOWARD STERN (1954–   ), U.S. radio personality
By age seven Howard, an amateur puppeteer, was putting on shows for family and friends. His father, Ben, built a stage for the boy's productions, and the shows became so professional that Howard took them to some senior citizen homes. As he grew older, however, "Howie" realized that his friends "went wild" when the marionettes became engaged in sexual antics, and the shows took on more of a pornographic flavor. Stern said, "Once I started doing the dirty puppet shows, I really lost interest in regular puppeteering, and pretty soon, all the puppets were wrapped up in storage. I had ruined a beautiful, innocent part of my life."

BARBRA STREISAND (1942–   ), U.S. singer, actor, and film director
Barbra had very few toys when she was growing up, and her only doll was a hot water bottle. A neighbor, who sometimes acted as Barbra's babysitter, knitted an outfit for the doll. When asked about the doll on the television show *Oprah*, Streisand said, "She [the neighbor] knit me a little tiny pink hat and a little pink sweater for the hot water bottle. And I used to fill it with warm water and it felt like a real baby. . . . I collect antique dolls today. I love dolls because I never had one."

GLORIA VANDERBILT (1924–   ), U.S. clothing designer
She was born into great wealth and at age ten captured national attention when she was the object of a scandalous custody trial that pitted her mother against her aunt. In her memoir, *Once upon a Time,* Vanderbilt discusses her traumatic childhood and all the people who were involved in her upbringing. She says that as a young girl she made her own paper dolls and that each one represented someone in her life—her mother, father ("who was in Heaven"), grandmother, aunts, nurse. According to Vanderbilt, she planned to put all the paper dolls in a big dollhouse where she could control all their movements. She says, "I'll stand outside the dollhouse looking in at them—because I'll be the one who's big and they'll be the ones who are tiny. They'll belong to me—all of them—and stay put, right where I want them to be—forever and ever and ever. . . ."

BELOVED PETS

ALVIN AILEY (1931–1989), U.S. choreographer
When he was nine or ten, he and his mother, Lula, were living in an abandoned house built on stilts near the Brazos River in Texas. They were very

poor. Lula picked cotton to provide three meals a day. She noticed that Alvin was putting some of his food—biscuits and syrup, for instance—to one side, even though she told him to clean his plate. The food, it turned out, went to hand-feed a huge chicken snake that lived under the house and had become Alvin's pet. When Lula later decided to move, she told Alvin that they would come back for his snake—but they never did.

MARLON BRANDO (1924–   ), U.S. actor

Young Marlon had a special way with animals, especially those that were hurt. The family kept a large menagerie—chickens, a Bantam rooster called Charlie Chaplin, cats, a cow, a mare (Peavine's Frenzy), a Great Dane called Dutchie, and some goats. Marlon was the only one who could milk one of their cows, who was mean. He could even ride her.

Once, when a special chicken died and someone buried it, Marlon dug it up; his father buried it again; Marlon dug it up. According to a friend, "he had liked the chicken and wanted to be the one to bury it."

Did you know that Steven Spielberg had a collection of parakeets all named Schmuck?

JACKIE COOPER (1922–   ), U.S. actor

On the set of *Skippy*, made in 1930 when Cooper was about nine, Jackie kept a little dog, given to him by one of his mother's friends. He was a very obedient dog. Jackie kept him tied to his chair, where he usually slept all day.

One day the script called for Jackie to cry, but Jackie could not. The director, Norman Taurog, suddenly focused on the dog. He said he did not want the dog around and threatened to take it to the dog pound. He said if Jackie could cry, ending the day's work on time, then maybe Jackie could get to the pound in time to save the dog before it was euthanized. Jackie sensed that it was a trick. He watched his grandmother take the dog and put it in the car. The dog yelped, but Jackie knew that his grandmother had pinched it. Jackie flew into a rage. Taurog said that if Jackie didn't calm down, the security guard would be ordered to shoot the dog. The guard unholstered his gun and set off in the direction that Jackie's grandmother had gone. Then Jackie heard a shot.

Jackie started sobbing. Taurog said that if Jackie did the scene right, they could go to see if the dog was alive. After he did the scene, Jackie found that the dog was unharmed and that, as he had suspected, it had been a trick all along—the director, Jackie's grandmother, and the security guard had been in cahoots. That night, Jackie couldn't eat or sleep or stop crying. A doctor was called in to give him a shot that put him to sleep. Jackie's grandmother told him in the morning that everyone had been worried. "I felt very bad about that," he wrote in his description of the incident.

STEPHEN CRANE (1871–1900), U.S. writer

He was the fourteenth child and baby of the family. His father, Jonathan, a minister, and his mother, Mary Helen, were so busy doing good works that they left Stephen in the care of his sister, Agnes Elizabeth, fifteen years older than he.

His father died in 1880 and his beloved sister Agnes died in 1884. Perhaps to assuage his grief, his brother Townley gave Stephen a trick circus pony named Pudgy. Stephen rode him bareback into the ocean waves at Asbury Park, New Jersey, where the family lived. Stephen "would almost rather ride a horse than play ball," said his friend C. K. Linson, noting that Stephen would have been a mounted policeman if he had not become a writer. When he went to military school four years later, he took Pudgy with him.

DALAI LAMA (LHAMO THONDUP) (1935–   ), Tibetan religious leader

Chosen as the next incarnation of Dalai Lama, he went off to live in the monastery in Lhasa at age four. In spring and summer, he stayed in Norbulingka, another monastery where there was a menagerie in the park—tame musk deer, Tibetan mastiffs, a Pekinese dog, mountain goats, a monkey, camels, leopards, a tiger, peacocks, geese, cranes, parrots. His special favorites were the fish that lived in the lake. He would call them to come for bread. Sometimes they came, sometimes not. When they did not come, he punished them with a shower of stones. When they did come, he used a stick to keep off the larger fish so that the smaller ones would receive their fair share.

WILLIAM FAULKNER (1897–1962), U.S. writer

Buster Callicoat, a 200-pound retarded man, and Willie Faulkner, about twelve, bought a horse at an auction for $4.75. It was untamed, but they gentled it. Finally, when Buster said it had been fully tamed, they put a sack on its head, hitched it up to a cart, and got in the cart. But when their friends took the sack off the horse's head, the horse bolted. The cart dropped a wheel during a sharp turn and finally scattered all over the lane. Buster grabbed Willie by the neck, threw him out of the cart, and then jumped out after him. The horse finally came to a halt in a dead-end street. Faulkner later said, "But we kept that horse and gentled him to what I finally rode him. But I loved that horse because he was my own horse. I bought him with my own money."

URI GELLER (1946–   ), Israeli psychic

Young Uri liked to explore caves near his home in Cyprus, where the family had moved when he was eleven. One day, all alone, with a flashlight and chalk to mark his way, he entered a new cave. When he turned around to go back, after exploring for quite a distance, he lost his way. His chalk arrows seemed to have disappeared. Panicked, he prayed and waited for about an hour, playing the light around the cave to see if he could spot any of his arrows. Then he heard a dog bark. When he shone his light toward the sound, he saw his dog, Joker, a wire-haired fox terrier. Joker led him out of the cave. Though Geller himself is a psychic, he could not figure out how Joker knew where he was or that he was in trouble.

JEAN PAUL GETTY (1892–1976), U.S. businessman and art patron

At eleven, he went off with his father to Indian Country (now Oklahoma) to watch an oil well at Bartlesville being drilled. It was not the Wild West he expected, but quite tame, even boring—just an oil town—though the wells themselves and the oil drillers fascinated him. In town he made friends with a yellow mutt, whom he named Jip. Jip slept in the hotel corridor outside Paul's room. He took Jip on walks and recorded them in his diary: "In the morning I saw the funniest thing. A lot of burros came along with four cowboys driving them. I set Jip on them and soon a dozen dogs were barking and snapping at their heels. . . ." A week later: "In the afternoon I walked four miles out into the country. Jip followed me and nearly got a rabbit. . . ."

After the well was drilled, the family went back to Minneapolis. Paul left Jip with a friend, but when they returned to Bartlesville in the fall, Jip was overjoyed to see his pal again. Paul later had a black greyhound named Prince, but he said that Prince never "quite took the place of my beloved Jip."

D. H. (DAVID HERBERT) LAWRENCE (1885–1930), English novelist

David, called "Bert," was given two white rats by a friend. Since the rats were tame, and very cute, Bert's parents said he could keep them as pets and give them a proper home—a nice, big wooden box. The rats were great playmates, and Bert let them sleep in his pockets and run up and down the inside of his coat sleeves. They sometimes hid in his sister's long hair, and all the Lawrence children were convinced that the rats recognized their voices. The rats, however, multiplied at such an alarming rate that Bert's father finally had to get rid of the beloved rat family.

CHARLES LINDBERGH (1902–1974), U.S. aviator

A quiet, bashful boy with not many friends, Charles was, however, very devoted to his pets, especially the dogs. Over the years he had at least five dogs, but a mongrel named Dingo always remained his favorite. Charles first encountered Dingo when he found the puppy tearing apart the garbage at the Lindbergh farm in Little Falls, Minnesota. The boy and dog became instant pals.

One morning when Charles was thirteen, he found the dog lying dead on the family's property. No one was ever able to prove that the dog had been shot intentionally. However, Charles's father was a member of Congress with controversial opinions, and it was possible that Dingo was a victim of an angry voter.

GEORGE C. MARSHALL (1880–1959), U.S. general and statesman

When the World War II hero was growing up in Uniontown, Pennsylvania, he wasn't allowed to have a dog because his parents had watched a relative die from rabies after a dog bite. So George became buddies with a friend's dog, a terrier named Trip. George would secretly let Trip out of the dog's fenced yard, and the two companions would head out for a day of fun—hiking, fishing, hunting. Trip was more devoted to George than he was to his unsuspecting real master.

As a young man, George moved away from his hometown and had a hard time saying goodbye to Trip. Several years later, when he returned to Uniontown for a visit, George went to see Trip, who had become an old, frail dog.

Charles Lindbergh and his beloved dog, Dingo.

Courtesy of the Minnesota Historical Society.

At first Trip ignored George, treating him as a complete stranger. Devastated and depressed, George sat and talked to the dog, petted him, and let the dog sniff him. After a while, Trip's memory returned and he couldn't stop jumping all over George. Or, as Marshall said, "He had finally gotten a scent in his old nostrils and he remembered me. That was the most flattering thing that occurred to me on that short visit home."

MARGARET MITCHELL (1900–1949), U.S. novelist

Growing up in Atlanta, Georgia, Margaret had her own pony and a number of other pets, including dogs, ducks, turtles—even a few alligators. But she spent the most time with her cats. Her first cat, named Piedy, was often hauled up (in a basket "elevator") to a tree house built by Margaret and her brother, Stephens. When Piedy died, two more cats, Hypatia and Lowpatia, joined the Mitchell menagerie. Lowpatia was usually the center of attention because Margaret had taught him how to stand up, put his right paw next to his ear, and give a military salute. As a reward, the cat was fed cantaloupe, one of his favorite treats.

GERALDO RIVERA (1943–   ), U.S. broadcast journalist

The man who would become an aggressive, outspoken, controversial, and award-winning journalist didn't have it easy as a kid. He was too skinny, suffered from acne and asthma, and was allergic to a number of things, including dogs.

The family pet, a Labrador named Patty (rescued from certain death at an animal shelter) was Geraldo's good buddy and companion, but too many hours with Patty caused Geraldo severe breathing problems and landed him in a hospital emergency room. Unable to return the dog to the pound or find a suitable home for her, Geraldo's father let Patty loose far from home, hoping she would find a new family. Several days later, however, Geraldo's uncle returned Patty to the Rivera doorstep—bloody, worn out, and dirty. Apparently, Patty had been hit by a car but had made her way to within a block of the Rivera home. The dog's courage and devotion was awarded with reinstatement in the household and a special doghouse in the yard.

STEVEN SPIELBERG (1946–   ), U.S. film director

His bedroom was a mess, with clothes, toys, junk food, and unidentifiable objects lying all over the floor (just like Eliot's room in *E.T.*). Also in the room were eight parakeets, which were supposed to remain in their cages. Steven couldn't stand to keep the birds in captivity, however, so he let them fly around and even trained them to perch on a curtain rod. As a result, bird droppings as well as birdseed were sprinkled atop the mounds of clutter in his room. According to Spielberg, he wasn't very imaginative when naming the parakeets. He'd call one Shmuck, the next Shmuck II, and so on.

JOHN STEINBECK (1902–1968), U.S. novelist

When he was ten, John received a surprise present from his father: a bay pony. He happily accepted all responsibility for the care and feeding of the pony, whom he named Jill, and spent endless hours grooming her and talking to her. The pony made John a neighborhood celebrity in Salinas, California. Every day he carefully chose the friends who would be allowed to ride Jill. Many years later, Steinbeck would immortalize some of his feelings for the animal in his work *The Red Pony.*

Here we are, Mary, John + Jill - Salinas Aug 28 07

John Steinbeck and his sister, Mary, atop his bay pony, Jill.

Courtesy of the Steinbeck Archives, Salinas (CA) Public Library.

JOHN WAYNE (1907–1979), U.S. actor

He was born Marion Morrison but asked the kids in grade school to call him "Morrison," since he was embarrassed by his girlish first name. When Marion was eleven, he was dubbed with a nickname that stuck with him for the rest of his life.

The name "Duke" was coined by firemen at a Glendale, California, fire station, which Marion passed every day on his way to school. Always with the boy was his Airedale terrier Duke. The dog was devoted to Marion and continually followed him to school. Worried that school authorities would impound his pet if they caught Duke hanging around the school, the boy asked the firemen to help out by distracting the dog until he was well past the station and on his way to school. The firemen knew the dog's name but not Marion's, so they called the Airedale "Little Duke" and Marion "Big Duke." The sixth grader liked his new nickname, because it sounded manly and important.

HOBBIES

INGMAR BERGMAN (1918–   ), Swedish film director

When he was about ten, a relative gave his brother, Dag, a movie projector. Ingmar swapped him most of his tin soldiers for it. He ran the first piece of film he was able to acquire—about three feet of a woman waking up in a meadow, stretching, then disappearing off the frame—so many times that it was ruined. When he obtained a better projector, he began to buy films, but more important, he started to make them. He and a friend, Rolf Åhgren, pasted together snapshots to make their first film. Ingmar also used films he was tired of watching as raw material for his own little movies with new story lines. He even soaked exposed film in soda solution to take off the emulsion, so that he could draw on the frames to make a kind of animation.

Did you know that J. Robert Oppenheimer was asked to speak, at age eleven, before the New York Mineralogical Club?

JOHNNY CARSON (1925–   ), U.S. comedian and talk show host

A neighbor and friend, Phil McNeely, brought a deck of marked cards and a magician's supply house catalog back from a visit to Omaha. When he showed them to twelve-year-old Johnny, the boy promptly ordered a kit of magic tricks from the catalog. From then on, Carson said, "Magic became my all-consuming interest." He practiced for hours, commandeering family members to watch his tricks. His stage name was The Great Carsoni. For Christmas, his mother gave him a magician's table and a black velvet cloth cover on which she had embroidered THE GREAT CARSONI in Oriental-looking letters. His signature sentence, "Take a card, take a card," became a family joke.

DALAI LAMA (LHAMO THONDUP) (1935–   ), Tibetan religious leader

As a child, the future leader of Tibetan Buddhism liked to take things apart and put them back together. Though he eventually became very good at it, he made mistakes at first. One day he found a broken old music box that had been given to the former Dalai Lama by the tsar of Russia. When he worked at loosening the overwound mainspring with a screwdriver, the spring, once freed, broke loose in a frenzy of clanging shards of metal.

At the monastery, four cars—a Dodge, two Baby Austins from the late 1920s, and a Willys Jeep—rusted away unused. The young Dalai Lama wanted to get them running again. He and a driver succeeded in fixing one of the Austins by using parts from the other. The Dodge and the Willys needed only a little tinkering. But the boy was not allowed to drive the cars. One day, however, he defied orders, taking the crank-operated Austin out, running it into a tree, and breaking the glass on one of the headlights. He fixed it as best he could. The driver, who must have seen the damage, never said a word.

ALFRED HITCHCOCK (1899–1980), English-born U.S. film director

Maps and timetables fascinated him. By the time he was eight years old, he had ridden every London tram line and had traveled on the river steamers to the mouth of the Thames. Timetables were "literature" to him. Before he went to school, he knew by heart the schedules of most British train lines. He also kept track of the positions of British ships on a huge wall chart.

When he was older, his interests expanded to include murder trials. He took voluminous notes at the Old Bailey, a London court. At Scotland Yard's Black Museum he spent hours looking at exhibits of crime and criminals, which, he noted, included gaslight-era prostitutes' shoes, whose heel colors advertised their owners' specialities.

C. EVERETT KOOP (1916–   ), U.S. surgeon general

The young Everett collected everything, especially sharp objects and human body parts. He cluttered his room with Indian pottery, Indian arrowheads, Civil War cavalry swords, stamps, an Italian stiletto. His high school science lab teacher said he could have some molars from the skull of a South American Indian woman if he could get them out. When he was unable to find a tool to extract the teeth, he finally did so by taking them in his own jaws. One of his prized possessions was a foot he had obtained while working as a teenager in a hospital. Amputated from a diabetic patient, it rested in a gallon jar of formaldehyde. He planned to dissect it but never did. His mother made him take it with him when he left home to get married. He decided to get rid of it and dropped the jar over a sewer grate, thinking that the glass would break and the foot would fall in the sewer. The foot did not drop through, but stood there, and for all he knows is standing there still.

Did you know that Henri de Toulouse-Lautrec completed three hundred drawings and fifty paintings when he was only sixteen?

GEORGE LUCAS (1944–   ), U.S. film director and producer

When George was eight, he and his friends put together backyard carnivals that featured a zoo, a fun house, and a six-foot-high roller coaster. They also built what Lucas calls "elaborate little environments." The forerunners of the filmmaker's elaborate movie sets, these environments were made up of farms, hills, towns, and roads. The boys used berries, wood, metal, and cement to construct them. Endless games and battles took place within the confines of these make-believe civilizations.

J. ROBERT OPPENHEIMER (1904–1967), U.S. physicist

For many years Oppenheimer, who would one day develop an atomic bomb for the United States, had an interest in mineralogy. When he was five, he got his first set of minerals from his grandfather. After that, he collected specimens wherever he went, and quite a few samples came from the rock formations in New York City's Central Park. When Robert was eleven, he began writing letters to a number of leading geologists, who were so impressed by his interest and knowledge that they wrote back. Not realizing that Robert was only a boy, one geologist proposed to the New York Mineralogical Club that J. Robert Oppenheimer be invited to become a member of the organization. After being accepted, Robert received a letter asking him to speak before the group. Members of the club were quite astonished when the featured speaker arrived and turned out to be a shy, curly-haired boy.

RONALD REAGAN (1911–   ), U.S. president

Ron became fascinated by birds' eggs when he was five years old. The landlord of a house that the Reagan family rented had left behind a collection of birds' eggs and butterflies in the attic. When Ron grew older, he started his own collection of birds' eggs, which he carefully placed in a display case. Reagan later wrote that he clearly remembered the hours he spent looking at the landlord's attic collection and that "the experience left me with a reverence for the handiwork of God that never left me."

THEODORE ROOSEVELT (1858–1919), U.S. president

Theodore (called "Teddie") became interested in zoology when he was seven, after he saw a dead seal displayed on a plank in an open-air market in New York City. He talked the owner of the seal into letting him buy the seal's head to put in his "Roosevelt Museum of Natural History," which was located on a porch in his parents' home. An avid naturalist, Teedie was always observing wildlife, and in a notebook he wrote descriptions of all sorts of creatures—spiders, turtles, frogs, mice, birds.

When Teedie was thirteen, he was given his first rifle and began shooting prey, mostly birds, for his collection. Since he had taken lessons in taxidermy, he was able to stuff and preserve his own specimens. Most of his family and friends were somewhat appalled by the sight of the boy skinning his victims, but Teedie was enthusiastic and meticulous as he worked on the additions to his museum.

HENRI DE TOULOUSE-LAUTREC (1864–1901), French painter

A very sickly child, Henri spent a lot of time in bed as he recuperated from various ailments. To keep himself occupied, he collected stamps and toy carriages and built model ships. He pursued each hobby with great enthusiasm and called them his "furias," because his devotion to them was almost obsessive. However, the "furia" that remained in first place was his love of art. At a very early age he was making sketches of animals and experimenting with watercolors. When he was only sixteen, Henri completed three hundred drawings and fifty paintings.

Did you know that as a child, the Dalai Lama's hobby was fixing cars?

ANDY WARHOL (1928–1987), U.S. artist

Eight-year-old Andy loved to go to the movies and sat transfixed by the larger-than-life actors on the big screen. He especially idolized Shirley Temple and wrote to her asking for an autographed photograph. The photograph, which was signed with a personal inscription, was to become one of his most treasured possessions. It inspired a lifelong hobby of collecting autographed pictures of movie stars.

When Warhol died at the age of fifty-nine, his estate was inventoried for auction. His New York townhouse resembled a warehouse stuffed with innumerable collections. There were statues and paintings, furniture and rare books, autographs and jewelry—even cookie jars. Some of the boxes and crates uncovered had never been opened. He had been an obsessive collector, whether the items concerned were priceless works of art or pure junk. In all, more than ten thousand items were discovered.

ORSON WELLES (1915–1985), U.S. actor and film director

He got his first magic set when he was four years old, and Orson loved to entertain his mother's friends with his tricks, always performed with great flamboyance. When he was a teenager, Orson attended a magic show starring Harry Houdini and was allowed to go backstage to meet the world-renowned magician. The precocious boy immediately tried to impress Houdini with a handkerchief trick. Houdini was courteous but told Orson never to perform any trick in public until it had been perfected in private. Orson heeded the advice; some time later, when he had another opportunity to talk to Houdini, he showed him the new, improved handkerchief trick.

PRANKSTERS

JACK BENNY (1894–1974), U.S. comedian

He was a great violin player in the high school orchestra, but he was a lousy student. Benny talked while the teachers were talking, continually cracked jokes, and was frequently caught passing notes during class. He played hooky as often as he dared and loved concocting pranks, such as hiding Limburger cheese behind the radiator on cold winter days when the heat was going full blast. When the high school principal learned that Benny was flunking all of his courses, the boy was expelled.

Did you know that John Lennon once gatecrashed a nuns' garden party dressed as a monk?

MARLON BRANDO (1924–   ), U.S. actor

His mother was a bohemian alcoholic and his father was not home much. Young Marlon ("Bud") thus had plenty of freedom to concoct pranks. When he was ten, he wrote *shit* on the blackboard with lighter fluid and lit it up when the teacher came in. By the time he was in junior high, his mother said, "He is a grand kid but living with him is like climbing a greased pole in war-torn Shanghai. And the worst won't come for another two or three years." She was right. In high school, his devilment escalated. When a teacher called, "Order!" he answered, "A hamburger, french fries, and a Coke!" He threw strings of firecrackers into classrooms and hung a dead skunk on the football scoreboard. The principal, Henry E. Underbrink, said to him, "Bud, you're a bum. You're good for nothing, you'll never be good for anything. You'll never do anything but dig ditches!"

JERRY FALWELL (1933–   ), U.S. evangelist leader

Born in Lynchburg, Virginia, he had the luck to have a rich father. Casey Falwell had made money on bootleg liquor and ran several businesses in town—the bus line, gas stations, a nightclub, a motel. He was self-confident, and so were his boys, Jerry and Gene. With .22 rifles, they regularly shot out the railroad company's water tank. Jerry put a rat in the teacher's cookie drawer and stole the physical education teacher's pants. Because of his father's power, however, no one dared touch him.

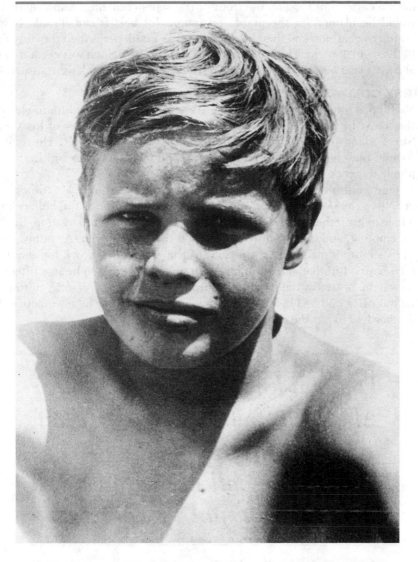

Marlon Brando, up to no good.

Courtesy of Archive Photos.

ERLE STANLEY GARDNER (1889–1970), U.S. mystery writer

The lawyer and writer who created Perry Mason attended high school in Oroville, California. The school's principal was a Professor Fogg, a skinny, middle-aged man with a Vandyke beard; the students called him "Fuzzy Fogg." Erle, who was an amateur cartoonist, thought that it would be a great idea to draw a cartoon of Fogg on the front of the school building. Knowing that he would be blamed for the prank, he taught his best friend, Frank, how to sketch the cartoon and then held the lamp as Frank performed the dirty deed in the dead of night. The students loved the picture, which was certain to last at least a year because it was done on stucco. Erle and Frank were suspended.

BARRY GOLDWATER (1909–1998), U.S. politician

He flipped butter pats on the ceiling. When his mother told him to clean up the mess, he talked back to her. At his suggestion, members of his Center Street Gang put rocks in the mudballs they threw at rivals. He took his friends' bicycles apart and hid the parts, and he pawned his brother's saxophone to get enough money to take a girl out.

One Fourth of July, at seven in the morning, he shot holes through the ceiling of the sleeping porch with his mother's gun. One of the bullets bored a hole in his father's barrel of whiskey, set there to age. Drop by drop, the barrel emptied, and the moisture also ruined the ceiling paint. As punishment, Barry's mother made him sit in front of the grandfather clock for about sixteen hours. But that didn't put an end to his pranks. When he was fifteen, at a party he hosted at the Phoenix Country Club, he drew a circle on the wall with lipstick and had his friends throw ice picks at it for target practice. His mother had to pay the damages.

> *Did you know that as a Yippie, Abbie Hoffman advocated that "children kill their parents" but would then call his parents and tell them not to worry?*

STEVE JOBS (1955–   ), U.S. computer entrepreneur

In his junior year in high school, he joined the Buck Fry Club, whose sole reason for existence was to stage practical jokes. The group found a way to disarm the school's locks and to get the fire alarm system to buzz continuously. The group set up a table for breakfast on the cafeteria roof and hoisted a Volkswagen up onto it using a winch. They painted a toilet seat gold and glued it to a planter box.

To celebrate graduation, Jobs and his friends Steve Wozniak and Allan Baum hung up a sheet the size of a building, on which they had painted a hand with one finger up, flipping the bird. On the sheet they put their collective signature, "SWABJOB."

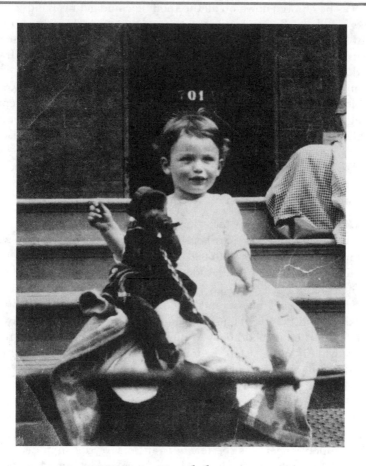

Barry Goldwater,
pre-Center Street Gang,
with monkey.

Courtesy of the Arizona Historical Society.

JOHN LENNON (1940–1980), English singer and songwriter

He grew up in a town on the outskirts of Liverpool and was raised mostly by his Aunt Mimi, his mother's sister. From a very early age, John was a chronic troublemaker and always needed to be the center of attention. In grammar school he became notorious for his "misdeeds." Many of them were fairly harmless, like using a peashooter in the classroom or making cardboard dog collars for his fellow students to wear. Once, dressed as a monk, he sneaked into a garden party hosted by a group of nuns and mingled with the other monks as he chowed down on all the food he could get his hands on. But his pranks could also be cruel and sometimes dangerous. He tripped runners on the athletic field, threw rocks and bricks at glass lamps, and frightened people with anonymous phone calls. During his school days, John was frequently placed in detention and was the object of numerous canings.

John's artistic talent was showcased in a book he created, the *Daily Howl*, in which he drew outrageous caricatures of the teachers. Surreptitiously passing the book among the students usually caused fits of laughter and general classroom disruption. Despite all of his antics, John was miserable in school. In an interview he gave after the Beatles became famous, he said, "In school, didn't they see that I'm cleverer than anybody else in this school? . . . Why would they keep forcing me to be a cowboy like the rest of them? I was different. I was always different. Why didn't anybody notice me?"

JAY LENO (1950–   ), U.S. talk show host and comedian

In his autobiography Leno writes, "There were two things that were true about my childhood—I loved to make trouble and more than that I loved getting a reaction." He grew up in Andover, Massachusetts, an adorable boy with curly hair and a large head. Jay got his first big laugh at age four when he pointed to his aunt's blouse and asked, "How come girls have humps like camels?" When he was about ten or eleven, Jay loved to harass two sisters who lived in the neighborhood. At night he used to climb up on their roof, lower himself into the sisters' bedroom window, locate their underwear, and tie all the underwear up in knots.

In junior high school, Jay was the king of pranksters, one of his classics being the "faked suicide" routine. A friend would stand at the edge of a wide-open third-floor classroom window and hold Jay's empty shoes over the edge. The accomplice would then yell, "Jay Leno's hanging out the window! I can't hold on much longer!" As the teacher ran to save the supposedly dangling Leno, the accomplice would let go of the shoes and let out a horrific scream. Jay, according to the plan, was already lying "dead" on the ground below. The heart-stopping episode, said Jay, naturally worked best on substitute teachers who weren't aware of his naughty reputation.

DAVID LETTERMAN (1947–   ), U.S. talk show host and comedian

While he pulled off some pranks in high school, the host of *Late Show with David Letterman* really hit his stride at the Atlas Super Market in Broad Ripple, Indiana, where he had an after-school job. One day he concocted a fake raffle and had shoppers fill out entry blanks to win a new automobile (some customers actually showed up on the designated prize day). On another occasion Dave set up a massive display of canned goods all the way to the ceiling; pulling just one can out of the display would have caused the entire wall of cans to crash to the floor. He loved to use the market's intercom system. Some days he announced Sunday mahjongg tournaments (the store was closed on Sundays). And when he was really bored, Dave conducted practice fire drills, instructing customers how to exit the store and proceed to the parking lot. Apparently, the store manager had a good sense of humor and Dave never got fired.

HENRY LOUIS MENCKEN (1880–1956), U.S. editor and critic

Henry inherited his love of practical jokes from his father, August. The elder Mencken once bought a piece of land, called it "Pig Hill," and told all the surrounding neighbors that he was going to blanket the property with pigsties. August even concocted a set of plans for the atrocity and applied for a building permit.

Growing up in Baltimore, Maryland, Henry was a member of the Hollins Street Gang, whose members stole produce from vegetable stands, made and exploded fireworks, harassed all the pets in the neighborhood, and performed daredevil stunts near freight trains. Henry also loved to perpetuate the myth of "Uncle Fred" (invented by his father). Uncle Fred was a minister who ultimately became a bishop and was subsequently murdered in a foreign country.

Even after Mencken became a respected journalist, he still loved practical jokes. His "bathtub hoax" is considered to be one of the greatest hoaxes in American journalistic history. In 1917 Mencken wrote an elaborate article celebrating the seventy-fifth anniversary of the bathtub and made up outrageous details: It was introduced in America at a stag party in Cincinnati; it was dangerous to one's health; some cities had outlawed the installation of bathtubs. For years afterward "facts" from Mencken's article were treated as the truth and reappeared in numerous books, scholarly articles, and newspapers.

DAVID NIVEN (1910–1983), English actor

One parent-teacher day, David brought a young prostitute to school. On another occasion he sent a package of dog excrement to a friend at another school. He "borrowed" cars and drove into town looking for adventure. His endless impersonations and jokes taxed the patience of every teacher he ever encountered. While he was a fun-loving and popular student, David was expelled from a number of British boarding schools for his outrageous behavior.

• Ironically, one of the greatest pranks in the history of the Academy Awards happened when Niven was on stage. The year was 1974, and the Oscar-winning actor was about to present an award when a naked "streaker" ran across the stage. To the millions of viewers watching the televised awards, Niven, with a straight face, quipped, "Just think. The only laugh that man will probably ever get is for stripping and showing his shortcomings."

Did you know that Jay Leno would routinely fake suicides to freak out his substitute teachers?

STEVEN SPIELBERG (1946–   ), U.S. film director

The victims of Steven's pranks were his three younger sisters—Nancy, Sue, and Anne. One of his all-time favorite pranks was the skull-in-the-closet routine: Steven stuck lights in a plastic skull and dressed the head to look like a World War II aviator, complete with a hat and goggles. After luring his sisters into a pitch-dark closet, he slammed the door shut, plugged in the lights, and gleefully listened to them scream. Once he snapped off the head of one of his sister's beloved dolls, placed the head atop a plate of lettuce leaves, and brought the nightmarish meal to the dining room table.

Steven wrapped toilet paper around and around his head, pretended to be a mummy, sneaked into a bedroom where his sisters were gathered, and slowly unwrapped his face, tossing the crumbled paper at the girls. He also liked to stand outside at night and cry out over and over again in a devilish voice, "I am the moon." Recalling how he had terrorized his sisters, the Oscar-winning director once said, "It's amazing that they even grew up. It's amazing that I grew up and they didn't kill me."

BOOKS THEY READ

JANE ADDAMS (1860–1935), U.S. social reformer

Her mother died in 1863, before Jane reached the age of three. The baby of the family, Jane was her father's little darling, and she adored him. He was a miller, and she tried to develop a flat miller's thumb like his by feeling the flour at the mill between thumb and forefinger. When she learned to read, she haunted the library, reading as many books as she could. Her goal was to read every book there. Why? Because her father had read through the library in the village where he grew up.

ISAAC ASIMOV (1920–1992), Russian-born U.S. science writer

His father gave him *The World Almanac* for his eleventh birthday. It fitted right in with one of his favorite activities, counting. Using the statistics from *The Almanac* as a source, he began to draw graphs on graph paper with a red-and-blue pencil. He made bar graphs and circle graphs and line graphs—graphs of the heights of mountains, populations, national debts. He didn't care what the subject was; he just wanted the graphic picture. He read other books of course—he was mad about science fiction—but the almanac was one of his favorites.

W. H. (WYSTAN HUGH) AUDEN (1907–1973), English poet

His favorite books were *Edinburgh School of Surgery, Mrs. Beeton's Book of Household Management,* and *Dangers to Health,* a book about plumbing that contained colored plates. He also liked the classic children's writers such as Edward Lear and Beatrix Potter. And as he grew older, he enjoyed adventure stories and Sherlock Holmes mysteries. His father read him poetry aloud, and he said later that poetry was meant to be read that way. He also thought that it should be fun. One of his favorite verses was by Harry Graham: "In the drinking well / Which the plumber built her, / Aunt Maria fell; / We must buy a filter."

CHARLES DICKENS (1812–1870), English writer

When he was little, *Little Red Riding Hood* was his "first love" of the books with "deliciously smooth covers of bright red or green." As he grew up, he started reading the books his father kept in the room next to his: "From that blessed little room, *Roderick Random, Peregrine Pickle, Humphrey Clinker, Tom Jones, The Vicar of Wakefield, Don Quixote, Gil Blas,* and *Robinson Crusoe* came out, a glorious host, to keep me company. They kept alive my fancy, and my hope of something beyond that place and time. . . ." He used to act out the characters in books to the furniture. "I recollect everything I read then as perfectly as I forget everything I read now," he later wrote. Perhaps the book that was most important to him was *The Arabian Nights.* References to its magical landscape show up throughout his writings. Later, in his adolescence, he had a penchant for horror stories from the nineteenth-century equivalents of the *Enquirer,* with headlines like "All of Us in Danger of Being Buried Alive." He liked *Terrific Register,* a weekly concentrating on tales of murder, which he later praised for ". . . frightening my very wits out of my head, for the small charge of a penny weekly, which, considering that there was an illustration to every number, in which there was always a pool of blood, and at least one body, was cheap."

THEODORE GEISEL (DR. SEUSS) (1904–1991), U.S. writer and illustrator

After his high school English teacher, Edwin A. "Red" Smith, encouraged him to become a writer, he discovered the poet Hilaire Belloc. Belloc's rhymes delighted him, and he read *The Bad Child's Book of Beasts* and *Cautionary Tales* several times. Walking home from school, he would recite one of his favorite Belloc verses: "As a friend to the children, commend me to the Yak. / You will find it exactly the thing; / It will carry and fetch, you can ride on its back, / Or lead it about with a string." The young man who became the world-famous author of *Cat in the Hat* and *How the Grinch Stole Christmas* had found his alter ego.

ADOLF HITLER (1889–1945), Austrian-born German dictator

Karl May, a German ex-convict, wrote books about the American West, which he had never seen. The books' hero, Old Shatterhand, hated Redskins, especially the southwestern Ogellallahs, and liked to kill them. May painted the Ogellallahs as mean, vulgar, and immoral thieves. On the other hand, he admired the Apaches, led by Winnetou. After his kills, Old Shatterhand would say, "I am great, I am marvelous!" Old Shatterhand's justification for killing Indians came from the Bible, which, he thought, gave him the right to wipe out so-called inferior races.

At twelve, Adolf Hitler was so addicted to May's novels that at night he used a magnifying glass to read them by moonlight. He claimed that he owed his grasp of geography to May (who had invented the geography in the books) and said that "he opened my eyes to the world." He continued to read the novels after he grew up. While fighting the war with the Soviet Union, he called the Russians "Redskins."

JOHN LENNON (1940–1980), English singer and songwriter
He had terrible eyesight and was probably dyslexic, but young John devoured books and frequently used his library card. He liked the *William* books, a series about an eleven-year-old boy who was always getting into trouble; and he was fascinated by Lewis Carroll's *Alice in Wonderland*. According to his Aunt Mimi, who raised him, John also read encyclopedias, newspapers, and classic literature such as the works of Balzac. She said, "He'd read most of the classics by the time he was ten. He had such an imagination and built up the stories himself when he and I talked them over."

JACK LONDON (1876–1916), U.S. novelist and short-story writer
Jack told tales about his youth that rivaled the adventures he made up in his books and short stories. According to Jack, he grew up in abject poverty, bought a ship and became an oyster pirate at age fifteen, raiding company-controlled oyster beds in San Francisco Bay. He was continually involved in some sort of life-threatening escapade. Although the general outline of his tales is probably true, it is likely that the details were often embellished. It's also likely that he gleaned the details from the numerous books he read. A regular patron of the public library in Oakland, California, he loved Horatio Alger stories (*From Canal Boy to President* was his favorite), Washington Irving's *Alhambra*, and volumes of books about travel and sea voyages. Jack always had a book in his hands. In fact, he spent so much time reading that he sometimes overstimulated his mind, causing a nervous reaction, which he called "the jerks."

GEORGE LUCAS (1944–   ), U.S. film director and producer
The only books George was interested in were comic books. He loved to read pictorial tales of Scrooge McDuck and Superman. He and his sister Wendy saved their allowance money to add to their comic book collection, which grew so large (totaling about five hundred) that their father had to build a shed in the backyard to store them. Inspired by the imaginative graphics of the comics, George sketched pictures, created small sculptures, and made his own greeting cards.

COLE PORTER (1891–1964), U.S. composer and lyricist
His mother, Kate, was the daughter of a millionaire. She devoted her life to seeing that Cole, her only child, had an upper-crust upbringing and insisted that he become a famous musician. As a baby, Cole was dressed in velvet and silk. When he went off to elementary school in Peru, Indiana, he wore a suit, starched shirt, and tie—and arrived atop his own Shetland pony. At age six, Cole was taking violin and piano lessons and had a private tutor for French classes.

Not satisfied with Cole's progress as a violinist, Kate decided to send the boy to a music conservatory in Marion, Indiana, thirty miles from Peru. The boy took an early morning train to Marion by himself. His lessons finished at noon, however, and he had to wait six hours for a return train to Peru. Bored and restless, Cole soon discovered that the candy vendors in Marion sold "spicy books." He bought the risqué stories and hid them in his violin case. Once he had a steady supply of titillating material, he never complained about the train trips or the long wait for the train back to Peru.

Porter said that the "naughty" books inspired some of the lyrics in his songs, probably tunes like "Love for Sale" and "But in the Morning, No!" Porter became one of the greatest songwriters in American history. His long list of hits includes "Night and Day," "Begin the Beguine," and "I've Got You Under My Skin."

JANET RENO (1938–   ), U.S. attorney general

Janet grew up in a rural area southwest of Miami, Florida, the eldest of four children. Her mother, Jane, a newspaper reporter and avid book lover, was always reading aloud to her young children. The family library included everything from fairy tales and adventure stories to poetry. Janet's all-time favorite was *The Wind in the Willows* by Kenneth Grahame. The enraptured Janet listened intently as her mother read about the adventures of Toad, Mole, and Rat and how they got themselves in and out of trouble, always surviving the forces of nature. As with most children's tales, there were usually a few moral lessons embedded in the story line.

When people ask Reno what books she read as a child, she inevitably recalls *The Wind in the Willows* and sometimes buys a copy for friends and colleagues who haven't read it. Asked to make a guest appearance on an episode of public television's *Reading Rainbow* series, Reno accepted and read from the Grahame classic to a group of children.

B. F. SKINNER (1904–1990), U.S. psychologist

As a boy B. F. (Burrhus Frederic) read whatever he could get his hands on— from adventure stories to classic literature. Fred especially liked tales such as *Robinson Crusoe* by Daniel Defoe and *Swiss Family Robinson* by Johann Wyss, in which the characters had to be creative and innovative to survive. At age ten he built his own private reading room out of a large box. Inside the enclosed space Fred was immune to anything happening in the outside world. As an adult, the behavioral scientist would become world renowned for his experimental boxes, the most famous of which was the "Skinner box" used to study the behavior of rats.

HARRY S TRUMAN (1884–1972), U.S. president

There were approximately three thousand books in the public library in Independence, Missouri, where Harry Truman grew up. By the time he finished high school, Harry had read every one of them, including the encyclopedias. While he pored over everything from Mark Twain books to the Bible (he had read the Bible three times by the end of grade school), he particularly liked history books and biographies. Sometimes he read five or six books at a time, jumping from one to another as his interests changed. Truman once said, "The main reason you read a book is to get a better insight into the people you're talking to."

Harry's bookworm days paid off enormously when he became president of the United States. Both allies and adversaries were routinely astounded at how Truman could draw analogies between current world problems and events of the past, effortlessly recalling what he had read about Marcus Aurelius, or Thomas Jefferson, or Charlemagne, or King Henry IV. When Truman retired to Independence, he frequently strolled into the public library to talk to groups of children. He told them exciting stories taken from the pages of American history and on occasion picked up one of his favorite books and read aloud to them.

CHAPTER FOUR

SCHOOL LIFE

"And then the whining school-boy, with his satchel,
And shining morning face, creeping like snail
Unwillingly to school. . . ."
WILLIAM SHAKESPEARE, *AS YOU LIKE IT*

I t's surprising how many successful people, like Shakespeare's re-
luctant schoolboy, hated school. But not all. To the school haters,
the minute hand on the wall clock jerked its slow and agonizing
way to the end of the school day—and freedom. The French writer
Guy de Maupassant said his Catholic school "smelled of prayers the
way a fish market smells of fish." His compatriot Gérard Depardieu
took his failing report card, tore it up, and put it back in the teacher's
mailbox.

Several distinguished individuals were thrown out of school. Some
were just bad, but others were unfairly punished; for instance,
Langston Hughes was kicked out of school for protesting segregation.

Some of our subjects did very well in school. It doesn't surprise us
that Bill Gates scored a perfect eight hundred on math SATs. But it
seems odd, at first glance, that Raymond Chandler, who wrote so con-

vincingly of a tough Los Angeles detective, was a top student at a prestigious English prep school. And that Madonna was a straight-A student.

Several of our subjects attribute a good part of their success to their teachers. Lionel Hampton remembered with affection his teacher Sister Petra, a drum virtuoso, even though she kicked him in the behind with her pointy shoes when he didn't hold the drumsticks correctly. Years after he graduated from school, Tom Wolfe wrote his teacher Margaret Roberts a letter, calling her "the mother of my spirit who fed me with light."

And at the end of school? Some of the captions under the high school yearbook photos of those who became famous capture their personalities beautifully; Richard Feynman's was "Mad Genius," for instance. Others seem like a bad joke, like the one for triple-murder suspect Gerald Lee Clemons, "Make a Rainy Day Sunny." So much for predictions.

FAVORITE OR MOST INFLUENTIAL TEACHERS

RICHARD BURTON (1925–1984), Welsh actor
His father, Richard Walter Jenkins, was a collier. His mother died when he was two. At eleven, he won a scholarship to attend secondary school, the ticket to a better life than mining. In his fifth year at school, he had to leave school and go to work to help support the family. For eighteen months he worked at a job he hated; his only outlet was acting at the youth center. Then one of his teachers from Infants (primary) school, Meredith Jones, arranged for him to go back to school. Jones asked teacher Philip Burton to keep an eye on Richard. Burton did far more than that. He nurtured the boy's intelligence and natural acting talent, and in 1943 he took him into his home and became his surrogate father. Utterly devoted to the boy, he would even go so far as to sprinkle sugar on Richard's cereal for him. He helped Richard develop his voice until it was "memorably beautiful." Eventually, Richard became Philip Burton's legal ward and took his name. In 1957, when the actor heard that his father had died, he asked, "Which one?" It was Jenkins.

ALBERT CAMUS (1913–1960), Algerian-born French writer
Albert Camus dedicated his Nobel Prize acceptance speech and lecture to Louis Germain, his teacher when he was nine and ten. Germain, a tall man with steely blue eyes, was authoritarian and tough; he stood for no nonsense. A student who failed to behave or do his best was rapped with a stick he called his peppermint stick. But Germain saw something in Albert, who was always best in literature and spoke with great facility.

In that school, most students were destined for jobs in trade. Germain saw a different future for Albert and went to talk to Albert's family about it. He told them to try to keep Albert in school as long as they could and gave them information about a scholarship that would allow him to continue his education. Albert's grandmother objected, saying that Albert had to work to help support the family, but his mother intervened. Albert went on to attend the University of Algiers and became a world-renowned writer.

MILES DAVIS (1926–1991), U.S. musician

Miles's father thought Miles would be a dentist like him. Musician Elwood Buchanan, one of his father's patients, said no: "Doc, Miles ain't gonna be no dentist. He's gonna be a musician." He gave Miles trumpet lessons when Miles was still in junior high. At Lincoln High School, Miles played in the band under Buchanan's tough direction. He copied his tone from Buchanan, and others told him he had imagination. Buchanan told him not to play with a vibrato sound, "Look here, Miles. Don't come around here with that Harry James stuff, playing with all that vibrato. Stop shaking all those notes and trembling them, because you gonna be shaking enough when you get old. Play straight, develop your *own* style. . . ." Always critical, Buchanan was a tough teacher, but that was how he was "if he thought you could play."

EDWARD VII (1841–1910), British monarch

As the child of Queen Victoria and Prince Albert, he was a royal prince, but his childhood was nevertheless austere, even harsh. He lived under an extremely structured regimen, informed by the most rigid of moral principles. The queen disliked her oldest child's personality: "He is my caricature," she said, "that is the misfortune." She wanted to change him, as did her husband. They sought to "train every shoot of a young mind." It was no wonder that the prince, nicknamed Bertie, became a difficult child, prone to tantrums.

In 1849, Bertie's parents chose Henry Birch to be his tutor. Prince Albert said then, not without some disapproval, "I can imagine that children would easily attach themselves to him." Bertie did eventually attach himself to Birch, who tried to understand the boy, not change him. "I seem to have found the key to his heart," Birch said, and it was true—but it was also his undoing. Albert decided to get someone else, someone stricter, to be his tutor. Lady Canning, one of Victoria's ladies-in-waiting, said, "It has been a trouble and sorrow to the Prince of Wales, who has done no end of touching things since he heard that he was to lose him [Birch]. He is such an affectionate dear little fellow; his notes and presents which Mr Birch used to find on his pillow were really too moving." Birch said of Bertie, the future king, that he "will eventually turn out to be a *good* and, in my humble opinion, a *great* man."

MICHEL FOUCAULT (1926–1984), French philosopher

In Poitiers secondary-level school, Saint-Stanislas, run by the Frères des Ecoles Chrétiennes, young Paul-Michel had an outstanding history teacher, Father de Montsabert. Michel's mother said that de Montsabert was the only teacher who influenced her son. A Benedictine monk and priest at a village nearby, de Montsabert went everywhere on foot, pilgrim's staff in hand, dressed in a large, muddy monk's habit. Michel's mother said, "Once I gave him a ride but he left the car full of fleas." Despite his eccentricity, he was highly erudite and a brilliant teacher. One student said of him: "He would let himself get carried away by the subject, by his own hot-headed thought and picturesque images, until, inevitably, he would set off an explosion of laughter that rapidly degenerated into a complete madhouse. Feeling totally overwhelmed and incapable of restoring order, he would leave the room in tears like a child, repeating, 'I can't take it, dear boys, I can't take it.' " The students would promise to behave, and he would come back to class and start over. As another student said, "history taught like this could not help but stick in your mind."

LIONEL HAMPTON (1913–   ), U.S. musician

The Hampton family moved to Chicago around 1919. They were in the bootleg whiskey business, and young Lionel helped out by stirring the mash. His mother did not like having her son involved in an illegal business; moreover, Chicago was a tough place. So she decided to send Lionel away to Holy Rosary Academy, a Catholic boarding school in Wisconsin dedicated to helping African Americans and Indians.

The teachers were Dominican nuns. Of them all, Sister Petra had the most influence on him. A demanding teacher—and a drum virtuoso—she taught Lionel to play drums. When Lionel did not hold the sticks evenly, she made him stand, and then kicked him in the behind with her pointy shoes. The school had a fife and drum corps, whose members practiced four hours a day. After being a group for only two months, they won second prize in their first Catholic band competition.

PETER MARTINS (1946–   ), Danish ballet dancer

In his 1982 autobiography, *Far from Denmark,* the dedication read, "To my mother and Stanley Williams." In the opening chapter he wrote, "Stanley Williams is my teacher. When a dancer says, 'So-and-So is my teacher,' he means this is the one who determined my style, who gave me the clue to the art and to my way of performing. . . . It was Stanley Williams who made me feel the challenge, the potential achievement, the importance of being a dancer."

Peter was accepted into the Royal Danish Ballet School when he was eight years old. By the time Williams became his teacher four years later, the boy had a reputation for being rude, independent, and rebellious. Although Peter was unruly, he was a model student when Williams was the teacher and worked hard to gain Williams's respect and approval.

Peter's training hit a catastrophic turn when another teacher at the ballet school tried to get him expelled for misbehaving in class. Even though the offense Peter had committed was minor, the teacher, a strict disciplinarian, took a tough stand: Either Peter would be expelled, or he would quit. Then Williams stepped in with another ultimatum: If Peter was thrown out, *Williams* would quit. Peter was subsequently suspended temporarily.

DAVID NIVEN (1910–1983), English actor

David's father, a military officer, was killed during World War I when David was only five years old. From an early age David was sent off to a number of prep schools, where his outrageous behavior led to expulsion on more than one occasion. His academic record was terrible, and his mother and stepfather were soon running out of schools to send him to.

A substitute father finally appeared when David was thirteen and entered Stowe House, a public school. This was the school's headmaster, J. F. Roxburgh, a kind, tolerant man who looked beyond David's jokes and pranks and tried to give him a sense of honor and responsibility. When David was caught cheating in an exam, however, Roxburgh was forced to whip him, a punishment that bothered the headmaster more than it bothered the student. Instead of expelling David, though, Roxburgh sat the boy down and talked to him. When graduation day neared, Roxburgh helped to get David into the Royal Military College by writing a letter of recommendation, saying that David was "an excellent type of boy, enormously improved since he came here."

As an Oscar-winning actor, Niven, who appeared in approximately ninety films, was known for his impeccable dress, his urbane wit, and his debonair style. He owed much of his sophistication to his former headmaster. Even when he attained international fame, Niven never forgot Roxburgh and regularly wrote letters to him until the headmaster died in 1954.

JESSE OWENS (1913–1980), U.S. track-and-field athlete

Jesse was fourteen when he first met Charles Riley, track coach at Fairmount Junior High School in Cleveland, Ohio. Of Irish descent, Riley recognized Jesse's raw talent and set out to teach him technique, style, and concentration. Since Jesse, the youngest of ten children, had an after-school job, Riley worked with him every morning before school began. On weekends, Riley often took Jesse to his home to have lunch with the Riley family. Jesse called Riley "Coach" or "Pop." In little over a year, Jesse was setting world records—the first two in the high jump and long jump. Riley continued to coach Jesse throughout his high school years.

When Jesse, a student at Ohio State, broke three world records and tied one at a meet in Ann Arbor, Michigan, Charles Riley was in the stands. After Jesse won four gold medals (three running events and the broad jump) at the 1936 Olympics in Berlin in front of Adolf Hitler, Riley met the conquering hero when he returned to the United States on board the *Queen Mary.* When Jesse was the surprise guest on Ralph Edwards's television program *This Is Your Life,* Riley, then eighty-two, was at the studio to honor his protégé.

Throughout his life Jesse Owens was very vocal about his admiration and respect for Riley. Riley had taught him to run "like the ground was a burning fire." Riley, Owens said, "was the first white man I really knew, and without even trying, he proved to me beyond all proof that a white man can understand—and love—a Negro. He trained me to become a man as well as an athlete."

RICHARD PRYOR (1940–   ), U.S. comedian and actor

At a very early age his comedic genius was evident. Whether he was contorting his face or making jokes, Richard Pryor was just plain funny. At school, however, the teachers didn't appreciate his Tarzan yells, silly pranks, and overall disruptive behavior. When Richard was thirteen, he discovered the Carver Community Center, close to his home in Peoria, Illinois, and it became a focal point of his life—a place where all of his unbridled talent and energy would begin to take shape and make him into a professional performer. Supervising the stage plays at the center was Juliette Whittaker, who became Richard's mentor and lifelong friend.

Whittaker remembers Richard as "a skinny little kid" who was willing to take any part in any play. He was quick to memorize all his lines and brought a great deal of imagination and innovation to every role he performed. She said, "He had a quick mind, was very good with puns. He could see the biting satire in things people would say." For four years Richard remained under Whittaker's tutelage. On the few occasions that Richard skipped rehearsals, she would head out into the streets to find him and then haul him back to the Center.

When Pryor became a celebrated comedian and actor, he often invited Whittaker to his opening nights. When he won an Emmy award for comedy writing, he presented it to his teacher, saying, "If it hadn't been for you, I would not have learned anything about the theater. And I certainly wouldn't have learned how to write."

BEVERLY SILLS (1929–   ), U.S. opera singer

Beverly, who grew up in Brooklyn, New York, was already a child star on radio programs when she started taking singing lessons from former opera singer Estelle Liebling. When Beverly was seven, she and her mother, Sonia, saw Liebling's picture on the cover of a magazine in which she was called "coach to the world's greatest voices." Beverly auditioned for Liebling, and although the teacher was amused at the young girl's rendering of an Italian accent, she was nonetheless impressed by the fact that Beverly had learned twenty-two arias just from listening to records.

The student-mentor relationship lasted for thirty-four years until Liebling died at the age of ninety-two. Estelle Liebling not only taught Beverly how to sing but also expanded the girl's cultural horizons by recommending books for her to read. She gave Beverly tickets to the opera and showed her pictures of the kinds of costumes that leading opera stars were wearing. In addition, Liebling often hosted dinner parties attended by celebrities, including opera singers; Beverly would often be invited and asked to sing for the guests.

In her autobiography, *Bubbles,* Sills wrote that Liebling "refused to take a penny for any of my lessons in all the years I was with her, even when I was able to afford it." Sills always thought of Liebling as a "second mother," and the teacher, who was as charming as she was talented, often attended Beverly's premiere performances. After Liebling died, Sills began to end her recitals with a short eulogy to her mentor, followed by a Portuguese folk song which Liebling had arranged for her as a gift on Beverly's tenth birthday.

THOMAS WOLFE (1900–1938), U.S. novelist

The man who wrote *You Can't Go Home Again* grew up in Asheville, North Carolina. His father, William, an alcoholic, sold tombstones. His mother, Julia, ran a second-rate boardinghouse. When William was sober, he would take Tom to the movies or buy him an ice cream soda; when he was drunk, he often exploded into a rage, ranting about his miserable life. Julia either pampered Tom or ignored him. One moment she would praise him; another time she would tell Tom that he had a "queer, freaky little face."

When Tom was twelve, he entered a private school, where he was taught by Margaret Roberts, wife of the school's principal. She immediately recognized his talents, encouraged him to write, and recommended books for him to read. Roberts became a stabilizing force in Tom's life, and he adored her. Under her guidance, Tom gained confidence, which not only helped him socially but also helped him to compete, and win, a number of debating and writing honors. Years after he graduated from school, he wrote Roberts a letter, telling her that she was "the mother of my spirit who fed me with light."

HONOR STUDENTS

KAREEM ABDUL-JABBAR (1947–   ), U.S. basketball player

An only child and good boy, Lew Alcindor (who later took the name Kareem Abdul-Jabbar) had parents who expected the best of him. He learned to read quickly and well. He did his homework because of pressure from his mother and the nuns at the Catholic schools he attended—and because he wanted to. The nuns doted on him. Not only taller than the other kids (he was six feet, eight inches by age fourteen), Lew was also smarter. In his first semester at Power Memorial Academy (a Catholic high school), he made the honor roll, and his grades were excellent throughout school. With his athletic talent and his mind, he could have gone to any college, and chose UCLA.

LEWIS CARROLL (CHARLES LUTWIDGE DODGSON) (1832–1898), English mathematician and writer

He said of school, which involved learning Latin, that it was "hours upon hours spent by many boys in the moiling evolution of one or two wintry and wooden elegiacs . . . boys whose inability might have been predicted at thirteen, kept at the same galley-work up to eighteen or nineteen, as unprogressive as the seamen who plied the oar upon the land." But Charles was good at it, so good that Mr. Tate, his principal from Richmond School in Yorkshire, where he went when he was twelve, wrote, "He possesses, along with other excellent and natural endowments, a very uncommon share of genius . . . he is capable of acquirements and knowledge far beyond his years, while his reason is so clear and so jealous of error, that he will not rest satisfied without a most exact solution of whatever appears to him to be obscure. . . . You may fairly anticipate for him a bright career."

Charles's headmaster from Rugby, which he attended for three years after completing Richmond, would have agreed with Tate's assessment. He said: ". . . His mathematical knowledge is great for his age, and I doubt not he will do himself credit in classics. As I believe I mentioned to you before, his examination for the Divinity prize was one of the most creditable exhibitions I have ever seen." At Rugby, Charles won prizes in classics, composition, divinity, history, and mathematics. Yet he said of his experience at the school, ". . . I cannot say that I look back on life at a Public School with any sensation of pleasure, or that any earthly considerations would induce me to go through my three years again."

RAYMOND CHANDLER (1888–1959), U.S. mystery writer

The creator of tough Los Angeles detective Philip Marlowe was educated at an exclusive English school. After his parents divorced, he and his mother went to England to stay with relatives, whom even he identified as snobs. He went to Dulwich College Preparatory School, which, though not socially in a class with Eton and Rugby, had a very good academic reputation at the time. Many of its students won scholarships to Oxford and Cambridge. He began his school career there in 1900. Records show that he consistently placed first or second among the boys in his form. He won a special prize in mathematics and one in general achievement.

Chandler felt that the training he received affected him for the good. He said, "It would seem that a classical education might be rather a poor basis for writing novels in a hard-boiled vernacular. I happen to think otherwise. A classical education saves you from being fooled by pretentiousness, which is what most current fiction is too full of."

AGNES DE MILLE (1905–1993), U.S. choreographer

Even the doll clothes Agnes and her sister Margaret sewed had to be perfect—the seams had to be French, for instance. Their mother, Anna, insisted on it. She brought the girls up to be obedient and precise. As Agnes said, "the way [Mother] did things was The Way." After all, they had something to live up to—they came from a distinguished family. Agnes's maternal grandfather was Henry George, inventor of the single tax (a controversial proposal to tax only land and natural resources, not labor). Her father, William, expected her to get As. He wrote in her autograph book, "I'd rather love you for what you do than because you're mine."

When Agnes attended the Hollywood School for Girls, she was a star. She was editor of the school paper, editor of the yearbook, best player on the tennis team, head of the upper school, and vice president of the drama club. She also earned top grades. Margaret's friend Irene Mayer Selznick put it well: "She had ambition, and a great appetite. She wanted to read, to know, to prevail. She had zeal and application. She was heroic! She put some of her teachers to shame."

BILL GATES (1955–   ), U.S. software entrepreneur

His IQ is somewhere in the 160s or 170s. By age nine, he had read the entire *World Book* encyclopedia. His response to a command to hurry up was, "I'm thinking. I'm thinking."

In fourth grade, the teacher assigned a four- to five-page report on a part of the human body. Bill wrote more than thirty pages. "Everything Bill did, he did to the max," said Carl Edmark, a childhood friend. "What he did always went well, well beyond everyone else."

In 1967, Bill's parents sent him to a private school in Seattle, Lakeside, which arranged for its students to have access to computers. He was the top

The gifted Agnes de Mille with Douglas Fairbanks.

Courtesy of the Performing Arts Research Center, New York Public Library at Lincoln Center.

student in math at Lakeside, and he scored a perfect eight hundred on the math section of the SATs. Fred Wright, who was chairman of the math department when Gates went to Lakeside, said, "He could see shortcuts through an algebraic problem or a computer problem. . . . He's as good an analytical mathematician as I've worked with in all my years of teaching. But Bill was really good in all areas, not just math. He's got a lot of breadth. It's one of the unusual things about him." Even then, Gates was incredibly smart and he knew it.

VLADIMIR LENIN (1870–1924), Russian revolutionary leader
He was a very bright child and a model student. Vladimir was reading at age five and playing chess at eight. Gifted with an excellent memory, he easily mastered foreign languages, and in the eighth grade he received an evaluation of "excellent" in ten out of eleven subjects (he only received a "good" in logic). His home life was stable, nurturing, and financially stable. His father was a teacher and school supervisor.

When Vladimir graduated from high school at the age of seventeen, his final school report read, "Quite talented, invariably diligent, prompt and reliable, Vladimir was first in all his classes, and upon graduation was awarded a gold medal as the most meritorious pupil in achievement, growth, and conduct. There is not a single instance on record, either in school or outside of it, of Vladimir's evoking by word or deed any adverse opinion from the authorities and teachers of this school."

What caused the transformation of an obedient schoolboy into a revolutionary has been the subject of endless speculation. Some historians think that the execution of his older brother, Alexander, for participating in an assassination attempt on Tsar Alexander III (when Lenin was seventeen) was a turning point. Others find no evidence that the death of his brother led to any radical thoughts. However, in his first year of college, Lenin was expelled for participating in a student demonstration. Subsequently, he did earn a college degree and graduated with honors.

Marilyn Monroe's
high school nickname
was "The Mmmm Girl."

MADONNA (1958–   ), U.S. singer and actor
Born Madonna Louise Ciccone, "the Material Girl" grew up in a strict Catholic household. Her mother died when little "Nonnie" was five; and it was her father, Tony, who made sure that all of his six children went to church every day, did their chores, and paid attention to their schoolwork. All of the Cic-

cone children competed for their father's attention, and getting good grades not only earned their father's respect but also paid off financially (50 cents for every A). Madonna always reaped the most money. She once said, "I was a straight-A student, and they all hated me for it because I did it more for the position I was going to have in my father's eyes than for whatever I was going to learn by studying."

Until she was fifteen, Madonna attended parochial schools and consistently shocked the nuns with her rebellious nature. She tried to wear go-go boots with the school uniform, rolled up her skirts to make them into miniskirts, sneaked into the restroom to put on makeup. Far from shy with the boys, she chased them around the playground, flirted outrageously, and hung upside down from the playground equipment so that members of the opposite sex could get a good view of her panties. When she was ten, Madonna entered a school talent contest and performed a go-go dance clad in a bikini and covered with body paint (applied so that she appeared to be naked). The routine was a big hit with the audience but not with her father, who grounded her for two weeks.

In 1973 Madonna entered a public high school in Rochester, Michigan. She became a cheerleader, joined the French club and the choir, and was one of the founders of the school's drama club. Her singing and dancing talents were showcased in theatrical productions such as *My Fair Lady* and *Godspell*. Although she was always striving to assert her independence, to rebel against the norm, she nonetheless remained a straight-A student. At graduation her grades, plus excellent recommendations from her teachers, won her a scholarship to the University of Michigan.

GOLDA MEIR (1898–1978), Israeli political leader

Her parents thought that school was an "unwarranted luxury" for the young Golda, and she wasn't allowed to attend a school until she was almost nine and living in the United States. When her family moved from Russia to Milwaukee, Wisconsin, Golda's mother put her to work in the family grocery store and would have kept her there, but a truant officer came by one day and said that all children under the age of fourteen had to attend school. Golda proceeded to earn excellent marks in elementary school and was class valedictorian at graduation exercises.

Once enrolled in high school, Golda was pressured by her mother to drop out, work in the store, and start looking for a husband. Her father said that "men don't like smart girls." The arguments over education became so intense that Golda ran away from home and took the train to Denver, where she moved in with her older sister Shana. Back in school, she was again an A student. Disagreements with Shana caused Golda to move out, and because she was on her own, she again had to quit school and go to work.

At seventeen she returned to Milwaukee. By this time, her parents had dropped their opposition to further schooling, and she graduated from high school at the top of her class in 1916. She then went on to college and became a teacher.

RICHARD NIXON (1913–1994), U.S. president

Even in the first grade, the thirty-seventh president of the United States was an outstanding student. According to his first-grade teacher, "He absorbed knowledge of any kind like a blotter." A serious boy, Richard skipped the second grade, was reading newspapers at six (not the comic strips), and at seven was discoursing on the merits of political candidates running in national elections. He was valedictorian for his grammar school and in the seventh grade won his first debate, defending a "yes" position on the question, "Is it more economical to rent a house than to own one?"

In high school in Whittier, California, Richard scarcely had time to sleep, maintaining a backbreaking schedule of studying, sports (he was on the football team), working at his father's grocery store, and attending church. But he was a dogged worker and even found time to win numerous debating and oratory contests. For the most part he was an A or B-plus student and graduated third in a class of 207.

As winner of the "best all-around student" award bestowed by the Harvard Club of California, Richard was virtually guaranteed a tuition scholarship to the prestigious university. But the Nixon family's finances were stripped to the bone because Richard's brother Harold, who was suffering from tuberculosis, had been placed in a private sanitorium in Arizona. There were no spare dollars to put toward living expenses at Harvard. So Richard chose to live at home and attend nearby Whittier College. Many years later, when writing his memoirs, former president Nixon claimed that he wasn't disappointed that he hadn't gone to Harvard or Yale (yet another tuition scholarship he might have had). Yet the missed opportunity must have had an impact on the ambitious man of humble origins when he constantly ran up against members of the political elite such as John F. Kennedy—wealthy, charismatic, and Harvard-educated.

---

*Did you know that Bill Gates
scored a perfect 800
on his math SATs?*

SYLVIA PLATH (1932–1963), U.S. poet

Her childhood resume seemed to predict fame and fortune for Plath, who at a very early age was displaying signs of genius. At eight weeks old, she was struggling to talk; at age five she was composing full-length poems. In elementary school the teachers were astounded by her speaking and writing abilities. In the sixth grade she won an award from the public library system

Richard Nixon, young musician.

Courtesy of Whittier College.

in Massachusetts for reading a large number of books in one year. By the time she finished junior high school in Wellesley, Massachusetts, young Sylvia had racked up a number of awards in English composition, had been elected president of her homeroom class, and had been given a "special student" commendation for overall excellence. In addition, her drawing abilities had earned her first prize in a national art contest.

In her last three years of high school, the overachieving Sylvia continued to outclass everyone (IQ test scores ranked her a genius). For the most part she got straight As in all her classes, except for an occasional B in subjects like orchestra. She won more awards for composition and drawing and was even published in the *Christian Science Monitor* and *Seventeen* magazine. A member of the National Honor Society, Sylvia graduated first in her class and won a number of scholarships to the prestigious Smith College.

Sylvia was not a stereotypical "brain." An attractive, energetic girl, she loved to hike and swim, belonged to the Girl Scouts, and went to summer camp every year. In school she was on the basketball team, played in the orchestra, and was a member of the school newspaper staff. In addition, she joined a high school sorority, acted in school plays, and even wrote the words to the school song. She had plenty of girlfriends and was quite popular with the boys, never lacking a date to school dances.

The fact that she seemed destined for success and happiness contrasts sharply with her tragic early suicide. In her college years she began to suffer from fits of depression and insomnia. At age nineteen she tried to commit suicide but failed. Then at age thirty, married with two children, she succeeded in killing herself by locking herself in the kitchen of her home, sealing the doors and windows, and breathing gas fumes from the oven. After her death, her poems and novel *The Bell Jar* enjoyed worldwide acclaim. She was posthumously awarded a Pulitzer Prize in 1982, nineteen years after her death.

H. NORMAN SCHWARZKOPF (1934–   ), U.S. general

His father was a West Point graduate, and from the time he was born, Norman was expected to attend West Point too. But in elementary school his grades were only average; the teachers, recognizing that he was exceptionally intelligent, encouraged him to try harder. When he entered Bordentown Military Academy (New Jersey) in the sixth grade, his marks shot up to straight As.

When his father accepted a number of military assignments abroad, Norman attended schools in the Middle East and Europe, and his grades began to drop a little. Worried that the boy wouldn't qualify for West Point, Norman's father sent him back to the United States and put him in Valley Forge Military Academy (Pennsylvania). Back in a disciplined environment, Norman once again made it to the honor roll. At Valley Forge he played football and track, was named valedictorian of the senior class, and won an "Honor Military Appointment" to West Point.

At West Point, the future hero of the Gulf War didn't have to study too much to make the dean's list. He graduated forty-third out of a class of 480. Schwarzkopf (who has a genius IQ of 170) could have ranked higher, but he didn't like being called a "hive" (an overachiever type of student who only cared about grades). In his autobiography, the general writes: "I wanted to be accepted as a regular guy. My goal was to be good academically, good socially, good athletically, and good militarily—but not to get carried away."

MISERABLE REPORT CARDS

BIX BEIDERBECKE (1903–1931), U.S. musician

At three he could play the theme from Liszt's Hungarian Rhapsody No. 2 on the piano after hearing it only once. His kindergarten teacher said of her "musical pet": "Bix loved to stand by the piano and play with the class pianist, imitating on the high notes whatever she was playing." Three people tried and failed to teach the young genius to play music according to traditional methods. This experience convinced him that no teachers of any kind were of much use to him. In school he could not keep his mind on his work and daydreamed constantly. In June 1914, when Bix was eleven, he failed to pass into the next grade and was held back. By age fourteen he was only in the fifth grade. He could read well, but he was terrible at arithmetic. Instead of the teacher's voice, all he heard was music in his head. Even then Bix knew he wanted to play jazz. In 1920, he took eight dollars he had saved and bought a used cornet, which he took home in a paper bag. It was the beginning of his brilliant career as a musician. School did not matter anymore.

GÉRARD DEPARDIEU (1948–   ), French actor

As Gérard Depardieu grew into adolescence, he became the class troublemaker. The teacher, stern Le Père Durand, put the miscreant in the front row. There he could keep an eye on him and discipline him more easily by hitting him on the fingers or head with his dreaded bamboo pointer. To get even, Gérard broke the pointer and then glued it back together so that the break would not show. When Durand rapped Gérard with the pointer the next time, the pointer broke, the end dangling impotently in his hand. Durand was furious. In another incident, Durand accused Gérard unjustly of stealing. After the two—teacher and pupil—engaged in a pushing match, Durand told the rest of the class not to speak to Gérard.

At the end of that year, Durand gave Gérard a failing grade in every single class, which meant that the boy could not move on to the next grade. Gérard took the report card, tore it up, and put it back in the teacher's mailbox. He did eventually succeed in passing but then quit school at only thirteen.

F. SCOTT FITZGERALD (1896–1940), U.S. writer

He lasted one day in nursery school because he cried so hard. It was an omen. Throughout his school life, he was a poor and unhappy student. However, he was a voracious reader, and he liked to write: ". . . I wrote all through every class in school in the back of my geography book and the first year Latin and in the margins of themes and declensions and mathematics problems."

In 1911, his parents decided to send him to the Newman School, a Catholic boarding school in Hackensack, New Jersey. No one liked him there—not teachers, not students. He was boastful, cowardly, irritating. In his first year he passed only four of his final exams. In his second year, he redeemed himself socially, but not academically. In two years, he failed four of his sixteen courses (Algebra I, Caesar, French B, and Physics); he received Ds in Latin Grammar and Virgil. His only A was in Ancient History. Most surprising, in English, the future novelist received no more than a C and a B.

ADOLF HITLER (1889–1945), Austrian-born German dictator
As a small boy, he was the star of his class, even in deportment. Then in 1899, his brother Edmund, died of measles at age five, and over the next year Adolf changed from a happy, outgoing, good student to a high-strung, withdrawn, poor student who was constantly at odds with his teachers.

In September 1900, Adolf entered *Realschule,* a technical high school that led to careers in engineering and technology. He had to repeat the first year. After the death of his father in 1903, Adolf continued to do badly in school; he was insolent to teachers and received low grades. After being expelled from the *Realschule* at Linz, he transferred to one at Steyr. In the first semester there, he received eight 4s and 5s out of 12 grades. (Grades were on a scale of 1 to 5, with 5s standing for "inadequate.") At the end of the next semester, he received a certificate from school and celebrated heartily on wine. Afterward, he had to go back to the *Realschule* and ask for a duplicate of his certificate, thinking he had lost it. Actually, the original was in the hands of the director. Torn in four pieces and used for toilet paper, it had come in the mail, probably sent by Hitler himself in his drunken state. That was the end of Hitler's school career.

JOHN FITZGERALD KENNEDY (1917–1963), U.S. president
Though the young John F. "Jack" Kennedy seemed intelligent, he did poorly on tests and lacked good study habits. His housemaster at Choate, a distinguished Connecticut prep school, said in a letter to his father, "Jack studies at the last minute, keeps appointments late, has little sense of material values, and can seldom locate possessions." His grades were abysmally low—he failed Latin, for instance. No motivation seemed to help. His father gave him expensive presents when he received good grades: a sailboat, a trip to Europe, a horse. But after he received the gifts, the grades dropped again. Consequently, the future president graduated 64th in a class of 112 from Choate—yet he was still dubbed "most likely to succeed."

GEORGE LUCAS (1944–   ), U.S. film director and producer
The cinematic genius behind *American Graffiti, Star Wars,* and *Raiders of the Lost Ark* has joked that the only reason he graduated from high school was because his teachers felt sorry for him after he was involved in a near-fatal car crash shortly before commencement exercises. In the eighth grade he failed spelling and arithmetic and had to go to summer school; in high school he got a lot of Ds. Nonetheless, George managed to get into a junior college and then went on to film school at the University of Southern California. A short, skinny youth (he weighed about one hundred pounds at age seventeen), George once said, "I wanted to enjoy school in the worst way and I never could."

GEORGE C. MARSHALL (1880–1959), U.S. general and statesman

The U.S. chief of staff during World War II was a gifted military strategist. He was also a persuasive negotiator, who stood his ground before the likes of Franklin D. Roosevelt, Joseph Stalin, and Winston Churchill. After the war, Marshall designed an economic recovery plan for Europe, called the Marshall Plan, an effort that won him the Nobel Peace Prize.

George was a lousy student. He was a slow reader, a slow learner, and always ranked at the bottom of his class. When he was nine years old, George had to take an oral exam in front of his father and was humiliated that he wasn't able to answer "rather simple questions." George's older brother and older sister, as well as his father, treated him as the family dunce. Only George's mother, Laura, provided the boy with approval and encouragement.

GAMAL ABDEL NASSER (1918–1970), Egyptian political leader

He went to public school, boarding school, and private school, but he failed over and over again. By the time Gamal was sixteen, he had been in school for ten years but had only passed through four grades. He frequently skipped school, and when he did attend, Gamal often engaged in verbal confrontations with the teachers. In his last year of secondary school he was expelled for taking part in a demonstration against the British, who at that time controlled Egypt, but his fellow students threatened a general strike if Gamal was not readmitted. He returned and did graduate, even though during his entire final year he attended classes for only forty-five days. Gamal managed to get himself admitted to law school but dropped out after several months. Then he applied, and was accepted, to the Royal Military Academy.

SPENCER TRACY (1900–1967), U.S. actor

On the first day of second grade, Spencer climbed out of his bedroom window, ran away, and got into a fight with a neighborhood boy. Skipping school and getting into fistfights became a recurring pattern in his life. By the time he finished the eighth grade, Spencer had been to sixteen schools. Sometimes he was expelled; sometimes his parents pulled him out of one school and put him in another one, hoping the boy would adjust. Spencer's parents came to know just about all the truant officers in Milwaukee, Wisconsin.

Spencer simply hated school. When he disappeared, he would roam the neighborhood, hang out at saloons, or go to the movies. He once said, "I wouldn't have gone to school at all if there had been any other way of learning to read the subtitles in the silent films." As early as age twelve, he was trying to talk his parents into letting him drop out of school to get a job.

In high school at Marquette Academy, a Jesuit prep school, Spencer began to show academic improvement. His failing grades started to get better overall, and he received good marks in his theological classes; for a short while, he thought he wanted to become a priest. He dropped out to join the navy in World War II but did eventually graduate from high school. Then he went on to college, where he acted in some theatrical productions and received rave reviews. Once again he dropped out of school, this time to pursue an acting career.

PAUL WHITEMAN (1890–1967), U.S. bandleader

The "King of Jazz" grew up in Denver, Colorado. His father, Wilberforce, was a superintendent of music education in the public school system, and his mother, Elfrida, was a singer. Paul's life was continually ruled by an exacting set of standards and rules imposed upon him by his father. Although Wilberforce did encourage Paul's musical talents, he wanted his son to become a mechanical engineer.

Unable to live up to his father's expectations, Paul rebelled. He smashed his violin (after being locked in a room to practice), skipped school, and got terrible grades. In high school he was overweight and began to lose some of his hair (as a result of a bout of typhoid fever). Always at odds with his teachers and at the bottom of the list academically, Paul ended up going to three different high schools in four years. The unhappy boy decided that music was the only ticket out of his miserable existence. Years later, when Paul had become incredibly successful, Wilberforce somewhat grudgingly admitted that even though he didn't particularly like Paul's "jazzed up" music, his son had indeed become a popular and respected musician.

SUSPENDED OR EXPELLED FROM SCHOOL

HUMPHREY BOGART (1899–1957), U.S. actor

In spite of his "tough guy" screen image, he grew up in a cultured and wealthy family. His father was a doctor and his mother was an artist. Hoping that their son would eventually go to Yale, the Bogarts sent Humphrey for a "rounding out" year at Phillips Academy, a prep school in Andover, Massachusetts. According to his schoolmates, he never cracked a book. At the end of his first semester he was failing three out of five subjects. In February 1918, the faculty voted to put him on probation because of his poor record. His father, replying to the school's letter informing him of this decision, suggested that "the harder the screws are put on the better it will be for my son." The screws did no good. In May, Humphrey was expelled for "failing to meet the terms of his probation." A schoolmate remembers him saying, as he was leaving school, "I'm leaving this goddamned place, and for good. It's a waste of time here." After a few weeks spinning his wheels at home, he enlisted in the navy. Many years later, after he had become a Hollywood legend, he said, "The bastards threw me out" and suggested that they did so because of "excessive high spirits" or "infractions of the rules."

JOHN CHEEVER (1912–1982), U.S. writer

In 1930, self-described "intractable student" John Cheever was expelled from Thayer Academy, a prestigious Massachusetts prep school. It was the spring of his junior year. His grades were mediocre, to say the least: The future American novelist received Cs and C minuses in English; and he failed French, Latin, and math. Only when he felt like it did he work at his lessons.

One of his teachers, Grace Osgood, said, "John was not happy at Thayer nor was Thayer happy about his achievement or attitude."

After his expulsion, Cheever, just eighteen, wrote a short story about his experience, called it "Expelled," and sent it to Malcolm Cowley at the *New Republic*. Cowley accepted it for the October 1, 1930, issue. Thayer students

Humphrey Bogart as a child.

Courtesy of Archive Photos.

and faculty were enraged at the story, which criticized the lackluster curriculum, lack of courage, and puny imagination of prep schools. Cheever himself later said the story could just as well have been titled "Reminiscences of a Young Sorehead."

CARY GRANT (1904–1986), English-born U.S. actor

At thirteen, he wanted to join a troupe of acrobats supervised by Bob Pender. His father agreed that when he was old enough to leave school legally, he could join the troupe. So in 1915, he went on scholarship to Fairfield Secondary School against his will. He tried to fail everything except gym.

In March 1918, he committed some serious offense. There are three versions of what happened: (1) He got caught sneaking into the girls' lavatory; (2) he and two other boys were on the girls' playground; (3) he stole. The following day, at the school assembly, his name was called. "I was marched up the steps onto the dais and taken to stand next to the headmaster. Through a trance-like mixture of emotions, I hazily heard such words as 'inattentive,' 'irresponsible,' 'incorrigible' and 'discredit to the school.' I suddenly realized that I was being publicly expelled."

Although he might not have chosen the route of humiliation, he had achieved his goal of leaving school. Not long after, he joined the Pender troupe.

ABBIE HOFFMAN (1936–1989), U.S. political activist

He chose to be a hood—he shot pool, wore pegged pants and shirts with big collars, liked fast cars. His hero was Marlon Brando in *The Wild One,* a film about a rebellious gang of motorcyclists, the precursors to Hell's Angels. However, Abbie's hood persona was something of a pose; he was actually a smart, middle-class kid.

On a college-bound track at Seaver Prep, a public junior high school in Worcester, Massachusetts, for gifted students, and at Classical High, he received As and Bs even though he studied very little. Still, he was a behavior problem. He challenged his teachers and refused to accept their authority. When his mother was called to school about his behavior, one of the administrators said to him, "It's a wonder half of us aren't in the insane asylum because of you." "What about the other half?" asked Abbie.

In his sophomore year, he wrote a paper for his English class defending atheism. He called it "Reward, Punishment, and God." Abbie claims that the teacher objected to the paper, called him "a little Communist bastard," grabbed him, and ripped his collar off his shirt. Abbie then overturned the teacher's desk and started hitting the teacher. He was suspended from school. Later, when he fought "the system" with his radical politics, he liked to tell the story.

LANGSTON HUGHES (1902–1967), U.S. poet

The African-American poet Langston Hughes faced discrimination early in his life. When it was time for him to start school in Topeka, Kansas, authorities told his mother that he would have to go to the school for black children, which was way across town. She fought the ruling, on the grounds that since she had to work every day, she couldn't take him to school, and he was too young to go by himself. She won. However, the teacher at the white school put Langston at the end of the last row, making him feel so isolated that his mother took him out of school before the end of the year.

Six years later, in another school, Langston and all the African-American children in his class were moved into a row separate from the white children. He wrote signs saying "Jim Crow Row" (referring to laws allowing discrimination) and gave them to the other African-American students to put on their desks. He was expelled from school, but when parents protested, he was reinstated and his class was desegregated.

MARY LEAKEY (1913–1996), British archaeologist

Her father, Erskine, was a landscape artist, and Mary's early years were spent in England, Switzerland, France, and Italy. Erskine died when Mary was thirteen, and Mary, who worshipped her father, was devastated and inconsolable. She was sent off to a convent school in England but was thrown out after she refused to recite poetry. Sent to another convent school, Mary deliberately set off an explosion in chemistry class and was expelled. The incident ended her formal education. Years later, when asked about the chemistry explosion, Leakey said that it "was quite loud and quite a lot of nuns came running, which will have been good for some of them."

JERRY LEWIS (1926–   ), U.S. comedian

He was expelled in his first year of high school in Irvington, New Jersey. After causing an explosion in the chemistry lab, Jerry was called to the principal's office. First, the principal asked Jerry if he was a "wise guy"; then he called the boy a "dumb Jew." Without hesitation, the boy punched the principal in the mouth and knocked out one of his teeth. Jerry was quickly booted out of school and subsequently was enrolled in a nearby vocational school.

GUY DE MAUPASSANT (1850–1893), French short-story writer and novelist

When he was thirteen, de Maupassant was sent to study at a small seminary at Yvetot near Rouen, even though he had no intention of becoming a priest. He was a good student but hated the religious atmosphere, saying that the school "smelled of prayers the way a fish market smells of fish." A year before he was due to graduate, de Maupassant was expelled for bad behavior. Among his sins: performing a parody on a lecture about the torments of hell, writing an indecent poem, and drinking the Father Superior's wine. Years later, de Maupassant often talked about the school, whose motto was, "Severe as Sparta, elegant as Athens."

BENITO MUSSOLINI (1883–1945), Italian dictator

As a boy, the Italian dictator and founder of Europe's first Fascist party was seen as vicious and rebellious. He was always picking fights and bullying everyone around him. Some of his biographers claim that he plucked live chickens and blinded captive birds. To control Benito's violent streak, his parents sent him, at age nine, to a boarding school run by a religious order. There he was repeatedly punished for causing trouble. He led a revolt against the quality of the food and threw an inkwell at a teacher who hit him with a ruler. He was finally thrown out of school after he pulled a knife on another boy and stabbed him in the buttocks.

ARISTOTLE ONASSIS (1906–1975), Greek shipping magnate

Born into a prosperous and influential family, Aristotle was frequently suspended from school and never did graduate. Once he was suspended for pinching the backside of a pretty English teacher. Another time he was kicked out for switching on all the electric bells at school. Even private tutors abandoned him after a few short lessons. The headmaster at the school said: "He was a really naughty person, a disorderly child, shocking all around him, and bothered all the other students in the school. He wouldn't listen to anybody. During the whole time I spent at the school, I never had such a child. He was the most difficult one there."

SIR WILLIAM OSLER (1849–1919), Canadian physician and educator

As a student, William was a prankster, once locking a flock of geese in the classroom. His most daring escapade, and the one that got him expelled, happened over a school weekend: Osler sneaked into the classroom and unscrewed all the desks and benches from the floor. He then hoisted them up through a trapdoor into the garret, thus leaving the room completely empty when his teacher returned on Monday. Osler went on to become the first professor of medicine and chief physician at Johns Hopkins Hospital in Baltimore.

RICHARD PRYOR (1940–   ), U.S. comedian and actor

When he was six, Pryor was expelled from a Catholic grammar school when school authorities learned that his grandmother operated a string of whorehouses (called "ho-houses"). The boy who would become one of America's most popular comedians did manage to get back into school, but at age sixteen he was once again expelled, this time for punching out a science teacher.

WILHELM KONRAD ROENTGEN (1845–1923), German physicist

He was expelled at sixteen for refusing to tattle on a classmate. When Roentgen's teacher discovered a caricature of himself, he demanded that Roentgen name the culprit, since the teacher suspected that the artist was Roentgen's friend. The boy refused to talk and was thrown out of school. The expulsion made it difficult for him to get admitted to a university, but he finally succeeded. Roentgen became one of Germany's foremost scientists, and in 1901 he was awarded the first Nobel Prize in physics for his discovery of X-rays.

FRANK SINATRA (1915–1998), U.S. singer

He made it through junior high school but lasted only forty-seven days in senior high. The world-famous crooner once said: "To my crowd, school was very uninteresting, and homework was something we never bothered with. The few times we attended class, we were rowdy. So it isn't surprising that a bunch of us were expelled."

LEON TROTSKY (1879–1940), Russian revolutionary leader

The Russian communist leader was expelled from the second grade when he took part in howling at a teacher who was treating a German student unfairly.

Frank Sinatra
at his First Communion.

Courtesy of Archive Photos.

While almost the entire class howled, some of the boys, when questioned, pointed to Trotsky as the ringleader (he wasn't). How his fellow students betrayed or defended him was something the child never forgot. He later wrote: "Such, one might say, was the first political test I underwent. These were the groups that resulted from that episode: The tale-bearers and the envious at one pole, the frank, courageous boys at the other, and the neutral, vacillating mass in the middle. These three groups never quite disappeared even during the years that followed. I met them again and again in my life, in the most varied circumstances." Because Trotsky was the school's star pupil, he was kept out of school for a short while and then readmitted.

ORVILLE WRIGHT (1871–1948), U.S. aviator
Because he was always involved in some sort of trouble, teachers would put him in the front row to keep an eye on him. No one really knows what incident tipped the scales, but in the sixth grade he was expelled for "mischievous behavior." The American inventor and aviator was allowed back into school in the seventh grade, upon a promise from his parents that he would behave.

BORIS YELTSIN (1931–), Russian president
Boris asked for and was granted permission to speak at his primary school graduation. Before an assembled group of teachers, parents, and students, he launched into a full-scale verbal attack on one teacher, saying that she had subjected students to "cruel, unusual punishment." He ended with a demand for her dismissal. Instead, he was expelled. However, he appealed the expulsion and was allowed to return to school.

YEARBOOK CAPTIONS

ISAAC ASIMOV (1920–1992), Russian-born U.S. science writer
"When he looked at the clock, not only did it stop, but it started going backwards."

RACHEL CARSON (1907–1964), U.S. biologist and writer
"Rachel's like the mid-day sun / Always very bright / Never stops her studying / 'Til she gets it right."

GERALD LEE CLEMONS (1942–), U.S. triple-murder suspect
"Make a Rainy Day Sunny."

AMELIA EARHART (1897–1937), U.S. aviator
"A.E.—the girl in brown who walks alone."

RICHARD FEYNMAN (1918–1988), U.S. physicist
"Mad Genius."

GRETA GARBO (1905–1990), Swedish-born U.S. actor
"Miss Gustafsson always looks clean and well-groomed and has such a good face."

GEORGIA O'KEEFFE:
"O is for O'Keeffe, an artist divine;
her paintings are perfect
and her drawings are fine."

JACQUELINE KENNEDY ONASSIS:
"Best Known For: wit; Ambition:
not to be a housewife;
Always Saying: play a rhumba next."

GLORIA STEINEM:
"A gal of many talents . . . smart and stylish
. . . enjoys dancing and cooking."

ANDY WARHOL:
"As genuine as a fingerprint."

THEODORE GEISEL (DR. SEUSS) (1904–1991), U.S. writer and illustrator
"Next comedy appeared with great applause."

MARTHA GRAHAM (1894–1991), U.S. dancer and choreographer
"Capable, generous, willing to do—To the noblest standards, faithful and true."

J. EDGAR HOOVER (1895–1972), U.S. FBI director
"A gentleman of dauntless courage and stainless honor."

LYNDON BAINES JOHNSON (1908–1973), U.S. president
The yearbook staff didn't use his photo but instead printed a picture of a jackass; the caption read, "As he looks to us on the campus every day."

ALFRED KINSEY (1894–1956), U.S. sexologist
"Man delights not me; no, nor woman neither."

WLADZIU VALENTINO LIBERACE (1919–1987), U.S. pianist
"Our Wally has already made his claim with Paderewski, Gershwin, and others of fame."

Lyndon Baines Johnson,
in his cowboy hat,
age seven and a half.

Courtesy of the Lyndon Baines Johnson Library.

VINCE LOMBARDI (1913–1970), U.S. football coach
"Lombardi—to be strong is to be happy."

CLARE BOOTHE LUCE (1903–1987), U.S. writer and diplomat
"Yes, yes, she is our prodigy and our genius . . . yet just the same, she is as lovable as she is brilliant."

GEORGE MCGOVERN (1922–　), U.S. politician
"For a debater, he's a nice kid."

BETTE MIDLER (1945–　), U.S. singer and actor
"Her ambition is to join the Peace Corps and, perhaps, someday become another Bette Davis."

EDWARD R. MURROW (1908–1965), U.S. broadcast journalist
"A man in the world's new fashion planted, that hath a mint of phrases in his brain."

RALPH NADER (1934–　), U.S. reformer
"Anything for peace. . . . Quiet—smart—can be found either at home or at the restaurant—woman hater."

JACK NICHOLSON (1937–　), U.S. actor
"Nick . . . jolly and good-natured . . . enthusiastic writer of those English compositions . . . his participation added to our plays."

GEORGIA O'KEEFFE (1887–1986), U.S. painter
"O is for O'Keeffe, an artist divine; her paintings are perfect and her drawings are fine."

JACQUELINE KENNEDY ONASSIS (1929–1994), U.S. first lady
"Best Known For: wit; Ambition: not to be a housewife; Always Saying: play a rhumba next."

TYRONE POWER (1914–1958), U.S. actor
"Ty is a good student, but his acting makes him a logical successor of John Barrymore."

ELVIS PRESLEY (1935–1977), U.S. singer
"Doing a bit of picking and singing."

JANET RENO (1938–　), U.S. attorney general
"Janet Reno . . . debater and scholar. In both, extraordinary."

JOHN STEINBECK (1902–1968), U.S. novelist
"The church of a far off city / Came towering into view / Where John was preaching in solemn tones / To many a well-filled pew."

GLORIA STEINEM (1934–　), U.S. writer/publisher and feminist
"A gal of many talents . . . smart and stylish . . . enjoys dancing and cooking."

BARBARA WALTERS (1929–　), U.S. broadcast journalist
"The glory of a firm, capacious mind."

ANDY WARHOL (1928–1987), U.S. artist
"As genuine as a fingerprint."

CHAPTER FIVE

$\mathcal{D}$BEING IFFERENT

"If there is anything that we wish to change in the child, we should first examine it and see whether it is not something that could better be changed in ourselves."
KARL GUSTAV JUNG, *THE INTEGRATIONS OF THE PERSONALITY*

Real childhood is not like *The Brady Bunch* or even *The Wonder Years*. We are as likely to be the nerdy friend as the cute protagonist. This goes in spades for the famous, who often were a little bit different as children. Some refused to play by the rules. Others suffered from being ugly ducklings—and not all were transformed into swans, at least not physically. Some responded to their situations by turning into loners.

As children, our subjects sometimes didn't fit into the gender roles society assigned to them. Tomboys named themselves after boys (Margaret "Jimmy" Mitchell and Marlene "Paul" Dietrich), or played rough sports in times when girls did not do such things (like singers Mary Martin and k. d. lang). Particularly in the distant past, some mothers tended to treat their little boys like girls. And some boys were by nature "girlish"—for example, Hans Christian Andersen had a propensity toward quiet dreaminess, Christopher Isherwood toward cross-dressing.

Ugly ducklings may grow up to be swans, but they aren't always aware of their transformation. No matter how good-looking they grew up to be, some kids who thought of themselves as ugly, like James Baldwin, suffered in this respect all their lives.

Many of our subjects were different because they were sickly. Strangely, ill health could confer advantages. G. W. Carver probably had opportunities he would not otherwise have had because he was too sickly to do heavy work. But for most, illness was a hardship. After Bobby Darin's last attack of rheumatic fever, his doctor predicted that he wouldn't live to see sixteen—and Bobby heard him say it.

Perhaps more than most of us, the famous felt the anguish (or superiority) of being loners, of sitting on the edge. Perhaps Jawaharlal Nehru put it best. He was, he said, "never an exact fit." John Denver saw himself "as a dot: round and flat, without edges or depth." As we see, fame and international reknown do not necessarily erase insecurities nor chase away personal demons.

TOMBOYS

FRIEDERIKE VIKTORIA (JOY) ADAMSON (1910–1980), Austrian naturalist

The Gessners wanted their second child to be a boy, but the baby turned out to be a girl like their first. They called her Friederike Viktoria—Fifi, for short. Her moody, handsome father nicknamed her Fritz and treated her as a son. Her mother, Traute, withheld love. Sixty years later, Traute wrote her daughter a letter telling her that she had been a disappointment because she was a girl.

Fifi became a tomboy. She showered her thwarted affection on animals—fox cubs and other wild animals she adopted. Yet when Fifi was fifteen, she went hunting with the family gamekeeper. A young roebuck appeared in a glade, and at the urging of the gamekeeper she shot and killed it. She was horrified at herself. After that experience, she vowed she would never kill another animal for sport.

When she grew up, Fifi (now Joy) sought the love she had never had. In Africa, she found it. She and her husband, George Adamson, adopted an orphaned lion cub, whom they named Elsa. Joy said of Elsa, "In her I found the love I had always been seeking. I had never known anything like it before." Joy's book about Elsa, *Born Free*, published in 1960, sold five million copies.

BABE DIDRIKSON (1913–1956), U.S. golfer.

"I don't know where I got that 'ting,' " Babe's Scandinavian mother, who loved Babe dearly, would say. Babe was different. She herself once told a reporter, "As far back as I can remember, I played with boys rather than girls. . . . I guess the habit of playing with boys made me too rough for the girls' games. Anyway, I found them too tame." She could beat up boys, even those bigger than she was, and if they didn't do as she wished, she knocked them down and sat on them.

Athletic and brave, Babe climbed to the top of the school flagpole, jumped off moving freight trains, and caught a rat in cooking class. Yes, she made a dress that won a prize in a state fair, but she also cut the sleeves off a dress she made in home economics class because they got in her way. When she was fourteen, she and her sister, Lillie, traveled with a Ringling circus troupe to California, and Babe learned how to be a trapeze artist. She could turn flips in the air and walk a tightrope.

Always picked first for games, she was on the high school basketball, golf, and tennis teams. Football coach Lilburn "Bubba" Dimmit wanted to have her kick points after a touchdown, but she was not allowed to because she was a girl.

MARLENE DIETRICH (1901–1992), German-born U.S. actor

Her father, a policeman, left home before she went to school and died not long after. Little Marlene openly sought to take his place "against my mother's wishes." She called herself Paul.

As a child, she developed crushes on both males and females. Often she wanted to play the part of a boy. Like other German schoolgirls, she fell madly in love with movie star Henny Porten, the "Mary Pickford of Germany." But Marlene took her attraction to Porten a couple of steps beyond sending Porten postcards; she actually stalked the glamorous star. One day she serenaded Porten in the foyer of her house with a violin solo of "*Engelslied*" ("Angel's Song").

In her first public violin performance in June 1917, she dressed as a boy in a sombrero and played "La Paloma" for some dancers. The costume prefigured the famous and sexy gender-ambiguous costumes she wore in movies, like her tuxedo in *Blue Angel,* in which she sang "Falling in Love Again."

JANE FONDA (1937–   ), U.S. actor

Though she seemed to have ambivalent feelings toward her aloof father, Henry, Jane tried to be like him in every way. She wore blue jeans and flannel shirts, and she purposely stood and walked like him—long and rangy. As an adult, she said, "I didn't want to be a girl, because I wanted to be like my father." When she cut her hair short and someone asked her if she was a girl or a boy, she was overjoyed, so pleased she couldn't sleep.

She was a tough contender, the leader in childhood pranks. Once she broke her arm in a fight with a boy. She broke her arm again play-acting a fall off a horse, a fall like those her father took in movies. In sixth grade, after the family moved to Connecticut, she took other kids into the schoolyard shed and told them dirty jokes. She and her cousin Brooke Hayward were kicked out of the Girl Scouts for similar activities.

> ### *"Don't take life or its happenings too seriously. Lift up the corners of that mouth I gave you one moonlit night."*
>
> —*Katharine Hepburn's father*

By the time she was twelve, she had accepted being a girl, though she remained unruly. At Emma Willard School, which she entered when she was thirteen, she set a trail of lighter fuel from her room to that of one of her enemies and set it on fire. She even belonged to a gang of girls called the "Disorders"—and became its leader.

KATHARINE HEPBURN (1907–   ), U.S. actor

In 1915, when Katharine (Kathy) was eight, she called herself Jimmy, after a friend of her brother Tom. To keep kids from pulling her red hair, she cut it so that it was a half-inch long. She wore boys' clothes. She badly wanted to be a boy like Tom, who was two years older, and her two younger brothers, Dick and Bob.

When she went back to school wearing boys' clothes in the fall of that year, her teacher, "old lady Seymour," told her that she must wear a dress to school and sent her home to put one on. Fanny, the cook, found a dress for her, and she dutifully wore it back to school. However, the next day, she showed up again in boys' clothes. The teacher sent her home again to put on a dress. Kathy came back, still in her boys' clothes, with her mother, Fanny, who said, "Mrs. Seymour, you don't tell my daughter how to dress. That is my concern, not yours."

Kathy was a scrapper. When other children teased her about her mother's suffragist activities, she fought them with fists and words. Fanny bragged that Kathy and Tommy "beat up on those kids that plagued them. Kathy beat up on the biggest bully of the lot—beat up on him plenty."

K. D. LANG (1961–   ), Canadian singer

Kathryn Dawn Lang grew up in Consort, a very small town in Alberta, Canada. Her father recalls her as "a real bomb" because she was very independent and never took a back seat to anyone. At age nine she was racing around on a motorbike, and at age twelve she had her own .12-gauge shotgun. By the time she was thirteen, Kathy was playing both piano and guitar.

Most people in Kathy's hometown remember her as an outstanding athlete. A star volleyball player, she also excelled at basketball and badminton. In addition, Kathy turned in Olympic-level performances in javelin throwing. For three consecutive years she was voted Athlete of the Year in her high school. Many people who knew Kathy thought she was destined for a career in sports, but she directed all her energy and ambition toward another equally competitive field, the world of music, where she soon achieved superstar status.

MARY MARTIN (1913–1990), U.S. singer and actor

In the second grade Mary put on a pair of boxing gloves (which she got for Christmas) and took on the best fighter in her class at school; she won, knocking out the boy's two front teeth. All through her childhood in Weatherford, Texas, Mary wanted to be a boy. She rode bicycles and horses, played baseball, climbed trees, and ruined every lacy dress her mother gave her. Rather than simply walk the two-block distance between school and home, Mary often did cartwheels all the way down a hill. She also liked to sing and dance and act (always wanting to play the villain).

Mary made her Broadway stage debut when she was twenty-five and went on to appear in such hits as *Annie Get Your Gun, South Pacific,* and *The Sound of Music.* But most fans remember her best as the flying, crowing Peter Pan, the boy who wouldn't grow up. In her autobiography Martin wrote: "Like all children I was sure I could fly. One day I tried it, from the roof of our garage, and landed with a broken collarbone. It was years before I found out that I could fly, but only with the help of a beautiful idea and a very strong wire."

MARGARET MITCHELL (1900–1949), U.S. novelist

After her skirts caught fire when she was three, Margaret was dressed in boys' clothes. With her hair pushed up underneath a tweed cap, she looked, and walked, like a boy. Neighbors called her "Jimmy" because she looked like a character in a newspaper comic strip. By the time she was six, Margaret, atop her pony, was riding around the streets of Atlanta, Georgia. Many afternoons her riding companions were a bunch of old Confederate veterans; the little girl loved to listen to the soldiers' war stories, and it was on those riding excursions that she learned how to swear.

Margaret preferred boy playmates to girl playmates. With her friends, she built forts and castles, played war games, and engaged in mud-ball battles. She was a good swimmer, an excellent tennis player, and a pitcher on an all-boys baseball team. While Margaret's mother, May Belle, insisted that her daughter take dancing and etiquette lessons, she also made sure that Margaret knew how to ride a horse and shoot a rifle.

Margaret didn't like school. She didn't like "girl talk" and preferred to shoot spitballs across the classroom. By the time she reached her teens, however, she had become a lovely southern belle—a petite girl under one hundred pounds with a nineteen-inch waist. Fortunately, her adventurous, rebellious nature remained, and those traits were bestowed upon her fictional character, Scarlett O'Hara, who graced and raced across the pages of *Gone with the Wind.*

Did you know that Jane Fonda was the leader of a girls' gang called the "Disorders"?

CARRY NATION (1846–1911), U.S. temperance leader and social reformer

As an adult, Carry Nation, with hatchet held high, stormed into saloons in Kansas and nearby states and smashed everything in sight in the name of the temperance movement; she was arrested more than thirty times. Born on a farm in Kentucky, the young Carry showed early signs of being the hell-raiser she would become. Energetic and opinionated, she was always the leader among her friends, whether they were climbing the tallest trees or fishing along the riverbank. She organized elaborate funerals for dead mice and birds and yelled out instructions for all the roles her friends would play; Carry was always the preacher.

In school Carry was afraid of no one, including the teachers, and was always stirring up some kind of trouble. As one of her classmates remembered: "She used to delight in assuming the role of a conqueror. She would array herself and the other school children in paper-soldier caps, stain their faces with the juice from the pokeberries that grew in the yard, and then, armed with a wooden sword, lead us into the woods to do battle against imaginary foes."

ANNIE OAKLEY (1860–1926), U.S. rodeo performer

Annie (born Phoebe Ann Moses) was eight years old when she took her first shot with her father's old Kentucky rifle. No one had taught her how to shoot, but she loaded the rifle with enough powder "to kill a buffalo," sneaked outside, steadied the rifle on the porch railing, and shot a squirrel right through the head.

Growing up on a farm in Drake County, Ohio, she was a small child with dark hair and bright blue-gray eyes. Annie was never enamored of her sister's rag dolls but preferred to help her father make animal traps out of heavy cornstalks instead. In her teenage years Annie's trapping and shooting abilities enabled her to put food on the table for her widowed mother and siblings. She sold her surplus game to a shopkeeper, who in turn sold the meat to hotel restaurants. Hotel owners, according to legend, were eager to buy Annie's game because she was able to shoot small animals through the head, thus providing meat untainted with buckshot.

MARJORIE MERRIWEATHER POST (1887–1973), U.S. financier and philan-
    thropist

She was one of the world's richest women, and she enjoyed spending money. Her life style was lavish, her estates large and luxurious, yet she generously gave money to a multitude of charitable causes. Post inherited her fortune at age twenty-seven when her father, C. W. Post, salesman turned breakfast-food tycoon, died.

C. W. Post always wanted a male heir, but Marjorie was his only child. So he raised her the way he would have raised a son. He taught her how to hunt; she trapped and skinned moles to make fur coats for her dolls. He taught her how to box and brought her with him to sit ringside at boxing matches, dressed as a boy with her hair tucked under a cap. When she was eleven, Marjorie attended board meetings at the Postum Company and was sometimes called upon to participate. At a moment's notice, C. W. would take Marjorie on business trips, both in the United States and Europe. He taught her two important lessons about money: (1) Spend it but don't trust anyone; (2) Be very knowledgeable about all transactions or risk being cheated.

BOYS WHO LOOKED OR ACTED LIKE GIRLS

HANS CHRISTIAN ANDERSEN (1805–1875), Danish writer

Quiet and timorous, young Hans Christian Andersen lived within his imagination, sewing clothes of bright-colored cloth for his dolls, which became the actors in his plays. He was afraid of the dark and of graveyards. At Carsten's School for Boys, he later said, the teacher "took me by the hand while the other boys played, that I might not be run over. . . ." He knew he was "not suited at all to be put among other wild boys and girls."

But Hans was not entirely unpopular or shy. What saved him from being completely spurned by others was his beautiful, high soprano voice. When he sang in his parents' garden, people came to the fence to listen and called him "the little Funen Nightingale."

As a young boy, he got a job in a textile mill. On the first day he came to work, the journeymen asked him to sing and to recite, while the other boys reluctantly did his work for him. The following day he was put to work, but he did not do well. When the workers told dirty jokes or sang smutty songs, he blushed and then cried. His behavior inspired one of the journeymen to say that Hans must be a girl, not a boy. He grabbed Hans and took off the protesting boy's pants to see what sex he was. Andersen describes his reaction in his autobiography: "I screamed aloud, and was as much ashamed as a girl. . . ." He ran home to his mother, who told him that he did not have to go back to work in the mill.

ERSKINE CALDWELL (1903–1987), U.S. writer

Erskine was an only child, "saved for something special." His mother, Carrie, raised to be a very proper southern lady, dressed Erskine in clothing she thought proper for a young boy in Prosperity, South Carolina—a kind of Russian blouse and short pants. Her minister husband, Ira, did not comment directly, but his son's sissy clothing and long curls disturbed him. One day he and Erskine's aunt, who had come to visit, took Erskine to the barbershop and had his hair cut short. Ira also bought his son blue overalls and a yellow shirt. Erskine saw himself in a store window on the way home. ". . . I wondered what my mother would say when she saw that I no longer had the long curls she had so often combed and brushed with expressions of pleasure. As for myself, I felt like a different person—so different that I wondered if I had mysteriously passed from one life and had entered another." According to some sources, when the trio arrived at home, Carrie held up her hands and said to her son, "Don't come near!"

She did not entirely give up on her attempts to dress her son as she saw fit. Later, when Erskine was older, she forced him to wear knickerbockers. No other boys his age dressed that way. He was a large and awkward boy, and the short pants emphasized the difference between him and the other boys to the point that he had to fight ridicule on his way to school.

This child who was dressed in sissified clothes and forced into gentility grew up to become an author of books written in language so earthy and ribald that some critics accused him of immorality. Others praised his empathetic portrayal of the southern poor and disenfranchised. He knew what it was like to be on the outside.

DAG HAMMARSKJÖLD (1905–1961), Swedish secretary-general to the United Nations

Dag Hammarskjöld was meant to be the "stay-at-home daughter," the child destined to look after aging parents. Having already given birth to three sons, Dag's mother, Agnes, wished the fourth to be a girl and treated him as such. She kept Dag in girls' clothes long after the time most boys graduated to pants. Emotional and moral, an expert on the Gospels, she visited the sick regularly and attended church faithfully. Dag went with her because other members of the family were unavailable. His two much older brothers, Bo and Åke, were out of the nest. His other brother Sten, five years older, was often too ill. And his statesman father, a model of granite rectitude, spent long periods of time away from home.

It was said that after God, Agnes worshipped Dag. One of his biographers commented, "Dag was his mother's gentleman-in-waiting, her page, her faithful and considerate attendant." Dag himself said of his mother, "Her chief traits . . . [were] a radically democratic and, if one will, an 'evangelical' view of mankind; a child's open attitude to life; an anti-rationalism with strong emotional undercurrents."

Dag never left the family home. His mother died in 1940—he was with her until the end—and he stayed in the house with his father for another five years, setting up his own home only when he was forty years old. He never married.

ERNEST HEMINGWAY (1899–1961), U.S. writer

When he was three, Ernest Hemingway was worried that Santa Claus would not know he was a boy. This was because his mother, Grace, dressed her two older children, Ernest and Marcelline, as if they were twins, though Ernest was a year and a half younger, and male. Long past the time they were in kindergarten, she outfitted them sometimes in organdie hats and dresses, sometimes in overalls. Both had unisex Dutch bobs. It was not until he was seven that Ernest had a boy's haircut. In a sense, Grace made the two children into cross-dressers. Marcelline later said that they "played with small china tea sets just alike; we had dolls alike; and when Ernest was given a little air rifle, I had one too."

Ernest Hemingway (on right) in 1917, with mother, Grace, and little brother, Leicester.

Courtesy of the John F. Kennedy Library.

Strict and religious, both parents kept a careful watch on the children. As an adolescent, Ernest was backward with girls. In fact, he took Marcelline, his sister, to his junior prom. From his boyhood he was drawn to guns and explosives. As an adult, he wrote partly to glorify those activities he thought of as manly—shooting, bullfighting, womanizing, and mountain climbing. It was as if all his life he tried to make sure that he would not be mistaken for a girl.

CHRISTOPHER ISHERWOOD (1904–1986), English-born U.S. writer

When Christopher was little, his mother, Kathleen, dressed him in fancy baby dresses and big hats, as was then the custom. As he grew older, he wore plush suits with lace collars, like Little Lord Fauntleroy. Though he had a nanny, he spent a good deal of time with his mother. They played together at dressing up, acting out situations Kathleen made up. She taught him how to dance the Sir Roger de Coverley so that they could pretend they were at a ball. Christopher liked to wear her clothes more than his father's. Kathleen encouraged this, enveloping him in her furs or silk petticoats and teaching him how to clasp a "switch" for elaborate hairdos. Cross-dressing ran in the family. His father, Frank, a professional soldier, athlete, and accomplished knitter, liked to dress in drag in revues.

Christopher grew up to be a somewhat affected boy, with a pretentious way of speaking. This made him unpopular, and he compensated for it by playing the clown. In 1914 his parents sent him to St. Edmunds, a boarding school, to "flatten him out" and make him "like other boys." In a letter written in 1915, Frank, then fighting in World War I, had second thoughts: "I don't know if it is at all desirable or necessary, and I for one would much rather have him as he is."

A. A. MILNE (1882–1956), English writer

Alan Alexander's mother, Maria, steadfastly claimed that she didn't mind that all three of her children were boys, but she dressed all of them in Little Lord Fauntleroy velvet suits with big lace collars. Since other kids wore the silly suits too, Alan wasn't particularly bothered by the clothes, but he didn't like his long, flaxen curls.

One day Alan was late to school and missed the beginning of an important debate because his mother wouldn't let him leave home until his just washed long hair was completely dry. On another occasion, a visitor to the school, upon seeing his hair, treated Alan like a baby. When Alan was ten, Maria allowed the curls to be cut but refused to go to the barber shop to watch. The boy who would one day write Winnie-the-Pooh stories carefully collected his detached curls and took them home to his mother.

ROBERT PEARY (1856–1920), U.S. Arctic explorer

Robert, called "Bertie," was an only child. His father died when Bertie was only two years old, and his mother, Mary, pampered the little boy and often treated him as if he were a girl. To keep the sun from burning his fair skin, she sent him outside in frilly bonnets. His girlish clothing, plus an embarrassing lisp, were ridiculed by his playmates in Portland, Maine. Robert was often called a sissy.

To prove he was a boy, Bertie engaged in a lot of fistfights. His mother was terrified when he came home dirty and bruised, but Bertie looked upon the injuries as badges of honor. In addition, he rebelled against his overprotective mother by engaging in a lot of pranks and startling guests with outrageous, adultlike comments. However, by the time he entered school, "Bertie" had become "Bert," a well-behaved boy who had no trouble making friends.

RAINER MARIA RILKE (1875–1926), Austro-German poet
Rainer (called Rene) was a premature baby. His mother, Sophia, had given birth to a daughter the year before Rene was born, but the girl had died shortly after birth. Sophia dressed Rene in long, feminine dresses, bought him dolls and other girls' toys, and let his hair grow long. On one occasion, when the boy thought his mother was angry with him, he got all dressed up, fixed his hair into braids, and said to his mother, "Rene is not good. I sent him away. Girls are, after all, so much nicer."

Rene's father tried to counteract Sophia's influence by giving him toy soldiers to play with. When Rene entered school at the age of seven, his mother finally abandoned the dresses and bought him boys' clothing. Despite his change in appearance, for a while the other schoolchildren called him a "mama's boy." Throughout his life Rilke had a love-hate relationship with his mother. He recognized that it was Sophia who had encouraged his early interest in poetry, but he resented the fact that she often left him in the care of a servant and sent him off at age ten to a military boarding school. On one hand, she seemed doting and proud; on the other hand, she often seemed to be an absentee parent. Of Sophia he later wrote, "I think my mother played with me as though I were a big doll."

UGLY DUCKLINGS

JAMES BALDWIN (1924–1987), U.S. writer
Baldwin grew up in New York's Harlem, and the person who had the greatest impact on him was his stepfather, David Baldwin ("He formed me, and he raised me, and he did not let me starve"). However, David Baldwin also labeled his son "ugly" and was ruthless in pointing out James's big, prominent eyes and frail body. In grade school the kids called him "Frog Eyes," which only reinforced his father's taunting. One day the young Baldwin excitedly yelled to his mother to come and look out the window at a woman he had spotted in the street, "Look, there's someone who's uglier than you and me." Baldwin grew up to become a much admired and accomplished writer, but he was never able to shake off the physical image of his childhood. In his bestseller *Go Tell It on the Mountain* the boy character (based on Baldwin) dreamed of being "beautiful, tall and popular," a boy who would become "a poet or a college president or a movie star."

BRIGITTE BARDOT (1934–   ), French actor

No one would have guessed that the young Bardot would grow up to be an international sex symbol. Her hair was thin and frizzy, and she always seemed to be suffering from allergic rashes. She wore wire-rimmed eyeglasses because of astigmatism and braces to straighten her teeth. Bardot saw herself as homely, but in reality she was just a plain-looking girl. By the time she was fifteen, however, she was able to see the body and face that would make her famous. Nonetheless, she has never been satisfied with her appearance and once said: "My nose is a very bad nose. When I meet a man it wrinkles up, as if I was sniffing a bowl of milk. My mouth is not a good mouth. My upper lip is heavier and more swollen than the other. My cheeks are too round and my eyes are too small."

J. M. BARRIE (1860–1937), English writer

The man who created Peter Pan ("the boy who would not grow up"), Barrie was the runt of his family and extremely sensitive about his small stature. In school the girls voted him "the sweetest smile" in the class, but none was attracted to the frail-looking boy. When no one was looking, Barrie would sneak off and scrawl his name, along with a girl's name, on the walls of the school. Many years later, when he was both rich and famous, he wrote: "Six feet three inches. . . . If I had really grown to this it would have made a great difference in my life. I would not have bothered turning out reels of printed matter. My one aim would have been to become a favorite of the ladies which between you and me has always been my sorrowful ambition. The things I could have said to them if my legs had been longer. Read that with a bitter cry." Barrie's adult height was barely five feet.

DALE CARNEGIE (1888–1955), U.S. writer

The son of a poor farmer in Missouri, he was a skinny and gawky boy with a dimpled chin and huge ears. One of his classmates, Sam White, constantly made fun of Carnegie's ears and threatened to cut them off. Terrified that the bully would carry out the threat, the young Carnegie endured many sleepless nights and never forgot the name of his tormentor. Unable to afford new clothes, Dale wore hand-me-downs that never fit and often made him look silly. Of being called to the chalkboard to solve a math problem, he once told his mother, "I can only think of the fact that people are probably laughing at my clothes." But he was determined to make up for his lack of physical assets with his speaking abilities. A powerful orator, he won many public speaking contests, feats that transformed him from social failure to intellectual leader. The ungainly boy from Missouri would go on to write *How to Win Friends and Influence People*, one of the biggest nonfiction bestsellers of all time.

GEORGE ELIOT (1819–1880), English writer

Her real name was Marian Evans and she would become one of the foremost English novelists of the nineteenth century; her best known work is *Silas Marner*. When she was ten years old, Marian said, "I don't like to play with children. I like to talk to grown-up people." Behind that comment was a young girl who was not very popular with her classmates. They called her "little mama." Although she was an excellent student, Marian was a very serious child and not terribly attractive. She had a large fleshy nose, prominent chin, full lower lip, dull complexion, and dark clinging hair. As an adult she wrote: "When I was quite a little child I could not be satisfied with the things around me; I was constantly living in a world of my own creation, and was quite contented to have no companions that I might be left to my own musings and imagining scenes in which I was chief actress."

ALFRED HITCHCOCK (1899–1980), English-born U.S. film director

He called himself "an uncommonly unattractive young man." Film director and master of the suspense thriller, Hitchcock preferred not to talk about his childhood. He was pudgy, very plain looking, and a loner. Girls were never an important part of his life, and he ended up marrying the first girl he ever dated. Always unhappy with his overweight body, he learned to joke about it: "A New York doctor once told me that I'm an adrenal type. That apparently means that I'm all body and only vestigial legs. But since I'm neither a mile runner nor a dancer, and my present interest in my body is almost altogether from the waist up, that didn't bother me much." Oddly enough, his unattractive body turned out to be an incredible publicity tool and helped to make him a worldwide celebrity. Movie fans eagerly awaited the short cameo appearance he made in each film. And his television series, *Alfred Hitchcock Presents,* opened with a silhouetted image of Hitchcock stepping into a profile sketch.

JANIS JOPLIN (1943–1970), U.S. singer

She tried hard to "fit in" in high school. At first she conformed by wearing all the "right" clothes and makeup and joining all the right clubs. But she was always self-conscious about her underdeveloped body, her "pig" eyes, and her recurring bouts of acne. Joplin once remarked that she was unhappy in school "cause I didn't have tits at age fourteen." When she failed to break into the popular groups in school, Joplin changed course and created her own brand of popularity. She dyed her hair orange, donned a black leather jacket, and became known for her mastery of cusswords. Her code of nonconformity would later carry her into the hippie subculture of San Francisco and launch her career as a singer. Her most successful album was *Pearl,* which contains her number one hit "Me and Bobby McGee." Known for her loud, raspy vocal renditions, she said, "I'd rather not sing than sing quiet."

ABRAHAM LINCOLN (1809–1865), U.S. president

The sixteenth president of the United States was six feet tall by the time he was fifteen (his adult height was six feet, four inches). As a teenager, he was admired for his strength and athletic abilities. In addition, he was a glib talker, a good joke teller, and a natural leader among the boys. The girls, however, paid him no attention. One of his schoolmates, Kate Ruby, said that all the girls made fun of his appearance, and she described him as follows: "His skin was shriveled and yellow. His shoes, when he had any, were low. He wore buckskin breeches, linsey-woolsey shirt and a cap, made from the skin of a squirrel or coon. His breeches were baggy and lacked by several inches meeting the tops of his shoes, thereby exposing his shin-bone, sharp, blue and narrow." Abe, however, didn't seem too bothered by his lack of popularity with the girls. He said, "A woman is the only thing I am afraid of that I know can't hurt me."

ELEANOR ROOSEVELT (1884–1962), U.S. first lady

The opening sentence of her memoirs is: "My mother was one of the most beautiful women I have ever seen." Unfortunately, her mother, Anna Hall Roosevelt, thought Eleanor was far from beautiful. In front of friends and relatives, Anna called her daughter "Granny" because she was so serious, awkward, and old-fashioned. Anna cautioned her daughter, "You have no looks, so see to it that you have manners." Eleanor's mother died when she was eight, and after her father died two years later, Eleanor moved in with her grandmother, Mary Hall. Eleanor's cousin, Alice Roosevelt, once said: "Eleanor was always making herself out to be an ugly duckling but she was really rather attractive. Tall, rather coltish-looking, with masses of pale, golden hair rippling to below her waist, and really lovely blue eyes. It's true that her chin went in a bit, which wouldn't have been so noticeable if only her hateful grandmother had fixed her teeth." The future first lady of the United States, however, was never able to erase the negative image her mother had placed upon her; and it would forever affect her self-esteem.

STENDHAL (1783–1842), French novelist

Marie Henri Beyle (Stendhal) was always self-conscious about his appearance. As an adolescent, his only redeeming qualities were his expressive eyes and curly black hair; he had an oversize head, a thick nose, short legs, fat cheeks, and a heavyset, stocky body. His outgoing personality and vivid imagination, however, won over his classmates, and he never lacked for friends. As an adult, he made fun of his appearance, saying, "I'd rather be a chameleon than an ox." Yet he let it be known that he had always longed to be a tall, blond German.

BARBRA STREISAND (1942–   ), U.S. singer, actor, and film director

In grade school her classmates called her names—"Big Beak," "Cross-Eyes," and "Mieskeit" (Yiddish for ugliness). Although she was an excellent student, the young Barbra was small and thin, awkward, and had a rather large nose. When she graduated from high school and tried to get work as an actress, most casting directors thought she had talent but weren't impressed with her looks. Undaunted, she transformed herself with clothes, makeup, and a new hairstyle, taking full advantage of her striking blue eyes and long, slender neck. When the Broadway show *Funny Girl* made her a celebrity overnight, the homely Streisand suddenly found herself one of the world's most beautiful and glamorous entertainers. Women flocked to beauty salons to ask for the "Streisand look."

WOODROW WILSON (1856–1924), U.S. president

The son of an extremely handsome Presbyterian minister, Woodrow, however, was a homely boy with a long, drawn face, big ears, and a thrusting jaw.

The lovely Eleanor Roosevelt,
who considered herself
an "ugly duckling," age fifteen.

Courtesy of the Franklin D. Roosevelt Library.

In addition, at age eight, he was forced to wear eyeglasses. Wilson once told his cousin that if he had his father's looks, nobody would care what he said or did. As a child, he often recited the following limerick: "For beauty I am not a star / There are others more handsome by far / But my face, I don't mind it / You see, I'm behind it / It's the people in front that I jar." Even after he became the twenty-eighth president of the United States, Wilson was somewhat camera shy, telling reporters that he didn't like "pictorial publicity."

SICKLY KIDS

HENRY ADAMS (1838–1918), U.S. historian

On December 3, 1841, when Henry Adams was almost four, he developed a case of scarlet fever and was "for several days as good as dead," according to his classic autobiography, *The Education of Henry Adams.* His family nursed him back to health. Although he did not remember anything about his illness, he did remember vividly the baked apple on a saucer that his aunt brought into his sickroom on New Year's Day, 1842. He was feeling better—and hungry. Ten days later, wrapped in blankets, he was carried to a new house in his hometown of Boston. "He never forgot his acute distress for want of air under his blankets . . . ," says his autobiography, which is written in the third person.

In most cases, such a childhood illness comes and goes, a passing misery. But Adams gave his scarlet fever credit for "a certain delicacy of mind and bone" that permanently shaped his character and his body. He "fell behind his brothers two or three inches in height, and proportionally in bone and weight." His character altered too—he "was not good in a fight" and his nerves were delicate, "more than boys' nerves ought to be." He tended to avoid responsibility and developed an open-mindedness, along with "the hesitation to act except as a choice of evils." He learned "the love of line, form, quality," a "horror of ennui," and "the passion for companionship and the antipathy to society." This brilliant grandson of President John Quincy Adams soberly assessed his own traits—good and bad—and maintained that they were "stimulated by the fever." He was different, and his illness had exacerbated it.

GEORGE WASHINGTON CARVER (c. 1864–1943), U.S. botanist

Often called the "Peanut Man" because he found three hundred uses for peanuts and sweet potatoes, George Washington Carver certainly owed some of his opportunities in life to his ill health as a child. He and his slave mother were kidnapped by slave raiders while he was still a baby. Moses Carver, their owner, arranged for a neighbor, John Bentley, a Union scout, to find the two. Bentley returned with only George but was nevertheless given a valuable racehorse as a reward.

Moses and his wife, Susan, raised George and his older brother, Jim, as their own children in their home in Diamond Grove, Missouri. Jim was a robust child, able to help out with farm chores. George was sickly and frail—he had had a bad case of whooping cough and several bouts of croup. His growth was stunted and his vocal cords damaged, perhaps as a result of tuberculosis or pneumonia. All his life, his voice was high-pitched, giving credence to rumors that he had been castrated.

His childhood chores were light; he watered the animals and helped in the house. This gave him plenty of time to pursue his own interests: reading, experimenting, studying wild plants and animals in the woods. Susan taught him housewifely arts such as cooking, sewing, doing laundry. These skills came in handy later, when, on his own at about fifteen, he was hired to do cooking and other chores for a blacksmith and laundry for a hotel in Fort Scott, Kansas, a place where work was hard to find. "I found employment just like a girl," he said.

"Peanut Man"
George Washington Carver (left)
and his brother, Jim.

Courtesy of the Tuskegee University Archives.

Did you know that JFK was plagued by sickness his whole life, starting with appendicitis and diphtheria, followed by jaundice, and finally Addison's disease?

JACQUES-YVES COUSTEAU (1910–1997), French oceanographer and film-maker

Our image of Jacques Cousteau is of a wiry sailor, the picture of health, performing strenuous ocean dives. Yet shortly after his birth in a town near Bordeaux, France, young Jacques fell ill with enteritis, a painful intestinal inflammation. It plagued him throughout his early childhood, making him thin and sickly. After he recovered from the enteritis, he developed anemia.

His father, Daniel Cousteau, a notary (in France a legal expert) worked as an adviser to Eugene Higgins, the multimillionaire heir to an American carpeting fortune. Higgins required Daniel to travel with him to play sports such as golf and tennis, and often his children went along. But in the playgrounds of the rich and famous, Jacques was supposedly too frail to engage in sports and physical games. Doctors warned against overexertion. Higgins, however, going against doctor's orders, persuaded the Cousteaus to allow Jacques to learn to swim at Deauville, where Higgins kept his yacht. "I loved touching water. Physically. Sensually," Cousteau later said, "Water fascinated me, first floating ships, then me floating and stones not floating." This was the beginning of a love affair with the sea that lasted throughout his life.

After a stint in the French navy, Cousteau began his career as an oceanographer and adventurer. He wrote about thirty books and made about ninety films. Long beyond the age at which most people retire, Cousteau remained active as a diver. "When you dive, you begin to feel that you're an angel. It's a liberation of your weight," he said. Yet all his adult life, too, he was not well. He suffered from neurasthenia, which causes malaise and nervous tension, and he was always underweight and bothered by water pressure, cold, and high altitudes.

BOBBY DARIN (1936–1973), U.S. singer and actor

His mother, Nina, was only eighteen when she gave birth to the boy she named Walden Robert Cassotto. Because he was illegitimate, she passed him off as her mother's child. Until he was thirty-two, the boy who later became a teenage pop idol thought his grandmother was his mother. His grandfather (who he thought was his father), a racketeer and inventor of pop-up figures at shooting galleries, died at Sing Sing prison of heroin withdrawal the year before he was born.

The family was on welfare. Bobby was so sickly that neighbors predicted he would die in the cardboard box that served as his crib. His stepfather, Carmine (Charlie) Maffia, who married Nina in 1942, paid for doctors and imported goat's milk, the only food the baby could digest. Four times between the ages of eight and thirteen he contracted rheumatic fever, caused by a streptococcus infection that can ravage the heart muscle and cause damage to the heart valve. His sister Vivienne has said, "My earliest memory of Bobby as a child was about his rheumatic fever. We couldn't walk on the floor because just walking across the floor would put him in agony. I remember Bobby crying and screaming and my father having to pick him up and carry him to the bathroom, he was in so much pain." At his last attack, the doctor predicted he wouldn't live to see sixteen—and Bobby heard him say it.

As a youngster, Bobby didn't go to school for months. He couldn't play hard, couldn't climb stairs. For a year he was a patient at a mountain sanitarium for victims of tuberculosis and heart disease. His family babied him, calling him "the King," and his two younger half-sisters resented him.

Because of his illness, he was a man in a hurry; for instance, he wrote "Splish Splash," a big hit, when he was only twenty-two. In 1973, his life ended following surgery to correct the functioning of an artificial heart valve.

MARY BAKER EDDY (1821–1910), U.S. founder of Christian Science
Mary Baker Eddy suffered from illness, some of it probably psychosomatic, throughout her childhood. She suffered from fevers, backaches, cankers. She suffered from lung and liver problems. She suffered from ulcers, dyspepsia, and convulsions. Both her father and her doctor thought her afflictions resulted from too much reading and study. The doctor said, "Do not doctor your child. She has got too much brains for her body; keep her out of doors, keep her in exercise, and keep her away from school all you can." This probably suited her just fine, as she did not do particularly well in school.

When she went into convulsions, she sometimes screamed and writhed on the floor, whereas at other times she became cataleptic. When her father had to go to fetch the doctor, fearing the worst, he would stand up in the wagon, whipping the horses, shouting, "Mary is dying!" To avoid these attacks, the family gave in to her whims. Her doctor diagnosed the episodes as "hysteria mixed with bad temper." He claimed that he could control her by mental suggestion. "I can make that girl stop in the street any time, merely by thinking," he bragged.

Mary herself also discovered the power of mind over body. Once, after a particularly vehement religious argument with her father, she developed a high fever. Her mother laid cool cloths on her and suggested that she look to God for guidance. Mary obeyed, praying, and she felt "a soft glow of ineffable joy" that seemed to cure her. "The fever was gone," she wrote later, "and I rose and dressed myself, in a normal condition of health. . . ."

Critic Harold Bloom calls her "a monumental hysteric of classical dimensions, indeed a kind of anthology of nineteenth-century nervous ailments." It is no wonder that this textbook case created Christian Science, a religion that intimately links mental and physical health.

JOHN FITZGERALD KENNEDY (1917–1963), U.S. president

The Kennedy image of an athletic, healthy president belies the truth of his medical history. As a child, "Jack" was sickly, suffering from high fevers and seizures. He failed to make the football team at Canterbury, his Connecticut prep school, because he was too scrawny. As a young teenager, he contracted appendicitis, followed by diphtheria. Even after he grew up, illness continued to plague him. In 1935 he developed jaundice and had to drop out of the London School of Economics and come home to Hyannis Port, the family home on Cape Cod. After he injured his back playing football and suffered another bout of jaundice at Princeton, he was forced to go to Arizona for a rest.

Illness turned the young Kennedy into a foolhardy pleasure seeker who lived for the moment. Ashamed of his infirmities, he feared that if people knew about them it would hurt him politically. In 1947, he found out that he had Addison's disease, then often fatal, an ailment that affects the adrenal glands. He called it "slow motion leukemia." Sir Daniel Davis, his London physician, told Pamela Churchill, Winston Churchill's daughter, "That American friend of yours, he hasn't got a year to live." The illness was kept a secret, even when it brought him near death in 1954. Kennedy did not expect to live past forty-five. He did, of course, only to be killed by an assassin's bullet a year later.

THEODORE ROOSEVELT (1858–1919), U.S. president

As a child, the man who loved to shout "Bully" and led the Rough Riders during the Spanish-American War was delicate and suffered severe asthma attacks. The attacks usually happened in the middle of the night and left "Teedie" in a near-convulsive state, gasping for air. During those days, the treatments for asthma were primitive, for example, drinking strong, black coffee or smoking a cigar.

In addition to asthma, Teedie suffered from stomach problems, frequent colds and headaches, and insomnia (partly due to the asthma). Small in stature and in body frame, he had poor eyesight and was a nervous, frail boy. At age twelve, determined to improve his physical condition, Teedie began to work out in a gym, lifting weights, swinging on parallel bars, hitting punching bags. After two years of training, Teedie put his efforts to the test when he encountered a couple of boys about his own age on a stagecoach ride. The boys, who instigated a fight, didn't succeed in hurting Teedie but, as he later said, they were able "to prevent my doing any damage whatever in return."

Refusing to accept defeat, Teedie continued to work on his body. He went hiking, swimming, horseback riding, rowing, skating. He even took boxing lessons. Although he was never able to reach peak physical condition, he was able to erase the weakling image that had dogged him up till then. As an adult, Roosevelt was perceived as a rugged, robust man, ready to take on any challenge or adversary.

IRVING THALBERG (1899–1936), U.S. film producer

He was born with a defective heart, and doctors predicted that he would have a short life span. His mother, Henrietta, tried to treat him as a normal child but kept a watchful eye on his every move. In grade school, Irving did his best to participate in sports and games, but too much physical exertion led him to spend many days recovering in bed.

When Irving was in his early teens, a severe case of diphtheria kept him out of school for three years. Confined to bed, he made good use of his time, reading a prodigious number of books—from Shakespeare to Nietzsche to Dickens—and his concern over his physical condition was tempered by his enjoyment of these works. He did graduate from high school and thought about becoming a lawyer, but his doctors didn't think he could withstand the rigors of college.

Did you know that due to chronic rheumatic fever, Bobby Darin wasn't expected to live past age sixteen?

Leaving New York City for Los Angeles, the young Thalberg began a career in the motion picture industry. Ambitious and hardworking, he quickly worked his way upward, becoming an executive at Universal Pictures when he was only twenty-one and a vice president at MGM at age twenty-four. Responsible for such movie classics as *Ben-Hur* and *Mutiny on the Bounty,* he was driven to overcome his physical limitations. He died of pneumonia, not heart failure, at the age of thirty-seven.

HENRI DE TOULOUSE-LAUTREC (1864–1901), French painter

His parents were first cousins (a union at that time not forbidden by the Catholic Church), and Henri suffered from a kind of dwarfism that caused innumerable ailments during his childhood. In addition to regular illnesses such as colds and measles, Henri suffered terribly painful toothaches (probably caused by genetic defects in his sinus cavities) and chronic debilitating pain and weakness in his legs. Throughout his childhood, he frequently relied on canes, crutches, splints, and a wheelchair. When he was in his early teens, Henri broke one leg, then the other, in two separate accidents, leaving him permanently deformed.

Henri's mother was always in search of a cure of her son. On a number of occasions she took him to the miracle site of Lourdes. She took him to bathe in the waters of spas in France and throughout Europe, and she entrusted his care to a number of physicians. The boy showed a remarkable amount of courage and never indulged in self-pity. When he was feeling well, he rode horses and his tricycle, went swimming, and engaged in boisterous games with his friends. A charming boy, Henri rarely spoke of his maladies and remained cheerful during his frequent confinements in bed.

In addition to his very small stature, Henri was physically unattractive: his lips and nose were too big for his face; he had a lot of dark body hair; he wore glasses to correct nearsightedness. On one of the few occasions on which he referred to his appearance, Henri drew a funny sketch of himself and said, "Look at that figure, totally lacking in elegance, that fat derrière, that potato-nose. It's not pretty."

ANDY WARHOL (1928–1987), U.S. artist

When he was six years old, Andy contracted scarlet fever and two years later came down with St. Vitus's dance, a disease of the central nervous system. The disease caused his hands to shake and left him with brownish blotches all over his body. Confined to bed for months at a time, the boy read movie magazines and comic books and played with cut-out paper dolls. In grade school the students mercilessly teased and bullied the frail Andy, calling him "Spot" because of his skin blemishes.

In high school Andy was an outsider. Although his overall health had improved, his albino-looking skin was often plagued with acne. The boys snickered at his all-white hair, shrill voice, and hunched posture. Andy, however, was able to form friendships with a few girls who found him to be a bright, entertaining companion.

Andy's saving grace was his talent for drawing. Both teachers and students were impressed by the quality, and quantity, of the sketches he turned out. His artistic ability was the redeeming factor that kept him from becoming an outcast. Andy never forgot his emotionally painful years at school. He once commented, "I wasn't amazingly popular, although I guess I wanted to be, because when I would see the kids telling one another their problems, I felt left out. No one confided in me."

LONERS

ISAAC ASIMOV (1920–1992), Russian-born U.S. science writer

A spindly little child, he was also very bright and knew it. Other kids found him difficult to be around. At school, older children bullied him. His parents, who had emigrated with him to the United States in 1923, had little time to socialize with him. They owned a candy store, which took up most of his father's time.

One of Isaac's favorite places was the kitchen in the back of the candy store, because it had no windows. He could be totally alone there. He liked other enclosed spaces, too, like the furniture display "rooms" in department stores. He was attracted to the newsstands at subway stops underground—he imagined their proprietors lying on cots alone and reading magazines.

Isaac also loved cemeteries, especially the Cemetery of the Evergreens near his house. It was like a park without people—at least without live people. He thought it resembled a closed room, shut off from the outside. He would go there in the summer and read, usually a science fiction magazine, on his "favorite stone benches where [he] could sit under trees with no signs or sounds of human life or human artifacts in any direction."

JOHN DENVER (1943–1997), U.S. singer and songwriter

A military brat, shuttled from air force base to air force base, he felt "lost in America." When his father was stationed in Tucson, John would ride his bike into the Arizona desert, where he played alone, or he would climb a eucalyptus tree and look down on the rest of the world, feeling removed.

In 1957 the family moved to Montgomery, Alabama. When John played guitar and sang for the class at his music teacher's request, his loner status changed somewhat. Other students started to talk to him, and he joined a band. Yet he maintained distance, partly because he abhorred southern racism; he was already a social activist. When the family moved to Fort Worth, Texas, he started to date girls, but it was difficult because he was a year younger than most other kids in his class and too young to drive.

Emotionally fragile, when hurt or irritated or depressed John retreated to his room and played guitar. He was still very much a loner throughout high school. In his senior year, when he gave a party to celebrate the publication of the yearbook, not one person came. He was devastated, even though one of his friends did call to say they were at someone's house and invited him to come over. In his autobiography, *Take Me Home,* he comments that he would have described himself then "as a dot: round and flat, without edges or depth. That's how I felt and that's what I thought others saw, too. Only my music could redeem me."

Did you know that in the third grade, Bruce Springsteen was stuffed into a garbage can by his teacher, a nun?

ALFRED HITCHCOCK (1899–1980), English-born U.S. film director

From the time he was small, he was a cameo player, as he was in his films. He lived on the sidelines of life, a watcher, not a participant. At family gatherings, he sat in a corner quietly. "I was a loner—can't even remember having a playmate," he said. He lived a rich fantasy life in his head and was too reticent to take part in sports. "My exertion is all from the neck up," he once said. "I watch."

At St. Ignatius, a tough Jesuit school, a schoolmate, Robert Goold, remembered him "as a solidly built dumpling of a boy . . . a lonely fat boy who smiled and looked at you as if he could see straight through you."

In his last year at school, Hitchcock became a troublemaker, his nickname "Cocky." He was no longer shy, but still an outsider. With another student, he tormented the much younger Goold, then only nine, by tying him up, pinning a string of firecrackers to his underwear, lighting them, and leaving. When the firecrackers went off, Goold was terrified. However, he did not tell. He later said, "I guess you could say Alfred Hitchcock had a sense of the macabre even at school," but he never went to see a Hitchcock film.

STEVE JOBS (1955–   ), U.S. computer entrepreneur

When Steve was five, he started swimming. He was good at it, reaching the A team at the very competitive Mountain View Dolphins club in California. However, he was not much of a team player. One of the other team members, Mark Wozniak, said that he was "a loner, pretty much of a crybaby." According to Wozniak, Steve cried when he lost a race; "He wasn't one of the guys."

Steve's passion was electronics. He baffled the other kids with his esoteric knowledge. Jeff Eastwood, a neighborhood kid said, "He'd show me things that I couldn't understand with all the electronic gear he'd taken apart, and I'd go home to my dad and say, 'He's lying again.' "

In sixth grade he went to Crittenden, a school filled with the toughest kids in town. Fights broke out regularly. Steve's antics paled next to those of the other kids, and his high intelligence went unnoticed. He was so unhappy he swore he would not return the next year. Aware that he was already a discipline problem, his parents moved so that he could go to another, better school. At the new school, Steve was put on a track for gifted children. His only friend was Bill Fernandez, who later went on to work with him on the Macintosh computer.

Electronics experiments, often conducted in dark garages, provided the perfect escape for these young loners. The two boys hitched up with Steve Wozniak (brother of Mark), a real electronics genius five years older than Fernandez. Jobs and Wozniak became "wireheads," the Silicon Valley term for electronics club members. But even in electronics class, Steve was a loner, off doing something on his own in a corner. He was bright (a "brain") and was attracted to the counterculture (a "hippie"), but he never fit completely into either group. Terri Anzur, one of his classmates, says, "He was a kind of an outsider. In high school everything revolved around what group you were in. If you weren't in a carefully defined group, you weren't anybody. He was an individual in a world where individuality was still a little suspect."

THEODORE KACZYNSKI (1942–   ), U.S. mathematician and Unabomber

He was his parents' firstborn—a jolly, smiling baby—and they adored him. When he was nine months old, however, he was hospitalized for a week because of an allergy. Hospital regulations allowed few visits from parents, and often only for one hour at a time. Teddy came home from the hospital a changed child, detached and unresponsive.

In 1952 the family moved from Chicago to a suburb called Evergreen Park. A neighbor who knew Teddy then describes him as "strictly a loner. This kid didn't play. No. No. He was an old man before his time." Others concur. His only real friend was his younger brother, David, with whom he played and for whom he did kindnesses, like nailing a spool to the bottom of a door so that David, too short to reach the doorknob, could open and close it.

Teddy may have had no friends, but he was very smart. His mother, Wanda, read him articles from *Scientific American* when he was still in grade school. Skipping a grade exacerbated his social problems. In high school, his interests were those of a younger boy. A member of the math club said, "While the math club would sit around talking about the big issues of the day, Ted would be waiting for someone to fart." The relationships he did have tended to be antisocial. He showed one kid how to make a mini-bomb, which blew out two windows in the chemistry classroom. This was not the only explosion the adolescent Teddy was responsible for. His classmates saw him as a nerd, "a walking brain," as one said. Many afternoons and evenings, he would just stay in his room in a depressed mood. At sixteen, he went to Harvard, where he remained aloof and reclusive, foreshadowing his later life as a hermit in a Montana cabin.

LOUIS LEAKEY (1903–1972), African-born British archeologist and anthropologist

He was a premature baby, born in a mud hut at the church missionary station about ten miles outside Nairobi. Both of his parents were missionaries, and Louis grew up among the members of the Kikuyu tribe. With the Kikuyu boys, he learned how to shoot a bow and arrow and how to hunt and trap. Considered a "blood brother," Louis was given the name "Wakuruigi" (Son of the Sparrow Hawk). When he was fourteen, Louis built his own mud hut and lived in it by himself, according to the traditions of the Kikuyu. The young warrior had his own spear and club and spent many hours setting and checking the traps he set in the dense forest that surrounded his home.

The Leakey family returned to England when Louis was sixteen. Placed in a private boys' school, he was at an educational disadvantage, since his schooling in Kenya had been conducted by private tutors and had been limited in scope. His educational shortcomings, however, were minor compared to his inability to fit in with the other students. Instead of being impressed by Louis's adventures in Kenya, the other boys made fun of his Kikuyu accent. They joked about Louis's odd walk, modeled on a walking pattern that enabled the Kikuyu to navigate steep and narrow pathways.

Louis was miserable in school. He was at the mercy of the older boys, who always had some menial task for him to perform, and he felt smothered by rules: how to dress, when to attend classes, what hour to get up, what hour to go to bed. He had no friends and spent his free time studying alone and daydreaming of the days when he had been an equal among the Kikuyu. About his school days, Leakey later wrote, "I was being treated like a child of ten when I felt like a man of twenty, and it made me very bitter."

SINCLAIR LEWIS (1885–1951), U.S. novelist

Both as a child and as an adult, Lewis was always somewhat of a misfit. The son of a doctor in Sauk Centre, Minnesota, Sinclair (called Harry) tried hard to make other children like him, but they either made fun of him or ignored him. Although he was a bright, eager boy, he was also awkward and over-bearing. His classmates would create a make-believe type of game, play for a while, and then lose interest. But Harry would continue playing the game for several days, always trying to impress everyone. Once he organized a Robin Hood Club, making himself the president, but the other boys tossed him out because of his "imaginative exactions."

Harry tried to play various sports, but he either turned in a poor perfor-mance or got hurt. He couldn't dance, wasn't popular with girls, and was often the victim of practical jokes. In high school he was a good student and was even elected president of the debating club, but he remained an outsider. As a result, Harry spent a lot of time alone. He read all types of books and diligently recorded his daily activities and insights in a diary.

The first American ever to win the Nobel Prize for Literature, Lewis was both famous and rich during his lifetime. Yet he could never form close per-sonal relationships. When the author of *Main Street* died at the age of sixty-six in a clinic in Rome, Italy, neither friends nor family members were there to comfort him.

CHARLES LINDBERGH (1902–1974), U.S. aviator

He loved the outdoors and often went hiking or swimming or boating, but he was usually alone. Since his father was a U.S. congressman, Charles some-times lived in Washington, D.C., but he also grew up on the family farm in Little Falls, Minnesota. By the time he was eighteen years old, Charles had attended eleven different schools. He had no close friends and made no ef-fort to form friendships. In high school he didn't participate in sports activi-ties or clubs and never had a date.

Charles was a mechanical genius. At an early age, he could pull apart and fix farm machinery. He could figure out the number sequence to open com-bination locks and often took apart, then reassembled, the guns in his gun collection (he got his first rifle when he was six). Charles started driving when he was only eleven, and when he was fourteen, he took his mother on a cross-country trip to California in the family car. When the car broke down, he repaired it. Quiet and introspective, Charles spent a lot of time on his hob-bies and collected stamps, toy soldiers, and tin cans.

In 1927, when Lindbergh was twenty-five years old, he became the first aviator to make a solo transatlantic flight (from New York to Paris). "Lucky Lindy" became an American hero overnight, and journalists flocked to Little Falls to dig up the details of his childhood. The reporters interviewed Lind-bergh's teachers and classmates, but no one had any stories to tell. Some peo-ple recalled that Charles was a bit reckless when he drove around on his motorcycle. But most people simply said that he had been a shy boy who kept to himself. Or, as one classmate said, "He was not what could be called a buddy."

JAWAHARLAL NEHRU (1889–1961), Indian political leader
Jawaharlal's father, Motilal, was a lawyer who had very little leisure time to spend with his son. Most of Jawaharlal's cousins were much older than he and had little in common with him. He had a sister, but she was eleven years his junior. In addition, he was schooled at home until he was sixteen. Thus Jawaharlal had no real friends or companions, except for his mother and his tutors.

Jawaharlal spent a lot of time reading and daydreaming. He fantasized that he could fly, all alone and up very high. He once said, "This dream has indeed been a frequent one throughout my life; and sometimes it has been vivid and realistic and the countryside seemed to lie underneath me in a vast pano-rama."

When he went off to school at Harrow, one of Britain's top public schools, Jawaharlal did his best to be sociable but said he was "never an exact fit." He was reserved and intellectual, and most of the other boys were primarily in-terested in sports and games. Nonetheless, the boy who would become the first prime minister of India looked back on his days at Harrow with affection and nostalgia. One of his prize possessions was a book of school songs, which he liked to sing to his grandchildren. Among his favorites were "Forty Years On" and "When Grandpapa's Grandpapa Was in the Lower Lower First."

BEATRIX POTTER (1866–1943), English writer of children's books
The woman who created the immortal characters of Peter Rabbit, Jemima Puddle-Duck, and Squirrel Nutkin grew up in an affluent family in London. Surrounded by servants, nannies, and home tutors, Beatrix had only one childhood companion, her brother Bertram, who was six years younger. Her parents believed that associations with other children would only invite germs and illness, so the Potter children spent a lot of time at home sur-rounded by adults.

Summer vacations, however, spent in Scotland and in the English coun-tryside, were exciting times for Beatrix and Bertram. They collected all sorts of plants and animals and insects (some dead, some alive). After careful ex-amination of their treasures, the children would draw sketches and paint pic-tures of whatever they brought home. Beatrix's renderings were so accurate and beautiful that her parents eventually hired an art teacher to develop the young girl's talent.

While Beatrix was schooled entirely at home, as was not uncommon for girls of her class, Bertram was sent away to boarding school when he was eleven. With her only friend gone, the teenager spent a lot of time alone in her bedroom. She liked to draw and paint and doted on her menagerie of small pets—a rabbit, a few mice, and a hedgehog. She raised a family of snails and wrote down daily observations about them. From time to time she would go to a party hosted by her cousins but felt so socially awkward that she refused to dance or mingle and usually left early. Although Potter never complained about her solitary existence, her diary sometimes provides evidence that she was a depressed, lonely girl. When she was in her late teens, she wrote: "Oh, life, wearisome, disappointing, and yet in many shades so sweet, I wonder why one is so unwilling to let go this old year?—not because it has been joyful, but because I fear its successors—I am terribly afraid of the future."

BRUCE SPRINGSTEEN (1949–   ), U.S. singer and songwriter

He grew up in the working-class community of Freehold, New Jersey, and attended Catholic schools. A loner and an outsider, he wasn't a troublemaker; but he just didn't quite fit in. In high school Bruce's hair was long and shaggy (he was in a rock band), he daydreamed a lot, and he made little effort to blend into the social scene. He was a poor student. When the other kids were engaged in school activities or prowling around town, Bruce was usually alone, playing guitar in his room.

When Bruce was in the third grade, a nun stuffed him in a garbage can "because she told me that's where I belonged." Once, when he was an altar boy, a priest knocked him down the steps of the altar during mass, angry that Bruce was not performing his duties correctly. When his high school graduation drew near, one of Bruce's teachers stood up in the classroom and mocked his long hair: "Class, don't you have any pride in yourselves? Are you going to allow this boy to embarrass you and go to graduation looking like that?"

As Springsteen tours the world, playing to screaming fans in sold-out concert halls, he often tells stories about the old days in New Jersey. The musician who has made it to the covers of *Time* and *Newsweek* once said: "I lived half of my first 13 years in a trance or something. People thought I was weird because I always went around with this look on my face. I was thinking of things, but I was always on the outside, looking in."

CHAPTER SIX

SOCIAL LIFE

"Not anybody and everybody can be your friend. It must be someone as close to you as your skin, someone who imparts color, drama, meaning to your life, however snug and secure it may be."
HENRY MILLER

We ordinarily contemplate our childhood life through a cloud of nostalgia or intensified remembered anguish. Figuring into our remembrances are those other kids we loved—and hated.

Like most of us, the famous had best friends, to whom they told everything. Some of the pairings surprise us; they appear to be mismatches until we look more closely. Take Joan Baez's friendship with a grown man—weird, even sinister, until we see the deep activism that brought them together. Classmates could not understand the basis of the friendship between Calvin Klein and Barry Schwartz, but there was one: business. Some children encountered a hidden part of themselves through friendship; for example, Simone de Beauvoir discovered her propensity to rebel through her fascinating friend Zaza. Others just had best friends—Dolly Parton called her best friend Judy "sis" because "The two of us have been as close as any two sisters could ever hope to be."

Children's love lives may sometimes be sweet, but certainly not always. And yes, we see innocence there. Of his first kiss, Theodore Geisel (Dr. Seuss) said, "I don't know why I kissed Libby, and neither did she." Other first kisses have elements of humor (Alan Alda's braces created too much spit), or perplexity (Burt Reynolds's adolescent French kiss), or just plain delight (Mary Tyler Moore's first kiss). Like most of us, the famous remember their first loves forever. Some kids tended to focus on strange love objects. For example, Louisa May Alcott had a childish infatuation with philosopher Ralph Waldo Emerson, decades older than she; Edgar Allan Poe adored his best friend's mother. And of course, first loves were rarely responsible for first sexual experiences.

BEST FRIENDS

JOAN BAEZ (1941–   ), U.S. singer and civil rights activist

When sixteen-year-old Joan Baez was at a Quaker meeting, she met Ira, a bearded man "with a laugh like a goat," much older than she. He took over some classes at the meetinghouse. His "sermons on the pavement" were mainly about nonviolence, and he read to the students from Lao-tse, the Chinese philosopher: "The is is the was of what shall be."

She and Ira became friends. He came by her house on his bicycle every morning. She ditched first period of high school classes; he was late to work. When Baez's father asked Ira what he saw in a child so young, Ira said that Joan was extraordinary. The tie that bound them was the desire to help change the world. They planned to travel around together to accomplish that goal.

One day, Baez asked Ira to visit Palo Alto High School, where she was a student. The teacher was late to English class, so Ira began to discuss war and nonviolence and life and love with the students. The school administrator called Joan and Ira to his office. After telling them that Ira was not allowed to speak without going through bureaucratic channels, he commanded Joan to go to class. She resisted, claiming that she was learning more by watching the interaction between Ira and the administrator than she would in a classroom. It was an early manifestation of her lifelong rebellion against injustice and senseless conformity.

TRUMAN CAPOTE (1924–1984), U.S. writer

Harper (Nelle) Lee was Truman Capote's best friend when he lived in Monroeville, Alabama, where his promiscuous mother and con man father had left him with relatives. She lived next door. Her immensely obese mother did crossword puzzles, said strange things while aimlessly wandering down the street, and twice tried to drown Nelle in the bathtub. (Each time an older sister saved her.) Both children were lonely; both felt rejected. He was a sissy; she was a tomboy. They spent a good deal of their time in a tree house, acting out stories.

When they grew up, both Truman and Nelle became writers. One of the characters in Lee's novel *To Kill a Mockingbird* resembles the Truman of their childhood: "He wore blue linen shorts that buttoned to his shirt, his hair was snow white and stuck to his head like dandruff; he was a year my senior, but I towered over him. As he told us [an] old tale his blue eyes would lighten and darken; his laugh was sudden and happy; he habitually pulled at a cowlick in the center of his forehead. . . . We came to know him as a pocket Merlin, whose head teemed with eccentric plans, strange longings, and quaint fancies." In turn, for his novel *Other Voices, Other Rooms,* Capote created a character, Idabel, much like Harper Lee. Idabel is a tough tomboy, who calls the protagonist, Joel, "sissy-britches." When Joel, Truman's alter ego, kisses her, she pushes him away.

Harper Lee went with Capote to Kansas to help with the research for what turned out to be *In Cold Blood,* his nonfiction account of the Clutter murders. "It was deep calling to deep," she said, describing their mutual fascination with the crime.

SIMONE DE BEAUVOIR (1908–1986), French writer

Her best friend was Elizabeth Mabille ("Zaza"), whom she met at the Cours Adeline Désir, a Paris Catholic school, when she was ten. Zaza was glamorous and rebellious, an athletic tomboy with short hair, who did cartwheels and splits, rode horses, and played tennis. Zaza's parents were liberal with all their nine children. They let Zaza read literature forbidden to Simone. Zaza had been to Italy.

Mme. de Beauvoir kept her children, Simone and Hélène, enwrapped in French middle-class conformity and piety. M. de Beauvoir, trained as a lawyer, supported the extreme right wing. Simone was beginning to rebel against her bourgeois life when she met Zaza. A witty cynic, Zaza adopted left-of-center attitudes toward money and hypocrisy. She said what Simone thought, and they became close friends.

Once, when Zaza was away, Simone felt as if "the whole world had died." And when Zaza came back, "a thousand bright suns began blazing in my breast." She wrote: "I told myself, 'I needed Zaza!' So that had been my ignorance of the workings of the heart that I hadn't thought of telling myself: 'I miss her.' I needed her presence to realize how much I needed her. . . . I allowed myself to be uplifted by that wave of joy which went on mounting inside me, as violent and fresh as a waterfalling cataract."

Zaza died of an unknown fever, perhaps encephalitis or meningitis, barely out of her teens. On the last page of her autobiography *Memoirs of a Dutiful Daughter,* de Beauvoir wrote, ". . . for a long time I believed that I had paid for my own freedom with her death."

EMILY DICKINSON (1830–1886), U.S. poet

The reclusive poet, who found her world in her backyard, had a childhood best friend named Jane Humphrey, the daughter of a Southwick doctor. They met at Amherst Academy, where Emily was sporadically enrolled, and Jane often visited the Dickinson household as an overnight guest. A letter eleven-year-old Emily wrote to Jane reveals her feelings about the friendship:

". . . I miss you more and more every day, in my study in play at home indeed every where I miss my beloved Jane. I wish you would write to me. I shall think more of it than of a mine of gold . . . what good times we used to have jumping into bed when you slept with me. I do wish you would come to Amherst and make me a great long visit. . . ."

In April 1852, she wrote to Jane again: "I think I love you *more* when spring comes—you know we used to sit in the front door, afternoons after school, and the shy little birds would say chirrup, chirrup in the tall cherry trees, and if your dresses rustled, hop frightened away; and there used to be some farmer cutting down a tree in the woods, and you and I, sitting there, could hear his sharp ax ring. You won't forget it, Jennie, Oh no, I'm sure you won't, for when you are old and gray, it will be a sweet thing to think of, through the long winter's day! And I *know I'll* remember it, for it's so precious to me that I doubt if I *could* forget it, ever, if I should try."

CALVIN KLEIN (1942–   ), U.S. clothing designer

Growing up in the Bronx, Calvin Klein and Barry Schwartz were buddies from the time they were five or six. Barry has said, "I spent my whole life growing up in Calvin's house. Calvin spent the same amount of time in my house. We'd sleep over, we'd eat together, we'd meet after school."

In many ways the two could not have been more different. Calvin walked as if he were on a trampoline, did not have the standard Bronx accent, and seemed a little girlish. Barry was short, athletic, tough, and quite traditionally masculine. Calvin was a clotheshorse, Barry was not. The friendship puzzled their other friends. "The two didn't share anything in common that I could see," said Alan Cohen, one of Barry's childhood friends. But they did have one thing in common: From the time they were kids, they wanted to get rich. They planned enterprises—a chain of pet stores or supermarkets—with Barry designated to run the business and Calvin to supply the ideas. At age six, they had a business selling iced tea on the streets; at age eight, it was newspapers.

After he became an adult, Barry took over his father's Harlem Sundial Supermarket and made a success of it. Though Barry had little interest in fashion, he financially backed Calvin's first attempt to put together a line of clothes. In 1968 the two became partners in Calvin Klein, Inc. Today they each own 43 percent of the company. In 1996 the company's net profits were $41 million. The two friends have achieved their mutual childhood dream—they are both rich.

ROCKY MARCIANO (1923–1969), U.S. boxer

Eugene Sylvester, Izzy Gold, and Rocky Marciano. They called themselves "The Terrific Three," a term they got from a comic strip. The grammar school pals from the Ward 2 neighborhood in Brockton, Massachusetts, spent endless hours together. When they weren't playing baseball or football, they could usually be found in their clubhouse, which they built in Izzy's dirt cellar.

Eugene was the leader of the group and always seemed to instigate trouble. Izzy was the risk taker who loved to gamble. And Rocky was the somewhat shy star athlete who dreamed of being a professional baseball player and who got into plenty of fistfights in defense of Eugene and Izzy.

From grammar school through high school, the gang had lots of adventures but never got into any serious trouble. They sent in a false alarm to the fire department, stole quarts of milk from the porches of wealthy families, shoplifted small items from local stores. When Rocky, who had no aspirations about being a boxer, was goaded into a fight, he usually won. As Eugene once said, "Once Rocky was enraged, he was like an animal."

Although the youths worked hard at lots of odd jobs, money was scarce, and they constantly dreamed of becoming rich. When fourteen-year-old Izzy won hundreds of dollars in a crap game in "Gamblers' Woods," a clandestine outdoor haven for adult gamblers, The Terrific Three were giddy with excitement. They dug a hole in the clubhouse and hid the money for a month until the annual weeklong Brockton Fair. Then they went on a madcap spending spree—riding the rides over and over again, buying souvenirs, eating everything in sight. Until the last dime was gone, they felt like the richest kids on earth.

HENRY MILLER (1891–1980), U.S. writer

The novels that made him famous were full of explicit sex, but Miller also wrote two nonfiction books, filled with portraits of his childhood and adult friends. For Miller friends were the center of his life, and friendship was a lifelong bond. In *My Bike & Other Friends* he wrote, "Not anybody and everybody can be your friend. It must be someone as close to you as your skin, someone who imparts color, drama, meaning to your life, however snug and secure it may be."

Miller met his very first friend, Stanley Borowski (called "Stasiu") when the boys were five years old. They were an inseparable, but odd, combination. Henry, the son of a tailor, had fashionable clothes and plenty of toys and was a good student. Stanley, an orphan, was being raised by an uncle, a barber who was a drunk and often beat the boy and chased him through the neighborhood with an open razor in his hand. Stanley was a good liar and thief, had a terrible temper, and was the leader of the neighborhood gang.

Henry, no angel himself, seemed to revel in Stanley's audacity and sense of adventure. As little boys, the twosome played card games, cops and robbers, board games, and war games with toy soldiers and cannons. As they grew older together, the boys got into fistfights with kids from other neighborhoods and hung around outside a local burlesque house to listen to the patrons telling dirty jokes.

Despite his street urchin appearance, Stanley was polite to adults, had good manners, worked hard at numerous odd jobs, and had a soft spot for the underdog. In addition, he had a wonderful imagination and liked to concoct romantic tales of distant places. He and Henry had long talks about travel, religion, and sex. It was Stanley who took it upon himself to tell Henry that Santa Claus was a myth. And it was Stanley who corrected Henry's stork-delivers-the-baby theory by telling him that babies "come from the mother's belly." However, how a baby got into, and out of, a mother's belly was a question that Stanley, surprisingly, couldn't answer.

DOLLY PARTON (1946–   ), U.S. singer and songwriter
Dolly met Judy Ogle when they were in the third grade. They grew up together in the Smoky Mountains of Tennessee. Both were in the high school band (Dolly hauled around the snare drum), and the girls also played together on sports teams. Judy had bright red hair, green eyes, and a lively spirit. She helped Dolly through a lot of tough times in high school.

Dolly, according to her own recollection, was "actively disliked" in school by the other girls because of her sexy clothes, bleached hair, heavy makeup, and "unearned reputation for being a tramp." The boys ogled what they called the "headlights" on her five-foot-two frame. But Judy laughed at her jokes, wrote down the words to songs Dolly composed, and remained ever loyal. Indeed, the two are still best friends. Dolly calls Judy "sis" or "sissy" because, she says, "The two of us have been as close as any two sisters could ever hope to be."

DAN RATHER (1931–   ), U.S. broadcast journalist
He grew up outside Houston, Texas, the son of an oil pipeliner. Little Danny Rather loved trains and sports and outdoor adventures. From the age of three his best friend was Georgie Hoyt, who was a year older and lived across the street from the Rathers. In his autobiography, *I Remember,* the CBS news anchor says, "Friendships were true friendships then. Georgie was my leader and protector. I always felt safe when he was around. Besides, he was stimulating company."

The boys camped out, swung from grapevines in the woods, and pulled off a number of stunts, particularly on Halloween, which is also Dan's birthday. They dreamed of far-off places and made canoes and rafts to carry them to their destinations someday. They biked to the railroad tracks to watch the Sam Houston Zephyr streak by on its way from Houston to Dallas.

Dan and Georgie spent a lot of time on the flat end of the corrugated tin roof of a neighbor's barn. As Rather recalls, "Georgie and I perched on the roof, jabbering and dreaming on and on, often from the time school let out until after sunset. Time was limitless and we never, never ran out of things to talk about. Or to pretend."

GERALDO RIVERA (1943–   ), U.S. broadcast journalist
Raised on Long Island, New York, the future talk show host attended West Babylon High School, where he was a cocaptain of the football team and belonged to a car club called the Valve Grinders (he owned a 1947 Chevy convertible he had bought for $25). In his 1991 autobiography, *Exposing Myself,* he said he "fit in" somewhere between the All-American Bandstanders ("the dream of every parent and teacher") and the Hapless Hoods ("incorrigibly blue collar and usually headed to an early exit from academia").

The half-Puerto Rican and half-Jewish teenager had two best friends in his junior and senior years of high school, Frankie DeCecco and Vic Furio. DeCecco, who looked like pop singer Frankie Avalon, was a sharp dresser; he and Geraldo owned matching black mohair suits, which they wore on their excursions into New York City. Before graduation, Geraldo made a bet with Frankie that he (Geraldo) would be successful in ten years and would be earning a salary of thirty thousand dollars. The boys agreed to meet in ten years at the top of the Empire State Building (the idea came from the movie *An Affair to Remember*) to settle the wager. When the time came, Geraldo won, and Frankie had to pay for an Italian dinner.

Vic Furio, Rivera's other best friend, liked to hang out off Oak Beach on the south shore of Long Island. According to Rivera, "Most of our surfing days were spent roaming the dunes, our boards under our arms, passing ourselves off to the ladies as smooth surf-dudes. Even then, I understood the importance of self-promotion."

DYLAN THOMAS (1914–1953), Welsh poet

When he was fourteen, Dylan was standing in the schoolyard when another student, a stranger, for no reason gave him a big push. Dylan responded by throwing a stone at the boy, and in an instant the two were fighting. When the bout of fisticuffs was over, the stranger had a bloody nose and Dylan had a black eye. The stranger, Daniel Jenkin Jones, became Dylan's lifelong friend.

Like Dylan, Daniel loved to write poetry. Together the boys wrote more than two hundred poems—some funny, some serious. In their collaborations, they had an alternate line arrangement: Daniel wrote the odd-numbered lines, and Dylan composed the even-numbered lines. Their pen name was "Walter Bram" (*bram* means "fart" in Welsh). In addition to poetry writing, the boys played word games, listened to music, and put together "joke concerts."

> ## "A man, if he is any good, never gets over being a boy."
>
> —*Sherwood Anderson (from* Tar)

Although their long friendship had its share of difficulties, Dylan said that Daniel was always willing to listen to Dylan read one of his new compositions, whether it was a poem or an essay or a joke. Daniel, said Dylan, "listened wisely, like a boy aged a hundred, his head on one side and his spectacles shaking on his swollen nose. . . . Nobody had ever listened like that before." When Dylan Thomas's excessive drinking led to his early death at the age of thirty-nine, Daniel Jones was in charge of the funeral arrangements.

FRANK LLOYD WRIGHT (1867–1959), U.S. architect

Frank was walking home from school one day when he saw a group of classmates tormenting and ridiculing Robie Lamp, a boy they called "cripple" because he had lost the use of both of his legs to polio. The bullies had snatched Robie's crutches and had buried him in a huge pile of leaves. Frank mustered up his courage, drove the boys off, and helped Robie to his feet. From then on, the two fourteen-year-olds became good friends.

Together the boys roamed the streets of Madison, Wisconsin. They read books, played music—Frank on viola, Robie on violin—sang Gilbert and Sullivan songs. Frank had a small printing press, which he shared with Robie, and the two boys also sketched out designs of waterwheels and catamarans and all sorts of technological inventions. They built a long bobsled on double runners and created magnificent multicolored kites with long, fantastic tails. And they shared secrets, especially those about girls they worshipped from afar.

When Wright became an architect, he designed a home for Robie. Located in Madison, the house was built of cream-colored bricks, had a flower garden on the roof, and was engineered to meet Robie's physical needs. Robie lived in the home until he died at age forty-four.

FIRST KISS

ALAN ALDA (1936–   ), U.S. actor

He was thirteen, wore braces, and was in love with Antoinette (Toni) Dell' Olio, whose father owned show horses and hobnobbed with a Hollywood crowd. They had met when he was ten or eleven. It had been difficult for them to get to know each other because of the tough rules at her school, Villa Cabrini Academy in Burbank, California, where she was a boarder. For instance, she could play ball with Alan only by standing on one side of the school wall and throwing the ball over to him.

Did you know that Theodore Geisel (Dr. Seuss) said of his first kiss: "I don't know why I kissed Libby, and neither did she"?

She came to his thirteenth birthday party. They danced to "The Girl That I Marry," from *Annie Get Your Gun.* At the line, "and I'll whisper sweet nothings in her ear," Alan whispered in Toni's ear, "nothing, nothing, nothing." At the end of the dance, he kissed her. As Toni recalled later, "So when Alan's lips met mine in that special moment, because of his mouthful of silver [braces], his saliva ran down my face." She waited until he wasn't looking to wipe her mouth off.

JUDY COLLINS (1939–   ), U.S. singer

When she was four, the family moved from Seattle to Los Angeles, where her blind father had gotten a job working for NBC as a radio performer. She walked to and from Nora Sterry School on Sawtelle Boulevard, past the Lark Ellen Home for Boys. She would stop to watch the boys playing baseball. Some of them went to her school, so she was invited to the home's Hallowe'en hayride. The ride went to a mountain lodge, where she, with about a hundred other children, bobbed for apples. On the way back to Los Angeles, a boy demanded that she close her eyes. Then he kissed her. When she opened her eyes, he said, "Do you know what that was?" She said no, but she did know. As she says in her autobiography, *Trust Your Heart,* "It was the beginning of trouble."

MILES DAVIS (1926–1991), U.S. musician

At his sixth birthday party, or maybe his seventh, one of the pretty girls that he kissed was Velma Brooks. He kissed her with too much enthusiasm, according to his sister Dorothy. She told on him to their mother, who commanded their father to stop Miles from kissing Velma. Their father said, "If he was kissing on a boy like Junior Quinn, now that would be something to tell. But kissing on Velma Brooks ain't nothing to tell; that's what the boy supposed to be doing."

His sister, miffed, replied that someone had better stop Miles before he gave Velma a baby. His mother told him later that it was bad to kiss a girl with so much gusto; then she slapped him.

SANDRA DEE (1944–   ), U.S. actor

Her screen test for *The Restless Years,* when she was only twelve, but looked much older, called for her to walk down a path with twenty-year-old heart-throb John Saxon and kiss him at a certain tree. When they reached the tree, she called for the cameras to stop filming because she had to go to the bathroom. After she did this for the third time a woman in the crew got her to confess that she had never been kissed before. After the woman explained to the whole crew, Sandra "threw herself into it" and found the kissing easy. The test was successful. Her grandmother saw the test and said, "Wherever did you learn to kiss a boy?" The truth? Sandra said that kissing a man was like kissing a wall. Saxon said that he felt a little awkward about the scene, that she "seemed young and kind of delicate and perhaps inexperienced."

THEODORE GEISEL (DR. SEUSS) (1904–1991), U.S. writer and illustrator

When he was in high school in Springfield, Massachusetts, the famous writer-illustrator of *Cat in the Hat* and other children's books loved a girl named Thelma to distraction. He loved her, he said, "right down to the bottom of my boots." Who was she? Probably Thelma Lester, who was in the senior class play and a member of the debating club. The first girl he kissed was *not* Thelma, however; it was Libby Elsborg. He later said, "I don't know why I kissed Libby, and neither did she."

Did you know that because of Alan Alda's braces, his first kiss left his date with saliva running down her face?

MARY TYLER MOORE (1936–   ), U.S. actor

The world knows her as the all-American girl next door because of her phenomenally successful portrayals of Laurie Petrie on *The Dick Van Dyke Show* in the 1960s and Mary Richards on *The Mary Tyler Moore Show* in the 1970s. Although Moore has suffered far more hardships in real life than her TV alter egos ever did, her first kiss would undoubtedly be the envy of both of her sitcom characters.

Mary and Jack were both eleven and went to the same parochial school in Los Angeles. Jack, "a diminutive God" with big blue eyes and a beautiful smile, used a rose-smelling pomade on his hair. He was very popular; all the girls, including Mary, had a crush on him. The kiss took place at a picnic for the school's altar boys. As Moore tells it: "We kissed a full frontal lip-to-lip kiss. I was done for. Fireworks, heartbeats, streamers, and some kind of stringed instrument. I was to be forever changed in that moment. I was as filled with pleasure and validation by that kiss as any that would follow in adulthood."

BURT REYNOLDS (1936–   ), U.S. actor

According to Burt, his "first long, long kiss" happened when he was about fifteen. He and Margie, a cheerleader, were sitting under a tree in a park. He says, "Our lips met, pressed together, and it was heaven. Locked in passionate embrace, we mashed faces for what seemed like eternity. If I had died then, I would've been happy." Burt thought Margie was a pretty experienced kisser, but when she put her tongue in his mouth ("almost choked me to death"), he questioned her sophistication. Later on, his friend Mo explained to the naive Burt that Margie had French-kissed him.

H. NORMAN SCHWARZKOPF (1934–   ), U.S. general

As a young teenager, Norman was enrolled for a short period in a Swiss boarding school in Geneva. The fact that he played fullback on the soccer team gave him some social status, and an older girl named Claudine fell for him. One afternoon she asked Norman to take a walk with her and steered him by a particular tree where couples were always supposed to kiss. In his autobiography, the general wrote, "I'm sure that Claudine, being a sophomore and French, expected a passionate French kiss. But what she got was a mere peck from my puckered lips. That was it for romance; she dropped me the next day."

FIRST LOVE

LOUISA MAY ALCOTT (1832–1888), U.S. writer

The object of young Louisa's affections was the great Ralph Waldo Emerson (1803–1882), the "Sage of Concord," nearly thirty years her senior. In 1845, Emerson helped the poverty-stricken Alcott family find a house, Hillside (now Wayside), in Concord. The Alcotts were able to buy it only because Louisa's mother had inherited money. Louisa's father, Bronson, a transcendentalist like Emerson, tried to live his utopian beliefs but found it very difficult to support his family.

For three years the Alcotts were neighbors of Emerson and Henry David Thoreau. Louisa took lessons with Thoreau and her father. She also had the run of the Emerson house and spent hours in his library reading. Had Emerson known, he might have regretted his generosity. One of the books that Louisa read told the story of a girl, Bettine, who worshipped the poet Goethe. It fired up Louisa's already fertile imagination, and she began to work up a similar romantic ardor for Emerson. She often thought of him as she sat in a cherry tree watching the moon rise, even though the owls frightened her as they swooped by.

The shy and awkward girl, just entering adolescence, expressed her love by leaving bouquets on Emerson's doorstep and by singing a serenade in German beneath his window, her voice so low that he could not possibly have heard her. She also wrote letters to him that she never sent.

Emerson had no idea that he had inspired such passionate feelings. In 1848 the Alcotts, unable to make a living in Concord, moved to Boston, where Louisa's mother had found work as an official visitor to the poor. Years later, when Louisa confessed her girlhood infatuation to Emerson, he asked to see the letters, but she had already burned them.

JAMES BALDWIN (1924–1987), U.S. writer

Delicate and nurturing, young Baldwin took care of his eight younger siblings like a mother. He hated his preacher stepfather, but he himself was a young minister at a Pentecostal church. Impressed by Jimmy's talent, Countee Cullen, the black poet, befriended him.

Confused in his sexuality, Jimmy was both attracted to boys and drawn to girls—in fact, he contracted gonorrhea from a girl. At sixteen, Jimmy fell in love with a Harlem racketeer who was then in his late thirties. The racketeer seemed to represent a departure from the path on which this cultured young black boy was set. Four years before his death, Baldwin said, "Even now, I sometimes wonder what on earth his friends could be thinking, confronted with stingy-brimmed, mustachioed, razor-toting Poppa and skinny, pop-eyed Me when he walked me (rarely) into various shady joints, I drinking gingerale, he drinking brandy. . . . I know that he was showing me off and wanted his friends to be happy for him." The racketeer passed Jimmy off as a young relative, though he was not black himself. Jimmy showed him his secret poetry.

Gossip about his relationship with an underworld figure was undermining Jimmy's reputation as a preacher. Jimmy loved to be loved, and, truth be told, he loved the racketeer "in a boy's way," but he was conflicted about the "sinful relationship." He ended the affair. Shortly afterward, he stopped preaching, too. Yet forty years later, he wrote, "I will be grateful to that man until the day I die."

GIOVANNI CASANOVA (1725–1798), Italian lover and adventurer

When he was eleven, Casanova lived with the family of a priest, Dr. Gozzi, and there he met Bettina, the priest's sister, seven years older than he. She was in charge of taking care of him; she washed his clothes, his hair, and even the rest of his body. Though she encouraged him to make advances to her, Casanova, whose name later became synonymous with profligacy, was too innocent and shy to respond!

She told him his thighs needed washing and proceeded to clean them, along with his genitals, until he had an orgasm. He was afraid that he had somehow committed a grievous sin, one that would reflect on her. He saw her as an angel but eventually decided that she too felt desire, being a weak female, and he decided to save her soul.

However, before he could accomplish his goal, Casanova found Bettina in bed with a hairy fifteen year old and thought about killing both of them. Before he got around to it, Bettina contracted smallpox and passed the disease on to Casanova. When both were well, his love for her was over, though he always remembered her with great affection.

GERARD DEPARDIEU (1948–   ), French actor

Though Gérard Depardieu's hometown, Châteauroux, was located in a backwater of France, it boasted a U.S. military base under the aegis of NATO. His family was impoverished, and life at home was sometimes grim. At the age of thirteen, Gérard left school and went to work as an apprentice printer. He looked older than he was. Standing nearly six feet tall and weighing 155 pounds, he wore his T-shirt sleeves rolled up to show his muscles and kept his hair long. He smoked Gitanes.

Ronnie, his first real love, was an African American he met roller-skating at the base. She was tall, with a mouth he described as "magnificent." They skated, holding hands. Once in a while they stopped to drink a soda or to kiss behind the rink. He could not begin to tell her how he felt. To his biographer, he said, "Her lips were so soft and I could see a shine in her eyes, and I knew what I felt was love. But it was impossible to communicate to her my feelings." Once an American boy, Billy, approached them while they were necking and said, "Never do that, Gérard. Black is black, and white is white." The remark brought home to Gérard the horror of American racism; he never forgot it—or Ronnie.

ELIZABETH II (1926–   ), British monarch

The grave and dutiful Princess Elizabeth was thirteen when she fell in love with her husband-to-be, Philip, her second cousin. It happened at Dartmouth Naval College in Devon, the king's base in World War II, which the royal family had come to visit. An outbreak of mumps and chickenpox among the cadets confined them to the house of the commanding officer. The two princesses, Elizabeth and her younger sister, Margaret, were bored. Then eighteen-year-old Philip, a navy cadet, arrived. According to the princesses' nanny-governess, Marion Crawford ("Crawfie"), he was "a fair-haired boy, rather like a Viking, with a sharp face and piercing blue eyes." After the three young people had played with clockwork trains, Philip suggested "having some real fun jumping the nets" at the tennis courts. Crawfie later said, "She [Elizabeth] never took her eyes off him the whole time. I thought he showed off a good deal, but the little girls were much impressed. Lilibet said, 'How good he is Crawfie! How high he can jump!'" The visit over, the royal family boarded the royal yacht and sailed away while the cadets followed, rowing small boats. Philip was the last to give up. Elizabeth "watched him fondly through an enormous pair of binoculars."

After the meeting, Philip showed up at some royal occasions when he was not at sea. With his little green sports car, he cut a dashing figure. Elizabeth kept his photograph on her bedroom mantelpiece. In 1943, he came to see her play Prince Charming in *Aladdin*. Elizabeth made her entrance by jumping out of a laundry basket dressed in a kimono and silk pantaloons and later tap-danced and sang. Crawford had "never seen Lilibet more animated. There was a sparkle about her none of us had ever seen before."

Philip said to his captain, "my uncle Dickie has ideas for me; he thinks I could marry Princess Elizabeth" and when asked if he cared for her said, "Oh yes, very. I write to her every week." In 1946, he proposed to her, and they were married in November 1947 in Westminster Abbey.

HENRY MILLER (1891–1980), U.S. writer

Known to many as the author of "dirty books," Miller filled his novels with graphic sex scenes. His bestseller *Tropic of Cancer,* published in 1934, was banned in the United States until 1961, when Miller was seventy. Married five times, Miller called his novels "autobiographical romances"; his critics called his works pornographic and misogynistic.

When he was sixteen, Henry fell madly in love with Cora Seward, a girl in his high school. He never asked her out and mostly adored her from a distance. Occasionally at parties he would ask her to dance, becoming so nervous that his whole body trembled. Party games like "Kiss the Pillow" and "Post Office" filled him with both excitement and fear. For three or four years, every night after dinner, Henry would take a long walk to Cora's house and hope to catch a glimpse of her in the parlor window.

His love for her was chaste and idealized, and he marveled at the fact that he never thought of her as a sexual partner. When Cora married, Miller was devastated. Many years later, he wrote, "I have often said, and I repeat it now, that on my dying bed, Cora will probably be the last one I shall think of. I may die with her name on my lips."

Did you know that Louisa May Alcott's first love was Ralph Waldo Emerson, thirty years her senior?

EDGAR ALLAN POE (1809–1849), U.S. poet and short-story writer

His father abandoned him when he was a year old, and his mother died when he was two. Raised by John Allan, a wealthy merchant in Richmond, Virginia, Poe was an intelligent, athletic boy who did well in school and was liked by both classmates and teachers. The boy who would become "the master of the macabre" viewed women, especially his deceased mother, as angelic figures, and he was very susceptible to female charms.

When Edgar was thirteen, he met Jane Craig Stanard, the mother of his friend Rob. The very first words she spoke to him, according to Poe, "so penetrated the sensitive heart of the orphan boy as to deprive him of the power of speech, and, for a time, almost of consciousness itself." Several years later, when Mrs. Stanard died, Poe was distraught and claimed that he often went to visit her grave. As an adult, he said that one of his most famous poems, "To Helen," was really inspired and dedicated to Jane Craig Stanard, "the first, purely ideal love of my soul."

RONALD REAGAN (1911–   ), U.S. president

In his autobiography Reagan wrote: "Perhaps it was love at first sight, I'm not sure. . . . Her name was Margaret Cleaver and, like my mother, she was short, pretty, auburn haired, and intelligent. For almost six years of my life I was sure she was going to be my wife. I was very much in love."

Margaret was the daughter of the minister of Ron's church and was also in his high school class. On warm summer afternoons he would take her on canoe rides in the river near his home in Dixon, Illinois. In the canoe Ron would take a windup Victrola to play one of his favorite records, "Ramona." Margaret (Ron called her "Mugs") was the first girl he ever kissed. The couple went to the same college, and Ron gave Margaret his fraternity pin and, later, an engagement ring.

After college the couple drifted apart. They broke up after Margaret decided to take an extended vacation to France and fell in love with another man (whom she later married) while on her trip. She wrote a letter to Ron, told him of her new relationship, and enclosed his fraternity pin and engagement ring. He later said, "Margaret's decision shattered me, not so much, I think, because she no longer loved me, but because I no longer had anyone to love."

WALTER WINCHELL (1897–1972), U.S. journalist
Walter grew up in Harlem and at age thirteen quit school to sing and dance with a vaudeville show that was touring the United States. A handsome boy with big blue eyes, he earned fifteen dollars a week and sent a third of his earnings to his mother to help support his family. When he had been with the vaudeville show less than a year, he was fired for allegedly breaking a prop vase (he was innocent). Depressed and scared, Walter walked outside the theater, sat in a gutter, and cried. To his rescue came Irene Martin, one of the show's top performers; she listened to his side of the story and promptly got him reinstated.

Irene was eighteen and one of the most beautiful girls Walter had ever seen. When she smiled, he said, "the whole world lighted up." While on tour, Walter couldn't do enough for Irene; he carried her suitcases, ran errands for her. When the vaudeville troupe stayed in hotels, Walter got a room next to Irene's and often slept on the floor outside her door to be sure she was safe. He said, "I worried so much that someone might molest or bother her that I became her self-appointed G-man." When the show ended its tour, the two parted; Walter was very depressed. Many years later, when Winchell had become a celebrity, he tried to contact Irene but she didn't respond to his phone calls. A mutual friend told him, "She wants you to remember her as she was."

FIRST SEXUAL EXPERIENCE

JACKIE COOPER (1922–   ), U.S. actor
Jackie Cooper, Skippy in the *Our Gang* comedies, was "America's Boy," our perpetual pouting child. But his introduction to sex came early, when he was thirteen. His instructor was a twenty-year-old woman, who lived next door. In the morning, after her little brother left for school and her mother for work, Jackie would go over to the woman's house and talk to her. She would still be in her nightgown, a revealing one, and they would talk about sex, or rather, he would ask questions and she, laughing, would answer them. Finally she took him off to her bedroom to teach him more than words could say.

The affair went on for several weeks. However, his mother finally figured out what was going on, and that was the end of that.

Jackie had other relationships with women in his teenage years. He met and dated Judy Garland, while she, unbeknownst to him, lusted for bandleader Artie Shaw. He engaged in afternoon groping with his mother's friend, Mrs. Martin, and had a short affair with a chorus girl. At seventeen he made sultry, kinky love with love goddess Joan Crawford (then in her thirties), who bathed and powdered him and posed in front of him in high heels, a garter belt, a large hat, and not much else.

BOBBY DARIN (1936–1973), U.S. singer and actor

Bobby Darin, then a high school virgin, caught his stepfather, Carmine (Charlie) Maffia, at home in bed with a woman not his mother. The rest of the family were supposedly away for the summer, staying at a resort on Staten Island. Bobby had his own key to the house, so he was able to surprise the couple in flagrante. Charlie said (in his version of the event), "It's about time he [Bobby] got fixed up." The woman agreed, and Charlie left the room, figuring that if he let his stepson have sex with his girlfriend, then Bobby wouldn't tell. After a while, the woman came into the kitchen. "He's pretty good," she said. Charlie replied, "Well, he's green, you know. I think you took his cherry." She agreed. Bobby came in and said, "Boy, what I've been missing! Is it really this good?"

Charlie warned Bobby, whose heart was weakened by rheumatic fever, that he should "go easy . . . it takes a lot out of you." Bobby replied, "What a way to die!"

Even after Bobby became a singer, famous for hits like "Dream Lover," he and his stepfather shared women. Charlie would start things off, and then Bobby would come naked into the room, saying, "Honey, how about this?" and jump into bed with them.

JAMES DEAN (1931–1955), U.S. actor

At nine, James Dean lost his beloved mother, Mildred, to uterine cancer. She had taught him to play the violin, engaged him in games of make-believe, and painted with him. They had their own private vocabulary and were unusually close. Every night when she was dying, he put a finger on her eyelid to make sure that she was asleep. He never got over her death.

After she died, James's father, Winton Dean, not knowing what else to do, gave his son to his sister and her husband, Ortense and Marcus Winslow. All at once, the boy had lost both parents.

In Fairmount, Indiana, James lived on the Winslows' farm. He continued to paint and act, and he dreamed about being in the movies. When he was about ten, a neighbor told Ortense that Jimmy was "too fair for a boy." But though James was not typical in every way, he fit, roughly, the profile of a Fairmount teenager: He chased cows on his motorcycle, played basketball, and was a hurdle jumper on the track team. He dated girls, but not seriously.

Then he met handsome James DeWeerd, a Fairmount Wesleyan minister in his thirties, who had refined tastes like those of James's mother. DeWeerd had traveled in Europe and loved poetry. He also loved watching boys skinny-dipping in a YMCA swimming pool. DeWeerd entertained James at candlelit dinners, ending the evening with films of bullfights, music, or conversation. He was probably James Dean's first lover. The two had a sexual, romantic relationship, as DeWeerd admitted years later to a newspaper reporter, but of course it would have been disastrous for either of them to have mentioned it in the conventional town of Fairmount.

URI GELLER (1946–   ), Israeli psychic

After the death of her husband, Uri Geller's mother ran a hotel in Nicosia, Cyprus. One day two sisters, Eva and Ingrid, checked in. They were part of a dance troupe that was brave enough to perform in spite of the fighting be-tween Turks and Greeks then going on on the island. This is how Geller, then sixteen, described Eva: "Eva was really beautiful. She was Austrian or Ger-man, if I remember right. She had short black hair cut in a French style, and she had a wonderful perfumed smell about her."

On a late hot afternoon, Uri and Eva were watching television in the lobby. She drank several beers and then, a little tipsy, went to her room to change into her bathing suit. She called Uri into her room, where she stood half-clothed in a brief bathing suit and asked Uri to help her close the bra. Heart pounding, he tried, but failed, not knowing how to do it.

Eva turned around and tore off the bra, then embraced Uri, falling back on the bed. As he said, "I tried to act very experienced and worldly, but all I knew about this was what I had learned from pictures and movies." After they had sex, she said she was sorry. He said, "Don't tell my mother about it."

BUSTER KEATON (1895–1966), U.S. comedian and actor

Buster Keaton's father did not want him to become involved with local girls in Muskegon, Michigan, where the family was staying. Instead, he said, he would take Buster to a brothel that he knew was safe. So of course sixteen-year-old Buster, who starred with his father in their vaudeville act, did become involved with a local girl. He met her at a neighbor boy's house, where they first made molasses taffy and then went on to more exciting activities. She was, he said later, "cute as a bug's ear and dying for experience." Both boys had sex with her, after which they went to a soda fountain for banana splits. On their way home, with Buster at the wheel of his Peerless, they were nearly overtaken by a Model T Ford containing the sheriff and the girl's mother. Buster managed to outrun it. He stayed hidden in a cabin in the woods for two days. Meanwhile, the mother and the sheriff approached Buster's father, Joe, famous for his temper, with their complaints. On the attack, Joe questioned the girl's morals as well as the mother's. The sheriff found the confrontation funny and left. The mother gave up. Buster got a scolding.

JOHN LENNON (1940–1980), English singer and songwriter

In his Beatle biography, *The Lives of John Lennon*, author Albert Goldman states that John's first sexual experience happened when he was fifteen. Ac-cording to Goldman, the object of John's desire was "a very sexy girl, with a body that would give a teenage boy the bends." The girl was the same age as John and wore her hair in a long ponytail. Before he became involved with her, John once shouted at her, "Oh, there's horseface! Horse's tail and horse's face!"

As a teenager, John was a rebel and a troublemaker who was often on the edge of expulsion from school. Yet one of his girlfriends said that he was very romantic and often wrote beautiful poetry.

BURT REYNOLDS (1936–   ), U.S. actor

Burt was fourteen and his partner was in her mid-forties. He was from a lower-middle-class family in Riviera Beach, Florida; she was a wealthy so-cialite from the nearby, upscale Palm Beach. They met when Burt stopped to admire a model of a three-masted schooner in the window of her antique store. Blonde, beautiful, and friendly, she invited him to dinner at her home.

After several innocent dinners, Burt was seduced by the woman he later said "made me very, very happy." In his autobiography, Reynolds tells of his first encounter: "After dinner, she brushed my cheek with her lips, innocently, seemingly by accident. But it wasn't an accident. . . . It was my first time making love, and I couldn't have wished for anyone better to be with. Gentle, tender, and smart enough to make things last for what seemed like forever, she made me feel godlike. Of course, at that age, you're perpetually like a marble statue. From then on, she seduced me in countless ways. . . . By the end of the summer I was starting to feel like I had the keys to the kingdom."

MAE WEST (1893–1980), U.S. actor

She was provocative, flamboyant, and she oozed sexuality. Dressed in satin clothes, feather boas, platform shoes, and outrageous blonde wigs, the voluptuous Mae had an endless supply of one-liners like "My ego is breakin' records."

She grew up in Brooklyn, had very little schooling, and was a child star in vaudeville. According to Mae, she decided to lose her virginity before puberty so that she could experiment without risking pregnancy. Her first lover was a young male teacher who gave her music and dance lessons. The sexual episode happened on a staircase in the vestibule of her home, while her parents were upstairs. Because the teacher was apprehensive, Mae assured him that she had had sex before. Her account of the experience: "It hurt the first couple of times, but I wasn't frightened. What was there to be frightened of, for God's sake? I felt right doing it, and after the first couple of times it felt good."

RUTH WESTHEIMER (1928–   ), German-born U.S. sex therapist

The world knows her as "Dr. Ruth," the woman who has made a career out of talking candidly about sex. In her autobiography, *All in a Lifetime,* Westheimer says that as a child she believed that the stork brought babies and all you had to do to get one was to leave a piece of sugar out on an outside window ledge for the stork (she tried it; it didn't work). Her first foray into sex education came from the book *Ideal Marriage,* which was kept under lock and key in her parents' closet.

In her book Westheimer describes her first sexual encounter, which happened on a kibbutz in Palestine when she was seventeen: "I won't say whom it was with, because I am still good friends with him *and* his wife. But I can say that it was a beautiful, romantic experience. . . . One night, when we both were ready, we walked hand in hand under the starry sky to a barn on the kibbutz where hay was stored and climbed up a ladder to the second story. . . . We spent many nights in that barn, sleeping there till morning, but I remember that first time most vividly of all, because it shows that when two people are in love, the first experience can be very enjoyable. One thing I'm not happy about is the way we dealt with the issue of contraception. I know much better now, but in those days I thought that hoping was enough."

SHELLEY WINTERS (1922–   ), U.S. actor

Believing that her "lack of life experience" was hurting her "art," the aspiring young actress (born Shirley Schrift) decided to try sex. Not yet sixteen,

Shirley chose a young actor to be her first partner. After buying some potato chips, bottles of Coca-Cola, and a fifth of Southern Comfort (her "aphrodisiacs"), she invited him to a hotel room.

In her autobiography, the Oscar-winning actress writes: "He turned off the light. . . . By the dim light from the radio, he proceeded to make lovely and expert love to me. To the strains of 'The Moon Was Yellow,' a frightened girl became a fulfilled young woman. The next morning, when I looked at myself in the mirror, my eyes and cheeks were glowing."

MARRIED CHILDHOOD SWEETHEARTS

ARIEL DURANT (1898–1981), Russian-born U.S. writer
They were an unlikely pair. When Ada Kaufman was three, her family emigrated from Russia, where they had lived in a Jewish ghetto, to the United States. Will Durant was born in Massachusetts, the son of Catholic French-Canadians; he had studied for the priesthood. They met in September 1912 at New York City's experimental Ferrer Modern School, where he was her teacher, thirteen years older than she. He enlisted her help in keeping the class in order, and by February 1913 they were kissing on walks in Central Park. In March, he resigned his teaching position; in October, they married. She was fifteen. The marriage was a successful and brilliant collaboration. She took the name Ariel, and together they wrote the enormously popular eleven-volume series *The Story of Civilization*. She died in 1981, only thirteen days before he did. They had been together for sixty-eight years.

WILLIAM FAULKNER (1897–1962), U.S. writer
With little Willie Faulkner in the lead on a Shetland pony, the Faulkner family marched past the Oldham house, where seven-year-old Lida Estelle Oldham was looking out the window. Estelle said to her nurse, Magnolia, who was curling her charge's hair, " 'Nolia, see that little boy? I'm going to marry him when I grow up." The two children played together and were friends all through school. In high school they discovered that they both loved poetry, and he became one of her gentleman callers. In 1918, however, she married Cornell Franklin. By 1929 she was divorced, and she and William married.

SALLY FIELD (1946–   ), U.S. actor
Already deep into acting, she was so shy at thirteen that she hid out in the girls' bathroom at junior high, saying to herself, "You're a good person. . . . You're a good person." Then when she was fourteen, she met Steve Craig at Birmingham High School in Pasadena, California. He was older than she—sixteen—and popular. They went steady throughout high school and were married in 1968 in Las Vegas, Nevada. They had two children. In 1974, they were divorced.

ROBERT FROST (1874–1963), U.S. poet
He courted pale, dreamy, blue-eyed Elinor White in his last year of high school in Lawrence, Massachusetts, where they were covaledictorians. After

graduation, they exchanged wedding rings in an unofficial secret ceremony; then he persuaded her to make love. He himself admitted later that he had been "ruthless" with her. It had repercussions. In spite of his love tokens— poems he wrote and had bound in leather for her—she allowed another suitor to pursue her. In 1894, Frost, in despair, threatened to kill himself in the Dismal Swamp, North Carolina, but decided against it when he got there. He and Elinor reconciled and were married in 1895.

JOHN GLENN (1921–   ), U.S. astronaut and politician
The first American to orbit the earth was three years old when he met Anna Castor, a brown-eyed brunette, his future wife. The two children played together at the potluck suppers their families attended and became fast friends. As they grew up, they worked on school projects and went to parties together. In high school, she watched as he played on the basketball, football, and tennis teams. They married in 1943 and had two children.

RON HOWARD (1954–   ), U.S. actor, producer, and director
The kid who played Opie on *The Andy Griffith Show* and starred in *Happy Days* met his future wife, Cheryl Alley, when they were both sixteen and in high school. Neither was popular. He has said, "When I went out on a date with Cheryl, I just had the greatest time and fell in love right away." They married in 1975 and have four children.

GEORGE S. PATTON (1885–1945), U.S. general
George met Beatrice Banning Ayer when he was sixteen and vacationing on Santa Catalina, an island off the coast of southern California. Daughter of a socially prominent Boston family, Beatrice, also sixteen, was a beautiful, graceful, and vivacious young woman. For years afterward the teenagers wrote letters to each other, and the relationship turned serious when George was at West Point. They married in 1910.

WILMA RUDOLPH (1940–   ), U.S. athlete
Olympic gold medal sprinter Wilma Rudolph met her husband, Robert Eldridge, in elementary school. To get her attention, Robert threw rocks at her. She said, "He was a devil, but an all-right sort of devil, and I liked him." They dated in high school and were married in 1963.

NOLAN RYAN (1947–   ), U.S. baseball player
When he was in the tenth grade in Alvin, Texas, Nolan was a star athlete and vice president of his class. He asked a pretty cheerleader, Ruth Holdorff, for a date and the thirteen-year-old accepted. From then on they were inseparable; four years later they were married.

JOHN R. R. TOLKIEN (1892–1973), South African–born British novelist
Tolkien met Edith Bratt when he was sixteen and she was nineteen. Both were orphans, but aside from that, they didn't have very much in common. However, they were very strongly attracted to each other. Tolkien's legal guardian tried to keep the couple apart and for a while succeeded, but they were eventually married in 1916.

HARRY S TRUMAN (1884–1972), U.S. president
Harry was smitten with Bess Wallace the first time he saw her in his Sunday school kindergarten class, but it took him five years to get up the courage to talk to her. They were friends in high school but never dated. When Harry was twenty-seven, he proposed to Bess, but she turned him down. However, Harry persisted, and eight years later they were married. For as long as he lived, Harry thought Bess was "the most beautiful and sweetest person on earth." He lovingly referred to her as "the Boss."

NICKNAMES

JULIAN ADDERLEY (1928–1975), U.S. musician
His original nickname, "Cannibal" (because of his big appetite), became "Cannonball."

> ## Did you know that Norman Schwarzkopf's teenage nickname was "Cuddles"?

ALVIN AILEY (1931–1989), U.S. choreographer
He was called "Big Head" because his head seemed too big for his body.

MUHAMMAD ALI (1942–   ), U.S. boxer
When he was a baby, he used to say "gee, gee . . ." so his nickname became "GG." He later claimed he was saying the initials for the Golden Gloves.

LOUIS ARMSTRONG (1900–1971), U.S. musician
He had a big grin, so he was nicknamed "Dippermouth" and "Gatemouth."

SAMUEL BECKETT (1906–1989), Irish dramatist
His French teacher called him "Inky Sam" because of his sloppy papers.

CARL BERNSTEIN (1944–   ), U.S. journalist
He was nicknamed "Howdy Doody" because he had freckles like the television puppet.

JIMMY CARTER (1924–   ), U.S. president
His nickname was "Baby Dumplin' " for Dagwood's son in the comic strip *Blondie*.

JOHNNY CASH (1932–   ), U.S. singer
His father called him "Shoo-Doo."

CHARLES DARWIN (1809–1882), English naturalist

Toolshed chemical experiments with "Ras" (Erasmus), his older brother, earned him the nickname "Gas."

MILES DAVIS (1926–1991), U.S. musician

Because he was dark, short, and thin, kids called him "Buckwheat," after the African-American character in the *Our Gang* comedies. Anyone who called him Buckwheat had to fight him. He hated the image, a racial caricature— and he hated being ridiculed.

GERARD DEPARDIEU (1948–   ), French actor

His family called him "Pétarou" (Little Firecracker) from age three on because he was so devilish.

WILLIAM FAULKNER (1897–1962), U.S. writer

His father, who could be mean, called him "Snake-Lips."

JANE FONDA (1937–   ), U.S. actor

Her mother, Frances, who was proud of being descended from the English noble family Seymour, named her child Jane Seymour Fonda. She nicknamed her "Lady Jane." By the time Jane was six, she had dumped the nickname: "I just stood up in class and announced that I was to be known as Jane from then on."

JUDY GARLAND (1922–1969), U.S. singer and actor

Her mother called her "Little Miss Leather Lungs" for her big voice. Louis B. Mayer called her his "little hunchback," because of her posture—she had slight scoliosis.

BILL GATES (1955–   ), U.S. software entrepreneur

William Henry Gates III was called "Trey," the cardplayer's word for a three, because he was the third with that name.

BARRY GOLDWATER (1909–1998), U.S. politician

Sent away to Virginia's Staunton Military Academy, he collected so many demerits that the students called him the "Beat King" for the amount of punishment time he served.

Did you know that Dennis Rodman was only five feet tall at age fifteen?

JEAN HARRIS (1923–   ), U.S. convicted murderer

Her mother called her "Miss Infallible" because she had fits of self-righteousness.

J. EDGAR HOOVER (1895–1972), U.S. FBI director
He was called "Speed" because he thought fast and spoke with machine-gun speed. "I can take two hundred words a minute, but that man must be talking four hundred a minute," a court reporter said.

JACK KEROUAC (1922–1969), U.S. novelist and poet
As a French-Canadian child growing up in Lowell, Massachusetts, his parents nicknamed him "Ti Jean" (little Jack). Later, his classmates called him "Memory Babe" for his good grades and his ability to recall facts.

JERRY LEWIS (1926–), U.S. comedian and actor
In high school he was always clowning around, doing silly things and making funny faces. The kids called him "Id" (for idiot).

SINCLAIR LEWIS (1885–1951), U.S. novelist
When Lewis was thirteen, he tried to enlist as a drummer boy in the Spanish-American War. When his classmates learned of his failed effort, they sang "Yankee Doodle" to him; thus, he was nicknamed "Doodle."

ANDREW LLOYD WEBBER (1948–), English composer
His parents called him "Bumper" because he was an energetic toddler who was always crashing into things.

MARGARET MEAD (1901–1978), U.S. anthropologist
She was an alert, active baby and her father called her "Punk."

MARGARET MITCHELL (1900–1949), U.S. novelist
She was a nonstop talker and her parents called her "Chatterbox."

AUDIE MURPHY (1924–1971), U.S. soldier and actor
He grew up very poor and had only one pair of pants, which he had to wear even after he had outgrown them. The kids at school called him "Little Britches."

EDWARD R. MURROW (1908–1965), U.S. broadcast journalist
Even as a young boy, Edward (real name Egbert) was opinionated and boisterous. His brothers called him "Eber Blowhard."

RICHARD NIXON (1913–1994), U.S. president
He was a smart, serious, introspective kid who was called "Gloomy Gus."

SATCHEL PAIGE (1906?–1982), U.S. baseball player
To make money, Leroy Paige hung out at the train station and helped passengers carry their bags. One of his friends dubbed him "Satchel."

RONALD REAGAN (1911–), U.S. president
When Ron was born, his father, Jack, said that the boy looked like "a fat little Dutchman," and he continued to refer to the child as "the Dutchman." When Ron grew older, he asked his friends to call him "Dutch," a name that stuck with him for life.

NORMAN ROCKWELL (1894–1978), U.S. illustrator
He was a scrawny, pigeon-toed kid with a large Adam's apple. His mother called him "Snow-in-the-Face" because his skin was so pale, and his class-

mates called him "Mooney" because he wore glasses with big, round lenses. Rockwell said, "A lump, a long skinny nothing, a bean pole without the beans—that's what I was."

Did you know that Jimmy Carter was called "Baby Dumplin" as a child?

DENNIS RODMAN (1962–   ), U.S. basketball player
At age fifteen he was shy, skinny, and short (only five feet tall). His nickname was "Worm."

WILL ROGERS (1879–1935), U.S. humorist and actor
Because he had big ears and could run really fast, the kids called him "Rabbit."

H. NORMAN SCHWARZKOPF (1934–   ), U.S. general
When he was a teenager, Norman was called "Cuddles" after his friends saw him cuddling and kissing his girlfriend on a bus.

BEVERLY SILLS (1929–   ), U.S. opera singer
When she was born, Beverly had a big spit bubble in her mouth; the doctor promptly christened her "Bubbles."

HOWARD STERN (1954–   ), U.S. radio personality
In high school the radio "shock jock" was tall and lanky but not good at sports, not even basketball. The other guys called him "Gunkard" or "Big Gunk."

Did you know that Judy Garland's mother called her "Little Miss Leather Lungs" for her big voice?

HENRI DE TOULOUSE-LAUTREC (1864–1901), French painter
When he was growing up, Henri had a lot of different nicknames. Among them: "Tapajoo" (rowdy); "Petit Bonhomme" (little fellow); "Petit Bijou" (little jewel).

ANDY WARHOL (1928–1987), U.S. artist
He was a sickly kid whose skin was very white and marred with brownish blotches and acne. The kids called him "Spot," "Albino," and "Andy the Red-Nosed Warhol."

ORSON WELLES (1915–1985), U.S. actor and film director
   When he was born, Orson weighed in at ten pounds. Smart, sassy, and very cute, he was called "Pookles."

*Orson "Pookles" Welles,
child prodigy.*

Courtesy of the Kenosha County Historical Society.

FRANK LLOYD WRIGHT (1867–1959), U.S. architect
   He was called "Shaggy" because of his long, curly hair.

CHAPTER SEVEN

*H*ARD KNOCKS

"The school of hard knocks is an accelerated curriculum."
ANONYMOUS

B eing a kid can be tough, especially since kids so often don't yet have the skills needed to fight back against life's cruelty. Fear and pain, and sometimes death, stalk a lot of kids. No less with the famous.

The bully looms large in the waking nightmares of many children. Aaron Spelling was so traumatized by bullies that he stayed in bed for a year. Bullies stuffed Dylan Thomas in a wastebasket. Maybe being bullied has its advantages, in that kids thereby learn a way of dealing with oppressors. Spelling's solution was to tell stories but withhold the end in order to be set free.

No adult experience is ever quite as degrading as a youthful humiliation. Nicolas Cage vomited on his shoes while on a date. Kids at camp painted Robert Oppenheimer's backside green. And Dolly Parton's song "Coat of Many Colors" comes from a painful childhood experience.

Many of the eminent faced moments of terror and almost overwhelming despair as children. Abuse. Assault. Accident. Trauma.

Abused children break our hearts. We find among the famous terrible stories of being burned, beaten up (with whips, with two-by-fours), sexually molested, kicked down the stairs. Buster Keaton was billed as "The Little Boy Who Can't Be Damaged"—but he was.

There were those who came close to dying; either someone wanted them dead (before birth, in some cases), or they themselves did, or there was an accident (Boris Yeltsin almost drowned in the baptismal font, for instance).

Less deadly tragedies make us want to cry when we think of the kids themselves: Thirteen-year-old Katharine Hepburn finding her brother hanging dead in the attic. Mickey Mantle facing the amputation of his leg. A young Doris Day hearing her father commit adultery in the next room. Little Jerry Garcia watching his father drown in a rushing river.

VICTIMS OF BULLIES

KAREEM ABDUL-JABBAR (1947–   ), U.S. basketball player

One Sunday, Joe, a tough kid in jeans, started pushing and shoving six-year-old Lew Alcindor (later Kareem Abdul-Jabbar), even though Lew was a lot taller. Dressed in Sunday clothes, Lew wanted to avoid a fight. He turned to walk away. Joe pushed him from behind, and Lew turned and hit him on the arm. The fight began. Lew eventually escaped and ran home. His father, a policeman, was reading the paper. When Lew told him what had happened, he said there was nothing he could do for him. So Lew, who wanted to play outside, changed clothes and went out again. Joe was waiting for him. The two fought. Joe was hitting him unmercifully, so Lew went back inside the house and got his toy nightstick. With a weapon, he succeeded in running Joe off. Joe never bothered him again. Not so with Cecilia, a girl three years older than he, who lived in Lew's building. She chased him and beat him up more than once.

When Lew was nine, his parents sent him to Holy Providence School, a boarding school for African-American children outside Philadelphia. It educated approximately forty boys and three hundred girls. Lew was the star of the class, and the nuns loved him for his academic prowess. Once they asked him to read to the seventh grade (he was in fourth). The nuns may have been impressed, but the other boys hated Lew for the educated way he spoke and his A report card. After seventh-grader Sylvester Curtis, the school bully, beat him up, Lew decided to downplay his intelligence and learning. He concentrated more on playing basketball, because he was safe on the court. Two weeks before the end of school, two bullies lay in wait for him and beat him badly in the face. From then on, Lew did not smile so much, but he came back home tougher.

Did you know that John Wayne was frequently beaten up when he was young?

LEWIS CARROLL (CHARLES LUTWIDGE DODGSON) (1832–1898), English mathematician and writer

At twelve he was sent away to board at Richmond School in Yorkshire. As part of the hazing process (known as "fagging"), some boys proposed to him that they play a game called King of the Cobblers, with him as king. They sat around him in a circle and said, "Go to work"; then they proceeded to kick him and knock him around. Next they suggested "Peter, the red lion." They made a mark on a tombstone. In turn the boys walked or were led to the tombstone with their eyes shut, holding out their fingers, trying to touch the mark. When it was Charles's turn, the boy led him so that his finger went into another boy's mouth.

The hazing made him decide to stick up for boys who were being bullied. "Long after he left school his name was remembered as that of a boy who knew well how to use his fist in defense of a righteous cause," a classmate said.

Did you know that to avoid being beaten up by schoolyard bullies, Aaron Spelling would start to tell a story but not finish it, promising to finish it the next day if they would please let him go home?

NICOLAS CAGE (1964–   ), U.S. actor

In fourth grade, a bully kept extorting Nicolas's lunchbox Twinkie from him on the school bus. Nicolas made himself into someone else—his cousin Roy Wilkinson—by slicking back his hair, putting on sunglasses, and wearing his brother's jeans and cowboy boots. On the bus, he told the bully he was Roy and said, "If you mess with him [Nicolas] again, I'm going to kick your ass." It worked.

THOMAS DE QUINCEY (1785–1859), English essayist and critic

As Thomas and his older brother William crossed the Oxford Road Bridge by the cotton mill on their way to their tutor's house, a factory boy taunted them with "Boots! Boots!" probably because of their expensive Hessian boots, knee-high, with tassels.

Thomas would have ignored him. Not William. William stopped and challenged the boy to a fight, which the boy turned down with "a most contemptuous and plebeian gesture." So William threw some stones at him.

From that time on, twice a day, a little war, usually of stone throwing, took place between the De Quincey boys and the factory boys. On the De Quincey side, William claimed to be the leader, Thomas his foot soldier. Each day William planned a new strategy, but each day the De Quinceys had to run. Sometimes the factory boys took Thomas prisoner. Once they kicked him and sent him to William with an offensive message. Another time some factory girls picked him up and kissed him, which Thomas enjoyed. William was furious. In the newspaper he published twice a week for the housekeeper, he told how Thomas had given in to the enemy.

C. EVERETT KOOP (1916–   ), U.S. surgeon general

He was afraid to go to P.S. 40 in Brooklyn because it was in a tough neighborhood. So since he was a smart kid, his parents found a way to get him into the rapid advancement track at Dewey Junior High School, thinking it would be safer. It wasn't. Each day he rode the trolley and walked a half mile from the trolley stop to and from school, which was eight miles from his house. Because the majority of the other students in the class went to Hebrew school after class, he had to walk alone to the trolley through a rough neighborhood. Almost every afternoon, a gang of tough kids who hung out on street corners beat him up. He changed his allowance into nickels and frequented phone booths, hoping his tormentors would leave him alone, but it did little good. They waited for him. The next year, he went to a small private school much nearer home.

GREG LOUGANIS (1960–   ), U.S. diver

The dark-skinned Samoan boy was adopted when he was nine months old and grew up in the suburbs of San Diego, California. Before he was two years old, Greg was taking acrobatic classes, followed by dance classes and diving lessons. By the time he was nine, Greg had won numerous talent contests, and by age ten he had a full-time diving coach. His exceptional athletic and theatrical abilities, however, didn't shield him from constant ridicule from his elementary school classmates.

Did you know that as a young child Dylan Thomas was routinely stuffed into the classroom wastebasket?

The kids called him "nigger" because of his dark skin, "sissy" because he took dance lessons, and "retard" because he stuttered and had trouble reading (years later he was diagnosed with dyslexia). Greg was frequently beaten up at the school bus stop by thugs who liked to embarrass him in front of a crowd of students.

In his autobiography, *Breaking the Surface,* Louganis talks candidly about his difficult childhood. He says, "Being beat up at elementary school . . . proved to be a big motivator. The name-calling and the humiliation pushed me to strive to be better than everyone. It made me angry, and I learned to focus most of that angry energy on my acrobatics and diving." That drive and ambition spurred him on to become an Olympic gold medalist in diving.

AARON SPELLING (1928–   ), U.S. television producer
He has produced more than fifty television series, including such huge hits as *Dynasty, Melrose Place, The Love Boat,* and *Charlie's Angels.* His current, lavish life style, however, is a startling contrast to his humble beginnings in Dallas, Texas. The son of Jewish immigrants who spoke mostly Yiddish, young Aaron was a puny kid who grew up poor in a tough neighborhood populated with the families of cotton mill workers. He and his older brother, Danny, were the only Jews in school, and the kids called them "Jew boys." Unless Danny was around to rescue him, Aaron got his "butt kicked."

According to Spelling, when Danny moved on to another school, "I got chased every day of my life. There wasn't a day when I didn't get beaten up." The nine-year-old boy became so traumatized that he simply crawled into bed and stayed there for a year. The only diversions that alleviated his depression were books and movies, which inspired him to create his own fanciful stories. When he returned to school, he used those stories to protect himself from further attacks. Or, as Spelling writes in his autobiography, "Whenever they [the bullies] would try to pick a fight, I would just tell them a story and not finish it. I told them I would finish it the next day, and they let me go home. I'd run like hell before they changed their minds, and so I could change my shorts!"

STEVEN SPIELBERG (1946–   ), U.S. film director
A self-described nerd and wimp in school, thirteen-year-old Spielberg had a particularly hard time fending off attacks from the toughest kid in the class

(he even looked like John Wayne), who was a year older than he. The punishment varied: The bully pushed Steven's face in the water fountain, threw him down on the ground, shoved his head in the dirt, or gave him a bloody nose. Once the bully tossed a cherry bomb between Steven's legs when he was on the toilet (Steven escaped unscathed).

Did you know that to scare the bully who kept stealing his Twinkies, the young Nicolas Cage slicked-back his hair, dressed up in a leather jacket, sunglasses, posed as his cousin, and told the bully that if he messed with Nicolas again "I'm going to kick your ass"?

To save himself from further terror, Steven offered the thug a starring role (squadron leader) in a World War II movie that he was filming. The older boy accepted, and the young filmmaker dressed the bully in full battle array and showed him how to fight the Nazis. The tactic worked; the two boys learned to tolerate each other because, as Steven later said, "I was able to bring him over to a place where I felt safer—in front of my camera."

DYLAN THOMAS (1914–1953), Welsh poet
He was a frail child who suffered from asthma, anemia, and a host of other minor diseases. In grammar school, the older boys loved to terrorize him, sometimes throwing him in the bushes of the school playground. In addition, the older boys howled as they grabbed Dylan and stuffed him, butt first, into a wastebasket; they pushed him in so tight that he couldn't get out by himself. When the teacher entered the classroom, his first words were usually, "Take Dylan out of the basket."

JOHN WAYNE (1907–1979), U.S. actor
Marion Morrison (his real name) was seven years old when his family moved from Iowa to Palmdale, California, on the edge of the Mojave Desert. He was shy, very skinny, and taller than the other boys. In addition, his family was

> *Did you know that Kareem Abdul-Jabbar was not always such an imposing figure? As a boy, he was constantly taunted by bullies, one of the most daunting being his female neighbor, Cecilia.*

poor, he spoke with a Midwestern accent, and he had a "sissy" first name. The kids ridiculed him, and the boys loved to beat him up.

It wasn't until Marion's body filled out, he started playing football, and he learned to land a punch that the boy became more secure and outgoing. In a biography of her father, Aissa Wayne writes: "The older boys called Marion 'little girl' which he despised. They asked him why he wore pants instead of a skirt. I think one of the reasons my father frequently acted so macho in later life was to compensate for this boyhood torment; I believe it scarred him deeply."

HUMILIATING OR EMBARRASSING INCIDENTS

NICOLAS CAGE (1964–   ), U.S. actor
In an interview in *Playboy*, Cage tells about going to the prom at Beverly Hills High School, a school of rich kids. He lived on the not-so-rich edge of town, and his car was often broken down. Most of the good-looking girls would not date him because it meant riding on the bus. When a beautiful girl accepted his invitation to go to the prom, he cashed in the savings bonds his grandmother had given him in order to rent a tuxedo and a limousine for the occasion. When he kissed the girl, she responded to him. He was so nervous he started to throw up. The driver of the limo would not let Nicolas get back in because of the vomit on his shoes. He had to walk home.

DORIS DAY (1924–   ), U.S. singer and actor
When she was in kindergarten, she had a starring part, reciting and dancing, in a minstrel show. Her mother had made her a costume: a red satin top, red panties, and a tarlatan skirt. She had to be pinned into it. It was a long wait before her turn came, and she needed to go to the bathroom, but no one

could figure out how to get her out of the costume. Her mother was down in the audience. Doris wet her pants, turning the red satin black. When she came out and took her bow, she heard giggling from the audience. "I'm sorry, Mommy. I couldn't help it," she cried, and then ran off the stage. She still hates performing live.

HENRY FONDA (1905–1982), U.S. actor

Handsome movie star Henry Fonda did not have much luck with girls when he was an innocent adolescent in high school. His father had to drive him and his girl on his first date. When they arrived at the girl's house, Henry went up to the door, fetched her, put her in the back seat, and then tried to get into the front seat with his father. That was impossible, though, because his father, William, was holding the door shut so that Henry would have to sit in back with the girl.

THEODORE GEISEL (DR. SEUSS) (1904–1991), U.S. writer and illustrator

In 1918, Colonel Theodore Roosevelt came to Springfield, Massachusetts, to present awards to ten boy scouts in the Municipal Auditorium. Fourteen-year-old Ted Geisel was the last in the line. As Roosevelt presented medals to each scout in turn, each boy saluted and walked off stage. Finally only one scout—Ted—remained, and Roosevelt was out of medals.

"What's this little boy doing here?" Roosevelt roared at the scoutmaster. The scoutmaster, unwilling to disconcert the great man, motioned Ted to leave the stage.

Did you know that Jerry Lewis's childhood nickname was "Id," short for "Idiot"?

Geisel never forgot his sense of injustice, and to the end of his life feared public platforms. He turned down thousands of requests to appear in public. When he did accept such a request, he always asked himself, once onstage, what he was doing there.

JERRY LEWIS (1926–   ), U.S. comedian and actor

Jerry's parents were entertainers on the vaudeville and burlesque circuits. Since they were usually on the road, the boy was left in the care of various relatives. When he lived with his grandmother, Sarah Rothberg, in Irvington, New Jersey, he attended Union Avenue Grammar School. However, his no-madic life caused him to miss a lot of school, and even when he was in school, his grades were poor.

When Jerry was in the fifth grade, "promotion day" arrived, the day the fifth graders were ceremoniously sent into the sixth grade. One by one the students were called to line up along the blackboard ready to be marched out of the classroom. Everybody except Jerry. He recalls, "The entire class is standing against that wall, and all the seats are empty, except in the middle of the room at one desk is Jerry Lewis. That told the class, and me, that I was left back. So at the age of around 10, I knew what trauma meant—the humiliation that I felt."

In 1957, more than twenty years later, when Lewis had become a big star, part of the Dean Martin/Jerry Lewis comedy team as well as a movie actor, he returned to Irvington for "Jerry Lewis Day." Most of the town's 63,000 residents showed up for a big parade, and the board of regents from his grammar school honored him with a luncheon. Lewis, still smarting from his fifth-grade embarrassment, asked to meet with the members of the board of regents and as he later recalled, "I told them the story and what I went through, and the promotion process changed that day. They never, ever did it again. That was the upside. The downside is that I will never forget it."

RICHARD NIXON (1913–1994), U.S. president

He was a brilliant student and a prize-winning debater and orator, but he was not particularly good at sports and was shy and awkward with girls. In high school Richard, always the overachiever, joined lots of clubs, played in the school orchestra, and wrote for the school newspaper. In his senior year the Latin Club held a Roman banquet, followed by a three-act play based on Virgil's *Aeneid*. Richard won the star role of Aeneas, the Trojan hero, and played opposite the romantic lead, Queen Dido.

The play got off to a bad start; it was boring and none of the students had any acting ability. Richard's boots were two sizes too small, and he felt stiff and very self-conscious. During the tender, romantic scene between Aeneas and the Queen, Richard did his best when embracing his lover and later throwing himself on Queen Dido's bier. But the audience broke up in what Nixon later described as "catcalls, whistles and uproarious laughter." The entire play had to stop until the laughter finally subsided. When the play mercifully came to an end, the audience responded with mild applause. Mortified, Richard ran up to the Latin teacher and offered to play the piano. "I'll do anything," he said, "to make the party a success."

J. ROBERT OPPENHEIMER (1904–1967), U.S. physicist

As a kid, the "father of the atomic bomb" just didn't fit in. Growing up in New York City, he was shy, sickly, and an intellectual snob. In addition, he was an athletic disaster and either refused to participate in sports or was the worst player on any team. As a child, he said, he was "an abnormally, repulsively good little boy."

To help him become more sociable and more sports-minded, Robert's parents sent him to summer camp when he was fourteen. Fellow campers ridiculed him because he wrote letters home to his parents, and they called him all sorts of names when they discovered that he wrote poetry. But the worst attack came one evening, when the boys kidnapped Robert and dragged him into an icehouse. They stripped him naked, beat him up, and painted his derriere with green paint. Then they locked him in the icehouse, where he remained overnight.

Did you know that when Nicolas Cage kissed his prom date, he got so nervous that he threw up on his shoes. The driver of his limo wouldn't let Nicolas get back into the car, so he had to walk home.

DOLLY PARTON (1946–   ), U.S. singer and songwriter

In her autobiography, Dolly Parton writes, "The worst thing about poverty is not the actual living of it, but the shame of it." She was the fourth of twelve children and grew up in Sevier County, Tennessee. In the Parton household everything was scarce, from food to clothing.

When Dolly was in grade school, her mother made a patchwork coat for her, tailored from many bright-colored scraps of material. Truly a work of art, the coat was expertly hand-sewn, had a lining, and fit Dolly perfectly. She couldn't wait to go to school to show off her new treasure. But the kids mocked her, telling her that her coat was nothing more than a bunch of rags. She later wrote, "My heart was broken. I couldn't understand the cruelty, the ignorance that made them laugh at me that way."

Dolly, however, had the last laugh. Years later she turned the experience into a song, "Coat of Many Colors," which became her signature song. She said, "It was a big hit, and that did a lot to help me forget that early pain. It's amazing how healing money can be."

RONALD REAGAN (1911–   ), U.S. president

He was an all-American boy who grew up in the small town of Dixon, Illinois. Good-looking and popular, Ron (nicknamed "Dutch") played football and basketball in high school, took part in class plays, and had a summer job as a lifeguard. He also worked on the high school yearbook and was elected president of the senior class.

One childhood incident that Reagan loves to tell happened when he was about fourteen and was the drum major for the Dixon boys' band. Dutch and his band were the first attraction in a holiday parade, with only the parade marshal (on a horse) in front of them. Dressed in white duck pants and a brightly colored tunic, Dutch strutted down the street with his baton twirling. At one point the parade marshal left the front of the line, and Dutch proudly became the leader of the whole parade. Because he was concentrating so intently on his style and rhythm, minutes went by before Dutch realized that

Ronald Reagan, who had a summer job as a lifeguard in his hometown of Dixon, Illinois.

Courtesy of the Ronald Reagan Library.

the music behind him was not very loud. When he finally turned around, he was all by himself. The marshal had led the band and the rest of the parade onto another street. Reagan recalled: "When I saw what had happened, I started running, crossed several vacant lots and backyards, got in front of the band, and fell into step again." When he rejoined the parade, the crowd broke into laughter, but the embarrassed drum major just kept marching.

CARL SANDBURG (1878–1967), U.S. poet and biographer

He grew up in Galesburg, Illinois, the son of Swedish immigrants, and he desperately wanted to be American—to look and sound American. Toward that end he read books about American history and culture and practiced his English, even though Swedish was the language spoken in his home. He told his classmates that his name was Charles (or Charlie), not the Swedish-sounding Carl.

Charlie's chance to shine came when he was twelve and was one of eight contestants competing for a medal in a public-speaking contest. All contestants chose a speech from a particular book of speeches; Charlie chose a short one and practiced it over and over. He was especially proud of the way he would deliver the final dramatic line. When his turn came, the boy started out strong, then totally froze up. He couldn't remember anything. The crowd of two hundred people laughed. With the help of a prompter on the sidelines, Charlie stumbled through the speech. Then he slumped into his chair in utter disgrace.

Sandburg would grow up to become one of America's greatest poets, winning two Pulitzer Prizes—one for poetry and one for his multivolume biography of Abraham Lincoln. Yet the memory of his public childhood defeat never left him, and in his later years he would sometimes recite the speech, getting every word right. Even in his seventies, he was still thinking and writing about the incident: "Of course, I knew they didn't laugh at my ideas and my language. And yet—they laughed at me."

Did you know that Dolly Parton's hit song "Coat of Many Colors" is about a real patchwork coat she once owned that her classmates ridiculed as a coat of rags?

JULES VERNE (1828–1905), French science fiction and adventure novelist

He was a fun-loving boy who excelled at games and sports and making people laugh. But there was a serious side to young Jules. When he was sixteen, he began to write poems and even tried his hand at a full-length play, a tragedy full of passion and drama. After summoning up his courage, Jules gathered together some friends and family members in order to read his work to them. Sitting in the audience was Caroline Tronson, his first cousin, "a blinding beauty" who had stolen his heart.

Before he got very far into the first act, someone started to laugh. As Jules continued, the laughter got louder and louder; Caroline was practically hysterical. Either the play was horrible or the audience thought that Jules, an unlikely dramatist, had staged the whole performance as a practical joke. Whatever the truth, the teenager was devastated. He finished reading the first act and made a fast exit. Later on, he stacked up the pages of his play and burned them.

VICTIMS OF CHILD ABUSE

JOSEPHINE BAKER (1906–1975), U.S. singer and dancer

When Josephine's mother, Carrie McDonald, was seven months pregnant, she could put a glass of water on her head and dance without spilling a drop. She bequeathed her daughter grace and balance, but not much else. It was Josephine's fault, Carrie felt, that Eddie Carson, who had fathered the child, finally left her. Eddie, a freedom-loving drummer, never married Carrie and certainly did not want offspring. Unfortunately, Josephine looked like Eddie, reminding Carrie of the man she had loved and lost.

After the defection of Carson, Carrie met another man, Arthur Martin, and had three children by him. Josephine always felt like a stepchild. The family was so poor that Martin had to make shoes for the children from newspaper and sacks.

When Josephine was eight, her mother sent her away to work for a white woman, Mrs. Keiser. Josephine did chores from five until eight every morning before she went to school. If Josephine did not get up on time, Mrs. Keiser hit her, as she did for other infractions. Josephine's bedroom was a spot in the cellar, next to the coal and wood piles, with the dog to keep her company. Her only other friend was a chicken, Tiny Tim. When Tiny Tim was ready for the pot, Mrs. Keiser made her kill him. Josephine did as she was told, but when Tiny Tim was dead, she kissed his body.

One day Josephine put too much soap in the wash. To punish her, Mrs. Keiser stuck her hands in boiling water. Josephine screamed so loudly that the neighbors came to her rescue and she ended up in the hospital. Though Carrie brought her home, she was not allowed to stay, but was sent off to work for another white woman. It is no accident that Josephine Baker, in spite of all her fame and fortune, identified with Cinderella all her life.

DIRK BOGARDE (1921–   ), English actor and director

Barely into adolescence, Dirk Bogarde was living with his uncle in Glasgow and daringly ditching school to go to the Paramount Theatre, a place with a reputation as a den for crooks and white slavers. One day, he went to see *The*

Mummy starring Boris Karloff, and a freckled man in a beige raincoat came to sit next to him. The man bought Dirk an ice cream and put his arm around his shoulders during the scary parts of the movie. After the movie was over, the man identified himself as Alec Dodd. The two made an appointment to see the film again at the end of the week and then go to tea. At tea, Mr. Dodd confessed that he was a medical student and that he knew exactly how mummies were bandaged, a skill he attempted to reproduce with his napkin. That having failed, he offered to show Dirk how it was done at his place, where he had the bandages.

In the messy flat, which smelled of ether, Mr. Dodd said he would turn Dirk into a mummy just like Karloff. This he proceeded to do, rolling and wrapping the boy until he was giddy. Then he set Dirk on his feet so he could see the effect, a complete wrapping—all except for the genitals, which Dirk later described as "naked and as pink and vulnerable as a sugar mouse." Then Dodd swung the boy onto the bed and held before his eyes a pair of scissors, saying that "in real life they cut that off" but that he, Dodd, was too kind to do that; after all, how could Dirk masturbate without his penis? Terrified, Dirk said some "Hail Marys," but Mr. Dodd put down the scissors and went to work masturbating him. When it was over, he unwrapped a weeping Dirk. Dodd explained that it was all right because he was a medical student. Dirk did not go to the movies alone again for many years.

TRUMAN CAPOTE (1924–1984), U.S. writer
According to his father, who was a con man and jailbird, Truman Capote's mother, Lillie Mae, had at least twenty-nine extramarital affairs during their seven years of marriage. As a little boy, Truman saw one lover try to strangle his mother with a necktie; and he once heard her making love from the rumble seat of a car. He later said of Lillie Mae that "she was the single worst person in my life."

> *Did you know that when Josephine Baker was eight years old, she was sent away to work as a chore girl; her bedroom was a spot in the cellar next to the coal and wood piles?*

Neither parent had time for him. They would lock him up in their hotel room and tell the hotel staff to pay no attention to him, even if he screamed, which he did—often. He later wrote, "Every day was a nightmare, because I was afraid that they would leave me when it turned dark. I had an intense fear of being abandoned, and I remember practically all of my childhood as being lived in a state of constant tension and fear."

Just before he was six, his parents left him with Lillie Mae's relatives, three old maids and a bachelor, who lived in Monroeville, Alabama. Sometimes his mother came to visit, leaving in a mist of her perfume, Evening in Paris. Once he found a bottle she had left behind and drank it to the bottom. Sometimes his father showed up, making empty promises of presents, dogs, and other things.

Lillie Mae was ambivalent toward Truman. She despised his effeminacy, which was apparent from the time he was quite young. As he entered his teen years, his mother continued tucking him in every night. But she also tore up one of his manuscripts and said to his friends, "Well, my boy's a fairy."

SANDRA DEE (1944–   ), U.S. actor

Mary Zuck treated her beautiful brown-eyed daughter, Sandra, like a doll, dressing her in velvet dresses with lace collars and spoonfeeding her until the child was six.

Mary Zuck's new husband, Eugene Douvan, treated his stepdaughter like a woman, abusing her sexually from the time she was five until she was eleven. He said to Mary, "I married you just to get Sandy." It was the truth, though he did not mention just *how* he meant to get Sandy.

When Eugene and Mary were dating, Sandra went with them. The couple would put her in bed between them in his apartment in New York. At the wedding Sandy danced on Gene's shoes. She went on the honeymoon with them.

When she was eight, perhaps because of the abuse, Sandra had her first period. Her breasts started developing, and her mother told her to bind them up. Mary did not suspect.

In the morning, little Sandra would go into Gene's bedroom to say goodbye. This took forty-five minutes. After she came out of the room she asked her mother to button her up, even though she knew well how to do it herself. Mary did not suspect.

Sandra later told her son, "I reasoned that if I protested, that would dignify what was happening and make it real." In her mind, Eugene became two people: her daddy, and the monster who molested her.

By age eleven she was making $78,000 a year and had a fur coat. The abuse stopped. Eugene died the following year.

Sandra went on to become a teenaged movie star, playing the lead in movies such as *Gidget* and *Tammy Tell Me True*. When she was eighteen, she married singer Bobby Darin. On her wedding night, she sat on the couch all night, her coat on. It was not until after the two were divorced in 1967 that she told him about the abuse. He cried.

When, long afterward, Sandra told her mother that she had been abused, her mother said, "What the hell are you talking about?"

ROBERT FROST (1874–1963), U.S. poet

When his mother was in labor in San Francisco, where the Frosts were then living, his father, Will, drew a Colt pistol on the doctor, threatening to kill him if anything went wrong during the birth. Luckily, all went well. Robert was born on March 26, 1874. Though at first proud of the new baby, Will, who drank, did not exempt the child from his rages and silences. He was a strange man—for example, he kept a pair of pickled testicles on his desk at his newspaper office. He would not speak to his family for weeks at a time and cheated on his wife, Belle, who took refuge in religion.

Will Frost abused his young son as his own health and prospects as a politician deteriorated. When young Rob told a friend he was forbidden to have a Hallowe'en pumpkin, his father hit him with a metal dog chain. Home-schooled, Rob spent many of his days running errands for his father. Will beat him for small mistakes, while his indulgent mother prayed on her knees in the next room.

> ## "Children begin by loving their parents; as they grow older, they judge them. Rarely, if ever, do they forgive them."
>
> —Oscar Wilde

When Rob was eight, Will discovered the cause of his health complaints: tuberculosis. He would take Rob with him to a slaughterhouse, where he made the child watch as he drank glasses of black steers' blood from their slashed throats, thinking it would cure him. Lying on the couch, he asked Rob to join him for comfort, as he breathed in the boy's face. It is possible that Will transmitted the disease to Rob by this practice. Will died in 1885, when Rob was eleven.

EMMA GOLDMAN (1869–1940), Lithuanian-born U.S. anarchist

Emma Goldman was the child of an embittered mother, Taube, and angry father, Abraham. By an arranged marriage, Abraham was Taube's second husband. Emma, the Goldmans' first child, was a disappointment to Abraham, who had wanted a son. Within a few years, Taube gave birth to three sons, the first of whom died when he was six. Money was tight, Abraham's businesses did not do well, and Taube was often depressed.

At the age of eight, Emma went to live with her grandmother in Königsberg, East Prussia, in order to go to school there. Abraham threatened to whip her for any wrongdoings she committed during her stay there. Emma felt abandoned, and to make her feelings of abandonment even stronger, her grandmother went away, leaving Emma with her aunt and uncle.

Her cruel uncle kept Emma out of school to do housework. One day, when she refused to walk several miles to deliver a package for him, he kicked her down the stairs. Emma hid her anger but dreamed of cutting off his head, as the biblical character Judith had cut off the head of the oppressor Holofernes. Two women who lived in the downstairs apartment were so concerned about Emma that they took her in, cared for her, and wired her father to take her home.

Emma became a reader. One of her favorite books was *What Is to Be Done*, which inspired her to imagine a future different from that of her parents, a future in which women would not be oppressed by male cruelty and control. When Abraham tried to arrange a marriage for her, she resisted. He gave up only when Emma threatened to throw herself in the Neva River. When Emma was sixteen, she and her half-sister Helena, then twenty-four, emigrated to the United States, where she tried to accomplish her dream of a better life by becoming an anarchist.

JIMI HENDRIX (1942–1970), U.S. musician

When little John, as Jimi Hendrix was originally named, was two months old, his grandmother brought him with her on a cleaning job. It was winter in Seattle, and his diaper was frozen, his legs blue with cold. Lucille, John's mother, had momentarily disappeared, the grandmother explained. Her employer, Minnie, took Jimi in, saying, "Leave him here and tell Lucille to come and get him. I want to see why she's leaving this baby in this kind of fix." There were reasons: Lucille was a teenager who liked a good time; her husband, Al, was away in the army; his pay was not getting to her because of a bureaucratic foul-up; and she was a heavy drinker. Eventually, she reclaimed her child and began traipsing around the country with him and her new low-life boyfriend from one bad housing situation to another. Once, Little John developed pneumonia and had to go to the hospital. From time to time, she farmed him out to friends and relatives. Luckily, John was a charming child, with a round face and big eyes, and people liked taking care of him.

Al came back to the United States in November 1945, two weeks shy of John's third birthday, and reclaimed his son, renaming him James. He and Lucille renewed their relationship and had two more boys: Leon, born in 1948, and Joseph, born in 1949. Lucille continued to drink and run around. By 1951 the couple were divorced for good and Al had custody of the children. Though Al tried to take care of the children, he would often leave them alone while he spent his nights gambling. The neighbors reported him for child neglect. On a couple of occasions, Jimmy ran away to stay with friends or relatives. When he was about eight, he said to his Aunt Dorothy, "when I get big I'm going far, far away. And I'm never comin' back."

BUSTER KEATON (1895–1966), U.S. comedian and actor

The Keatons called their son "The Little Boy Who Can't Be Damaged" because in their vaudeville act, Joe, Buster's father, threw the clownish, rubber-legged child around the stage—apparently without harming him. The act, in which they featured Buster from the age of five, brought the family great success. It brought Buster cracked vertebrae and a deadpan expression that

Young Buster Keaton on the verge of becoming a star, age four, with his guitar.

Courtesy of the Photography and Film Collection, Harry Ransom Humanities Research Center, University of Texas at Austin.

made him a fortune in show business but may have hidden a damaged psyche.

In the act, Joe sometimes hurled Buster as far as thirty feet, into the orchestra. His mother, Myra, sewed a suitcase handle in the back of the child's suit so that Joe could grab him more easily. Buster was not allowed to laugh or smile or cry; if he did, he was beaten.

One night hecklers made fun of Myra's saxophone solo. Incensed, Joe Keaton said to Buster, "Tighten up your asshole, son," grabbed the suitcase handle, and threw the boy into the audience, feet first. Buster's shoes hit the face of one of the hecklers and broke his nose. "I was just a handy ballistic missile," Buster later said. Another time, Joe accidentally kicked Buster and knocked him out for eighteen hours. Famous actress Sarah Bernhardt threatened to report Joe to the police for mistreating Buster. A minstrel on the bill with the Keatons said that "it looked as though his dad would break his neck." In fact he did; a 1935 X-ray showed cracked vertebrae.

When Buster was sixteen, the act grew even rougher. Joe punched Buster and hit him over the head with a chair and Buster hit back, all to the tune of "The Anvil Chorus."

Buster never blamed his father for throwing him around. In 1913 he said, "Dad has had a sprained wrist for years from throwing me. I've only been hurt a few times."

RUDYARD KIPLING (1865–1936), Indian–born British writer

When Rudyard was five and a half and his sister, Alice (Trix), almost three, their happy lives in tropical Bombay, India, came to an end. As was the custom with India-based British colonials, their parents boarded the children out in England, probably to get them away from oppressive summer heat and local disease. Unfortunately, they chose a family called the Holloways, whom they did not know.

The children called the Holloways' house in Southsea, where they lived for more than five years, "House of Desolation" or "Forlorn Lodge." The little house smelled of cabbage, mildew, and what Rudyard called a "buried-alive smell." The stingy Holloways ("Aunty Rosa" and "Uncle Harry") did not spend enough on fuel to keep the house warm. Aunty Rosa, who had always wanted a daughter, doted on Trix and picked on Rudyard. The son of the house, Harry "Devil-Boy," much older than the Kipling children, hit Rudyard, using religious correction as his excuse. If the children spilled something at the table or cried when hearing letters from their parents, Aunty would sentence them to twenty-four hours in solitary confinement.

In March 1877, Aunty, on the pretext that Rudyard was a "moral leper," put him in solitary confinement in the attic for two days. On the morning of his release, Trix looked out the window and saw her brother walking out of the yard with a large cardboard placard stitched to his clothes. It read "Kipling the Liar." Trix ran out of the house and took Rudyard's knife to cut the stitches. Then she put the placard on the ground and jumped on it. Rudyard went on to school and Trix went back to the house to confront Aunty, threatening to tell authorities about her treatment of the children. Later that month Mrs. Kipling came to see the children. When she walked into the bedroom to kiss Rudyard goodnight, he automatically threw his arm up in fear of being hit. That was the end of their stay at Desolation House.

Did you know that when Robert Frost was eight years old, his father would take him to a slaughterhouse—where he would make Robert watch as he drank glasses of blood from the slashed throats of steers? His father thought this would cure his own tuberculosis.

PEGGY LEE (1920–   ), U.S. singer

For eleven years she endured beatings from her stepmother, "Min." In her autobiography Lee said that Min had "bulging thyroid eyes" and was "obese—strong as a horse. She beat everyone into a fright. Even the men were afraid of her." According to Lee, her stepmother poured scalding water over Peggy's hands, hit her over the head with a cast-iron skillet, beat her with a leather strap, and dragged her around by the hair.

When Peggy was ten, she spent ten days in a hospital to recover from appendicitis and peritonitis. On the day Peggy returned home, Min immediately told her to scrub the floor, but Peggy had a hard time working because she was so weak. Lee says: "My abdomen was fairly heavily bandaged and had drain tubes for the peritonitis. But that didn't stop her. Suddenly she was kicking me in the stomach, and she just kept kicking me until she broke the incision." Peggy survived her childhood by taking refuge in school and daydreaming about the day when she would become a famous singer.

MAO TSE-TUNG (1893–1976), Chinese communist leader

He grew up in a peasant family that lived in Hunan province. Even as a very young boy, Mao was stubborn, argumentative, and rebelled against whatever he thought was an unjust act. Those traits led to a lot of beatings from his father and his schoolteachers.

When Mao was ten, he was called upon by his teacher to recite some lessons he had learned. It was customary for students to stand beside the teacher's desk and face the class. Instead the defiant boy said, "If you can hear me well while I sit down, why should I stand up to recite?" The enraged teacher ordered the boy to stand at the front of the room, but Mao dragged his desk and stool up to the teacher's desk and promptly sat down. The teacher grabbed the boy and tried to make him stand, but Mao broke free and raced out of the school. He hid in the hills for three days before he was located and forced to return home. When interviewed many years later, he said, "After my return to the family, to my surprise conditions somewhat improved. My father was slightly more considerate, and the teacher was more inclined to moderation. The result of my act of protest impressed me very much. It was a successful strike."

MARY McCARTHY (1912–1989), U.S. novelist and critic

The controversial and outspoken writer was orphaned at the age of six when both of her parents died in an influenza epidemic. The care of Mary and her three brothers was entrusted to their aunt and uncle, Margaret and Myers Shriver, of Minneapolis.

Mary and her brothers weren't allowed to play with other children and were given only a few broken-down toys to play with, even though they had some wonderful playthings given to them by their grandparents. They weren't permitted to read anything but religious books, the food they ate was horrible, and candy was forbidden. The Shrivers believed that children needed fresh air and would lock the kids outdoors for hours, even in subzero temperatures. To prevent "mouth breathing," the Shrivers taped the children's mouths shut at night. When the children did anything wrong, Uncle Myers beat them with a hairbrush or razor strop.

At age ten Mary won first prize—and twenty-five dollars—in an essay contest with her entry "The Irish in American History." Uncle Myers took away her prize money and beat her so that she wouldn't "become stuck-up." After two years of unrelenting abuse, Mary and her brothers were finally rescued by their grandparents. She later wrote about her aunt and uncle: "It was as though these ignorant people, at sea with four frightened children, had taken a Dickens novel—*Oliver Twist*, perhaps, or *Nicholas Nickleby*—for a navigation chart."

HENRY MILLER (1891–1980), U.S. writer

As a boy, the famed novelist was consistently rejected or ignored by both parents. Although he was always dressed in fashionable clothing (his dad was a tailor) and had more toys than anyone else in his Brooklyn neighborhood, Henry received no affection, encouragement, or praise. Heinrich, his father, was an easygoing man who had a drinking problem and stayed away from home as much as possible. His mother, Louise, was an unstable, Puritanical disciplinarian who had rules for everything and watched over the household with an autocratic hand. Overall, Miller would later say that his parents and relatives combined added up to "a galaxy of screwballs."

Did you know that in his family's vaudeville act, five-year-old Buster Keaton was known as "the little boy who can't be damaged"? Buster's father would throw him around the stage without apparently hurting him. Buster's mother even sewed a suitcase handle onto his costume so his father could grab him more easily.

Mental illness was rooted in his mother's side of the family, and Louise often flew into unpredictable, uncontrollable rages that could last for days. Often she took out her anger on Henry's younger sister, Lauretta, who was mentally retarded. When his mother beat or screamed at Lauretta, Henry would hypnotize himself and mentally drift off into another world. Almost every evening his mother and father would fight at the dinner table, causing Henry to go into a gagging fit. (Even as an adult, Miller would sometimes find his throat contracting when he tried to swallow food.)

Because he got so little nurturing or love at home, Henry devoted himself to his neighborhood friends. A generous boy, he felt guilty that he had so many toys when most of his friends had none. So he gave away his toys one by one, even his most prized possessions such as the drum he got for his fourth birthday. When Louise learned of her son's benevolence, she grabbed him by the ear and dragged him to the home of every child who had received a toy and made Henry ask for everything back.

Henry was fond of one of his friend's mothers, who always had kind words and sweet treats for the boys. He later wrote, "I was in seventh heaven. . . . She was affectionate, a quality I didn't know mothers were supposed to possess in dealing with their offspring. All I knew was discipline, criticism, slaps, threats."

BERNARD LAW MONTGOMERY (1887–1976), British general

Son of an Anglican bishop, Montgomery spent his early years in Tasmania, where his mother, Maud, ran the household according to a strict code of behavior and bullied her children and her husband. Bernard and his siblings had to adhere to a daily set of rules: when to pray, play, eat, do chores. Of all the children, Bernard rebelled the most against his mother's tyrannical rule. Once, when the children were lined up and listening to Maud's instructions, the young boy bellowed, "Silence in the pig market, the old sow speaks first."

Maud hit Bernard with a cane or a whip or a stick. According to Montgomery, the beatings were "constant" and he would later say, "My early life was a series of fierce battles from which my mother invariably emerged the victor." Yet some of her traits—her ironclad will, fierce determination, and unwavering self discipline—became a part of Montgomery's character and served him well as he advanced through the military hierarchy. As an adult, Montgomery tried to establish a better relationship with his mother, but she was incapable of bestowing love and affection. After he became famous following the British defeat of Rommel's German army at El Alamein in North Africa during World War II, he often shunned Maud; and when she died, he did not attend her funeral.

MARY TYLER MOORE (1936–   ), U.S. actor

Mary was six and living in Flushing, New York, when she was molested by a family friend. In *After All*, her autobiography, she gives an account of the incident saying, "I was paralyzed as I remembered where I was and who was making me feel this way. It had to be bad what he was doing, really bad . . . I was ashamed and scared because I couldn't stop him."

She told her mother what had happened, but she was too young to know all the right words to describe what the man had done to her. Nevertheless, she got the message across. According to Moore, "My mother said, 'No! That's not true.' My mother said, 'It didn't happen.' . . . I never felt the same about her after that. My mother, by her denial, had abused me far more than her friend."

JOHN MUIR (1838–1914), Scottish-born U.S. naturalist

John Muir was one of the world's greatest conservationists and founder of the Sierra Club. He was born in Dunbar, Scotland, where he lived for eleven years until his family sailed to the United States in 1849. In his Scottish grammar school all of the boys were taught by teachers who believed that sparing the rod spoiled the child. Students were punished for a multitude of infractions—failure to get to school on time, misbehavior in class, failure to learn lessons fast enough, involvement in a playground fistfight. The instrument of punishment was a *tawse*, a whip with thongs at one end to make the flogging hurt more (cuts could be inflicted if enough force was used). Johnnie Muir, an adventurous and outspoken lad, got more than his fair share of thrashings at school.

Beatings at home were worse than beatings at school, however. Johnnie's father, a corn merchant, was a stern taskmaster and religious fanatic. He beat his son with a strap or cane for everything from failing to memorize a Bible passage to taking a short rest while working, from expressing an opinion not asked for to forgetting to do a small task. Often the father yelled, "The Deevil's in that boy." According to Muir, the punishments were "outrageously severe."

As an adult, Muir sometimes claimed that the floggings may have served some good purpose, like instilling in him a sense of discipline and fortitude. In reality, he had a lifelong hatred of child beating. He once wrote: "When the rod is falling on the flesh of a child, and, what may oftentimes be worse, heartbreaking scolding falling on its tender little heart, it makes the whole family seem far from the Kingdom of Heaven. In all the world I know of nothing more pathetic and deplorable than a heartbroken child, sobbing itself to sleep after being unjustly punished by a truly pious and conscientiously misguided parent."

ANNIE OAKLEY (1860–1926), U.S. rodeo performer

When Annie was six years old, her father died, leaving her mother to care for seven children, all under the age of fifteen. Three years later Annie was sent to the county poor farm in Greenville, Ohio. She was there for only two weeks when a nearby farmer offered to take her into his home to help care for his newborn baby; the workload would be light, he promised, and Annie would be able to attend school.

Annie's new family never sent her to school but treated her as a slave. She took care of the baby, prepared meals, fed the livestock, worked in the garden, trapped and hunted game for food. The couple—Annie called them "he-wolf" and "she-wolf"—beat her often, and at times she was unable to sleep because of the welts on her back. One night "she-wolf" threw a barefoot Annie outside into the snow because the girl almost fell asleep while darning some socks. Annie would later write, "I was held a prisoner. They would not let me go."

For two years Annie was at the mercy of "the wolves," until she finally ran away. After that, she lived part-time with her mother and part-time at the poor farm. She married at age fifteen and went on to become a professional sharpshooter and the star of Buffalo Bill Cody's Wild West Show.

RICHARD PRYOR (1940–), U.S. comedian and actor

When he was six years old, Richard was raped by a sixteen-year-old neighborhood kid named Hoss. The boy was playing in the alley behind his house in Peoria, Illinois, when Hoss appeared and told Richard what he intended to do. Paralyzed with fear, Richard was unable to run away. Pryor later said, "I cried and shook and tried to make sense of what had happened. I knew something horrible had happened to me. I felt violated, humiliated, dirty, fearful, and most of all, ashamed. I carried that secret around for most of my life."

Many years later, when Pryor was famous and making a movie in Peoria, Hoss stopped by the movie set and asked to see Pryor. Richard agreed, though he had spent a lifetime hating the guy and had no idea what he would say to him. When Hoss arrived, he had his son with him and explained to Richard that the son was a big fan and would like an autograph. The visit was short and no words about the past were spoken. Ironically, Hoss's son was about six years old.

BRIAN WILSON (1942–   ), U.S. musician
The genius behind the Beach Boys singing group, Wilson wrote in his auto-biography, *Wouldn't It Be Nice:* "I've always thought my dad never should have had kids. . . . He abused us psychologically and physically, creating wounds that never healed." Brian's father, Murray, himself a victim of child abuse, beat all three of his sons; but Brian, the oldest, was the most severely victimized. On one occasion, when Brian (age nine) unleashed the neighbor's dog, his father brutally hit him with a splintered two-by-four.

Murray Wilson, an aspiring songwriter, wrote beautiful songs with lovely melodies, and Brian said that the only time his father seemed calm and nor-mal was when he was composing music. According to Wilson, "The rest of the time he was pure danger, a land mine waiting to be detonated." After the Beach Boys recorded their first hit song, "Surfin'," Murray appointed himself manager of the group. He worked long, hard hours and, as Wilson put it, "My dad deserves credit for getting us off the ground." Wilson says his father's vi-olent behavior left him "indelibly scarred" and with "a predisposition to men-tal illness that left me a cripple." When Wilson was thirty-one, his father died. Upon hearing the news, Wilson wrote, "I buried my head in the pillow and cried."

OPRAH WINFREY (1954–   ), U.S. talk show host and actor
By the time she was fourteen, Oprah had been sexually molested by a cousin, an uncle, and the boyfriend of another relative. Since revealing these inci-dents, Oprah has relentlessly crusaded on behalf of the victims of child abuse and has testified before the U.S. Senate Judiciary Committee.

In an interview with *Good Housekeeping* magazine, Oprah was asked what she would change in the world if she could change one thing. Her reply: "I would stop people from beating their kids. Not just beating, but molesting kids, verbally abusing kids, neglecting kids. The dishonor of children is the single worst problem in this country."

CHILDHOOD TRAUMAS

FATTY ARBUCKLE (1887–1933), U.S. film actor
Born weighing fourteen pounds, Roscoe Arbuckle early earned the nickname "Fatty." Even when he was little, his irascible father, William, beat him often. Fatty was just a toddler when William moved the family to Santa Ana, Cali-fornia, where he opened a small hotel and promptly left for Watsonville, about three hundred miles north, perhaps to look for gold. He eventually opened another hotel there.

As Fatty grew up in Santa Ana with his mother and siblings, he hung out at the local theater, where he often took part in productions. One by one, his older brothers and sisters left home. When he was twelve years old, his mother died. His married sister Nora comforted him, and then she put him on a train for Watsonville to go to live with his father. When Fatty arrived, however, he found that his father had left town—leaving no forwarding address, even though he knew Fatty was coming. Fatty sat crying at the station beside his cardboard suitcase. Luckily Sam Booker, the man who had bought his father's Watsonville hotel, took pity on him and gave him room and board in exchange for work around the hotel. Booker traced William Arbuckle to San Jose. On the day he received word of where his father was, Fatty overturned a meat wagon by taking a corner too fast. Booker told him to move on, so Fatty went to San Jose to join his father, who had given him plenty of evidence that he was unwanted.

> *Did you know that the one time Mohandas Gandhi left his father's sickbed, his father died? And for that, Gandhi never forgave himself.*

ETHEL BARRYMORE (1879–1959), U.S. actor

When they were little, Ethel, Lionel, and John Barrymore barely knew their mother, Georgie; she was too busy acting. Ethel said, "I looked at her in worship and silence as a small girl, longing to talk with her, but fearing out of the very shyness of my nature to speak to her."

At the peak of her career, Georgie became ill with tuberculosis. When nothing else seemed to help, doctors advised her to go to California for the drier air. Ethel, then thirteen, was chosen to go with her.

No one told Ethel how ill her mother was, but she had an inkling. During the three-week trip to Santa Barbara, California, Ethel could hear her mother coughing at night. Once her mother said to herself, "What's going to happen to my children?" Though she said nothing, Ethel was frightened.

In Santa Barbara, a doctor came to the house. After listening to Georgie cough, he asked who was going to take care of her. When Georgie told him that Ethel would do it, a strange look came over the doctor's face. It filled Ethel with panic. At first Georgie seemed to get better. One day she even went out for a drive in a carriage with the mayor. Ethel went to mass, and as she came home, a child ran to her to tell her that her mother had had a hemorrhage. Georgie died soon after.

It was Ethel who packed up the house, with the help of their Chinese cook. It was Ethel who sent telegrams to her father and uncle, telling them what happened. It was Ethel who made arrangements with the undertaker and for the return trip by train for herself and the coffin containing her mother's body. Because she had no money for mourning clothes, she wore her black uniform from convent school.

For four days and nights on the trip back east, Ethel sat up in day coach. In Chicago, her father met the train, but it was Ethel who made the arrangements for the rest of the trip to New York—he was too hysterical.

ANGELA DAVIS (1944–   ), U.S. political activist

In 1948, the Davises moved out of the projects of Birmingham, Alabama, into a big house on Center Street. They were the first African-American family to move into the neighborhood, and the white people did not like it. They drew a line down the center of the street, letting it be known that only if the black people stayed on the east side would they be safe from harrassment.

White people began to move out and black people to move in. One African-American family, the Deyaberts, bought a house on the verboten west side of the street, right next to the Montees, an elderly white couple who were in the habit of sitting on their front porch staring with hate at the black people.

One evening in spring 1949, Angela was washing out her white shoelaces in the bathroom when a terrible explosion rocked the house. It threw medicine bottles off the shelves and sent her running into the kitchen where her mother was. Crowds of African Americans assembled on the east side of the street. The Deyaberts' house was in ruins. That was the first bombing of several, as more African-American families moved into the "white" side of the street. Sometimes Police Chief Bull Conner would announce on the radio that a "nigger family" had moved to the white side and predict, "There will be bloodshed tonight." The neighborhood was christened Dynamite Hill.

Though Angela's mother, a teacher, tried to tell her that not all white people were hateful and that peace between the races was possible, Angela and her friends stood on the lawn and shouted "cracker" and "redneck" at cars of white people when they drove by. She and other neighborhood children took turns ringing the Montees' doorbell and hiding in the bushes while the Montees screamed, "You little niggers better leave us alone." She became intensely aware of discrimination, and she also decided that she would never want to be white. She had a fantasy in which, in whiteface, she went wherever she wanted, before dramatically pulling off the face and calling people fools.

DORIS DAY (1924–   ), U.S. singer and actor

William Kappelhoff, a music teacher and opera lover, didn't get along with his wife, Alma Sophia, so he spent much of his time away from home. His daughter, Doris (later Doris Day), admired him but didn't see much of him.

Did you know that when Mickey Mantle was a sophomore in high school, the future baseball great was faced with the horrible possibility that his leg would be amputated?

Nonetheless, the Kappelhoff house was full. Doris often brought her friends home, especially Jane and Virginia. Jane and Virginia needed looking after—their tall, auburn-haired mother, a classical singer and Mrs. Kappelhoff's best friend, was having an affair with Mr. Kappelhoff.

One night when she was ten, Doris's parents hosted a big party, an unusual thing for them to do. She was half-asleep in her bedroom when she heard whispering, then saw her father peek into the room. Doris didn't move, pretending to be asleep.

Kappelhoff and his inamorata tiptoed through Doris's bedroom into the spare room, where they made love. Doris heard it all. She burst into tears, but muffled her sobs when the two came back out through her room. And she never told.

Alma soon found out about the affair anyway. Within a year, Doris's father moved out. From then on Doris and her brother took turns sleeping in her father's bed. Her father married the lover.

Did you know that Adlai Stevenson, at twelve years old, accidentally shot and killed a young girl with a .22 rifle?

MOHANDAS K. GANDHI (1869–1948), Indian nationalist and spiritual leader
The man who would become an international symbol of peace and tolerance was a shy, serious boy who was very devoted to his parents. At thirteen he

was married to Kasturbai, a thirteen-year-old girl from his hometown of Porbandar (Hindu child marriages were not unusual). Even though the marriage had been arranged by his parents, Mohandas was passionately in love with his wife and often had sex on his mind. He thought about Kasturbai all the time at school and couldn't wait to get home for what he called "lustful love."

When Mohandas was sixteen, his father became seriously ill. Every day the teenager acted as nurse to his father; he gave him medications and at night massaged his legs until his father fell asleep. One night while giving the massage, Mohandas's uncle approached him and offered to take over. Obsessed by "carnal desire" for his pregnant wife who was sleeping nearby, Mohandas agreed. Shortly afterward, a servant knocked on the bedroom door and informed Mohandas that his father had died.

His absence from his father's deathbed would forever torment Gandhi. He later wrote, "I saw that, if animal passion had not blinded me, I should have been spared the torture of separation from my father during his last moments. . . . It is a blot I have never been able to efface or forget." When Kasturbai gave birth, the baby lived for only three or four days—which to Mohandas was another tragedy, another "shame," that happened because he had been self-indulgent and had given in to his passions.

JERRY GARCIA (1942–1995), U.S. musician
Jose Garcia, Jerry Garcia's father, owned a bar called the Four Hundred Club on the San Francisco waterfront. He was also a clarinet player. At night he played the clarinet for little Jerry, who looked just like him, to help him go to sleep.

When Jerry was five, the family went on a camping trip. Jose went fly-fishing in the fast-moving river, slipped, went under, and was swept away. Jerry, playing on the riverbank, saw it all. "I couldn't even stand to hear about it until I was ten or eleven," he later said. "I didn't start to get over it till then, maybe because of the way it affected my mother."

His mother, Ruth, went to work full-time at the bar, but she found she could not handle it all—grieving, child care, and full-time work. She sent Jerry to live with her parents, who lived nearby, and they raised him for the next five years. They did not discipline him very much, which may have been responsible for his poor performance in school and his flirtation with gangs in high school. The lack of discipline was probably also partly responsible for his streak of independence. In 1952, Ruth remarried and took Jerry back.

KATHARINE HEPBURN (1907–   ), U.S. actor
After eating breakfast, thirteen-year-old Kathy Hepburn went up to her Aunt Mary's attic room to wake up her adored brother Tom, two and a half years older than she. She found him dead, hanged by a braided sheet tied to a rafter, his knees bent, his feet on the floor, his face blue.

Tom had given only a little indication, and that ambiguous, that he would kill himself that night. He and Kathy, the two oldest of the six Hepburn children, had been on a pleasure trip to New York City to visit their aunt. Two nights before he killed himself, they went to see a movie based on Mark

Twain's *A Connecticut Yankee in King Arthur's Court.* It contained a hanging scene, which gave Tom "the horrors."

Dr. Hepburn, the children's father, insisted that Tom's death had been an accident. Yet Tom had had a lifelong history of nervous problems and had been found hanging the year before. (Though he had said it was a stunt, some doubt existed about why he had done it.) The family grieved in Victorian silence. Dr. Hepburn would not talk to Kathy about suicide or what she had seen and experienced.

Kathy changed. She became moody and buried herself in her schoolwork but somehow could not keep up with it. She tried to become Tom. She said she planned to be a doctor like her father, as Tom had, and even took Tom's birthday, November 8, as her own. Nothing helped much. The little girl who had shouted, "I am going to change the world! I am going to change the world!" when she was six could not change the incomprehensible fact of her brother's death.

MICKEY MANTLE (1931–1995), U.S. baseball player

The legendary New York Yankees center fielder was named "Mickey" after Detroit Tigers catcher Mickey Cochrane. Mantle's father, Elvin, a miner and semiprofessional (weekend) baseball player, was determined that Mickey would one day become a major league baseball player. Mickey was always told to "practice, practice, practice," and by the time he was in the second grade, Mickey was a standout player. Every day his father worked out with him and spent endless hours teaching him to be a switch-hitter. On the sideline stood Mickey's mother Lovell, who shared her husband's passion for the game. The young boy never felt pressured or intimidated; he adored his parents and loved baseball.

In his sophomore year in high school in Commerce, Oklahoma, Mickey played football, and during one game was kicked really hard in the left shin. The next day his temperature was 104 degrees, and his ankle was double its normal size. For weeks he was treated at two hospitals, but none of the various treatments improved the condition. Doctors finally said he had osteomyelitis—an infection of the bone marrow—and that his leg would have to be amputated. Mickey, horrified, saw his entire future dissolving before his eyes. His mother adamantly refused the operation.

Mickey's condition finally improved after being injected around the clock (every three hours) with penicillin, the new wonder drug. Full recovery took almost a year, but he finally gained back the weight he had lost and was able to stop using crutches. Referring to the proposed leg amputation, he later wrote, "I would have rather seen mine rot off than have somebody cut it off without at least trying to find an alternative."

PABLO PICASSO (1881–1973), Spanish artist

The child prodigy knew he was destined to become a great artist; no other profession ever entered his mind. When he was thirteen, Pablo's seven-year-old sister Conchita contracted diphtheria. Her transformation from a healthy, bright-eyed little girl to a very sickly, bedridden child terrified Pablo. As her death grew near, the boy made a deal with God: Spare his sister, and he would never paint again.

Once Pablo had made the secret pact, he was tormented by his offer. He truly wanted his sister to live, yet he desperately wanted to paint. When Conchita died, he felt overwhelming guilt because he figured God knew of his ambivalence and that it was his lack of real commitment that had caused God to allow his sister to die. On the other hand, he also felt that the death had confirmed his destiny to be an artist, no matter what obstacles and consequences he might face.

WILHELM REICH (1897–1957), Austrian psychiatrist

Twelve-year-old Wilhelm adored and idolized his mother, Cecilia, and hated and feared his tyrannical father, Leo. Wilhelm's father was obsessively jealous of any attention paid to his wife and always suspected that she was cheating on him. In truth, Cecilia had had an affair with a younger man who had been hired as a live-in tutor for Wilhelm. The couple made love in the tutor's bedroom, and Wilhelm stood outside the room and listened. In his autobiography, Reich writes, "I heard them kissing, whispering, and the horrible creaking of the bed in which my mother lay. Ten feet away stood her own child, a witness to her disgrace."

Did you know that when Margaret Sanger's father wanted to make a bust of her dead brother, her father took young Maggie to the cemetery and made her hold the lantern as he dug up the body and made a death mask of the brother's face?

One afternoon Wilhelm's father flew into a rage and demanded that Cecilia confess to any love affairs she had ever engaged in. She denied everything. When Leo asked Wilhelm if he had any evidence of Cecilia's infidelity, Wilhelm told everything he knew about his mother and the tutor, including how he had spied on them and what he had seen and heard.

For months after Wilhelm's disclosures, Leo inflicted both verbal and physical abuse upon Cecilia. Finally, she committed suicide by swallowing poison. Wilhelm was never able to exonerate himself from the part he played in his mother's death. When he was forty-seven, he wrote, "I wish my mother were alive today so that I could make good for the crime I committed."

MARGARET SANGER (1879–1966), U.S. social reformer

Margaret Higgins Sanger, the woman who would spearhead the birth control movement in the United States, was born in Corning, New York. Her father, Michael, was a stonemason. Her mother, Anne, who suffered from tuberculosis, was a devout Irish Catholic who became pregnant eighteen times; she died when she was forty-nine, after having suffered seven miscarriages and given birth to four girls and seven boys. With her father often out of work and her mother always ill, Maggie Higgins was burdened at an early age with adult responsibilities. When she grew up, Sanger got stomach pains whenever she rode on a train that merely passed through her hometown—an attack of "Corningitis," she said.

When Maggie was very young, her four-year-old brother died and was buried in a local cemetery. In an attempt to console Anne Higgins, Maggie's father decided to make a bust of the boy, but before he could create the work of art, he needed a plaster cast of the boy's face. Taking Maggie with him, Michael Higgins went into the cemetery at midnight and dug up the boy's body. As he diligently worked on the death mask, Maggie stood by, silently holding a lantern.

ADLAI STEVENSON (1900–1965), U.S. politician

Stevenson, the governor of Illinois, was the Democratic candidate for president of the United States in 1952 and 1956, and he later served as U.S. ambassador to the United Nations. Born into a socially prominent family, Adlai grew up in Bloomington, Illinois. He loved sports and trains and stamp collecting. Overall, he was a normal, active child with an inquisitive mind and a love of American history. Adults were often impressed with his conscientious nature; he was a nice kid and had good manners.

When Adlai was twelve, his older sister, Buffie, threw a Christmas party at the family home. As the party got under way, Adlai's parents left to visit a neighbor and Adlai spent most of the time in his room, since he was "too young" to mix with the older kids. However, one of the boys at the party wanted to demonstrate the manual of arms, which he had learned at military school, so Adlai was called upon to fetch an old .22 rifle from the attic. After supposedly checking the gun to make sure it wasn't loaded, the older boy performed his demonstration and then gave the rifle back to Adlai. However, the gun was loaded, and while Adlai was handling the gun, it went off. The bullet hit one of the female guests in the forehead, and she fell to the floor and died.

No one ever doubted that the tragedy was an accident, and the dead girl's parents held no animosity toward Adlai. From then on, no one in the Stevenson family ever mentioned the incident. Many years later a magazine reporter unearthed the story and asked Stevenson about it. Reportedly, the statesman said, "You are the first person who has ever asked me about that since it happened—and this is the first time I have spoken of it to anyone." Ten years before he died, Stevenson learned about a woman whose son had been involved in a similar accident. He wrote a letter to the woman with advice for her son, "Tell him that he must live for two."

ATTEMPTED SUICIDES

JUDY COLLINS (1939–   ), U.S. singer

Her father, Charles, who had lost his sight as a boy, refused to use a cane. He performed on radio, telling funny stories, philosophizing, and singing songs. Judy took after him. He said of her, "This tyke can harmonize with anything, even a car horn, a train whistle." However he had other, more ambitious plans for her. When Judy was five, she began taking piano lessons. By the time she was eleven, she had displayed such talent at classical piano that Dr. Antonia Brisco, who had studied in Berkeley music schools, took her on as a pupil. In 1951, her father asked her to play on his radio show. She chose Mendelssohn's "Arabesque," and they sang a song together.

In 1953, Judy played Mozart's *Concerto in E-flat* in a piano duet with Brisco's orchestra. Some months later she started learning a difficult Liszt transcription of a Paganini violin piece. Her father asked her to play it on a program he was giving in June, a month away. She said that she couldn't do it, that she wasn't ready. He insisted that she could do it if she wanted to. A week went by, while she agonized over disappointing her father, either by refusing to play or playing badly. While she was ironing shirts, she decided that only one solution to her dilemma was possible: death. She took handfuls of aspirin, thinking they would kill her. After a while, she started to feel sick and frightened. She called a friend, Marcia Pinto, whose father was a doctor. Mrs. Pinto told her to induce vomiting and said that she was sending her husband over. When he came, Dr. Pinto said that even though Judy had taken about a hundred aspirin, she would be all right. When her mother asked her why she had attempted to kill herself, she said she was afraid of failing her father.

GRAHAM GREENE (1904–1991), English writer

His family home was attached to Berkhamsted School, in Berkhamsted, England, where his father, Charles, who looked a little like a walrus, was headmaster. Charles thought boys were naturally sinners, probably believed that masturbation led to madness, and ran the school so that no homosexual acts could take place.

Just before Graham turned fourteen, he became a boarder at the school. He felt abandoned by his parents. The fact that he was the headmaster's son complicated his life enormously. The dormitory was cold. He had no privacy: ". . . no moment of the night was free from noise, a cough, a snore, a fart." He could not sleep. He didn't play games. He was not popular. He was odd.

One of the boys, L. A. Carter, tormented Graham by calling him names, testing his loyalty to his father, and pricking him with dividers (a tool for doing geometry). Other boys joined in. Graham felt he had two choices: to betray his father or to put up with the teasing.

He had to escape. He tried to cut his knee open with a penknife, but he could not bring himself to stab himself hard enough. Turning to poison, he drank a hypo from the photography dark room and a whole bottle of cocaine-laced hayfever medicine. He ate deadly nightshade and a box of hair pomade. He swallowed handfuls of aspirin.

None of this worked.

So he decided to run away. He wrote a note saying he was hiding out on the Commons until his parents agreed not to send him back to St. John's. His sister Molly found him. His father listened kindly to him as he complained about the "filth" in the dormitories. Graham meant the unlocked bathrooms and the farting. His father thought he meant that there was a masturbation ring.

In 1921, the family sent Graham away to be psychoanalyzed by the spiritualist-psychologist Kenneth Richmond. Richmond's wife, Zoe, claimed that "People are often suicidal and unbalanced if they have impossible parents. . . . His [Graham's] father had a frightful instinct against homosexuality. Graham wasn't homosexual but he was feminine and sometimes you cannot tell the difference. . . . In Graham's case, he wanted to commit suicide in the end because he couldn't love himself or anybody else."

MARTIN LUTHER KING, JR. (1929–1968), U.S. civil rights leader

His father, Martin Luther, ruled the house as a stern patriarch, while his subdued mother, Alberta (Mother Dear), was deliberate and calm. His "saintly grandmother" Williams was warm and comforting, and she adored M. L. (as he was then called). "She was very dear to each of us," King later wrote, "but especially to me. I sometimes think that I was her favorite grandchild." When his father beat him with a strap for infractions of the rules, M. L. would cry without uttering a sound. Grandmother Williams—M. L. called her "Mama"—would go to another room and begin to cry herself.

One day, his little brother, A. D. (Alfred Daniel), came sliding down the banister right into Mama. She fell and did not move. M. L., thinking she was dead, frantically ran upstairs, threw himself out of a window, and fell twelve feet to the ground. When his relatives called his name so that he would get up, he did not move. When he heard that Mama was all right, he finally stood.

On May 18, 1941, M. L. sneaked off to watch a parade. While he stood there enjoying it, a messenger came and told him that something had happened to his grandmother. M. L. ran home and saw a crowd of people at his house. Grandmother Williams had died of a heart attack on the way to the hospital.

M. L. thought God was punishing him, partly because he had sneaked off to watch the parade without telling anybody. Laden with guilt and sorrow, he went upstairs and threw himself out of the window, falling to the ground. He had thought he could follow Mama to heaven that way.

GREG LOUGANIS (1960–   ), U.S. diver

There was never any doubt that young Greg possessed superior athletic skills. At the age of eighteen months he was taking acrobatic lessons, and at age nine he was taking diving lessons. However, because of his dark skin (he was Samoan) and learning difficulties (he was dyslexic but didn't know it), his classmates called him names, and he was often beaten up by the school bullies. An introspective kid, Greg had a terrible self-image. In his autobiography, *Breaking the Surface,* he writes: "When I looked in the mirror, I saw an ugly kid who had a hard time reading. I felt terribly isolated and depressed, and was convinced that nobody could or would want to understand me."

When Greg was twelve, he was told by the family doctor that he would have to give up all sports except diving because of knee injuries. According to Louganis, he went into a depression that "hit a real low point" and decided to kill himself. He swallowed a bunch of pills ("mostly aspirin and Ex-Lax"), used a razor to inflict some minor cuts, and waited to die. When his effort failed, he decided to tell no one, not even his adoptive parents, about the suicide attempt.

Did you know that Graham Greene was so miserable at school (where his father was the headmaster) that he cut his knee open with a pen knife, then consumed solution from the darkroom, handfuls of aspirin, cocaine-laced medicine, deadly nightshade, and a box of hair pomade—all with hopes of escaping from life's pain?

Greg made another suicide attempt when he was a senior in high school and another when he was a college student (both drug attempts). In his autobiography, the Olympic diving gold medalist talks openly about his childhood days, his homosexuality, the fact that he is HIV-positive, and his need to uncover and face all the facts about his past. About his suicide attempts, he writes, "After having tried unsuccessfully to kill myself three times, I started thinking that there must be a reason why I was still alive, and maybe I should try to figure out what that reason was."

ALMOST ABORTED

TRUMAN CAPOTE (1924–1984), U.S. writer

His mother, Lillie Mae Faulk, was seventeen when she married Arch Persons in Monroeville, Alabama. She married him partly to get away from her family. Also, she reasoned, with his big, expensive cars, he must be prosperous. Their honeymoon came to an abrupt end when Arch ran out of money.

Determined to take care of herself and jettison Arch, Lillie Mae entered business school in Selma. During an exercise class at the school, she fainted and found out she was pregnant. She left school and returned to Monroeville, set on having an abortion. All that spring, she worked on Arch to achieve her goal, but Arch "wanted a little son more than anything else in the world." He sent her to Colorado. By the time she came back to Monroeville, it was too late—she had the baby, Truman.

Arch and Lillie Mae divorced after seven years of marriage. Although she loved Truman she despised his girlishness. He was small and pretty, with a little high voice; he wanted to be a girl until he was nine.

After her second marriage, to Joe Capote, who adopted Truman, Lillie Mae, renamed Nina, aborted two other pregnancies. "I will not have another child like Truman," she said, "and if I do have another child it will be like Truman." One of those abortions harmed her reproductive organs so badly that when she did decide to have a child, she was unable to become pregnant again.

JOHN CHEEVER (1912–1982), U.S. writer

John Cheever's mother didn't want him. "If I hadn't drunk two manhattans one afternoon, you would never have been conceived," she once told him. But it was his father, Frederick Lincoln Cheever, who suggested that she get an abortion. He even invited the abortionist to dinner. Nonetheless John William Cheever was born—on May 27, 1912. His mother, Mary, was thirty-nine; Frederick was forty-nine. Frederick thought one son was enough, and he favored Fred, born seven years before. John felt unwanted. He wrote in his novel *Falconer,* "Farragut's father, Farragut's own father, had wanted to have him extinguished as he dwelt in his mother's womb, and how could we live happily with this knowledge?" His mother was usually too busy with charity work to pay him much attention. She had tuberculosis and may have passed it on to young John; he felt that she neglected him when he was ill. Cheever's wife, Mary, said, "He never had any love. His parents never paid much attention to him."

His father's rejection poisoned his relationship with his brother, which was paramount in his life. He once said to his biographer, Scott Donaldson, "Some people have parents or children. I had a brother. . . . For a long time I couldn't take him. I still can't." Yet as young men they spent a good deal of time together. Fred supported John when he was writing in obscurity. In the year John finished his novel *Falconer,* he said to Fred, "I killed you off in *Falconer.*" Fred replied, "Good, you've been trying all these years." That year, Fred died of alcoholism in spite of John's attempts to save him.

CHER (1946–   ), U.S. singer and actor

At eighteen, Jackie Jean Crouch (later Georgia Holt) a country-and-western singer, was besotted with a handsome, alcoholic farmer, John Sarkisian. She married him in Reno. Though she soon realized that the marriage was a mistake, pregnancy prevented her from leaving Sarkisian. She decided to abort the baby and even went to the clinic to have the procedure done. However, the clinic was too dirty. Perhaps it was reminiscent of the grimy shelters she had slept in with her alcoholic father when she was singing in bars to support both of them. In any event, she decided to remain with her husband and have the baby. The child, Cherilyn, was born on May 20, 1946.

Still a star-struck teenager, Jackie put Cherilyn in orphanages and foster homes while she tried to break into show business. She gave Cherilyn the impression that having children kept her from success as an entertainer. Yet she did not seem to feel that way about husbands, of whom she had four. And in spite of the fact that Sarkisian, a morphine addict, did time in the penitentiary for passing bad checks and drug use, Jackie married him again—twice.

Cher said of her father, "He didn't have any features that I think are important; he had no character. So even though he could be cute and adorable, he had no backbone." However, she resembles him in looks and charisma.

At sixteen, Cher left home and moved in with twenty-eight-year-old Sonny Bono. Bono reminded Georgia of Sarkisian, and he was still married, to boot.

GERARD DEPARDIEU (1948–   ), French actor

Lilette Depardieu had to give up a trip she had planned—a trip that represented her movie-magazine-inspired dreams of exotic travel—in order to give birth to her third child, Gérard, in 1948. She and her husband, Dédé, were living in poverty in Châteauroux, a village in midwestern France. Though Dédé had a job as a sheet metal worker in a factory, the family also had to accept welfare in order to feed and clothe themselves. Perhaps partly because he had been unwelcome and his mother tended to ignore him, Gérard was a mercurial, irrepressible clown. When Lilette was in an irascible mood, she would tell him that he had ruined her Christmas with his birth. When he really irritated her, she would tell him that she had tried to abort him with knitting needles. Sometimes he would look in the mirror for scars of the needles on his face and top of his head. The notion that he had been unwanted disturbed him for years. He withdrew into himself.

Ironically, like his mother, the young Gérard, who liked to hang around the the nearby U.S.-manned NATO base, also dreamed of foreign lands. But his dream was of *le rêve américain* (the American Dream), an escape to a land of popcorn, rock, and James Dean.

JUDY GARLAND (1922–1969), U.S. singer and actor

In November 1921, Frank Gumm took the train nearly two hundred miles from Grand Rapids to Minneapolis. His mission was to ask a favor of his friend Marc Rabwin, a medical student at the University of Minnesota. He arrived late at night and went directly to Rabwin's boarding house, where he blurted out his problem. His wife, Ethel, was about two months pregnant. They did not want another child. After all, they already had two girls. Ethel had tried home remedies—castor oil, bouncy wagon rides—but nothing had worked. Could Marc help them out? Did he know of an abortionist? Marc, who knew the dangers of illegal abortion, talked Frank out of it. "After the baby's born," he said, "you wouldn't take a million dollars for it." Frank agreed to talk Ethel into having the baby. Frances Ethel Gumm, who became Judy Garland, was born on June 10, 1922.

Later, Rabwin moved to California, where he completed his residency. The Gumms followed in 1926 when Frank, who was bisexual, was forced to leave Minnesota in the wake of an affair with a boy.

Then Frances, just a kindergartener, came down with a dangerous infection. Rabwin knew how dangerous it was—when she was only one year old, a similar infection had nearly killed her and kept her in the hospital for almost a month. He rushed her by ambulance the sixty miles to Los Angeles County Hospital, where he had done his residency and where Oscar Weiss, a famous pediatrician, had his practice. Though the hospital usually took only charity cases, Rabwin found a way to bend the rules and get the child admitted. He and Weiss saw her through the crisis. He had saved her life again.

SADDAM HUSSEIN (1937–   ), Iraqi dictator

Her husband gone, Saddam Hussein's mother, Subha, "renowned for her ugliness and vile tongue," tried to kill herself—and Saddam—while he was still unborn. She even banged her stomach against walls to try to induce a miscarriage. But the baby stayed stubbornly in her womb. On April 28, 1937, she gave birth to Saddam in a mud brick house outside Tikrit belonging to her brother, Khayrallah Tulfah, and left him there. His life did not improve much after that. An Arab nationalist and schoolteacher, Khayrallah was jailed for five years for taking part in an uprising, so Saddam went to live with his mother, who had remarried. Her new husband, Ibrahim al-Hasan, known as "Hasan the Liar," tormented his stepson by making him dance around to avoid blows with an asphalt-covered stick. He would wake him up in the morning yelling, "Get up, you son of a whore, and look after the sheep."

Hussein makes up for his neglected and brutal youth with a cult of personality. A Swiss analyst claims that Hussein's name is mentioned fifty times an hour on radio Baghdad. Two huge sculptures of Hussein's arms stand over the main street in Baghdad, and giant portraits of him framed in brocade hang over streets. A statue of him, with spy cameras behind the eyes, stands in almost every town square in Iraq.

JACK LONDON (1876–1916), U.S. novelist and short-story writer

Jack's biological father, William H. Chaney, was an astrologer, and his mother, Flora Wellman, was a spiritualist. It's not certain that the couple were ever legally married, but when Flora became pregnant, Chaney was adamant that she get an abortion. Flora refused and was so distraught that she almost killed the fetus when she attempted, but failed, to kill herself, first by taking laudanum and then by shooting herself in the forehead with a gun.

Did you know that Truman Capote, until he was nine years old, wanted to be a girl?

The *San Francisco Chronicle* ran a long story, "A Discarded Wife" about the scandalous incidents. When Jack (who got his last name from his stepfather John London) was twenty-one, he tracked down Chaney and wrote him a letter, asking for his side of the story. Chaney denied that he was ever married to Flora and said that Jack was not his son.

ARTHUR RUBINSTEIN (1887–1982), Polish-born U.S. pianist
There were already six children in the family when Arthur's mother became pregnant again. It had been seven years since her last pregnancy, and her oldest daughter was about to be married. Arthur would have been aborted if not for the intervention of his Aunt Salomea, who persuaded his parents to change their minds. In his autobiography, *My Young Years,* Rubinstein states that he was never very close to his parents and that they never really appreciated him or his music, even though they recognized his genius. When he was ten, Arthur was sent away to Berlin to study music. About his parents, he later wrote, "I suppose that the main reason for the estrangement from my family lay in the fact that my parents sent me to live among strangers, who made a strong impact on my mind and my character at an age when I was most vulnerable."

ALMOST DIED

ALFRED ADLER (1870–1937), Austrian psychiatrist
He saw death up close twice before he was six. When he was nearly four, his one-and-a-half-year-old brother died in the bed next to his. Alfred then decided never to cry or scream again, to avoid having the spasms that brought him close to suffocation. At the age of five, he was privy to his own death sentence. Suffering from a bad case of pneumonia, he overheard the doctor say

to his father that there was "no point in going to the trouble of looking after [him] as there was no hope of [his] living." A "frightful terror" came over the little boy. He did get well, though. A few days later, he decided to become a doctor in order to "have a better defense against the danger of death and weapons to combat it superior to my doctor's." Adler went on to get a medical degree and become a leading psychiatrist and psychologist.

ISAAC ASIMOV (1920–1992), Russian-born U.S. science writer

He was born in Petrovichi, Russia. At the age of two, he developed double pneumonia. He was treated by cupping, a procedure in which a glass cup heated by a lighted paper is put on the skin. (The burning of the paper consumes oxygen and creates a vacuum to encourage circulation.) He was also wrapped to bring on sweating. Later, his mother told him that of the seventeen babies in the town who became ill with pneumonia, sixteen died. The doctor said Isaac would not live and told her to resign herself to it. Her own mother told her Isaac was "only a baby" and that there would be other children (he was the first). But he had taken three days and two nights to be born, and his mother was not about to give up. She sent her mother and the doctor packing and held Isaac in her arms until he recovered.

Did you know that Boris Yeltsin almost drowned at his baptism? The priest lowered the baby into the holy water, got distracted in an argument, and forgot to take Boris out of the water!

JOAN BAEZ (1941–   ), U.S. singer and civil rights activist

In 1951, Joan developed a high fever and diarrhea. She was so weak that reaching the glass of lemonade on the bedside table seemed impossible for her. Her devoted mother brought her the lemonade and otherwise took care of her, never leaving her side.

During the illness Joan dreamed that she was riding a bicycle on a vast, prairielike meadow. The road became smaller and smaller, finally becoming nothing but a potholed track so that she had to use her feet to guide the bike. On the edge of the meadow was a canyon, and on the other side of the canyon was a beautiful field of green grass. Without hesitating, Joan pushed with her foot and sailed off over the cliff to the field. As she floated toward it, she woke up. Her mother told her later that the dream had to do with dying.

ALBERT CAMUS (1913–1960), Algerian-born French writer

As a student in high school, Albert Camus excelled in sports as well as in academics. His ambition was to be a soccer player. He was obsessed with soccer—he even dribbled a can of shoe polish along the sidewalk to practice at odd moments. Then, sometime in the winter of 1930–1931, he became very ill. He coughed blood for two days, and his grandmother Catherine took the boy to his Uncle Gustave's house. The doctor came, and Albert ended up at Mustapha Hospital. His right lung was tubercular, a doctor told his uncle, adding, "You are the only one who can save the boy's life." He meant that Gustave, a butcher, could offer Albert not only a comfortable home but also lots of red meat. The doctor told Albert that he must rest; he should not even read. Albert, just seventeen, said, "What will I do, if I don't get better?" In 1930 there was no treatment for tuberculosis except rest and artificial pneumothorax, a collapsing of the lung.

"I don't want to die," said Camus to his Uncle Gustave, who did take him in. He later wrote in *Entre Oui et Non* (Between Yes and No): "At the worst of his illness, the doctor showed no hope for him. He had had no doubts about it. Besides, the fear of death troubled him considerably." In those days, before antibiotics, tuberculosis could kill someone in two or three years.

Albert lived. But because of the disease, he missed out on a professorship and was not allowed to join the military in World War II—perhaps not unmixed blessings. However, he never became a world-renowned soccer player, either.

JOSEPH CONRAD (1857–1924), Polish writer

His father, Apollo Korzeniowski, belonged to a Polish not-quite-aristocratic hereditary class, the *szlachta*. Impoverished but landed and a Polish patriot, he dressed in a peasant smock and spoke against Russian oppression. On October 20, 1861, he was arrested and jailed for seven months; then in May 1862 he and his wife, Eva, were sentenced to exile in Vologda, 250 miles northeast of Moscow. On the journey, near Moscow, four-year-old Joseph became ill with pneumonia. His parents refused to move on, in spite of the guards' refusal to let them stop. A doctor came from the city, sent by a sympathetic traveler, and saved the boy's life with calomel (a purgative) and leeches. Joseph felt better, but Apollo wanted to stay behind until the child was completely well. As Apollo said, "Naturally I protest against leaving, particularly as the doctor says openly that the child may die if we do so. My passive resistance postpones the departure but causes my guard to refer to the local authorities. The civilised oracle, after hearing the report, pronounces that we have to go at once—as children are born to die."

LIONEL HAMPTON (1913–   ), U.S. musician

His strong grandmother, Mama Louvenia, who belonged to the Holiness Church, was a healer. She prayed for sick people in the congregation; sometimes white people asked her to come to their houses to heal them. While she

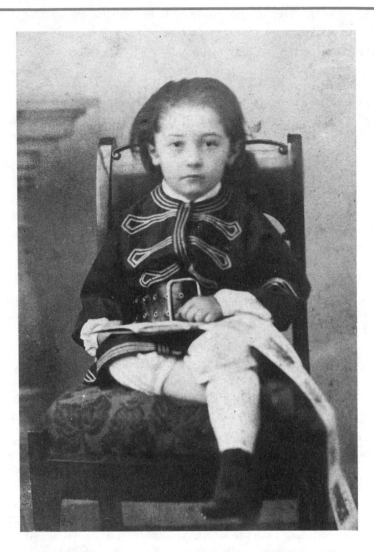

A healthy Joseph Conrad in 1863.

Courtesy of the Beinecke Rare Book and Manuscript Library, Yale University.

lived, according to Lionel, no one in the family went to a doctor. Her cohort was a woman named Sister Draper.

When Lionel was five or six, he developed pneumonia. Mama Louvenia was away, so his mother, who doubted her own power to heal, called a pharmacist to the house. The pharmacist diagnosed his illness and prescribed a medicine. Lionel wouldn't take it. His Mama Louvenia had trained him well, and over his bed hung a reminder of the power of faith to heal: a drawing of

Jesus with the words, "The great physician who forgiveth sins and healeth our diseases."

Lionel's mother could not persuade or force him to take the medicine, and he developed a very high fever. That night Mama Louvenia and Sister Draper came home and started working over him. Mama asked him, "Do you really believe in Jesus?" When he said yes, she made the sign of the cross with castor oil on his forehead and then got everyone in the family praying. The fever broke in about four hours.

Did you know that when psychiatrist Alfred Adler was five years old, he overheard his doctor tell his father that there was "no point in going to the trouble of looking after [him] as there is no hope of [his] living"? It was those words that made him decide to become a doctor in order to "have a better defence against death . . ."

HENRY JAMES (1843–1916), U.S. novelist

A terrible accident in the childhood of his father shadowed the lives of his sons. A flaming experimental air balloon fell into a hay loft, and thirteen-year-old Henry, who would become the novelist's father, climbed up and started to stamp it out. His trousers, which had been splashed with turpentine, caught on fire and he suffered dreadful burns over his whole leg. The leg failed to heal, and the boy suffered two amputations. As a result, he ended up with a cork leg, a sense of terror, and a drinking problem. It is not surprising that he overprotected his own children. He was determined that they would have a happier childhood than he had had.

Yet in the summer of 1857, when the James family was living in Boulogne, France, fourteen-year-old Henry, his son and namesake, came down with typhoid fever, which the future novelist later described as "the gravest illness of my life . . . an all but mortal attack." It marked, he said, "the limit of my state of being a small boy" and as he recovered, he discovered that he had access "into a part of myself previously quite unvisited and now made accessible as by the sharp forcing of a closed door." He was delirious for several days. His parents feared he would die. It took him eight weeks to recover. In a letter to his mother, Henry, Sr., wrote that they had "trembled more than once for the issue."

GEORGE LUCAS (1944–   ), U.S. film director and producer
He loved to drive fast and got more than his fair share of speeding tickets from the police in Modesto, California, where he grew up. On June 12, 1962, George was driving home on a country road in his Fiat Bianchina. As he made a left turn, a Chevy Impala hit him broadside. The small Fiat flipped over five times and ended up crashing into a walnut tree. On the third roll, George's seat belt broke loose, and he was miraculously thrown free of the car. He spent two weeks in the hospital, missed his high school graduation, and spent the summer undergoing extensive physical therapy. The car was totaled, and on top of it all, George got a ticket for making an illegal left turn.

PABLO PICASSO (1881–1973), Spanish artist
One of the most revered artists of the twentieth century, Pablo Picasso was stillborn. His mother's midwife made repeated efforts to get the baby to breathe, to move, to cry. When nothing worked, the midwife set the child aside and tended to his mother. However, standing on the sidelines watching the birth was Dr. Salvador Ruiz, Pablo's uncle. Smoking a cigar, the uncle blew smoke into the baby's nostrils and, as the story goes, Pablo began to move, coming to life "with a grimace and a bellow of fury."

MARJORIE MERRIWEATHER POST (1887–1973), U.S. financier and philanthropist
Marjorie grew up in Battle Creek, Michigan, where her father, C. W. Post, founded his cereal empire. When she was very young, Marjorie and her friend Myra often crossed railroad tracks on their walk home from school. One day Marjorie caught her shoe in the tracks as a train barreled toward the girls. Marjorie was so scared that she was unable to move. Myra took charge and was able to get Marjorie's foot out of the shoe—not a moment too soon. For years afterward, Post lavished presents on Myra, and when her friend grew old and had to be placed in a nursing home, Marjorie made sure that Myra was well taken care of.

BILL SHOEMAKER (1931–   ), U.S. jockey
As a child, Bill almost died on two occasions. The first time was on the day he was born. A premature baby, his skin had a bluish cast, and he weighed a mere two and a half pounds. Although the doctor said the baby had no hope of survival, he lived. Then, when Bill was about five or six and living on a ranch in Texas, he fell into a large tank, filled with water for cattle. Unable to swim, Bill screamed for help as his lungs filled with water. He was saved by his aunt, but it was a very close call.

Did you know that Pablo Picasso was stillborn and only after a healthy blast of smoke from his uncle's cigar was blown up Pablo's nose did he come to life?

JOHN STEINBECK (1902–1968), U.S. novelist

The acclaimed author of *The Grapes of Wrath* caught a bad case of the flu, which quickly brought on pneumonia, when he was sixteen. Antibiotics didn't exist at that time, and John was put into bed and watched around the clock by his parents. When his fever became dangerously high and he became delirious, a local surgeon was called in. The doctor, thinking the boy would soon die, performed surgery in the bedroom. He cut into John's chest and had to remove a rib in order to drain the infected lung. Of his illness, Steinbeck later wrote, "I went down and down, until the wingtips of angels brushed my eyes."

LAWRENCE WELK (1903–1992), U.S. bandleader

When he was eleven, Lawrence woke up in the middle of the night with an excruciating pain in his right side. Because it was harvest time on his family's farm in North Dakota, the boy tried to ignore the pain and nausea, since he knew how much the family needed him to work the following day. However, after breakfast the next morning, Lawrence passed out. By the time he was taken to the nearest hospital, seventy-five miles away, he had a ruptured appendix and a bad case of peritonitis. After an operation, the boy slipped in and out of consciousness for weeks. He remained in the hospital for seven weeks and then had to spend another two months in bed at home. Recovery from the life-threatening attack took almost a year.

BORIS YELTSIN (1931–   ), Russian political leader

On the day Boris was baptized, a drunken priest lowered him into a basin of holy water, got into an argument with a church member, and forgot to retrieve the boy. When Boris's parents, who were standing across the room, realized what was happening, they raced to the font, pulled the baby out, and frantically shook the water out of his body. When the child resumed normal breathing, the priest said: "Well, if he can survive such an ordeal, it means he's a good, tough lad, and I name him Boris." (*Boris* means "warrior.")

CHAPTER EIGHT

BEYOND THE ORDINARY

"Why not go out on a limb? Isn't that where the fruit is?"
FRANK SCULLY

This chapter is about the exceptional among the exceptional: Extraordinary kids encounter extraordinary experiences. Extraordinary kids do extraordinary things.

Kids see strange things adults don't. Life hasn't yet taught the lesson of what to see, what not to see. This might partly explain the supernatural experiences of Barbara Cartland (she saw a ghost), Robert Goddard (he had a vision of a spaceship), George S. Patton (he remembered past lives).

In the childhoods of some prominent people can be found the seeds of their future claims to fame. Warren Buffet and Armand Hammer showed entrepreneurial talent very early. Bill Gates and Linus Pauling started companies when they were teenagers.

Early promise? Indeed. *Promise*, rather than *genius*, is often the right word. Take Thomas Edison, the prolific inventor: As a kid, he spent days experimenting, usually with dangerous materials. Often, his experiments ended in something spectacular—an explosion, perhaps. Some of our subjects were true child prodigies, who did not flame with genius and then burn out but went on to fulfill their potential. Mozart was playing and composing music at the age of four; Michael Jackson was appointed lead singer for his group at age five; at four Pablo Picasso was drawing animals and flowers, and by six he was signing and dating his works.

They fill us with awe.

HAD A SUPERNATURAL EXPERIENCE

SHERWOOD ANDERSON (1876–1941), U.S. writer

As a teenager, young Sherwood lived under terrible pressure to earn money for his impoverished family. He also worried about his sexuality, wanting love but not wanting to degrade women. One clear fall day, as he sat under a tree, he experienced a strange, floating feeling: "I became faint and weak. I had my own life in my hand and it slipped out of my grasp," he later wrote. "It became like a bird. . . . My life was flying away from me. It was going, going, going. It got very small, far out there in the clear blue sky. It was a very speck in the distance. . . . I had the definite feeling that, if it went quite out of sight, out there, I would be dead. My eyes clung, with desperate intensity, to the little dark speck against the blue out there. Then it came back, slowly at first, and then, suddenly, with a rush. It flew back to me."

Sherwood experienced the floating feeling several times. Once his hands floated off; on another occasion a tree, and still another time voices that he heard; then they would come back. The episodes stopped when he was sixteen but came back twenty years later.

According to one scholar, these were mystic episodes; but some psychologists call them fugue states, spells of "dreaming-while-awake" that often occur in teenagers.

Did you know that General George S. Patton believed he had been a Viking and a Roman legionnaire in former lives?

WILLIAM BLAKE (1757–1827), English poet, engraver, and mystic
Visions ran in his dissenter family. James, his older brother, a "mild madman," talked of seeing Abraham and Moses. When William was a child, he saw things too. At four, according to one biographer, he saw God, who "put His head to the window" and set William "a-screaming." Another biographer claims that, when William was eight or ten, he had a vision of a tree of angels. When he told his parents of this miraculous experience, his father threatened to beat him for telling a lie, but his mother interceded. Later, as William walked among a group of haymakers, he saw angels again.

In 1772, his parents apprenticed him to an engraver. As part of his job, he sketched the tombs in Westminster Abbey. Working there one day, he had a strange and wonderful vision. His eyes beheld a procession of ghostly priests, singers, and monks suddenly filling the galleries and aisles. They sang unearthly songs while the organ played unearthly music and the odor of incense wafted from censers.

BARBARA CARTLAND (1901–   ), English writer
Always a little fey, at the age of thirteen Barbara Cartland saw an angel while staying with a family in Bath. A devout High Church Episcopalian, she had set up an altar with two candles in her room. One night, an angel visited her. She wrote, then: ". . . I was in my bedroom thinking of my mother and praying, when on the wall in front of me I saw the huge outline of an angel. His head nearly touched the ceiling and his feet were only a few inches off the floor. He was outlined in light like a line drawing and only his wings had any substance." After about a minute, he faded away. She later described him to her biographer as a "very masculine looking angel," remarking that he was much like a Michaelangelo drawing of an angel that she first saw in the Sistine Chapel *after* the experience.

THOMAS DE QUINCEY (1785–1859), English essayist and critic
He adored his sisters, particularly Elizabeth, two years his senior, who played games and fantasized with him. When he was seven, she developed what doctors then called "hydrocephalus," probably cerebrospinal meningitis. The children were not allowed to see her. A nurse told him she was going to die, and he was devastated.

The day after Elizabeth died, Thomas climbed the back stairs to the room where her body lay. He turned the key in the lock and entered. The sun was shining in through the window. He walked to the side of the bed and looked at her dead face and "the stiffening hands, laid palm to palm." A sound of wind put him into a trance. "A vault seemed to open in the zenith of the far blue sky, a shaft which ran up forever; and the billows seemed to pursue the throne of God; but that also ran before us and fed away continually . . . some mighty relation between God and death struggled to evolve itself." After what seemed like a long time, he came back to his normal self. He heard what sounded like a footstep on the stairs, so he kissed Elizabeth on the lips and sneaked away.

After that, on Sunday mornings in church, Thomas's dazzled eyes saw in the clear glass in the midst of the stained glass "white, fleecy clouds sailing over the azure depths of the sky," which became "visions of beds with white lawny curtains; and in the beds lay sick children, that were tossing in anguish, and weeping clamorously for death. God, for some mysterious reason, could not suddenly release them from their pain; but he suffered the beds, as it seemed, to rise slowly into the clouds."

ROBERT FROST (1874–1963), U.S. poet

His mother believed in Swedenborgianism, a mystical faith that he later described as her "incipient insanity." But Robert too was prone to an occult experience. He wrote that when he was a boy, "he often knelt in an armchair and, holding his hands over his ears, buried his face in the back of the chair to drown out the mystical voices calling to him." Because the voices were incomprehensible to him, they troubled him deeply. When he grew up, he continued to hear voices. Though these voices ridiculed him, echoing what he said with a different inflection, he still wanted to figure them out, because he thought they might inspire his writing.

URI GELLER (1946–   ), Israeli psychic

In the late afternoon in a wild Arabic garden in Tel Aviv, Uri Geller, aged three or four, was playing alone. He heard a high-pitched, loud ringing in his ears, but no other sound. Everything was still, as if time had stopped. He looked up and saw a mass of brilliant silver light. What has happened to the sun? he wondered. The light dropped lower and closer, and as he later said, "I felt as if I had been knocked over backward." After feeling a pain in his forehead, he lost consciousness. When he came to, he ran home to tell his mother what happened. Though he kept going back to the garden, he never saw the light again.

ROBERT GODDARD (1882–1945), U.S. physicist

As a boy growing up in Worcester, Massachusetts, Goddard was always interested in space flight. H. G. Wells's *War of the Worlds,* which was running in installments in the local paper, further piqued his curiosity. He knew that Wells's story of evil Martians in spaceships was pure fiction, but his mind was haunted by the question the story suggested: "How did that spaceship function?" Robert worked away in his mind at the underlying problems: How could a necessarily heavy ship overcome gravity, how could it land, how could the problem of airless space be overcome by air-breathing humans?

His interest became a burning ambition on October 19, 1899, when he was a seventeen-year-old sophomore in high school. After climbing a decrepit cherry tree to prune it, Robert experienced a mystical vision in which he saw a space vehicle spin and lift straight up into the sky.

Partly inspired by the vision, Robert worked away at the knotty problems space flight represented. Seventeen years later, in 1926, he launched the world's first liquid-fuel rocket.

CARL JUNG (1875–1961), Swiss psychologist

The father of analytical psychology and a contemporary of Sigmund Freud, Jung was the son of a minister. When Carl was twelve, he had a mystical experience, which he said marked the end of his childhood and the dawning of his "ego-consciousness." In his autobiography he wrote: "I was taking the long road to school . . . when suddenly for a single moment I had the overwhelming impression of having just emerged from a dense cloud. I knew all at once: now I am *myself!* It was as if a wall of mist were at my back, and behind that wall there was not yet an 'I.' But at this moment *I came upon myself.* Previously I had existed, too, but everything had merely happened to me. Now I happened to myself. . . . Previously I had been willed to do this and that; now *I* willed. This experience seemed to me tremendously important and new: there was 'authority' in me."

Did you know that when Robert Frost was a boy he often heard mystical voices calling to him, and that he continued hearing voices throughout his life?

Carl also had another vision, of God sitting on a golden throne above a cathedral, but when he tried to picture what would happen next, his mind was stopped by the thought that to go further was a sin. He felt as if he were choking. After several days, his mind was liberated, and he saw what he had been avoiding: "from under the throne an enormous turd falls upon the sparkling new roof, shatters it, and breaks the walls of the cathedral asunder." He felt "indescribable relief" and "an unutterable feeling of bliss." To him, this vision demonstrated that God did not conform to any tradition and that it was more important than anything to fulfill God's will.

HORATIO NELSON (1758–1805), British naval commander
Horatio was one of eight children. His mother died when he was nine years old, and his father was a poor country clergyman. Small and frail, Horatio was a sickly boy who was something of a hypochondriac. Nonetheless, at age twelve, he was accepted as a midshipman on his uncle's warship, the *Raisonable.* Aside from getting seasick, he turned out to be a remarkably good sailor.

Five years and several voyages later, Horatio came down with malaria. He slipped in and out of consciousness, running a high fever, and sometimes his body became partly paralyzed. When he finally began to recover, he found himself weak and depressed. Then, while lying in bed on the *Dolphin*, the listless Horatio had a supernatural experience. At first he saw a bright light, which he called "a radiant orb." Then, as he told it, "After a long and gloomy reverie, in which I almost wished myself overboard, a sudden glow of patriotism was kindled within me, and presented my king and country as my patron. My mind exulted in the idea. 'Well then' I exclaimed, 'I will be a hero, and confiding in Providence, I will brave every danger.' "

GEORGE S. PATTON (1885–1945), U.S. general

When "Georgie" Patton was ten years old, he gathered his cousins together to play some war games. During the "battle," Patton pushed an abandoned farm wagon down a hill into the enemy line (a flock of turkeys). Many of the turkeys were killed or injured, and his angry mother demanded to know what he was doing. Georgie said he was copying the fifteenth-century battle tactics of John the Blind of Bohemia. When asked how he knew about John the Blind, the child triumphantly declared, "I was there." Patton's belief in psychic experiences and reincarnation remained with him throughout his life. When he was in his forties, his dead father appeared to him on at least two occasions. "Old Blood and Guts," one of the generals instrumental in defeating the Germans in World War II, always contended that in his former lives he had been both a Viking and a Roman legionnaire.

Did you know that part of Robert Goddard's decision to pursue physics and rocket science was based on a vision he had when he was seventeen? While pruning the branches of a tree, Robert saw a spacecraft spin and lift straight up into the sky.

GRIGORI RASPUTIN (1871?–1916), Russian mystic

The man who would wield great influence over the court of Tsar Nicholas II grew up in a village in western Siberia. When he was eleven, Grigori and his older brother, Dmitri, almost drowned while swimming in a river. Both were rescued, but Dmitri got pneumonia and died. According to legend, it was after his brother's death that Grigori's personality began to change. He became moody and withdrawn.

Evidence of his special powers was first displayed one evening in his father's home. A bunch of villagers had gathered to discuss the theft of one of the villagers' horses. Grigori, who was ill with a fever, suddenly sprang forward and, pointing his finger, accused the wealthiest man in the room of stealing the horse. Thinking that the boy was delirious, no one paid any attention to him until later that evening, when the wealthy man was caught leading the horse out of his barn. Grigori's father demanded to know what evidence had led Grigori to make the accusation. The boy replied, "I just knew it."

JOSEPH SMITH (1805–1844), U.S. founder of the Mormon Church
Raised in Palmyra, New York, Joseph had his first religious vision when he was fourteen. He mentioned the experience to a number of people, including a Methodist preacher, but he was distressed when everyone was skeptical and mocked him. Three years later he had another vision, in which the angel Moroni appeared to him. According to Smith, "A personage appeared at my bedside, standing in the air, for his feet did not touch the floor. He had on a loose robe of most exquisite whiteness . . . his whole person was glorious beyond description. . . . I was afraid; but the fear soon left me. He called me by name, and said unto me that he was a messenger sent from the presence of God to me and that his name was Moroni; that God had a work for me to do."

CHILD ENTREPRENEURS

WARREN BUFFETT (1930–   ), U.S. billionaire
A multibillionaire, he was always fascinated by money, talented in understanding it, and dogged in his pursuit of it. By the time Warren was six, he was making a profit selling Coca-Cola to his friends. At age eleven, he bought three shares of Cities Service stock for thirty-eight dollars each; he made a profit of five dollars when he sold it. He had five different newspaper routes when he was a teenager, so that he could accumulate enough money to play the stock market in earnest. Talented at mathematics, he was always figuring the odds, and he even created a scheme with a friend to bet on the horses.

BILL GATES (1955–   ), U.S. software entrepreneur
In eleventh grade, he said that he would be a millionaire by age thirty. He had reason for such confidence. When he was nine, he negotiated a formal contract with his sister for the rights to use her baseball glove, paying her five dollars for the privilege. For his sixth-grade economics class, he developed a report called "Invest with Gateway Incorporated." In it, he was a young inventor trying to market a coronary care system to hospitals. He wrote, "If my idea is good and I am able to hire good people and raise enough money, I should be successful."

In 1971, when Bill was still in Seattle's prestigious prep school, Lakeside, he and his friend Paul Allen developed a company called Traf-O-Data to analyze the tapes municipalities used to count cars traveling over their roads. They hired students to transcribe the numbers, which they then keyed in.

Eventually, they designed a computer program to analyze the tapes directly. They made about $20,000 from Traf-O-Data in only two years.

In May 1972 Gates and Allen worked out a class scheduling computer program for Lakeside. It worked. Through clever scheduling, some seniors had no Tuesday afternoon classes. They wore T-shirts with the slogan "Tuesday Club" over a keg of beer. The program placed young Bill in classes with girls he liked. He even started marketing the system to other schools.

By 1983 Gates's company, Microsoft, had made more than ten million dollars from MS-DOS alone. Bill Gates, true to his prediction, was not yet thirty.

ARMAND HAMMER (1898–1990), U.S. businessman
During the holidays, the Hammer family went to Metuchen, New Jersey, to stay at a farm owned by friends Malka and Mendel Kornblatt. Mendel Kornblatt introduced young Armand to the ins and outs of trade when Armand was seven or eight. Carrying produce to sell, they would leave the house at eleven or twelve o'clock at night to get to the market in Jersey City, about thirty miles away, before dawn. Once there, Armand helped Mendel display the produce and created rudimentary market reports by comparing competitors' prices with theirs. That was when he started to become fascinated with business, "the harmony, in business, of theory *in* practice." He "seemed to recognize by instinct the immutable laws of supply and demand, the importance of good products, and the advantage of intelligent salesmanship over dumb optimism."

Armand was sixteen when he fell in love with a car, a used 1910 Hupmobile. The car cost $185, about six months' salary then, and he borrowed the money to buy it from his brother Harry. He used the car to deliver candy during the Christmas holidays. In two weeks, he made enough to repay his brother plus more. It was an "early lesson that you can get most things you want if you plan the right strategy, make the right deal and work your socks off."

Did you know that Linus Pauling won two Nobel Prizes: the chemistry award in 1954 and the Nobel Peace Prize in 1962?

ALGER HISS (1904–1996), U.S. public official accused of spying
In financial trouble and overwhelmed with responsibility for his brother's six children and widow and his own five children, Alger's father committed sui-

cide by cutting his own throat ear to ear with a razor when Alger was only two and a half. His mother and aunt raised him, and he helped by making money when he could. He and his friend Fritz Geyer had a spring water route. They built a long wagon, with a bottle rack to hold a dozen quart bottles and one huge bottle at the end. The two boys got up at 5:30 A.M. three or four days a week, pulled the wagon fifteen blocks to Baltimore's Druid Hill Park, and dragged it to the spring at the top to fill the bottles. They then rode the brakeless wagon back down. Alger and Fritz sold the water for fifteen cents a quart, making a tidy profit.

STEVE JOBS (1955–   ), U.S. computer entrepreneur

He always had the chutzpah of the entrepreneur. When he was in junior high, he needed parts for an electronic device he was building, so he called Bill Hewlett, of Hewlett-Packard, at his home. Hewlett got him the parts—and a summer job working on the Hewlett-Packard assembly line. In high school, Steve called Burroughs for components, with the story that he needed such components for a new electronic design he was creating and was considering using theirs in the final design. They sent the parts at no cost. A born haggler, he liked to trade in electronic parts. He had honed his skills throughout a childhood of watching his father, a car buff, negotiate for cars and parts. Steve kept up with the prices of thousands of electronic parts in order to buy them at bargain prices at swap meets and sell them to supply stores for a profit.

In 1971, Steve and his friend Steve Wozniak became involved in making and selling Blue Boxes, electronic gadgets to tap into the phone system illegally. They sold the boxes to high school students at Homestead High and to college students at Berkeley. When the police and the phone companies began cracking down on such illegal operations, they quit.

JOE MCCARTHY (1908–1957), U.S. politician

After finishing the eighth grade, Joe dropped out of school to work on the family farm outside Appleton, Wisconsin. A few years later the teenager started his own chicken farm and singlehandedly built housing for the animals, cared for them, and sold their eggs to local grocery stores. Once he began to make a tidy profit, he expanded the business and sold poultry as well as eggs. At one time he had ten thousand broilers and two thousand laying hens. When Joe was twenty, however, a disease killed off the majority of his flock, and he decided to reassess his plans for the future.

He wanted to go to college, but because he hadn't finished high school, he had to go back at age twenty-one and attend class with fourteen-year-olds. He was allowed to finish required courses at his own pace, though. He studied seven days a week around the clock, and in less than one year he completed grades 9 through 12. And he was an honor roll student. Intelligence and ambition eventually led McCarthy to become a U.S. senator. His reputation, however, was irreparably damaged in the 1950s when he zealously led a hunt for Communists within the U.S. government based on unfounded information.

"Sometimes you have to waltz around your enemy to fox-trot on his back."

—*Gordon Parks's father*

LINUS PAULING (1901–1994), U.S. scientist

Linus was nine when his father, a pharmacist in Portland, Oregon, died. To help support his family, Linus was forced to take a number of part-time jobs—delivering newspapers, setting up pins in a bowling alley, running the projector at a movie theater. In addition, he worked in a grocery store and in a butcher's shop. Linus, a whiz at both science and math, was always dreaming up ways to go into business for himself and earn some significant money.

Fifteen-year-old Linus and his friend Lloyd Simon set up a company called Palmon Laboratories (Palmon was a combination of the boys' last names) to test the butterfat content of milk. They set up a lab with all the proper equipment and tried to drum up work from the local dairies. Their youthful appearance, however, put them at a big disadvantage, and Palmon was a short-lived venture. Refusing to give up, the boys, along with another friend, moved on to the photography business. Once again they set up a lab, this time to develop pictures, hoping to get work from drug stores and local photography studios. This time they actually made some money, but not enough to keep them afloat.

Pauling's boyhood optimism and entrepreneurial mindset served him well. He became one of only a handful of people ever to win two Nobel Prizes. In 1954 he won the chemistry award for his work in molecular structure. In 1962 he won the peace prize for his political activism.

EDWARD RICKENBACKER (1890–1973), U.S. aviator

World War II hero Eddie Rickenbacker started his first business when he was six years old, before he entered school. The idea came from Sam the junkman, who roamed the neighborhoods in Columbus, Ohio, collecting rags, bones (to grind up for fertilizer) and all sorts of metal objects. Eddie called his friends together, and each boy began to collect junk to turn over to Eddie, who then sold the junk to Sam on their behalf. Eddie's own stash was always the biggest, so he made the most money. Also, because he was the go-between, Eddie siphoned off a percentage of the other boys' profits. Since the money paid out was based on weight, Eddie needed to be sure that Sam's scales were accurate. Since he suspected that they weren't, he bought his own set. Sure enough, Sam's scales were "off," a fact the little businessman was quick to point out. The reason the six-year-old wanted to save money? He wanted to buy Bull Durham tobacco so that he could smoke like his older brother, Bill.

NELSON ROCKEFELLER (1908–1979), U.S. politician

The governor of New York and U.S. vice president grew up in the lap of luxury, heir to the Rockefeller oil fortune. The homes he lived in were huge estates filled with luxurious furnishings and hordes of servants. However, Nelson's father, a strict Baptist, was something of a penny pincher and insisted that all six of his children learn the value, and responsibility, of wealth. Each child got an initial allowance of thirty cents a week (upped in five-cent increments) and had to keep a weekly journal of money earned and money spent. In addition, part of the allowance had to be earmarked for charity and part for a savings account. To earn money around the house, Nelson swatted flies (a dime for every one hundred flies) or shined shoes (a nickel a pair). Once a week the servants vacated the kitchen and the Rockefeller children were responsible for preparing dinner.

Since Nelson was always short of spending money, he frequently had to borrow from his classmates. To alleviate his financial woes, the boy decided to start up his own business, breeding rabbits. First he got some male and female rabbits from the Rockefeller Institute for Medical Research. Then he set up some makeshift facilities and let the rabbits multiply. Finally, he sold all the rabbits back to the institute and made a respectable profit.

SHOWED EARLY PROMISE

JANE AUSTEN (1775–1817), English writer

From 1787, when she was eleven or twelve, until she was eighteen, Jane produced three notebooks of writings, of which about 90,000 words survive. They include tales, sketches, fragments of novels and plays, and some idiosyncratic history. A cynic at a tender age, she saw the fiction of her time as hopelessly sentimental and excessive. She hated its false values and often bad writing. One critic has observed that she "began by defining herself through what she rejected."

As a young adolescent, the writer of *Pride and Prejudice, Emma,* and *Sense and Sensibility* knew how to ridicule fear of spinsterhood, marriage for money and position, and ignorant arrogance. Her stories show both a biting satirical wit and a youthful silliness. Surgeon Lady Williams, in Jane's story "Jack & Alice," advises the heroine, a claret addict, "Preserve yourself from first Love & you need not fear a second." Yet when a female character pursues a certain Charles Adams against his will, he sets a bear trap and catches her in it. A duke asks this lady to marry him, and she is tempted: ". . . one should receive obligations only from those we despise." However, she dies of poison, and the duke "mourned her loss with unshaken constancy for the next fortnight."

"Love and Freindship [sic]," written when she was fourteen, parodies the glorification of sensibility and emotional excess: "She was all Sensibility and

*Nelson Rockefeller, age twelve,
an entrepreneur who started his
own rabbit-breeding business.*

Courtesy of the Rockefeller Archive Center.

Feeling. We flew into each others arms and after having exchanged vows of
mutual Freindship for the rest of our Lives, instantly unfolded to each other
the most inward secrets of our Hearts . ." The characters faint at the drop
of a hat. In fact, one dies of catching a chill while passed out. Expiring, she
warns her friend, "Beware of fainting-fits . . . though at the time they may
be refreshing and agreeable yet beleive [sic] me they will in the end, if too

often repeated and at improper seasons, prove destructive to your Constitution. . . . One fatal swoon has cost me my Life. Beware of swoons Dear Laura."

SAMUEL BARBER (1910–1981), U.S. composer

NOTICE to *Mother and nobody else*
Dear Mother: I have written this to tell you my worrying secret. Now don't cry when you read it because it is neither yours nor my fault. I suppose I will have to tell it now without any nonsense. To begin with I was not meant to be an athlet [sic]. I was meant to be a composer, and will be I'm sure. I'll ask you one more thing. —Don't ask me to try to forget this unpleasant thing and go play football.—*Please*—Sometimes I've been worrying about this so much that it makes me mad (not very),

Love,
Sam Barber II

He wrote this when he was nine, and he meant it.

This child whom a cousin described as "an unusually handsome child, strong, lively, and intelligent" was only six when he began composing melodies at the piano. His mother, Daisy, helped him to write down some of his first efforts. When Sam was seven, he wrote them down himself. When he was ten, he started to compose an opera, *The Rose Tree,* but did not get past the first act. At twelve, he was the organist at the Westminster Church in West Chester, Pennsylvania, his hometown. His salary was one hundred dollars a month, not bad for that time.

Sam entered the Curtis Institute of Music at fourteen. By then he had composed many pieces. He was a serious boy and looked it: hair parted in the middle, square chin, big spectacles. At Curtis he studied piano, voice, and composition and music theory, in all of which he distinguished himself. His fellow students were in awe of him; many considered him to be a genius. Fellow student, longtime associate, and friend Gian Carlo Menotti called him "the star" of the institute.

ALEXANDER GRAHAM BELL (1847–1922), Scottish-born U.S. inventor

Young Aleck Bell was friends with Ben Herdman, who had been sent to Aleck's father, a professor of elocution, to have his stammer corrected. One day they were at Bell's mill, owned by Ben's father, fooling around. Mr. Herdman called them into his office and suggested that they do something useful. Aleck asked for a hint, and Mr. Herdman showed them some grain and said, "If only you could take the husks off this wheat, you would be of some help." Aleck conceived of a machine with rotating paddles, made of nailbrushes. It worked. Aleck later wrote, "So far as I remember, Mr. Herdman's injunction to do something useful was my first incentive to invention, and the method of cleaning wheat the first fruit."

GEORGE WASHINGTON CARVER (c. 1864–1943), U.S. botanist

Moses and Susan Carver, George's white owners, raised him as their own child in Diamond, Missouri. He early began to comb the woods, picking up treasures, usually reptiles or insects. He secreted these in the house until,

267

after a couple of unfortunate experiences, Susan Carver made him empty his pockets before he could come inside. In the woods, he established a little garden of native plants and learned the special needs of each. Neighbors called him the "plant doctor," because he knew how to make sick plants healthy. He said, "I wanted to know the name of every stone and flower and insect and bird and beast. I wanted to know where it got its color, where it got its life—but there was no one to tell me."

At about the age of twelve, George left Diamond to go to school in Neosho, and by 1896 he had earned a master's degree from the State Agricultural College in Ames, Iowa, then went on to an illustrious career as a botanist.

THOMAS ALVA EDISON (1847–1931), U.S. inventor

He showed early promise, no doubt about that. He was always experimenting, and his experiments were innovative. The problem? They all too often ended in disaster; for example, when he was little he started a fire that burned down his father's barn.

At age twelve Alva started working on a train, the Grand Trunk Railway, that went from Port Huron, Michigan, to Detroit. During layovers in Detroit, a center of the chemical industry, Alva experimented with chemicals in the baggage car. Though very inventive, he had no mind for details. He forgot to keep his phosphorus bottle covered with water, so it burst into flame, fell from the shelf, and started a fire. The baggage master put out the fire, burning his fingers in the process, and threw out all the chemicals.

Alva moved his base of operations to his house, where he built various devices. One was a rudimentary cannon. He hollowed out a log near an icehouse, filled it with gunpowder, plugged it, and told his friend to put his cap on top of the plug. When he lit the fuse, the explosion slammed the boys to the ground, sent the cap to the top of the light tower, and blew out the side of the icehouse.

At sixteen, Alva had a job working in a telegraph office, which did not take up much of his time. So he again started experimenting, this time with new concoctions. The result: another explosion. Luckily no one was hurt, but Alva lost another job.

Of course, the experimenting paid off in the end. From Edison's "invention factory" in New Jersey came the phonograph, new ways of manufacturing chemicals, an improved storage battery, and much more.

THEODORE GEISEL (DR. SEUSS) (1904–1991), U.S. writer and illustrator

He said he always looked at the world through "the wrong end of a telescope." Even as a boy, the future writer of *Cat in the Hat* had a talent for exaggeration, absurdity, and verbal rhythm. He loved the place-names around his hometown of Springfield, Massachusetts: Wickersham, McEligot, Terwilliger. At night his mother read to him and his sister, Marnie, in the same singsong she had used to sell pies in her father's bakery: "Apple, mince, lemon . . ." It was she, Ted said, who gave him "the rhythms in which I write and the urgency with which I do it."

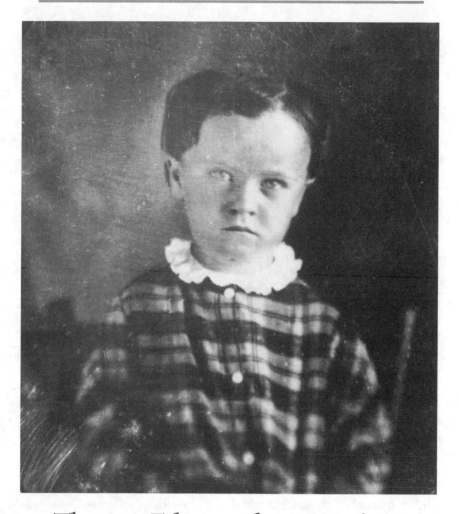

Thomas Edison, about age four.

Courtesy of the U.S. Department of the Interior, National Park Service, Edison
National Historic Site.

He could draw, too, and in a style that anticipated the imaginative illustrations he created as an adult. When he went with his father to the Springfield Zoo in Forest Park, he took a pad and pencil with him to sketch the animals—the bearded African sheep, the monkeys, the bears. His pictures were caricatures, much like his adult drawings of fantastic animals such as the Grinch. In high school, he drew cartoons for the school paper, eventually signing his work as T. S. LeSieg (his name spelled backwards).

Did you know that Sam Barber started to compose his first opera at the age of ten?

URI GELLER (1946–   ), Israeli psychic

He was only in first grade when he began having psychic experiences. When his mother came home from playing cards, he knew whether she had won or lost and by how much. He also seemed able to read her mind, saying what she was going to say before she said it.

His parents gave him his first watch when he was about six. Somehow the watch jumped forward in time—to time for recess, which he was eagerly looking forward to—before the wall clocks did. Once the hands furiously swept around the dial. His parents bought him another watch; but it, too, kept time in tune with his desires.

Uri learned to bend spoons—the ability for which he is perhaps best known—when he was still very small. Other objects yielded to his mind as well; for instance, when he was thirteen, he mentally unlocked a combination lock to a bicycle that was to be his bar mitzvah present.

His talents gave him the chance to become an exceptional cheater. He read the minds of A students, seeing answers written on a gray screen in his head, and then copied the answers on his own paper. Even when teachers isolated him, he could use other students as crib sheets.

STEPHEN HAWKING (1942–   ), English physicist

Odd and thin, messy in his habits, he jabbered with a slight lisp in what his fellow students at St. Alban's School called "Hawkingese." One of the students bet another a bag of candy that the twelve-year-old Stephen would never amount to anything, and in truth in his earliest years at St. Albans his teachers considered him bright but nothing out of the ordinary.

He hung out with students like himself. They invented and played games like War Game and Feudal Game, for which Stephen devised the rules. But a problem arose: The rules were so complicated that a move resulted in consequences so complex that it would take an afternoon to figure them out.

At fourteen, Stephen's genius started to show. He knew he wanted to study mathematics but spent very little time doing his mathematics homework; yet, he always did very well. One of his contemporaries has said, "He had incredible, instinctive insight. While I would be worrying away at a complicated mathematical solution to a problem, *he just knew the answer*— he didn't have to think about it."

Stephen and his group began to develop an interest in electronics. Stephen had no talent for the mechanics of electronics—once he got a 500-volt shock while trying to convert an old television set into an amplifier. But he did have enormous talent for the mathematics of it. In 1958, they built a computer from recycled parts of an office telephone exchange and called it LUCE (the Logical Uniselector Computing Engine).

Hawking was twenty-one when he developed ALS (amyotrophic lateral sclerosis), better known as Lou Gehrig's disease, which has now disabled him to the point where he has to use a voice synthesizer to communicate. But he dominates his field of astrophysics.

MICHAEL JACKSON (1958–   ), U.S. singer

When he was five, his four older brothers voted him lead singer for their group. That year he sang "Climb Every Mountain" for his kindergarten class; his mother and teacher cried.

Michael had enormous talent, as did his siblings. To further their talent, their father, Joe, acted as a severe taskmaster, demanding long rehearsals and excellence in school. Michael has said that if children made a mistake at rehearsals, Joe would beat them.

Joe's efforts paid off, in success if not in happiness. The group, known as the Jackson Five, began to win talent contests. In 1968, they performed at amateur night at the Apollo Theater in Harlem, where they won a standing ovation from a traditionally tough audience and a chance to come back as paid performers. They were also signed by Motown Records. Ten-year-old Michael could dance so well and sing with such mature emotion that some people started the rumor that he was actually an older midget, not a young boy.

In 1970, before Michael had entered his teens, the group had four number one hit singles: "I Want You Back," "ABC," "The Love You Save," and "I'll Be There." Michael began to do solo albums. By the time he was fourteen, he was famous and a millionaire.

MARTIN LUTHER KING, JR. (1929–1968), U.S. civil rights leader

Small but athletic, young M. L., as he was called as a child, showed signs of genius early. Adults noted his intelligence and his precocious sensibilities. Sometimes he talked like a grownup. "You just wait and see," he said to his parents. "When I grow up I'm going to get me some big words." His memory impressed everyone. By the age of five, M. L. could recite whole passages from the Bible. At six, he sang hymns in church; his favorite was "I Want to Be More and More Like Jesus." Sometimes people cried when he sang, but, according to his father, he "didn't get puffed up."

Did you know that Mozart was only six years old when he went on his first performance tour—and that it lasted for three and a half years?

Young star Michael Jackson.

Courtesy of Archive Photos.

He encountered racism in his home city of Atlanta, Georgia, early on, when his best friend's parents told him he could no longer play with their boy. When he asked why, they said, "Because we are white, and you are colored." M.L.'s parents, though, did not accept the notion of white superiority and told him that he must always feel like *somebody*. His father said, "Nobody can make a slave out of you if you don't think like a slave."

In high school, he dazzled teachers with his huge vocabulary and his rich baritone voice. He liked to study oratory and literature. He said later that his "greatest talent, strongest tradition, and most constant interest was the eloquent statement of ideas."

When M.L. was only fifteen, he entered Morehouse College. He wanted to spend his life helping his people. He fulfilled this ambition when he became a civil rights leader, able to inspire crowds with his fiery oratory.

CALVIN KLEIN (1942–   ), U.S. clothing designer
At age eleven, skinny, freckled Calvin Klein loved going to Loehmann's, a women's discount clothing store in the Bronx. He followed his mother, Flore (Flo), up and down the aisles, going through the racks with her and trying to figure out how the designer clothing was made. Passion for clothes ran in the family—on the female side. Flo was a clotheshorse, and her mother, Molly Stern, had been a seamstress for dress designer Hattie Carnegie.

Calvin liked to watch his grandmother guide fabric through the teeth of a sewing machine. Flo gave him his own sewing machine, and every day after school he sewed. First he sewed clothes for the dolls of his younger sister's friends; then he made clothes for his mother. He says he knew when he was five that he wanted to be a clothing designer.

WOLFGANG AMADEUS MOZART (1756–1791), Austrian composer
When Wolfgang was three years old, he loved to imitate his older sister, Nannerl, who was taking clavier lessons from their father Leopold, a violinist and composer. By the age of four Wolfgang was playing with amazing proficiency and began to write his own compositions, making up his own system of music notation. Music permeated every hour of the boy's life. When he had to move his toys from one room to another, he did so with great ceremony and made everyone present sing or play music to accompany his short sojourn.

When Wolfgang was six, Leopold took him and his sister on a performance tour that lasted for three and a half years. The children played in public concert halls, but they were also courted and hosted by the royal families of Europe. Wolfgang was heralded everywhere as a genius. He had an amazing ability to sight-read music, he displayed phenomenal talent playing the violin and harpsichord, and he was able to improvise with breathtaking sophistication. Toward the end of the tour, when Wolfgang was in England, the Royal Society of London appointed a special committee to determine whether the boy was truly a prodigy. After careful examination, the committee members concluded that of all the music prodigies who had ever lived, Wolfgang was "the most astonishing of all" and that his talent seemed "almost supernatural."

Wolfgang was a charming child who loved to be the center of attention. Kissed and cuddled by kings and queens, he never complained about his grueling schedule and happily accepted all the presents that were bestowed upon him—gold medals, jewelry, and elaborate, velvet costumes. When critics speculated about when his popularity would subside, he astonished them with a new achievement; at eight he wrote his first symphony, at twelve he wrote his first opera.

For many years Wolfgang was the chief breadwinner in his family. The money he earned enabled his parents and sister to enjoy a comfortable, sometimes lavish, life style. The remarkable composer, however, died penniless at the young age of thirty-five. He is credited with 626 musical compositions.

ISAAC NEWTON (1642–1727), English scientist

The genius who would formulate the laws of gravitation and the laws of motion was a small, weak, quiet child. In his early school days he was so uninterested in his studies that he was ranked second to last out of eighty students in his school. However, once he started to apply himself, Isaac quickly shot up to the top of the class.

Isaac rarely participated in sports and games, since he knew he would always lose. However, one day, when the other boys were engaged in a long-jump contest, he noticed how hard the wind was blowing. After carefully observing the timing and direction of the wind gusts, he stepped forward to announce that he wanted to play. When his turn came, he positioned himself to take full advantage of the wind force, which propelled him forward to victory. He later said that the feat was one of his earliest experiments.

The boy had his own tool set of saws and hammers and was always constructing mechanical toys and knickknacks. His paper kites were aerodynamically perfect, and sometimes he attached lanterns, which he made from paper and candles, to the tails of the kites. When flown at night, the kites lit up the sky. At age eleven he was drawing extraordinary renderings of birds and ships on the stone walls of his room.

Did you know that by the time he was five, Michael Jackson was voted the lead singer of the Jackson Five, and that he recorded four hit singles before he was a teenager?

Fascinated by the movement of wind and water, Isaac incorporated the forces of nature into his inventions. He built a water clock activated by drops of water falling on a sliver of wood. After watching the construction of a windmill near his home, Isaac built a model windmill that, when placed in the wind, mimicked the rotation of the big windmill. To make his toy work without wind, Isaac put a mouse inside the mill and strategically placed food above the wheel so that the mouse made the wheel turn when it went after the food.

J. ROBERT OPPENHEIMER (1904–1967), U.S. physicist

At a very young age, Robert was studying architectural books, writing poetry, and creating oil paintings on his own small easel. It was evident that he had a very good memory, since he could easily recite long passages from books he had read or hum music from the works of great classical composers. His vocabulary was extensive. Recognizing that Robert was not an ordinary boy, his parents did everything they could to encourage his development. For example, they bought him everything from a piano to a microscope, enrolled him in the best schools, and took him to Europe.

At school Robert excelled in all subjects except sports. By the time he entered the fifth grade, he was working on problems in elementary physics. At seventeen, when he graduated from high school in New York City, his straight-A grade status won him the honor of valedictorian. At that time he knew five languages and had completed college-level work in many subjects, including chemistry and Latin. The boy genius would go on to become a member of the Manhattan Project at Los Alamos, New Mexico, during World War II and earn the title "father of the atomic bomb."

PABLO PICASSO (1881–1973), Spanish artist

His first word was "piz" for *lapiz* (a pencil), but according to his biographers, Picasso could draw before he could speak. When he wanted a *churro* (a twisted, sugar-coated fritter), he would draw long spirals and would be rewarded with the tasty treat. At four he was drawing animals and flowers, and by six he was signing and dating his works. His first oil paintings, completed when he was eight, were technically very sophisticated.

School was a long and torturous ordeal for the boy. Because he was a poor, inattentive student, Pablo was frequently punished by being sent to the "cells," a room where he sat on a bench, isolated from the other students. But he loved the punishment, because he "could take a pad of paper and draw nonstop." Until he was eleven, Pablo was given art instruction solely by his father, an art teacher. Then he entered formal training in a succession of art schools. When he applied to the Barcelona School of Fine Arts, Pablo was asked to do a series of drawings, which had to be completed in thirty days; he said he finished the assignment "all in one day."

Pablo's first "one-man" show, arranged by his father, took place when he was a mere thirteen years old. Looking back, the adult Picasso once said, "My first drawings could never be exhibited in an exposition of children's drawings. The awkwardness and naivete of childhood were almost absent from them. . . . Their precision, their exactitude frightens me."

ARTHUR RUBINSTEIN (1887–1982), Polish-born U.S. pianist

When Arthur was three, his parents bought a piano and hired an instructor, Madame Kijanska, to teach his older sister Jadwiga how to play. Every time Jadwiga made a mistake, the instructor slapped the sister's hands. Arthur instinctively knew when his sister hit a wrong note, and soon he began to slap her hands. Even though no one in Arthur's family had any musical talent, it was apparent to everyone that the boy was gifted.

Arthur's father preferred the violin to the piano and gave the boy a small fiddle to get him started. But Arthur wanted nothing but the piano, and he promptly destroyed the fiddle. Shortly afterward, Arthur was taken to Berlin to have his talent evaluated by noted violinist Joseph Joachim, who gave the child a number of tests. At one point Joachim hummed the second theme of Schubert's Unfinished Symphony and then had Arthur play it on the piano. Impressed by the boy's performance, Joachim kissed him and gave him chocolate candy. Arthur, said the violinist, showed great promise, but he was still too young to take formal lessons.

Did you know that when Uri Geller was thirteen, he unlocked a combination lock to a bicycle with the powers of his mind?

Arthur started taking piano lessons at age six and made his concert debut a year later. At ten he was sent from his hometown of Lodz, Poland, to Berlin, where Joseph Joachim supervised his education. A solo concert, which Arthur gave when he was thirteen, solidified his standing in the music world; music critics wrote that he was "a coming star." Rubinstein lived to be ninety-five years old, and for more than eighty of those years he appeared in concerts throughout the world.

STEVEN SPIELBERG (1946–   ), U.S. film director

When he was twelve, Steven started to make short movies, using his father's 8-mm Kodak camera. His first creations featured his Lionel trains, which he crashed into each other with amazing precision and drama. Then he advanced to movies with actual story lines, cajoling his three sisters and his friends to dress up in elaborate costumes and act out the roles he had created. Once he convinced his mother, Leah, to don an army uniform and pith helmet for a war movie. Driving the family Jeep, she furiously raced across mountain roads, her body jolted from hitting numerous potholes—while her son meticulously filmed the action.

Leah was a loving and overindulgent parent who allowed Steven to skip school, especially on Mondays, when he would piece together the footage he had shot over the weekends. His films became increasingly sophisticated and were always full of action and primitive special effects. The teenage filmmaker was obsessively dedicated to his hobby and was surprisingly adept at getting everyone around him to go along with his elaborate schemes. When he needed to go "on location" for airplane scenes, he got an airport to shut down a runway temporarily. When he needed to shoot medical scenes, he went to a hospital and talked his way into the emergency room. According to

Leah, "No one ever said no to him, and it's a good thing. Steven doesn't understand no."

One of Steven's high school efforts, *Escape to Nowhere,* a World War II movie, won first prize in a film festival; it was twenty-two minutes long and shot in color. Another film, *Firelight,* a science fiction adventure, was even shown in a local movie theater with paid admission. After deducting production costs, Steven earned one hundred dollars. The boy genius eventually earned far more handsome profits with box office sensations like *E.T., Jaws, Jurassic Park, Raiders of the Lost Ark,* and *Close Encounters of the Third Kind.* His net worth is now estimated at over one billion dollars.

ORSON WELLES (1915–1985), U.S. actor and film director

When Orson was eighteen months old, he looked up at the family doctor and said, "The desire to take medicine is one of the greatest features which distinguishes men from animals." The tot's verbal sophistication was no surprise to his mother, Beatrice, who always showered her son with praise and encouragement. A gifted pianist and opera lover, Beatrice decided not to send her genius son to school but to teach him herself. She read poetry and Shakespeare to the boy, not fairy tales. She hired a teacher to give him piano lessons and took him to the theater and to art museums. When Beatrice died, Orson was enrolled in school in Madison, Wisconsin. Shortly after his arrival, a local newspaper ran an article about him; the headline read, "Cartoonist, Actor, Poet—and Only 10."

When Orson was eleven, he went to the Todd School in Woodstock, Illinois, an all-boys' school for exceptional students. The talkative boy was a standout, even when surrounded by other gifted students. He challenged practically everything his teachers said, and his deep, resonant voice exuded confidence and authority. However, it was the talent he displayed in theatrical productions that would solidify his reputation and determine his future.

The Todd School had a two-hundred-seat theater used for all types of productions, from Shakespearian plays to musical comedies. Orson put himself in charge of the theater. He designed the sets, staged the lighting, rewrote scripts, and directed the acting. He moved around the stage, bellowing orders to everyone in sight. As one student later put it, "It was Simon Legree. . . . If you had a lead [part], you did exactly as you were told. He choreographed everything." The shows were so professional that when Orson was fourteen, he took them on the road, placing the shows in theaters and movie houses in Chicago. In addition to singlehandedly directing the plays, Orson also acted in them. He was as comfortable playing the Virgin Mary as he was playing dual roles (Cassius and Antony) in *Julius Caesar.*

A Chicago drama critic, after seeing one of Orson's plays, predicted that the teenager would grow up to distinguish himself in the world of acting. The prophecy turned out to be accurate. At sixteen Orson became a professional actor. At twenty he was a radio star. And at twenty-five Welles directed and cowrote his masterpiece, *Citizen Kane,* which is generally considered to be the best film ever made.

PUBLISHED AT AN EARLY AGE

ELIZABETH BARRETT BROWNING (1806–1861), English poet

Just before her fourteenth birthday, her father had fifty copies of her long epic poem, *Battle of Marathon,* printed. It turned her into a poet rather than someone who just liked to write poetry. She wrote the story of her life soon after, so sure was she that she would become a famous writer. "Literature was the star which in prospect illuminated my future days . . . it was the spur . . . the aim . . . the very soul of my being."

Did you know that Mozart composed his first symphony when he was eight years old, and his first opera when he was ten?

DAVID BRINKLEY (1920–   ), U.S. broadcast journalist

In high school he was enrolled in an intern program, which got him a job working a couple of hours a day for the Wilmington (Delaware) *Star-News,* a morning and afternoon paper with a circulation of about ten thousand. A woman who lived on North Fifth Street called the paper to say that her century plant would bloom the following night. The managing editor, Al Dickson, gave David the job of following up on the lead. "Could be a nice little local story," he said.

David did some research on century plants and found a definition indicating that they were "erroneously believed to flower only once every century." He decided to go to North Fifth Street anyway and "report whatever happens."

When David arrived at North Fifth, he found throngs of people jamming the street. The fire department had set up emergency floodlights. Food vendors worked the crowd. The plant's incipient flower, if that's what it was, "looked like a broom handle growing a little hair." The woman who owned the plant said that her grandfather had bought it in Mexico, but otherwise was vague about its age and whether it would bloom.

The plant did not bloom. The fire chief was angry about wasting time and money. The waiting people were angry about waiting up for something that didn't happen. The woman who owned the plant said she would never trust a Mexican again. David wrote the story, quoting one of the bystanders: "Look at this damn mess. Popsicle sticks and Eskimo Pie wrappers all over. Coca-Cola bottles. Broken glass. Because of that damn fool woman the taxpayers have to pay to clean this up? What's all this going to cost us? Don't we pay enough already? And that damned century plant never even bloomed." The *Star-News* published the story. But even better, the Associated Press picked it up, and it appeared in newspapers everywhere; the *Los Angeles Times* gave it three column inches.

PEARL BUCK (1892–1973), U.S. writer

When she was six, living with her missionary family in China, her little brother Clyde died. She wrote a letter about death to the editor of the *Christian Observer,* a religious publication. Headlined "Our Real Home in Heaven," it appeared in the April 5, 1899, issue: "I am a little girl six years old. I live in China. I have a big brother in college who is coming to China to help our father tell the Chinese about Jesus. I have two little brothers in heaven. Maudie went first, then Artie, then Edith, and on the tenth of last month my little brave brother, Clyde, left us to go to our real home in Heaven. Clyde said that he was a Christian Soldier and that Heaven was his bestest home.

Clyde was four years and we both loved the little letters in the Observer. I wrote this all by myself, and my hand is tired, so goodbye. Pearl.

After that, Pearl started writing for the children's pages of the *Shanghai Mercury.* The prizes provided pocket money for her. When she grew up, she became a Pulitzer Prize–winning novelist.

RACHEL CARSON (1907–1964), U.S. biologist and writer

When she was ten and in the fourth grade, *St. Nicholas* magazine, written for children, bought a story from her. It was published in the section of the magazine called "St. Nicholas League," containing contributions from young people. In later life she said that she doubted "any royalty check of recent years has given me as great joy as notice of that award. Perhaps that early experience of seeing my work in print played its part in fostering my childhood dream of becoming a writer." The story she wrote, "A Battle in the Clouds," was about World War I. It told of a Canadian aviator who was so skillful in avoiding a crash after being hit that the Germans respectfully stopped firing and let him land. While she was still in elementary school, *St. Nicholas* published two more of her stories. One was about a naval battle in the Spanish-American War of 1898. The other, winner of a Gold Badge for excellence, was set in World War I.

ALLEN WELSH DULLES (1893–1969), director of the CIA

"THE BOER WAR: A History" took up more than one hundred handwritten pages. Its author was eight-year-old Allen Dulles. He had taken two months to write it, inspired by his family's discussions about the war between Boer settlers in South Africa and the British. Allen took the side of the Boers, and his aim in writing the book was to make money for the Boer Relief Committee. He wrote: "The Boers want peace, but England has to have the gold so she goes around fighting all the little countries but she never dares to fight eather [sic] China or Russia. . . . I hope that the Boers will win, for the Boers are in the wright [sic] and the British are wrong in the War." His parents were proud of their son's work, though they didn't agree with his point of view. His grandfather, John Watson Foster, who had been secretary of state to President Benjamin Harrison, had thirty thousand copies of the manuscript privately published in a booklet, with a preface he wrote himself, telling of Allen's sympathy with the "suffering of the Boer women and children in African concentration camps and the destitution of Boer prisoners in the Bermudas." Several hundred dollars for Boer relief were raised from sale of the booklet. When Dulles became director of the CIA, the agency published a reprint.

Did you know that at age fifteen, Upton Sinclair was able to support himself and his parents by writing jokes?

HELEN KELLER (1880–1968), U.S. writer and educator

When she was twelve, Helen, who was both deaf and blind, wrote a story for Michael Anagnos, head of the Perkins Institute, an agency for the blind. Her family suggested that she call the story "The Frost King." It had taken Helen the better part of a month to write. Anagnos included it as part of the institute's annual report with the comment, "If there be a pupil in any of the private or public grammar schools of New England who can write an original story like this, without assistance from any one, he or she certainly is a rare phenomenon." The story was picked up by two other publications. *The Goodson Gazette,* a weekly for the education of the deaf and blind, ran it with the comment, "we believe it to be without parallel in the history of literature."

Unfortunately, the story resembled "The Frost Fairies," a story by Margaret Canby, and Helen was accused of plagiarism. It is possible that she had heard the story years before and had unconsciously reproduced it, or that the similarities between the two stories are just pure coincidence.

H. P. (HOWARD PHILLIPS) LOVECRAFT (1890–1937), U.S. writer

He was a very intelligent child who was reading at the age of three and writing stories when he was five. His first piece, "The Little Glass Bottle," was a fanciful, nautical tale that bore no resemblance to the science fiction and horror stories he would later write.

When Howard was sixteen, he began to write astronomy articles for a newspaper, the Pawtuxet *Valley Gleaner,* in West Warwick, Rhode Island.

Among the pieces that appeared were "Is Mars an Inhabited World?" and "Can the Moon Be Reached by Man?" While the boy probably received little or no pay, the published articles earned him some respect in high school. Howard's schoolmates stopped calling him "Lovey" and instead called him "the Professor."

The young author, Helen Keller, and Michael Anagnos, about 1891.

Courtesy of the Perkins School for the Blind.

Ironically, although Lovecraft was writing fiction and nonfiction throughout most of his life, his stories were not compiled and published in book form until after he died. Until the end of his life at age forty-seven, he believed he was a total failure.

Did you know that Allen Welsh Dulles hand wrote a one hundred page history of the Boer War when he was only eight years old?

SYLVIA PLATH (1932–1963), U.S. poet

She grew up in the suburbs of Boston, Massachusetts, and was writing full-length poems when she was five years old. When she was eight, Sylvia saw her name in print for the first time in the *Boston Herald*; she had submitted a work called "Poem," which appeared in a children's section of the newspaper. The short piece was, according to the little girl, "about what I see and hear on hot summer nights." Before she graduated from high school, Sylvia's poems and short stories would appear in a number of publications, including the *Atlantic Monthly* and *Seventeen* magazine. The budding poet would go on to create numerous poems and a novel, *The Bell Jar*. Critical acclaim for her work, however, eluded her during her lifetime. She committed suicide at age thirty. In 1982 her work was awarded a Pulitzer Prize.

MARY SHELLEY (1797–1851), English novelist

Both of her parents were writers. Her mother, Mary Wollstonecraft, was an ardent feminist and her father, William Godwin, was a political philosopher. When Mary was ten and a half, she wrote an expanded version of a funny song from a musical comedy, *The General Election*. The song, "Mounseer Nongtongpaw," was about a man who traveled to France and had some hilarious experiences with the language. Mary's father sent her creation to a publisher, who liked it and printed it.

UPTON SINCLAIR (1878–1968), U.S. novelist and social reformer

At age fifteen Upton was in his second year of college in New York City. An only child, gifted with extraordinary intelligence and a photographic memory, he supported both himself and his parents by writing jokes. He sent the jokes, in batches of ten, to national magazines and usually got paid one dollar for every published joke. Upton also sold several short stories, but the jokes remained his financial mainstay and he was obsessed with creating them. He wrote, "I would take my mother to church, and make up jokes on the phrases in the prayer-book and hymn-book. I kept my little notebook before me at meals, while walking, while dressing, and in college if the professor was a bore."

Sinclair lived to be ninety. His literary output included more than ninety books, twenty-nine plays, and hundreds of magazine articles and short stories. He became internationally famous after publication of *The Jungle,* an exposé of the squalid conditions of the meat-packing industry in Chicago.

E. B. WHITE (1899–1985), U.S. essayist and author
When he was ten, E. B. (Elwyn Brooks) White wrote a poem about a mouse,

A charming E. B. White
with his older sister Lillian.

Courtesy of the Division of Rare Books and Manuscript Collections, Carl A. Kroch Library, Cornell University.

which he sent to *Woman's Home Companion;* it won a prize. More honors were to follow in the next few years for other animal stories which appeared in a children's magazine, *St. Nicholas.* His "kindness-to-animals" themes, said White, were inspired by a boyhood friend, who said that animal stories were sure winners. Looking back on his early writing endeavors, White concluded, "I detect running through them an amazing note of friendliness toward dumb creatures, an almost virulent sympathy for dogs, cats, horses, bears, toads, and robins." In 1952, when White was fifty-three, he published *Charlotte's Web,* which has become a juvenile classic.

BIBLIOGRAPHY

GENERAL REFERENCES

Bowie, Walter Russell. *Women of Light*. New York: Harper and Row, 1963.

Ewen, David. *Men of Popular Music*. Chicago: Ziff-Davis, 1944.

Fellowes-Gordon, Ian. *Heroes of the Twentieth Century*. New York: Hawthorn, 1966.

Goertzel, Mildred George, Victor Goertzel, and Ted George Goertzel. *Three Hundred Eminent Personalities*. San Francisco: Jossey-Bass, 1978.

Harrington, Walt. *American Profiles: Somebodies and Nobodies Who Matter*. Columbia, Mo.: University of Missouri Press, 1985.

Illingworth, R. S. and C. M. *Lessons from Childhood: Some Aspects of the Early Life of Unusual Men and Women*. Baltimore, Md.: William and Wilkins, 1966.

Keyes, Ralph. *Is There Life After High School?* Boston: Little, Brown, 1976.

Kupferberg, Tuli and Sylvia Topp. *First Glance: Childhood Creations of the Famous*. Maplewood, N.J.: Hammond, 1978.

Lucaire, Ed. *The Celebrity Book of Lists*. New York: Stein and Day, 1984.

Lyons, Len and Don Perlo. *Jazz Portraits: The Lives and Music of the Jazz Masters*. New York: William Morrow, 1989.

Mallon, Thomas. *A Book of One's Own: People and Their Diaries*. New York: Penguin Books, 1986.

Moffat, Mary Jane and Charlotte Painter. *Revelations: Diaries of Women*. New York: Random House, 1974.

Prause, Gerhard. *School Days of the Famous*. New York: Springer, 1978.

Rose, Phyllis (ed.). *The Norton Book of Women's Lives*. New York: W. W. Norton, 1993.

Wallace, Amy, David Wallechinsky, and Irving Wallace. *The Book of Lists #3*. New York: William Morrow, 1983.

Wallace, Irving, David Wallechinsky, Amy Wallace, and Sylvia Wallace. *The Book of Lists #2*. New York: William Morrow, 1980.

Wallechinsky, David, Irving Wallace, and Amy Wallace. *The Book of Lists*. New York: William Morrow, 1977.

Wallechinsky, David and Amy Wallace. *The Book of Lists: The 90s Edition*. Boston: Little, Brown, 1993.

Whitcomb, John and Claire Whitcomb. *Great American Anecdotes*. New York: William Morrow, 1993.

Winokur, Jon. *Fathers*. New York: E. P. Dutton, 1993.

KAREEM ABDUL-JABBAR

Abdul-Jabbar, Kareem and Peter Knobler. *Giant Steps*. New York: Bantam, 1983.

HENRY ADAMS

Adams, Henry. *The Education of Henry Adams*. New York: Modern Library, 1918/1931.

FRIEDERIKE VIKTORIA (JOY) ADAMSON

Adamson, Joy. *The Searching Spirit*. New York: Harcourt Brace Jovanovich, 1979.

Cass, Caroline. *Joy Adamson: Behind the Mask*. London: Weidenfeld and Nicholson, 1992.

JANE ADDAMS

Bowie, Walter Russell. *Women of Light*. New York: Harper and Row, 1963.

Levine, Daniel. *Jane Addams and the Liberal Tradition*. Madison: State Historical Society of Wisconsin, 1971.

JULIAN "CANNONBALL" ADDERLEY

Ewen, David. *Men of Popular Music*. Chicago: Ziff-Davis, 1944.

ALFRED ADLER

Karier, Clarence J. *Scientists of the Mind: Intellectual Founders of Modern Psychology*. Urbana, Ill.: University of Illinois Press, 1986.

ALVIN AILEY

Ailey, Alvin (with A. Peter Bailey). *Revelations: The Autobiography of Alvin Ailey*. New York: Birch Lane Press, 1995.

Dunning, Jennifer. *Alvin Ailey, A Life in Dance*. Reading, Mass.: Addison Wesley, 1996.

LOUISA MAY ALCOTT

Meigs, Cornelia. *Invincible Louisa: The Story of the Author of* Little Women. Boston: Little, Brown, 1933.

Moffat, Mary Jane and Charlotte Painter. *Revelations: Diaries of Women*. New York: Random House, 1974.

Myerson, Joel and Daniel Shealy. *The Journals of Louisa May Alcott*. Boston: Little, Brown, 1989.

ALAN ALDA

Strait, Raymond. *Alan Alda*. New York: St. Martin's, 1983.

MUHAMMAD ALI

"Muhammad Ali." *Biography*, A&E Channel.

Fifty Who Made the Difference. New York: Villard Books, 1984.

Hauser, Thomas. *Muhammad Ali: His Life and Times*. New York: Simon and Schuster, 1991.

FRED ALLEN

Allen, Fred. *Much Ado About Me*. Boston: Little, Brown, 1956.

Taylor, Robert. *Fred Allen: His Life and Wit*. Boston: Little, Brown, 1989.

HANS CHRISTIAN ANDERSEN

Bredsdorff, Elias. *Hans Christian Andersen: The Story of His Life and Work, 1805–75*. New York: Noonday Press, 1994.

Reed, Gwendolyn (compiler). *Beginnings*. New York: Atheneum, 1971.

Stirling, Monica. *The Wild Swan: The Life and Times of Hans Christian Andersen*. New York: Harcourt, Brace and World, 1965.

MARIAN ANDERSON

Anderson, Marian. *My Lord, What a Morning: An Autobiography by Marian Anderson*. New York: Viking, 1956.

SHERWOOD ANDERSON

Townsend, Kim. *Sherwood Anderson*. Boston: Houghton Mifflin, 1987.

FATTY ARBUCKLE

Yallop, David A. *The Day the Laughter Stopped: The True Story of Fatty Arbuckle*. New York: St. Martin's, 1976.

ELIZABETH ARDEN

Lewis, Alfred Allan and Constance Woodward. *Miss Elizabeth Arden: An Unretouched Portrait*. New York: Coward, McCann and Geoghegan, 1972.

HANNAH ARENDT

Young-Bruehl, Elisabeth. *Hannah Arendt: For Love of the World*. New Haven, Conn.: Yale University Press, 1982.

LOUIS ARMSTRONG

Collier, James Lincoln. *Louis Armstrong: An American Genius*. New York: Oxford, 1983.

Ewen, David. *Men of Popular Music*. Chicago: Ziff-Davis, 1944.

ISAAC ASIMOV

Asimov, Isaac. *In Memory Yet Green: The Autobiography of Isaac Asimov: 1920–1954.* Garden City, N.Y.: Doubleday, 1979.

W. H. (WYSTAN HUGH) AUDEN

Bucknell, Katharine and Nicholas Jenkins (eds.), *W. H. Auden: "The Map of All My Youth": Early Works, Friends and Influences.* Oxford: Clarendon Press, 1990.

Carpenter, Humphrey. *W. H. Auden: A Biography.* Boston: Houghton Mifflin, 1981.

JANE AUSTEN

Austen-Leigh, William and Richard Arthur Austen-Leigh. *Jane Austen: A Family Record.* Boston: G. K. Hall, 1989.

Carpenter, Humphrey. *W. H. Auden: A Biography.* Boston: Houghton Mifflin, 1981.

JOAN BAEZ

Baez, Joan. *Daybreak.* New York: Dial Press, 1968.

Garza, Hedda. *Joan Baez.* New York: Chelsea House, 1991.

JOSEPHINE BAKER

Rose, Phyllis. *Jazz Cleopatra: Josephine Baker in Her Time.* New York: Doubleday, 1989.

JAMES BALDWIN

Campbell, James. *Talking at the Gates: A Life of James Baldwin.* New York: Viking, 1991.

Weatherby, W. J. *James Baldwin: Artist on Fire.* New York: Donald I. Fine, 1989.

SAMUEL BARBER

Heyman, Barbara B. *Samuel Barber: The Composer and His Music.* New York: Oxford, 1992.

BRIGITTE BARDOT

Lowry, Suzanne. "Betrayal, Jealousy, and the Dark Side of the Sex Siren Called Bardot . . ." *Daily Mail,* September 25, 1996.

Robinson, Jeffrey. *Bardot: An Intimate Portrait.* New York: Donald I. Fine, 1994.

J. M. BARRIE

Birkin, Andrew. *J. M. Barrie & The Lost Boys: The Love Story That Gave Birth to Peter Pan.* New York: Clarkson N. Potter, 1979.

ETHEL BARRYMORE

Alpert, Hollis. *The Barrymores.* New York: Dial Press, 1964.

SIDNEY BECHET

Chilton, John. *Sidney Bechet: The Wizard of Jazz.* New York: Oxford, 1987.

SAMUEL BECKETT

Bair, Deidre. *Samuel Beckett: A Biography.* New York: Harcourt Brace Jovanovich, 1978.

BIX BEIDERBECKE
Berton, Ralph. *Remembering Bix: A Memoir of the Jazz Age.* New York: Harper and Row, 1974.

ALEXANDER GRAHAM BELL
Bruce, Robert V. *Bell: Alexander Graham Bell and the Conquest of Solitude.* Ithaca, N.Y.: Cornell University Press, 1973.

RUTH BENEDICT
Modell, Judith Schachter. *Ruth Benedict: Patterns of a Life.* Philadelphia: University of Pennsylvania Press, 1983.

JACK BENNY
Benny, Mary Livingston and Hilliard Parks, with Marcia Borie. *Jack Benny.* Garden City, N.Y.: Doubleday, 1978.
Fein, Irving A. *Jack Benny: An Intimate Biography.* New York: G. P. Putnam's, 1976.

INGMAR BERGMAN
Gado, Frank. *The Passion of Ingmar Bergman.* Durham, N.C.: Duke University Press, 1986.
Kakutani, Michiko. "Ingmar Bergman: Summing Up a Life in Film." *New York Times,* June 26, 1983.
Sterritt, David. "Bergman's Images of Bergman." *Christian Science Monitor,* November 1, 1988.

CARL BERNSTEIN
Harrington, Walt. *American Profiles.* Columbia, Mo.: University of Missouri Press, 1985.
Schwartz, Tony. "Carl Bernstein: Interview." *Playboy,* September, 1986.

MARY MCLEOD BETHUNE
Bowie, Walter Russell. *Women of Light.* New York: Harper and Row, 1963.

HUGO BLACK
Newman, Roger K. *Hugo Black: A Biography.* New York: Pantheon, 1994.

SHIRLEY TEMPLE BLACK
Black, Shirley Temple. *Child Star: An Autobiography.* New York: McGraw-Hill, 1988.

WILLIAM BLAKE
Lindsay, Jack. *William Blake: His Life and Work.* New York: George Braziller, 1979.

DIRK BOGARDE
Bogarde, Dirk. *A Postillion Struck by Lightning.* New York: Holt, Rinehart and Winston, 1977.

HUMPHREY BOGART
Benchley, Nathaniel. *Humphrey Bogart.* Boston: Little, Brown, 1975.
Cooke, Alistair. *Six Men.* New York: Alfred A. Knopf, 1977.
Hyams, Joe. *Bogart & Bacall: A Love Story.* New York: David McKay, 1975.

NAPOLEON BONAPARTE
Cronin, Vincent. *Napoleon Bonaparte: An Intimate Biography.* New York: William Morrow, 1972.

MARLON BRANDO
Manso, Peter. *Brando, the Biography.* New York: Hyperion, 1994.
Schickel, Richard. *Brando: A Life in Our Times.* New York: Atheneum, 1991.

DAVID BRINKLEY
Brinkley, David. *David Brinkley: 11 Presidents, 4 Wars, 22 Political Conventions . . .* New York: Alfred A. Knopf, 1995.

ANNE, CHARLOTTE, EMILY, AND PATRICK BRANWELL BRONTË
Fraser, Rebecca. *The Brontës: Charlotte Brontë and Her Family.* New York: Crown, 1988.
Spark, Muriel and Derek Stanford. *Emily Brontë: Her Life and Work.* New York: Coward-McCann, 1966.

ELIZABETH BARRETT BROWNING
Forster, Margaret. *Elizabeth Barrett Browning: A Biography.* New York: Doubleday, 1988.

PEARL BUCK
Stirling, Nora. *Pearl Buck: A Woman in Conflict.* Piscataway, N.J.: New Century, 1983.

WARREN BUFFETT
Carricaburu, Lisa. "The World's Richest Man and Mister Rogers Have a Lot in Common." *Salt Lake Tribune,* September 25, 1996.
Madrick, Jeff. "How to Succeed in Business." *New York Review of Books,* April 18, 1996.

CAROL BURNETT
Burnett, Carol. *One More Time: A Memoir.* New York: Random House, 1986.

RICHARD BURTON
Bragg, Melvyn. *Richard Burton: A Life.* Boston: Little, Brown, 1988.

NICOLAS CAGE
Sheff, David. "*Playboy* Interview." *Playboy,* September 1996.

ERSKINE CALDWELL
Klevar, Harvey. *Erskine Caldwell: A Biography.* Knoxville, Tenn.: University of Tennessee Press, 1995.

ALBERT CAMUS
Lottman, Herbert. *Albert Camus: A Biography.* New York: Doubleday, 1979.

TRUMAN CAPOTE
Clarke, Gerald. *Capote: A Biography.* New York: Simon and Schuster, 1988.

ANDREW CARNEGIE
Wall, Joseph Frazier. *The Andrew Carnegie Reader.* Pittsburgh: University of Pittsburgh Press, 1992.

DALE CARNEGIE
Kemp, Giles and Edward Claflin. *Dale Carnegie: The Man Who Influenced Millions.* New York: St. Martin's, 1989.

LEWIS CARROLL (CHARLES LUTWIDGE DODGSON)

Bayley, John. "Alice, or the Art of Survival." *New York Review of Books,* February 15, 1996.

Cohen, Morton N. *The Letters of Lewis Carroll,* vol. 1, ca. 1837–1885. New York: Oxford, 1979.

Lennon, Florence Baker. *Victoria Through the Looking Glass: The Life of Lewis Carroll.* New York: Simon and Schuster, 1945.

Truss, Lynne. "Curiouser and Curiouser." (London) *Times,* August 1, 1996.

JOHNNY CARSON

Corkery, Paul. *Carson: The Unauthorized Biography.* Ketchum, Id.: Randt, 1987.

Leamer, Laurence. *King of the Night: The Life of Johnny Carson.* New York: William Morrow, 1989.

RACHEL CARSON

Fifty Who Made the Difference. New York: Villard Books, 1984.

Jezer, Marty. *Rachel Carson.* New York: Chelsea House, 1988.

JIMMY CARTER

Lasky, Victor. *Jimmy Carter: The Man and the Myth.* New York: Richard Marek, 1979.

BARBARA CARTLAND

Robyns, Gwen. *Barbara Cartland: An Authorized Biography.* Garden City, N.Y.: Doubleday, 1985.

GEORGE WASHINGTON CARVER

McMurry, Linda O. *George Washington Carver: Scientist and Symbol.* Oxford, U.K.: Oxford University Press, 1981.

GIOVANNI CASANOVA

Masters, John. *Casanova.* New York: Bernard Geis, 1969.

JOHNNY CASH

Cash, Johnny. *Man in Black: His Own Story in His Own Words.* Grand Rapids, Mich.: Zondervan, 1975.

RAYMOND CHANDLER

MacShane, Frank. *The Life of Raymond Chandler.* New York: E. P. Dutton, 1976.

CHARLIE CHAPLIN

Gehring, Wes D. *Charlie Chaplin: A Bio-Bibliography.* Westport, Conn.: Greenwood Press, 1983.

Gopnik, Adam. "You Have to Laugh." *New Yorker,* August 12, 1996.

JOHN CHEEVER

Donaldson, Scott. *John Cheever: A Biography.* New York: Random House, 1988.

CHER

Quirk, Lawrence J. *Totally Uninhibited: The Life and Wild Times of Cher.* New York: William Morrow, 1991.

AGATHA CHRISTIE

Christie, Agatha. *Agatha Christie: An Autobiography.* New York: Dodd, Mead, 1977.

Morgan, Janet. *Agatha Christie.* New York: Alfred A. Knopf, 1985.

GERALD LEE CLEMONS

Hillenmeyer, Kathleen. "The Clemons Some Knew." *Cincinnati Enquirer,* January 8, 1996.

JEAN COCTEAU

Cocteau, Jean and Robert Phelps, trans. Richard Howard. *Professional Secrets: An Autobiography of Jean Cocteau, Drawn from His Lifetime Writings.* New York: Farrar, Straus and Giroux, 1970.

Steegmuller, Francis. *Cocteau: A Biography.* Boston: Little, Brown, 1970.

ROY COHN

von Hoffman, Nicholas. *Citizen Cohn: The Life and Times of Roy Cohn.* New York: Doubleday, 1988.

SAMUEL TAYLOR COLERIDGE

Reed, Gwendolyn. *Beginnings.* New York: Atheneum, 1971.

JUDY COLLINS

Collins, Judy. *Trust Your Heart.* Boston: Houghton Mifflin, 1987.

DeVault, Russ. "Both Sides Now: Judy Collins Tries Fiction." *Sacramento Bee,* August 22, 1995.

Gilbert, Matthew. "From 'Amazing Grace' to 'Shameless.' " *Boston Globe,* September 1, 1995.

Small, Michael. "Switching from Singer to Scribe with Amazing Grace, Judy Collins Writes a Searing Self-Portrait." *People,* December 7, 1987.

JOSEPH CONRAD

Meyers, Jeffrey. *Joseph Conrad: A Biography.* New York: Charles Scribner's, 1991.

Tennant, Roger. *Joseph Conrad.* New York: Atheneum, 1981.

JACKIE COOPER

Cooper, Jackie (with Dick Kleiner). *Please Don't Shoot My Dog: The Autobiography of Jackie Cooper.* New York: William Morrow, 1981.

PATRICIA CORNWELL

Cantwell, Mary. "How to Make a Corpse Talk." *New York Times,* July 14, 1996.

Canty, Mary. "Take Me to the Morgue." *Irish Times,* July 27, 1996.

Fabrikant, Geraldine. "Talking Money with Patricia Cornwell." *New York Times,* March 23, 1997.

McElwaine, Sandra. "Autopsy, She Wrote; Author Patricia Cornwell." *Harper's Bazaar,* August 1992.

Sonmor, Jean. "Stranger than Fiction." *Toronto Sun,* July 28, 1996.

Weeks, Linton. "Death Sentences; Mystery Writer Patricia Cornwell Has Money, Power, Fame, and a Really Morbid Curiosity." *Sun-Sentinel,* August 18, 1996.

JACQUES-YVES COUSTEAU
Austin American-Statesman, June 26, 1997.
"Jacques-Yves Cousteau." *Houston Chronicle,* June 26, 1997.
"Obituary of Jacques Cousteau." *Daily Telegraph,* June 26, 1997.
Kraft, Scott. "An Appreciation: Cousteau Was Willing to Stand for Principles." *Los Angeles Times,* June 26, 1997.
Madsen, Axel. *Costeau: An Unauthorized Biography.* New York: Beaufort, 1986.
Munson, Richard. *Costeau: The Captain and His World.* New York: William Morrow, 1989.
————. "Obituary: Jacques Cousteau." *Independent,* June 26, 1997.
Thomas, Jack. "Jacques Cousteau, 1910–1997." *Boston Globe,* June 26, 1997.

NOEL COWARD
Hoare, Philip. *Noel Coward.* New York: Simon and Schuster, 1995.
Seymour, Miranda. "A Talent to Amuse." *New York Times Book Review,* August 25, 1996.

STEPHEN CRANE
Stallman, R. W. *Stephen Crane: A Biography.* New York: George Braziller, 1968.

DAVID CROCKETT
Burke, James Wakefield. *David Crockett: The Man Behind the Myth.* Austin, Tex.: Eakin Press, 1984.
Derr, Mark. *The Frontiersman: The Real Life and the Many Legends of Davy Crockett.* New York: William Morrow, 1993.

DALAI LAMA (LHAMO THONDUP)
Dalai Lama. *Freedom in Exile: The Autobiography of the Dalai Lama.* New York: HarperCollins, 1990.

SALVADOR DALÍ
Parinaud, André (as told to). *The Unspeakable Confessions of Salvador Dali.* New York: William Morrow, 1976.
Secrest, Meryle. *Salvador Dalí.* New York: E. P. Dutton, 1986.

BOBBY DARIN
"Ask the Globe." *Boston Globe,* May 7, 1994.
Cerio, Gregory. "Bobby Darin and Sandra Dee's Son Looks Back in Regret— and Some Anger." *People,* November 14, 1994.
Darin, Dodd. *Dream Lovers: The Magnificent Shattered Lives of Bobby Darin and Sandra Dee by Their Son.* New York: Warner, 1994.
Inman, David. "The Incredible Inman." *The Courier-Journal,* October 30, 1994.
Newlove, Donald. " 'Dream Lovers.' " *Hollywood Reporter,* October 20, 1994.
Wloszczyna, Susan. "For Star Couple's Son, a Mending of Aching Memories." *USA Today,* October 11, 1994.

CLARENCE DARROW
Tierney, Kevin. *Darrow: A Biography.* New York: Thomas Y. Crowell, 1979.
Weinberg, Arthur and Lila. *Clarence Darrow: A Sentimental Rebel.* New York: G. P. Putnam's, 1980.

CHARLES DARWIN

Bowlby, John. *Charles Darwin: A New Life.* New York: W. W. Norton, 1990.

ANGELA DAVIS

Davis, Angela. *Angela Davis: An Autobiography.* New York: Random House, 1974.

MILES DAVIS

Davis, Miles, with Quincy Troupe. *Miles: The Autobiography of Miles Davis.* New York: Simon and Schuster, 1989.

Lyons, Len and Don Perlo. *Jazz Portraits: The Lives and Music of the Jazz Masters.* New York: William Morrow, 1989.

DORIS DAY

Hotchner, A. E. *Doris Day: Her Own Story.* New York: William Morrow, 1976.

DANIEL DAY-LEWIS

Jenkins, Garry. *Daniel Day-Lewis: The Fire Within.* New York: St. Martin's, 1995.

SIMONE DE BEAUVOIR

De Beauvoir, Simone. *Memoirs of a Dutiful Daughter.* New York: Harper and Row, 1958.

Francis, Claude and Fernande Gontier. *Simone de Beauvoir: A Life . . . a Love Story,* trans. Lisa Nesselson. New York: St. Martin's, 1985.

AGNES DE MILLE

Easton, Carol. *No Intermissions: The Life of Agnes de Mille.* Boston: Little, Brown, 1996.

THOMAS DE QUINCEY

Lindop, Grevel. *The Opium-Eater: A Life of Thomas De Quincey.* New York: Taplinger, 1981.

JAMES DEAN

Alexander, Paul. *Boulevard of Broken Dreams: The Life, Times, and Legend of James Dean.* New York: Viking, 1994.

Holley, Val. *James Dean: The Biography.* New York: St. Martin's, 1995.

SANDRA DEE

Darin, Dodd. *Dream Lovers: The Magnificent Shattered Lives of Bobby Darin and Sandra Dee by Their Son.* New York: Warner, 1994.

Dee, Sandra and Todd Gold. "Learning to Live Again." *People,* March 18, 1994.

JOHN DENVER

Denver, John (with Arthur Tobier). *Take Me Home: An Autobiography.* New York: Harmony Books, 1994.

GERARD DEPARDIEU

Chutkow, Paul. *Depardieu: A Biography.* New York: Alfred A. Knopf, 1994.

CHARLES DICKENS

Ackroyd, Peter. *Dickens.* New York: HarperCollins, 1990.

EMILY DICKINSON

Whicher, George Frisbie. *This Was a Poet: A Critical Biography of Emily Dickinson.* New York: Charles Scribner's, 1938.

BABE DIDRIKSON

Cayleff, Susan. *Babe: The Life and Legend of Babe Didrikson Zaharias.* Urbana, Ill.: University of Illinois Press, 1995.

MARLENE DIETRICH

Bach, Steven. *Marlene Dietrich: Life and Legend.* New York: William Morrow, 1992.

Riva, Maria. *Marlene Dietrich.* New York: Alfred A. Knopf, 1993.

ALLEN WELSH DULLES

Mosley, Leonard. *Dulles: A Biography of Eleanor, Allen, and John Foster Dulles and Their Family Network.* New York: Dial Press, 1978.

ARIEL DURANT

Durant, Will and Ariel. *Will & Ariel Durant: A Dual Biography.* New York: Simon and Schuster, 1977.

Freeman, Jeanne. "Professor-Student Romance Is Tough Course to Follow." *San Diego Union-Tribune,* September 18, 1992.

Lindeman, Bard. "Loneliness Bodes Ill for Longevity," *The Record,* June 9, 1994.

ESTHER DYSON

Dreifus, Claudia. "The Cyber-Maxims of Esther Dyson." *New York Times Magazine,* July 7, 1996.

AMELIA EARHART

Lovell, Mary S. *The Sound of Wings: The Life of Amelia Earhart.* New York: St. Martin's, 1989.

Rich, Doris L. *Amelia Earhart: A Biography.* Washington, D.C.: Smithsonian Institution Press, 1989.

MARY BAKER EDDY

Cather, Willa and Georgine Milmine. *The Life of Mary Baker G. Eddy and the History of Christian Science.* Lincoln, Nebr.: University of Nebraska Press, 1993.

Fraser, Caroline. "Mrs. Eddy Builds Her Empire." *New York Review of Books,* July 11, 1996.

Peel, Robert. *Mary Baker Eddy: The Years of Discovery.* New York: Holt, Rinehart and Winston, 1966.

Silberger, Julius, Jr. *Mary Baker Eddy: An Interpretive Biography of the Founder of Christian Science.* Boston: Little, Brown, 1980.

Smith, Louise A. *Mary Baker Eddy: Discoverer and Founder of Christian Science.* Boston: Christian Science Publishing Society, 1991.

THOMAS ALVA EDISON

Clark, Ronald William. *Edison: The Man Who Made the Future.* New York: G.P. Putnam's, 1977.

Conot, Robert. *Thomas A. Edison: A Streak of Luck.* New York: Da Capo, 1979.

EDWARD VII

St. Aubyn, Giles. *Edward VII: Prince and King.* New York: Atheneum, 1979.

DWIGHT DAVID EISENHOWER

Brendon, Piers. *Ike: His Life and Times.* New York: Harper and Row, 1986.

Fifty Who Made the Difference. New York: Villard Books, 1984.

GEORGE ELIOT

Bell, Millicent. "George Eliot, Radical." *New York Review of Books*, April 18, 1996.

Haight, Gordon Sherman. *George Eliot: A Biography*. New York: Oxford, 1968.

Karl, Frederick Robert. *George Eliot, Voice of a Century: A Biography*. New York: W. W. Norton, 1995.

Uglow, Jennifer. *George Eliot*. New York: Virago/Pantheon, 1987.

ELIZABETH II

Bradford, Sarah. "Mother and Queen." *Newsweek*, March 11, 1996.

Higham, Charles and Roy Moseley. *Elizabeth and Philip: The Untold Story of the Queen of England and Her Prince*. New York: Doubleday, 1991.

Keay, Douglas. *The Queen: A Revealing Look at the Private Life of Elizabeth II*. New York: St. Martin's, 1991.

Riches, Steve. "101 Things You Didn't Know About the Queen. . . ." *The People,* March 31, 1996.

Zeigler, Philip. "Elizabeth: An Intimate Portrait." *Daily Mail*, February 17, 1996.

EDWARD KENNEDY (DUKE) ELLINGTON

Ewen, David. *Men of Popular Music*. Chicago: Ziff-Davis, 1944.

Lyons, Len and Don Perlo. *Jazz Portraits: The Lives and Music of the Jazz Masters*. New York: William Morrow, 1989.

Tucker, Mark. *Ellington: The Early Years*. Urbana, Ill.: University of Illinois Press, 1991.

MARIANNE FAITHFULL

Faithfull, Marianne (with David Dalton). *Faithfull: An Autobiography*. Boston: Little, Brown, 1994.

JERRY FALWELL

Harrington, Walt. *American Profiles: Somebodies and Nobodies Who Matter*. Columbia, Mo.: University of Missouri Press, 1985.

WILLIAM FAULKNER

Blotner, Joseph. *Faulkner: A Biography* (one-volume edition). New York: Random House, 1974, 1984.

Karl, Frederick Robert. *William Faulkner: American Writer: A Biography*. New York: Weidenfeld and Nicolson, 1989.

Minter, David. *William Faulkner: His Life and Work*. Baltimore, Md.: Johns Hopkins, 1980.

RICHARD FEYNMAN

Gleick, James. *Genius: The Life and Science of Richard Feynman*. New York: Vintage Books, 1992.

SALLY FIELD

Bonderoff, Jason. *Sally Field: A Biography*. New York: St. Martin's, 1987.

W. C. FIELDS

Gehring, Wes D. *Groucho and W. C. Fields: Huckster Comedians*. Jackson, Miss.: University Press of Mississippi, 1994.

Taylor, Robert Lewis. *W. C. Fields: His Follies and Fortunes*. Garden City, N.Y.: Doubleday, 1949.

PETER FINCH

Faulkner, Trader. *Peter Finch: A Biography.* New York: Taplinger, 1979.

F. SCOTT FITZGERALD

Bruccoli, Matthew J. *Some Sort of Epic Grandeur: The Life of F. Scott Fitzgerald.* New York: Harcourt Brace Jovanovich, 1981.

ERROL FLYNN

Higham, Charles. *Errol Flynn: The Untold Story.* Garden City, N.Y.: Doubleday, 1980.

Thomas, Tony. *Errol Flynn: The Spy Who Never Was.* New York: Carol, 1990.

HENRY FONDA

Collier, Peter. *The Fondas: A Hollywood Dynasty.* New York: G. P. Putnam's, 1991.

JANE AND PETER FONDA

Collier, Peter. *The Fondas: A Hollywood Dynasty.* New York: G. P. Putnam's, 1991.

Freedland, Michael. *Jane Fonda: A Biography.* New York: St. Martin's, 1988.

MALCOLM FORBES

Winans, Christopher. *Malcolm Forbes: The Man Who Had Everything.* New York: St. Martin's, 1990.

HENRY FORD

Nevins, Alan (and Frank Ernest Hill). *Ford: The Times, The Man, The Company.* New York: Charles Scribner's, 1954.

MICHEL FOUCAULT

Eribon, Didier, trans. Betsy Wing. *Michel Foucault.* Cambridge, Mass.: Harvard University Press, 1991.

Miller, James. *Foucault.* New York: Simon and Schuster, 1993.

ANNE FRANK

Levin, Meyer. "Life in the Secret Annex." *New York Times Book Review,* October 6, 1996.

Moffat, Mary Jane and Charlotte Painter (eds.). *Revelations: Diaries of Women.* New York: Random House, 1974.

Rose, Phyllis (ed.). *The Norton Book of Women's Lives.* New York: W. W. Norton, 1993.

SIGMUND FREUD

Clark, Ronald W. *Freud: The Man and the Cause.* New York: Random House, 1980.

Gay, Peter. *Freud: A Life for Our Time.* New York: W. W. Norton, 1988.

Karier, Clarence J. *Scientists of the Mind: Intellectual Founders of Modern Psychology.* Urbana, Ill.: University of Illinois Press, 1986.

ROBERT FROST

Meyers, Jeffrey. *Robert Frost: A Biography.* Boston: Houghton Mifflin, 1996.

INDIRA GANDHI

Jayakar, Pupul. *Indira Gandhi: An Intimate Biography.* New York: Pantheon, 1992.

MOHANDAS K. GANDHI

Ashe, Geoffrey. *Gandhi.* New York: Stein and Day, 1968.

Gandhi, Mohandas K. *An Autobiography: The Story of My Experiments with Truth.* Boston: Beacon Press, 1929.

Gold, Gerald. *Gandhi: A Pictorial Biography.* New York: Newmarket Press, 1983.

GRETA GARBO

Sands, Frederick and Sven Broman. *The Divine Garbo.* New York: Grosset and Dunlap, 1979.

JERRY GARCIA

"Jerry Garcia Left Behind Little-Known Hispanic Roots." *Rocky Mountain News,* August 14, 1995.

Colford, Paul D. "Rolling Stone Shows Garcia's 'Secret Life.'" *Los Angeles Times,* August 1, 1996.

Corliss, Richard. "The Trip Ends; The Pied and Tie-Dyed Piper of the Grateful Dead, Dies at 53." *Time,* August 21, 1995.

Le Draoulec, Pascale. "Rock 'n' Roll in His Blood." *Gannett News Service,* August 9, 1995.

Troy, Sandy. *Captain Trips: A Biography of Jerry Garcia.* New York: Thunder's Mouth Press, 1994.

ERLE STANLEY GARDNER

Hughes, Dorothy. *Erle Stanley Gardner: The Case of the Real Perry Mason.* New York: William Morrow, 1978.

JUDY GARLAND

"Judy Garland." *Biography.* A&E Channel.

Frank, Gerold. *Judy.* New York: Harper and Row, 1975.

BILL GATES

"Bill Gates Tops Forbes List of Billionaires." *Los Angeles Times,* July 1, 1996.

Isaacson, Walter. "In Search of the Real Bill Gates." *Time,* January 13, 1997.

Manes, Stephen and Paul Andrews. *Gates: How Microsoft's Mogul Reinvented an Industry and Made Himself the Richest Man in America.* New York: Doubleday, 1993.

Wallace, James and Jim Erickson. *Hard Drive: Bill Gates and the Making of the Microsoft Empire.* New York: Wiley, 1992.

THEODORE GEISEL

Beyette, Beverly. "Seuss: New Book on the Tip of His Tongue," *Los Angeles Times,* May 29, 1979.

Morgan, Judith and Neil Morgan. *Dr. Seuss and Mr. Geisel: A Biography.* New York: Random House, 1995.

URI GELLER

Geller, Uri. *My Story.* New York: Praeger, 1975.

JEAN PAUL GETTY

Henriquez, Diana B. "Poor Little Rich Boys." *New York Times Book Review,* December 10, 1995.

Miller, Russell. *The House of Getty.* New York: Henry Holt, 1985.

ALLEN GINSBERG

Schumacher, Michael. *Dharma Lion: A Biography of Allen Ginsberg.* New York: St. Martin's, 1992.

JOHN GLENN

Angel, Ann. *John Glenn: Space Pioneer.* New York: Fawcett, 1989.

Mashek, John W. "John Glenn Tries for a White House Landing." *U.S. News and World Report,* June 13, 1983.

McCombs, Phil. "John Glenn at Liftoff Plus 25 Years." *Washington Post,* February 20, 1987.

ROBERT GODDARD

Streissguth, Tom. *Rocket Man: The Story of Robert Goddard.* Minneapolis: Carolrhoda, 1995.

EMMA GOLDMAN

Falk, Candace Serena. *Love, Anarchy, and Emma Goldman.* New Brunswick, N.J.: Rutgers University Press, 1984.

BARRY GOLDWATER

Goldberg, Robert Alan. *Barry Goldwater.* New Haven, Conn.: Yale University Press, 1995.

Goldwater, Barry (with Jack Casserly). *Goldwater.* New York: Doubleday, 1988.

MARTHA GRAHAM

de Mille, Agnes. *Martha: The Life and Work of Martha Graham.* New York: Random House, 1956, 1991.

Graham, Martha. *Blood Memory: An Autobiography.* New York: Doubleday, 1991.

Stodelle, Ernestine. *Deep Song: The Dance and Story of Martha Graham.* New York: Macmillan, 1984.

CARY GRANT

Harris, Warren G. *Cary Grant: A Touch of Elegance.* New York: Doubleday, 1987.

Higham, Charles. *Cary Grant: The Lonely Heart.* San Diego: Harcourt Brace Jovanovich, 1989.

Nelson, Nancy. *Evenings with Cary Grant: Recollections in His Own Words and by Those Who Knew Him Best.* New York: William Morrow, 1991.

Schickel, Richard. *Cary Grant: A Celebration.* Boston: Little, Brown, 1983.

GRAHAM GREENE

Sherry, Norman. *The Life of Graham Greene, vol. 1 1904–1939.* New York: Viking, 1989.

DICK GREGORY

Gregory, Dick (with Robert Lipsyte). *Nigger.* New York: E. P. Dutton, 1964.

DAG HAMMARSKJÖLD

Söderberg, Sten. *Hammmarskjöld: A Pictorial Biography.* New York: Viking, 1962.

Stolpe, Sven. *Dag Hammmarskjöld.* New York: Charles Scribner's, 1966.

ARMAND HAMMER

Blumay, Carl (with Henry Edwards). *The Dark Side of Power: The Real Armand Hammer.* New York: Simon and Schuster, 1992.

Hammer, Armand (with Neil Lyndon). *Hammer.* New York: G. P. Putnam's, 1987.

Weinberg, Steve. *Armand Hammer: The Untold Story.* Boston: Little, Brown, 1989.

OSCAR HAMMERSTEIN II

Fordin, Hugh. *Getting to Know Him: A Biography of Oscar Hammerstein II.* New York: Random House, 1977.

LIONEL HAMPTON

Hampton, Lionel (with James Haskins). *Hamp: An Autobiography.* New York: Warner, 1989.

JEAN HARRIS

Alexander, Shana. *"Very Much a Lady": The Untold Story of Jean Harris and Dr. Herman Tarnower.* Boston: Little, Brown, 1983.

Harris, Jean. *Stranger in Two Worlds.* New York: Macmillan, 1986.

STEPHEN HAWKING

White, Michael and John Gribbin. *Stephen Hawking: A Life in Science.* New York: E. P. Dutton, 1992.

JOSEPH HAYDN

Landon, H. C. Robbins. *Haydn.* New York: Praeger, 1972.

WILLIAM RANDOLPH HEARST

Robinson, Judith. *The Hearsts: An American Dynasty.* Newark, Del.: University of Delaware Press, 1991.

Swanberg, W. A. *Citizen Hearst: A Biography of William Randolph Hearst.* New York: Charles Scribner's, 1961.

LILLIAN HELLMAN

Rollyson, Carl. *Hellman: Her Legend and Her Legacy.* New York: St. Martin's, 1988.

Wright, William. *Lillian Hellman: The Image, The Woman.* New York: Simon and Schuster, 1986.

ERNEST HEMINGWAY

Brian, Denis. *The True Gent: An Intimate Portrait of Ernest Hemingway by Those Who Knew Him.* New York: Grove Press, 1988.

Mellow, Ames R. *Hemingway: A Life Without Consequences.* Boston: Houghton Mifflin, 1992.

JIMI HENDRIX

Shapiro, Harry and Caesar Glebbeek. *Jimi Hendrix: Electric Gypsy.* New York: St. Martin's, 1991.

KATHARINE HEPBURN

Hepburn, Katharine. *Me: Stories of My Life.* New York: Alfred A. Knopf, 1991.

Leaming, Barbara. *Katharine Hepburn.* New York: Crown, 1995.

ALGER HISS

Hiss, Alger. *Recollections of a Life.* New York: Henry Holt, 1988.

Smith, John C. *Alger Hiss: The True Story.* New York: Holt, Rinehart and Winston, 1976.

Thomas, Evan. "An American Melodrama." *Newsweek,* November 25, 1996.

ALFRED HITCHCOCK

Spoto, Donald. *The Dark Side of Genius: The Life of Alfred Hitchcock.* Boston: Little, Brown, 1983.

ADOLF HITLER

Payne, Robert. *The Life and Death of Adolf Hitler.* New York: Praeger, 1973.

Prause, Gerhard, trans. Susan Hecker Ray. *School Days of the Famous: Do School Achievements Foretell Success in Life?* New York: Springer, 1978.

ABBIE HOFFMAN

Jezer, Marty. *Abbie Hoffman: American Rebel.* New Brunswick, N.J.: Rutgers University Press, 1992.

DUSTIN HOFFMAN

Diamond, Jamie. "The Arts: Neurotic Quest for Perfection . . ." *Sunday Telegraph,* November 10, 1996.

Gussow, Mel. "Dustin Hoffman's 'Salesman.'" *New York Times,* March 18, 1984.

Lenbueg, Jeff. *Dustin Hoffman: Hollywood's Anti-Hero.* New York: St. Martin's, 1983.

Travers, Peter. "Tootsie Drops His Guard." *Time,* January 17, 1983.

J. EDGAR HOOVER

Demaris, Ovid. *The Director: An Oral Biography of J. Edgar Hoover.* New York: Harper's Magazine Press, 1975.

Lyons, Eugene. *Herbert Hoover: A Biography.* Garden City, N.Y.: Doubleday, 1948.

Nash, Jay Robert. *Citizen Hoover: A Critical Study of the Life and Times of J. Edgar Hoover and His FBI.* Chicago: Nelson-Hall, 1972.

Summers, Anthony. *Official and Confidential: The Secret Life of J. Edgar Hoover.* New York: G. P. Putnam's, 1993.

Theoharis, Athan G. and John Stuart Cox. *The Boss: J. Edgar Hoover and the Great American Inquisition.* Philadelphia: Temple University Press, 1988.

HARRY HOUDINI

Fitzsimmons, Raymond. *Death and the Magician: The Mystery of Houdini.* New York: Atheneum, 1981.

Teller. "The Great Escaper." *New York Times Book Review,* December 15, 1996.

SAM HOUSTON

De Bruhl, Marshall. *Sword of San Jacinto: A Life of Sam Houston.* New York: Random House, 1993.

Williams, John Hoyt. *Sam Houston: A Biography of the Father of Texas.* New York: Simon and Schuster, 1993.

RON HOWARD

"Ron Howard." CNN *Larry King Weekend*, November 9, 1996.

"Ron Howard." *Playboy*, May 1994.

Brooks, David. "Kid from Mayberry Makes Good." *Insight*, March 31, 1986.

Rader, Dotson. "A Nice Guy and a Winner." *Parade*, November 10, 1996.

HOWARD HUGHES

Brown, Peter Harry and Par H. Broeske. *Howard Hughes: The Untold Story*. New York: E. P. Dutton, 1996.

LANGSTON HUGHES

Hughes, Langston. *The Big Sea: An Autobiography*. New York: Thunder's Mouth Press, 1940.

Hummel, Jack. *Langston Hughes*. New York: Chelsea House, 1988.

HUBERT HUMPHREY

Winokur, Jon. *Fathers*. New York: E. P. Dutton, 1993.

SADDAM HUSSEIN

"The Mind of Hussein." *Frontline* (PBS), February 26, 1991.

"Saddam Hussein." *Biography*. A&E Channel.

Braun, Stephen and Tracy Wilkinson. "What Sort of Man Is Hussein?" *Los Angeles Times*, February 10, 1991.

Bulloch, John. "The Violent Boy from Al-Ouja . . ." *The Independent*, January 6, 1991.

Hirst, David. "Saddam's Enemy Within." *The Guardian*, August 15, 1995.

Karsh, Efraim and Inari Rautsi. *Saddam Hussein: A Political Biography*. New York: Free Press, 1991.

Letter to the editor. *Charleston Daily Mail*, October 14, 1996.

Miller, Judith. "The Rise to Power." *Seattle Times*, January 31, 1991.

LEE IACOCCA

Iacocca, Lee (with William Novak). *Iacocca: An Autobiography*. New York: Bantam, 1984.

CHRISTOPHER ISHERWOOD

"Christopher Isherwood Is Dead at 81." *New York Times*, January 6, 1986.

Braun, Stephen. "Christopher Isherwood, Whose Tapes Inspired 'Cabaret,' Dies." *Los Angeles Times*, January 6, 1986.

Fryer, Jonathan. *Isherwood*. Garden City, N.Y.: Doubleday, 1978.

MICHAEL JACKSON

Campbell, Lisa D. *Michael Jackson: The King of Pop*. Boston: Branden Books, 1993.

MICK JAGGER

Andersen, Christopher. *Jagger Unauthorized*. New York: Delacorte, 1993.

HENRY JAMES AND WILLIAM JAMES

Allen, Gay Wilson. *William James: A Biography*. New York: Viking, 1967.

Bjork, Daniel W. *William James: The Center of His Vision*. New York: Columbia University Press, 1988.

Lewis, R. W. B. *The Jameses: A Family Narrative.* New York: Farrar, Straus and Giroux, 1991.

STEVE JOBS

Young, Jeffrey S. *Steve: The Journey Is the Reward.* Glenview, Ill.: Scott, Foresman, 1988.

LYNDON BAINES JOHNSON

Dallek. *Lone Star Rising: Lyndon Johnson and His Times, 1908–1960.* New York: Oxford, 1991.

JANIS JOPLIN

Friedman, Myra. *Buried Alive: The Biography of Janis Joplin.* New York: William Morrow, 1973.

Joplin, Laura. *Love, Janis.* New York: Villard Books, 1992.

CARL JUNG

Brome, Vincent. *Jung: Man and Myth.* New York: Atheneum, 1978.

Hannah, Barbara. *Jung: His Life and Work. A Biographical Memoir.* New York: G. P. Putnam's, 1976.

Jung, C. G. *Memories, Dreams, Reflections.* New York: Pantheon, 1963.

Wehr, Gerhard. *Jung, A Biography.* New York: Random House, 1987.

THEODORE KACZYNSKI

"Theodore Kaczynski." *People,* December 30 and January 6, 1997.

Johnston, David and Janny Scott. "The Tortured Genius of Theodore Kaczynski." *New York Times,* August 29, 1995.

ELIA KAZAN

Kazan, Elia. *A Life.* New York: Alfred A. Knopf, 1988.

BUSTER KEATON

Meade, Marion. *Buster Keaton. Cut to the Chase: A Biography.* New York: HarperCollins, 1995.

HELEN KELLER

Fellowes-Gordon, Ian. *Heroes of the Twentieth Century.* New York: Hawthorn, 1966.

Lash, Joseph P. *Helen and Teacher: The Story of Helen Keller and Anne Sullivan Macy.* New York: Delacorte, 1980.

Rose, Phyllis. *The Norton Book of Women's Lives.* New York: W. W. Norton, 1993.

JOHN FITZGERALD KENNEDY

Fellowes-Gordon, Ian. *Heroes of the Twentieth Century.* New York, Hawthorn, 1966.

Fifty Who Made the Difference. New York: Villard Books, 1984.

Klein, Edward. "Young Love." *Vanity Fair,* September 1996.

Steinberg, Alfred. *The Kennedy Brothers.* New York: G. P. Putnam's, 1969.

ELIZABETH KENNY

Cohn, Victor. *Sister Kenny: The Woman Who Challenged the Doctors.* Minneapolis: University of Minnesota Press, 1975.

Oppewal, Sonda Riedesel. "Sister Elizabeth Kenny, an Australian Nurse, and Treatment of Poliomyelitis Victims." *Image: Journal of Nursing Scholarship,* March 1997.

JACK KEROUAC

McNally, Dennis. *Desolate Angel: A Biography: Jack Kerouac, the Beat Generation, and America.* New York: Random House, 1979.

MARTIN LUTHER KING, JR.

Fifty Who Made the Difference. New York: Villard Books, 1984.

Oates, Stephen B. *Let the Trumpet Sound: The Life of Martin Luther King, Jr.* New York: Harper and Row, 1982.

STEPHEN KING

Geier, Thom. "The Obsession of Stephen King." *U.S. News and World Report,* September 23, 1996.

Kanfer, Stefan. "King of Horror." *Time,* October 6, 1986.

Reino, *Stephen King: The First Decade, Carrie to Pet Sematary.* Swansea, U.K.: University College of Swansea Press, 1988.

ALFRED KINSEY

Pomeroy, Wardell B. *Dr. Kinsey and the Institute for Sex Research.* New York: Harper and Row, 1972.

RUDYARD KIPLING

Birkenhead, Lord. *Rudyard Kipling.* New York: Random House, 1978.

CALVIN KLEIN

Black, Larry. "Fashion Kings Treading the Catwalk to a Quote." *Evening Standard,* June 26, 1997.

Gaines, Steven and Sharon Churcher. *Obsession: The Lives and Times of Calvin Klein.* New York: Carol, 1994.

Lockwood, Lisa. "Calvin's Credo." *WWD,* July 22, 1997.

Ryan, Thomas J. "Calvin Won't Follow Ralph onto the Big Board." *Daily News Record,* June 18, 1997.

C. EVERETT KOOP

Koop, C. Everett. *Koop: The Memoirs of America's Family Doctor.* New York: Random House, 1991.

BURT LANCASTER

Clinch, Minty. *Burt Lancaster.* New York: Stein and Day, 1984.

Windeler, Robert. *Burt Lancaster.* New York: St. Martin's, 1984.

K. D. LANG

Starr, Victoria. *k. d. lang.* New York: St. Martin's, 1994.

D. H. (DAVID HERBERT) LAWRENCE

Callow, Philip. *Son and Lover: The Young D. H. Lawrence.* New York: Stein and Day, 1975.

Worthen, John. *D. H. Lawrence: The Early Years.* Cambridge, U.K.: Cambridge University Press, 1991.

LOUIS LEAKEY

Morell, Virginia. *Ancestral Passions: The Leakey Family and the Quest for Humankind's Beginnings.* New York: Simon and Schuster, 1995.

MARY LEAKEY

Manning, Anita. "Mary Leakey. Her Discoveries Redefined Theories on Human Origins." *USA Today,* December 10, 1996.

Morrell, Virginia. *Ancestral Passions: The Leakey Family and the Quest for Humankind's Beginnings.* New York: Simon and Schuster, 1995.

PEGGY LEE

Lee, Peggy. *Miss Peggy Lee: An Autobiography.* New York: Donald I. Fine, 1989.

VLADIMIR LENIN

Trotsky, Leon. *The Young Lenin.* New York: Doubleday, 1972.

Volkogonov, Dmitri. *Lenin: A New Biography.* New York: Free Press, 1994.

JOHN LENNON

Coleman, Ray. *Lennon: The Definitive Biography.* New York: Harper Perennial, 1985.

Goldman, Albert. *The Lives of John Lennon.* New York: William Morrow, 1988.

Norman, Philip. *Shout! The Beatles in Their Generation.* New York: Warner Books, 1981.

JAY LENO

Leno, Jay (with Bill Zehme). *Leading with My Chin.* New York: HarperCollins, 1996.

ALAN JAY LERNER

Lerner, Alan Jay. *The Street Where I Live.* New York: W. W. Norton, 1978.

DAVID LETTERMAN

Adler, Bill. *The Letterman Wit. His Life and Humor.* New York: Carroll & Graf, 1994.

Rader, Dotson. "I Love Nothing More Than Being in Love." *Parade,* May 26, 1996.

JERRY LEWIS

"Jerry Lewis." *Biography.* A&E Channel.

Levy, Shawn. *King of Comedy: The Life and Art of Jerry Lewis.* New York: St. Martin's, 1996.

Lewis, Jerry (with Herb Gluck). *Jerry Lewis, in Person.* New York: Atheneum, 1982.

SINCLAIR LEWIS

Schorer, Mark. *Sinclair Lewis: An American Life.* New York: McGraw-Hill, 1961.

WLADZIU VALENTINO LIBERACE

Thomas, Bob. *Liberace: The True Story.* New York: St. Martin's, 1987.

ABRAHAM LINCOLN

Kigel, Richard. *The Frontier Years of Abe Lincoln.* New York: Walker, 1986.

Weiser, Marjorie P. K. and Jean S. Arbeiter. *Womanlist.* New York: Atheneum, 1981.

CHARLES LINDBERGH

Davis, Kenneth S. *The Hero: Charles A. Lindbergh and the American Dream.* New York: Doubleday, 1959.

Milton, Joyce. *Loss of Eden: A Biography of Charles and Anne Morrow Lindbergh.* New York: HarperCollins, 1993.

ANDREW LLOYD WEBBER

Walsh, Michael A. *Andrew Lloyd Webber: His Life and Works.* New York: Harry N. Abrams, 1989.

VINCE LOMBARDI

O'Brien, Michael. *Vince.* New York, William Morrow, 1987.

JACK LONDON

Perry, John. *Jack London: An American Myth.* Chicago: Nelson-Hall, 1981.

Sinclair, Andrew. *Jack.* New York: Harper and Row, 1977.

GREG LOUGANIS

Louganis, Greg (with Eric Marcus). *Breaking the Surface.* New York: Random House, 1995.

H. P. (HOWARD PHILLIPS) LOVECRAFT

de Camp, L. Sprague. *Lovecraft.* New York: Doubleday, 1975.

GEORGE LUCAS

Goldstein, Patrick. "The Force Never Left Him." *Los Angeles Times Magazine,* February 2, 1997.

Pollock, Dale. *Skywalking: The Life and Films of George Lucas.* New York: Samuel French, 1983.

CLARE BOOTHE LUCE

Sheed, Wilfrid. *Clare Boothe Luce.* New York: E. P. Dutton, 1982.

HENRY LUCE

Martin, Ralph G. *Henry and Clare: An Intimate Portrait of the Luces.* New York: G. P. Putnam's, 1991.

DOUGLAS MACARTHUR

Manchester, William. *American Caesar.* Boston: Little, Brown, 1978.

MADONNA

Bego, Mark. *Madonna: Blonde Ambition.* New York: Harmony Books, 1992.

Claro, Nichole. *Madonna.* New York: Chelsea House, 1994.

Wilkinson, Peter. "Madonna on Life Before and After Motherhood." *Redbook,* January 1997.

MALCOLM X

Brown, Kevin. *Malcolm X: His Life and Legacy.* Brookfield, Conn.: Millbrook Press, 1995.

Diamond, Arthur. *Malcolm X: A Voice for Black America.* Hillside, N.J.: Enslow Publishers, 1994.

Malcolm X (as told to Alex Haley). *The Autobiography of Malcolm X.* New York: Ballantine Books, 1973.

NELSON MANDELA

Mandela, Nelson. *Mandela: An Illustrated Autobiography.* Boston: Little, Brown, 1994.

Meer, Fatima. *Higher than Hope: The Authorized Biography of Nelson Mandela.* New York: Harper and Row, 1988.

THOMAS MANN
Hayman, Ronald. *Thomas Mann.* New York: Charles Scribner's, 1995.
Winston, Richard. *Thomas Mann: The Making of an Artist.* New York: Alfred A. Knopf, 1981.

MICKEY MANTLE
Falkner, David. *The Life of Mickey Mantle.* New York: Simon and Schuster, 1995.
Mantle, Mickey (with Herb Gluck). *The Mick.* New York: Doubleday, 1985.

MAO TSE-TUNG
Suyin, Han. *The Morning Deluge: Mao Tse-Tung and the Chinese Revolution.* New York: Little, Brown, 1972.
Terrill, Ross. *Mao: A Biography.* New York: Harper and Row, 1980.

ROCKY MARCIANO
Skehan, Everett M. *Rocky Marciano: Biography of a First Son.* Boston: Houghton Mifflin, 1977.

MARGARET ROSE OF YORK
Dempster, Nigel. *Princess Margaret: A Life Unfulfilled.* New York: Macmillan, 1981.
Higham, Charles and Roy Moseley. *Elizabeth and Philip.* New York: Doubleday, 1991.
Warwick, Christopher. *Princess Margaret.* New York: St. Martin's, 1983.

GEORGE C. MARSHALL
Mosley, Leonard. *Marshall: Hero for Our Times.* New York: Hearst Books, 1982.

MARY MARTIN
Martin, Mary. *My Heart Belongs.* New York: William Morrow, 1976.

PETER MARTINS
Martins, Peter (with Robert Cornfield). *Far from Denmark.* Boston: Little, Brown, 1982.

GUY DE MAUPASSANT
Steegmuller, Francis. *Maupassant.* London: Collins, 1950.

ROBERT MAXWELL
Bower, Tom. *Maxwell, the Outsider.* New York: Viking, 1988.
Greenslade, Roy. *Maxwell. The Rise and Fall of Robert Maxwell and His Empire.* New York: Birch Lane Press, 1992.

JOE MCCARTHY
Reeves, Thomas C. *The Life and Times of Joe McCarthy.* New York: Stein and Day, 1982.

MARY MCCARTHY
Brightman, Carol. *Writing Dangerously: Mary McCarthy and Her World.* New York: Clarkson Potter, 1992.
Gelderman, Carol. *Mary McCarthy: A Life.* New York: St. Martin's, 1988.

GEORGE MCGOVERN
Keyes, Ralph. *Is There Life After High School?* Boston: Little, Brown, 1976.

MARGARET MEAD
Mead, Margaret. *Blackberry Winter: My Earlier Years.* New York: William Morrow, 1972.

GOLDA MEIR
Martin, Ralph G. *Golda Meir: The Romantic Years.* New York: Charles Scribner's, 1988.

HENRY LOUIS MENCKEN
Bode, Carl. *Mencken.* Carbondale, Ill.: Southern Illinois University Press, 1969.
Hobson, Fred. *Mencken: A Life.* New York: Random House, 1994.

BETTE MIDLER
Mair, George. *Bette: An Intimate Biography of Bette Midler.* New York: Carol, 1995.
Whitcomb, John and Claire Whitcomb. *Great American Anecdotes.* New York: William Morrow, 1993.

HENRY MILLER
Dearborn, Mary V. *The Happiest Man Alive.* New York: Simon and Schuster, 1991.
Miller, Henry. *Henry Miller's Book of Friends.* Santa Barbara, Calif.: Capra Press, 1976.

A. A. MILNE
Milne, A. A. *Autobiography.* New York: E. P. Dutton, 1939.
Thwaite, Ann. *A. A. Milne: The Man Behind Winnie-the-Pooh.* New York: Random House, 1990.

MARGARET MITCHELL
Edwards, Anne. *Road to Tara: The Life of Margaret Mitchell.* New York: Ticknor and Fields, 1983.
Farr, Finis. *Margaret Mitchell of Atlanta.* New York: Avon Books, 1974.
Pyron, Darden Asbury. *Southern Daughter: The Life of Margaret Mitchell.* New York: Oxford University Press, 1991.

MARILYN MONROE
Guiles, Fred Lawrence. *Norman Jean.* New York: McGraw-Hill, 1969.
Mailer, Norman. *Marilyn.* New York: Grosset and Dunlap, 1973.
Spoto, Donald. *Marilyn Monroe.* New York: HarperCollins, 1993.

BERNARD LAW MONTGOMERY
Hamilton, Nigel. *Monty: The Making of a General.* New York: McGraw-Hill, 1981.
Horne, Alistair (with David Montgomery). *Monty: The Lonely Leader.* New York: HarperCollins, 1994.

MARY TYLER MOORE
Moore, Mary Tyler. *After All*. New York: G. P. Putnam's, 1995.

WOLFGANG AMADEUS MOZART
Kupferberg, Herbert. *Amadeus: A Mozart Mosaic*. New York: McGraw-Hill, 1986.
Solomon, Maynard. *Mozart*. New York: HarperCollins, 1995.

JOHN MUIR
Clarke, James Mitchell. *The Life and Adventures of John Muir*. San Francisco: Sierra Club Books, 1979.
Turner, Frederick. *Rediscovering America: John Muir in His Time and Ours*. New York: Viking, 1985.
Wilkins, Thurman. *John Muir: Apostle of Nature*. Norman, Okla.: University of Oklahoma Press, 1995.

AUDIE MURPHY
Audie Murphy Research Foundation (Santa Clarita, Calif.).
Graham, Don. *No Name on the Bullet: A Biography of Audie Murphy*. New York: Viking, 1989.

EDWARD R. MURROW
Persico, Joseph E. *Edward R. Murrow: An American Original*. New York: McGraw-Hill, 1988.

BENITO MUSSOLINI
Smith, Denis Mack. *Mussolini*. New York: Alfred A. Knopf, 1982.

RALPH NADER
McCarry, Charles. *Citizen Nader*. New York: Saturday Review Press, 1972.

GAMAL ABDEL NASSER
St. John, Robert. *The Boss: The Story of Gamal Abdel Nasser*. New York: McGraw-Hill, 1960.

CARRY NATION
Madison, Arnold. *Carry Nation*. New York: Thomas Nelson, 1977.
Taylor, Robert Lewis. *Vessel of Wrath*. New York: The New American Library, 1966.

JAWAHARLAL NEHRU
Moraes, Frank. *Jawaharlal Nehru*. New York: Macmillan, 1956.

HORATIO NELSON
Bradford, Ernle. *Nelson: The Essential Hero*. New York: Harcourt Brace Jovanovich, 1977.
Walder, David. *Nelson*. New York: Dial Press, 1978.

ISAAC NEWTON
Christianson, Gale E. *In the Presence of the Creator*. New York: Free Press, 1984.

JACK NICHOLSON
McGilligan, Patrick. *Jack's Life: A Biography of Jack Nicholson*. New York: W. W. Norton, 1994.

FLORENCE NIGHTINGALE

Cook, Sir Edward. *The Life of Florence Nightingale*. New York: Macmillan, 1942.

Smith, F. B. *Florence Nightingale: Reputation and Power*. New York: St. Martin's, 1982.

Woodham-Smith, Cecil. *Florence Nightingale*. New York: McGraw-Hill, 1951.

VASLAV NIJINSKY

Ostwald, Peter. *Vaslav Nijinsky: A Leap into Madness*. New York: A Lyle Stuart Book, Carol, 1991.

ANAIS NIN

Fitch, Noel Riley. *Anaïs: The Erotic Life of Anais Nin*. Boston: Little, Brown, 1993.

Kupferberg, Tuli and Sylvia Topp. *First Glance: Childhood Creations of the Famous*. Maplewood, N.J.: Hammond, 1978.

DAVID NIVEN

Morley, Sheridan. *The Other Side of the Moon: The Life of David Niven*. New York: Harper and Row, 1985.

RICHARD NIXON

Ambrose, Stephen E. *Nixon: The Education of a Politician*. New York: Simon and Schuster, 1987.

Morris, Roger. *Richard Milhous Nixon: The Rise of an American Politician*. New York: Henry Holt, 1990.

ANNIE OAKLEY

Kasper, Shirl. *Annie Oakley*. Norman, Okla.: University of Oklahoma Press, 1992.

Riley, Glenda. *The Life and Legacy of Annie Oakley*. Norman, Okla.: University of Oklahoma Press, 1994.

GEORGIA O'KEEFFE

Lisle, Laurie. *Portrait of an Artist: A Biography of Georgia O'Keeffe*. New York: Pocket Books, 1980.

Robinson, Roxana. *Georgia O'Keeffe: A Life*. New York: Harper and Row, 1989.

ARISTOTLE ONASSIS

Brady, Frank. *Onassis: An Extravagant Life*. Englewood Cliffs, N.J.: Prentice-Hall, 1977.

JACQUELINE KENNEDY ONASSIS

"Jacqueline Kennedy Onassis." *Biography*. A&E Channel.

EUGENE O'NEILL

Alexander, Doris. *The Tempering of Eugene O'Neill*. New York: Harcourt, Brace and World, 1962.

Gelb, Arthur and Barbara. *O'Neill*. New York: Harper and Brothers, 1960.

J. ROBERT OPPENHEIMER

Goodchild, Peter. *J. Robert Oppenheimer: Shatterer of Worlds*. London: British Broadcasting Corporation, 1980.

Royal, Denise. *The Story of J. Robert Oppenheimer*. New York: St. Martin's, 1969.

GEORGE ORWELL
Crick, Bernard. *George Orwell: A Life.* Boston: Little, Brown, 1980.

SIR WILLIAM OSLER
Illingworth, R. S. and C. M. *Lessons from Childhood: Some Aspects of the Early Life of Unusual Men and Women.* Baltimore, Md.: William and Wilkins, 1966.

JESSE OWENS
Baker, William J. *Jesse Owens: An American Life.* New York: Free Press, 1986.

SATCHEL PAIGE
Littlefield, Bill. *Champions: Stories of Ten Remarkable Athletes.* Boston: Little, Brown, 1993.

DOLLY PARTON
Parton, Dolly. *Dolly: My Life and Other Unfinished Business.* New York: Harper-Collins, 1994.

GEORGE S. PATTON
Blumenson, Martin. *Patton: The Man Behind the Legend.* New York: William Morrow, 1985.
Patton, Robert H. *The Pattons: A Personal History of the American Family.* New York: Crown, 1994.

LINUS PAULING
Hager, Thomas. *Force of Nature: The Life of Linus Pauling.* New York, Simon and Schuster, 1995.
Goertzel, Ted and Ben. *Linus Pauling: A Life in Science and Politics.* New York: Basic Books, 1995.

NORMAN VINCENT PEALE
Peale, Norman Vincent. *The True Joy of Positive Living.* New York: William Morrow, 1984.

ROBERT PEARY
Weems, John Edward. *Peary: The Explorer and the Man.* Cambridge, Mass.: Riverside Press, 1967.

PABLO PICASSO
Huffington, Arianna Stassinopoulos. *Picasso: Creator and Destroyer.* New York: Simon and Schuster, 1988.
Mailer, Norman. *Picasso as a Young Man.* New York: Atlantic Monthly Press, 1995.

MARY PICKFORD
Windeler, Robert. *Sweetheart: The Story of Mary Pickford.* New York: Praeger, 1973.

SYLVIA PLATH
Alexander, Paul. *Rough Magic: A Biography of Sylvia Plath.* New York: Viking, 1991.
Goertzel, Mildred George, Victor Goertzel, and Ted George Goertzel. *Three Hundred Eminent Personalities.* San Francisco: Jossey-Bass, 1978.

EDGAR ALLAN POE

Symons, Julian. *The Tell-Tale Heart: The Life and Work of Edgar Allan Poe.* New York: Harper and Row, 1978.

POPE JOHN PAUL II

Bernstein, Carl and Marco Politi. *His Holiness: John Paul II and the Hidden History of Our Time.* New York: Doubleday, 1996.

Pope John Paul II. *Gift and Mystery: On the Fiftieth Anniversary of My Priestly Ordination.* New York: Doubleday, 1996.

COLE PORTER

Eells, George. *The Life That Late He Led: A Biography of Cole Porter.* New York: G. P. Putnam's, 1967.

Grafton, David. *Red, Hot & Rich! An Oral History of Cole Porter.* New York: Stein and Day, 1987.

Schwartz, Charles. *Cole Porter.* New York: Dial Press, 1977.

MARJORIE MERRIWEATHER POST

Wright, William. *Heiress: The Rich Life of Marjorie Merriweather Post.* Washington, D.C.: New Republic Books, 1978.

BEATRIX POTTER

Lane, Margaret. *The Tale of Beatrix Potter.* London: Frederick Warne, 1968.

Taylor, Judy. *Beatrix Potter: Artist, Storyteller and Countrywoman.* London: Frederick Warne, 1986.

COLIN POWELL

Powell, Colin (with Joseph E. Persico). *My American Journey.* New York: Random House, 1995.

TYRONE POWER

"Tyrone Power." *Biography.* A&E Channel.

ELVIS PRESLEY

Goldman, Albert. *Elvis.* New York: Avon Books, 1981.

Guralnick, Peter. *Last Train to Memphis: The Rise of Elvis Presley.* Boston: Little, Brown, 1994.

Nash, Alanna (with Billy Smith, Marty Lacker, and Lamar Fike). *Elvis Aaron Presley: Revelations from the Memphis Mafia.* New York: HarperCollins, 1995.

MARCEL PROUST

Hayman, Ronald. *Proust: A Biography.* New York: HarperCollins, 1990.

RICHARD PRYOR

Haskins, Jim. *Richard Pryor: A Man and His Madness.* New York: Beaufort Books, 1984.

Pryor, Richard (with Todd Gold). *Pryor Convictions and Other Life Sentences.* New York: Pantheon Books, 1995.

GRIGORI RASPUTIN

De Jonge, Alex. *The Life and Times of Grigori Rasputin.* New York: Carroll and Graf, 1982.

Hook, Donald D. *Madmen of History.* Middle Village, N.Y.: Jonathan David, 1976.

DAN RATHER
Rather, Dan (with Peter Wyden). *I Remember*. Boston: Little, Brown, 1991.

RONALD REAGAN
Edwards, Anne. *Early Reagan*. New York: William Morrow, 1987.
Reagan, Ronald. *An American Life*. New York: Simon and Schuster, 1990.

WILHELM REICH
Reich, Ilse Ollendorff. *Wilhelm Reich: A Personal Biography*. New York: St. Martin's, 1969.
Reich, Wilhelm. *Passion of Youth: An Autobiography*. New York: Farrar, Straus and Giroux, 1988.

JANET RENO
Anderson, Paul. *Janet Reno: Doing the Right Thing*. New York: John Wiley, 1994.

BURT REYNOLDS
Reynolds, Burt. *My Life*. New York: Hyperion, 1994.

EDWARD RICKENBACKER
Rickenbacker, Edward V. *Rickenbacker*. Englewood Cliffs, N.J.: Prentice-Hall, 1967.

RAINER MARIA RILKE
Freedman, Ralph. *Life of a Poet: Rainer Maria Rilke*. New York: Farrar, Straus and Giroux, 1996.

GERALDO RIVERA
Rivera, Geraldo (with Daniel Paisner). *Exposing Myself*. New York: Bantam, 1991.

NELSON ROCKEFELLER
Reich, Cary. *The Life of Nelson A. Rockefeller*. New York: Doubleday, 1996.

NORMAN ROCKWELL
Rockwell, Norman. *My Adventures as an Illustrator*. New York: Harry N. Abrams, 1988.
Walton, Donald. *A Rockwell Portrait*. Kansas City, Mo.: Sheed Andrews and McMeel, 1978.

DENNIS RODMAN
People, August 26, 1996.

WILHELM KONRAD ROENTGEN
Illingworth, R. S. and C. M. *Lessons from Childhood: Some Aspects of the Early Life of Unusual Men and Women*. Baltimore, Md.: William and Wilkins, 1966.

WILL ROGERS
Yagoda, Ben. *Will Rogers*. New York: Alfred A. Knopf, 1993.

ELEANOR ROOSEVELT
Cook, Blanche Wiesen. *Eleanor Roosevelt*. New York: Viking, 1992.

FRANKLIN D. ROOSEVELT
Cook, Blanche Wiesen. *Eleanor Roosevelt*. New York: Viking, 1992.
Miller, Nathan. *FDR: An Intimate History*. New York: Doubleday, 1983.

Ward, Geoffrey C. *Before the Trumpet: Young Franklin Roosevelt*. New York: Harper and Row, 1985.

THEODORE ROOSEVELT

Busch, Noel F. *T. R.: The Story of Theodore Roosevelt and His Influence on Our Times*. New York: Reynal, 1963.

McCullough, David. *Mornings on Horseback*. New York: Simon and Schuster, 1981.

ARTHUR RUBINSTEIN

Rubinstein, Arthur. *My Young Years*. New York: Alfred A. Knopf, 1973.

WILMA RUDOLPH

Biracree, Tom. *Wilma Rudolph*. New York: Chelsea House, 1988.

NOLAN RYAN

Rolfe, John. *Nolan Ryan*. New York: Sports Illustrated for Kids Books, 1992.

CARL SANDBURG

Niven, Penelope. *Carl Sandburg*. New York: Charles Scribner's, 1991.

MARGARET SANGER

Gray, Madeline. *Margaret Sanger: A Biography of the Champion of Birth Control*. New York: Richard Marek, 1979.

H. NORMAN SCHWARZKOPF

Anderson, Jack and Dale Van Atta. *Stormin' Norman: An American Hero*. New York: Kensington, 1991.

Schwarzkopf, H. Norman (with Peter Petre). *It Doesn't Take a Hero*. New York: Bantam, 1992.

ALBERT SCHWEITZER

Marshall, George and David Poling. *Schweitzer*. New York: Doubleday, 1971.

Seaver, George. *Albert Schweitzer: The Man and His Mind*. New York: Harper and Brothers, 1947.

MARY SHELLEY

Sunstein, Emily W. *Mary Shelley: Romance and Reality*. Boston: Little, Brown, 1989.

BILL SHOEMAKER

Shoemaker, Bill and Barney Nagler. *Shoemaker*. New York: Doubleday, 1988.

BEVERLY SILLS

Sills, Beverly. *Bubbles: A Self-Portrait*. New York: Bobbs-Merrill, 1976.

Sills, Beverly and Lawrence Linderman. *Beverly: An Autobiography*. New York: Bantam, 1987.

FRANK SINATRA

Sinatra, Nancy. *Frank Sinatra: An American Legend*. Los Angeles: General Publishing, 1995.

UPTON SINCLAIR

Harris, Leon. *Upton Sinclair: American Rebel*. New York: Thomas Y. Crowell, 1975.

RED SKELTON
Marx, Arthur. *Red Skelton*. New York: E. P. Dutton, 1979.

B. F. SKINNER
Bjork, Daniel W. *B. F. Skinner: A Life*. New York: Basic Books, 1993.

JOSEPH SMITH
Brodie, Fawn M. *No Man Knows My History: The Life of Joseph Smith*. New York: Alfred A. Knopf, 1946.
Hill, Donna. *Joseph Smith: The First Mormon*. New York: Doubleday, 1977.

AARON SPELLING
Spelling, Aaron. *A Prime-Time Life*. New York: St. Martin's, 1996.

STEVEN SPIELBERG
Corliss, Richard and Jeffrey Ressner. "Peter Pan Grows Up, but Can He Still Fly?" *Time*, May 19, 1997.
Sanello, Frank. *Spielberg: The Man, the Movies, the Mythology*. Dallas, Tex.: Taylor Publishing, 1996.
Spielberg, Steven. "The Autobiography of Peter Pan." *Time*, July 15, 1985.

BRUCE SPRINGSTEEN
Gambaccini, Peter. *Bruce Springsteen*. New York: Perigee Books, 1985.
Marsh, Dave. *Glory Days: Bruce Springsteen in the 1980s*. New York: Pantheon Books, 1987.

JOSEPH STALIN
Conquest, Robert. *Stalin: Breaker of Nations*. New York: Viking, 1991.
Smith, Edward Ellis. *The Young Stalin: The Early Years of an Elusive Revolutionary*. New York: Farrar, Straus and Giroux, 1967.

SYLVESTER STALLONE
Rader, Dotson. "A Chance to Go the Distance." *Parade*, July 6, 1997.

JOHN STEINBECK
Parini, Jay. *John Steinbeck: A Biography*. New York: Henry Holt, 1995.
Valjean, Nelson. *John Steinbeck: The Errant Knight*. San Francisco: Chronicle Books, 1975.

GLORIA STEINEM
Heilbrun, Carolyn G. *The Education of a Woman: The Life of Gloria Steinem*. New York: Dial Press, 1995.
Keyes, Ralph. *Is There Life After High School?* Boston: Little, Brown, 1976.
Steinem, Gloria. *Outrageous Acts and Everyday Rebellions*. New York: Holt, Rinehart and Winston, 1983.

STENDHAL
May, Gita. *Stendhal and the Age of Napoleon*. New York: Columbia University Press, 1977.

CASEY STENGEL
Creamer, Robert W. *Stengel: His Life and Times*. New York: Simon and Schuster, 1984.

HOWARD STERN

Colford, Paul D. *Howard Stern: King of All Media.* New York: St. Martin's, 1996.

Stern, Howard. *Private Parts.* New York: Pocket Books, 1994.

ADLAI STEVENSON

Martin, John Bartlow. *Adlai Stevenson of Illinois.* New York: Anchor Books/Doubleday, 1977.

McKeever, Porter. *Adlai Stevenson: His Life and Legacy.* New York: William Morrow, 1989.

ROBERT LOUIS STEVENSON

McLynn, Frank. *Robert Louis Stevenson: A Biography.* New York: Random House, 1993.

JAMES STEWART

Ansen, David. "The All American Hero." *Newsweek,* July 14, 1997.

Dewey, Donald. *James Stewart: A Biography.* Atlanta, Ga.: Turner Publishing, 1996.

Wloszczyna, Susan. "Jimmy Stewart: Beloved Actor Dies at 89." *USA Today,* July 3, 1997.

BARBRA STREISAND

Riese, Randall. *Her Name Is Barbra.* New York: Birch Lane/Carol, 1993.

Spada, James. *Streisand: Her Life.* New York: Crown, 1995.

Streisand, Barbra. On *Oprah Winfrey.*

GLORIA SWANSON

Swanson, Gloria. *Swanson on Swanson: An Autobiography.* New York: Random House, 1980.

IDA TARBELL

Brady, Kathleen. *Ida Tarbell: Portrait of a Muckraker.* New York: Seaview/Putnam, 1984.

PËTR ILICH TCHAIKOVSKY

Warrack, John Hamilton. *Tchaikovsky.* New York: Charles Scribner's, 1973.

IRVING THALBERG

Flamini, Roland. *Thalberg: The Last Tycoon and the World of M-G-M.* New York: Crown, 1994.

DYLAN THOMAS

Ferris, Paul. *Dylan Thomas: A Biography.* New York: Dial Press, 1977.

Read, Bill. *Dylan Thomas.* New York: McGraw-Hill, 1964.

Tremlett, George. *Dylan Thomas: In the Mercy of His Means.* New York: St. Martin's, 1991.

JOSIP BROZ TITO

West, Richard. *Tito and the Rise and Fall of Yugoslavia.* New York: Carroll & Graf, 1994.

JOHN R. R. TOLKIEN

Carpenter, Humphrey. *Tolkien: The Authorized Biography.* Boston: Houghton Mifflin, 1977.

HENRI DE TOULOUSE-LAUTREC
Frey, Julia. *Toulouse-Lautrec: A Life*. New York: Viking, 1994.

SPENCER TRACY
Davidson, Bill. *Spencer Tracy: Tragic Idol*. New York: E. P. Dutton, 1987.

Swindell, Larry. *Spencer Tracy: A Biography*. New York: World, 1969.

LEON TROTSKY
Howe, Irving. *Leon Trotsky*. New York: Viking Press, 1978.

Trotsky, Leon. *My Life: An Attempt at an Autobiography*. New York: Pathfinder Press, 1970.

HARRY S TRUMAN
Merle Miller. *Plain Speaking: An Oral Biography of Harry S Truman*. New York: Berkley, 1974.

Miller, Richard Lawrence. *Truman: The Rise to Power*. New York: McGraw-Hill, 1986.

MARK TWAIN
Sanborn, Margaret. *Mark Twain: The Bachelor Years*. New York: Doubleday, 1990.

PETER USTINOV
Goertzel, Mildred George, Victor Goertzel, Ted George Goertzel. *Three Hundred Eminent Personalities*. San Francisco: Jossey-Bass, 1978.

GLORIA VANDERBILT
Vanderbilt, Gloria. *Once upon a Time: A True Story*. New York: Alfred A. Knopf, 1985.

JULES VERNE
Costello, Peter. *Jules Verne: Inventor of Science Fiction*. New York: Charles Scribner's, 1978.

Freedman, Russell. *Jules Verne: Portrait of a Prophet*. New York: Holiday House, 1965.

Jules-Verne, Jean, trans. and adapted by Roger Greaves. *Jules Verne: A Biography*. New York: Taplinger, 1976.

BARBARA WALTERS
Oppenheimer, Jerry. *Barbara Walters: An Unauthorized Biography*. New York: St. Martin's, 1990.

ANDY WARHOL
Bockris, Victor. *The Life and Death of Andy Warhol*. New York: Bantam, 1989.

Colacello, Bob. *Holy Terror: Andy Warhol Close Up*. New York: HarperCollins, 1990.

JOHN WAYNE
Shepherd, Donald. *Duke: The Life and Times of John Wayne*. New York: Doubleday, 1985.

Wayne, Aissa (with Steve Delsohn). *John Wayne: My Father*. New York: Random House, 1991.

Zolotow, Maurice. *Shooting Star: A Biography of John Wayne*. New York: Simon and Schuster, 1974.

LAWRENCE WELK
Welk, Lawrence (with Bernice McGeehan). *Wunnerful, Wunnerful!* Englewood Cliffs, N.J.: Prentice-Hall, 1971.

ORSON WELLES
Callow, Simon. *Orson Welles: The Road to Xanadu.* New York, Viking, 1995.
Corliss, Richard. "Praising Kane." *Time,* January 29, 1996.
Thomson, David. *Rosebud: The Story of Orson Welles.* New York: Alfred A. Knopf, 1996.

H. G. WELLS
Dickson, Lovat. *H. G. Wells: His Turbulent Life and Times.* New York: Atheneum, 1969.

MAE WEST
Eells, George and Stanley Musgrove. *Mae West: A Biography.* New York: William Morrow, 1982.

RUTH WESTHEIMER
Westheimer, Ruth K. (with Ben Yagoda). *All in a Lifetime: An Autobiography.* New York: Warner Books, 1987.

E. B. WHITE
Elledge, Scott. *E. B. White: A Biography.* New York: W. W. Norton, 1984.

PAUL WHITEMAN
DeLong, Thomas A. *Pops: Paul Whiteman, King of Jazz.* Piscataway, N.J.: New Century, 1983.

OSCAR WILDE
Knox, Melissa. *Oscar Wilde: A Long and Lovely Suicide.* New Haven, Conn.: Yale University Press, 1994.

HANK WILLIAMS
Escott, Colin. *Hank Williams: The Biography.* Boston: Little, Brown, 1994.

BRIAN WILSON
Wilson, Brian (with Todd Gold). *Wouldn't It Be Nice.* New York: HarperCollins, 1991.

WOODROW WILSON
Weinstein, Edwin A. *Woodrow Wilson: A Medical and Psychological Biography.* Princeton, N.J.: Princeton University Press, 1981.

WALTER WINCHELL
Gabler, Neal. *Winchell: Gossip, Power and the Culture of Celebrity.* New York: Vintage Books, 1995.
Klurfeld, Herman. *Winchell: His Life and Times.* New York: Praeger, 1976.

OPRAH WINFREY
Mair, George. *Oprah Winfrey: The Real Story.* New York: Birch Lane/Carol, 1994.
Taraborrelli, J. Randy. "How Oprah Does It All." *Redbook,* August 1996.
Smith, Liz. "Oprah Exhales." *Good Housekeeping,* October 1995.

SHELLEY WINTERS

Winters, Shelley. *Shelley: Also Known as Shirley.* New York: William Morrow, 1980.

THOMAS WOLFE

Donald, David Herbert. *Look Homeward: A Life of Thomas Wolfe.* Boston: Little, Brown, 1987.

FRANK LLOYD WRIGHT

Secrest, Meryle. *Frank Lloyd Wright.* New York: Alfred A. Knopf, 1992.
Wright, Frank Lloyd. *An Autobiography.* New York: Horizon Press, 1932.

ORVILLE WRIGHT

Crouch, Tom D. *The Bishop's Boys: A Life of the Wright Brothers.* New York: W. W. Norton, 1989.

WILLIAM WYLER

Herman, Jan. *A Talent for Trouble: The Life of Hollywood's Most Acclaimed Director.* New York: G. P. Putnam's, 1995.

BORIS YELTSIN

Otfinoski, Steven. *Boris Yeltsin and the Rebirth of Russia.* Brookfield, Conn.: Millbrook Press, 1995.
Solovyov, Vladimir and Elena Klepikova. *Boris Yeltsin: A Political Biography.* New York: G.P. Putnam's, 1992.

INDEX